Docker for Developers

Develop and run your application with Docker
containers using DevOps tools for continuous delivery

Richard Bullington-McGuire

Andrew K. Dennis

Michael Schwartz

BIRMINGHAM—MUMBAI

Docker for Developers

Commissioning Editor: Vijin Boricha

Acquisition Editor: Rohit Rajkumar

Senior Editor: Arun Nadar

Content Development Editor: Romy Dias

Technical Editor: Sarvesh Jayant

Copy Editor: Safis Editing

Project Coordinator: Neil Dmello

Proofreader: Safis Editing

Indexer: Priyanka Dhadke

Production Designer: Nilesh Mohite

First published: August 2020

Production reference: 1140820

Published by Packt Publishing Ltd.
Livery Place
35 Livery Street
Birmingham
B3 2PB, UK.

ISBN 978-1-78953-605-8

www.packt.com

Packt.com

Subscribe to our online digital library for full access to over 7,000 books and videos, as well as industry leading tools to help you plan your personal development and advance your career. For more information, please visit our website.

Why subscribe?

- Spend less time learning and more time coding with practical eBooks and Videos from over 4,000 industry professionals

- Improve your learning with Skill Plans built especially for you

- Get a free eBook or video every month

- Fully searchable for easy access to vital information

- Copy and paste, print, and bookmark content

Did you know that Packt offers eBook versions of every book published, with PDF and ePub files available? You can upgrade to the eBook version at packt.com and as a print book customer, you are entitled to a discount on the eBook copy. Get in touch with us at customercare@packtpub.com for more details.

At www.packt.com, you can also read a collection of free technical articles, sign up for a range of free newsletters, and receive exclusive discounts and offers on Packt books and eBooks.

Contributors

About the authors

Richard Bullington-McGuire is a software architect and DevOps practitioner with more than 28 years of professional experience in information technology. He has operated internet services continuously since 1995 when he established The Obscure Organization. He has used Docker to build, deploy, and run applications in production, including operating the Freezing Saddles winter cycling event since 2018. Richard is a member of the IEEE and the ACM. He holds 6 AWS certifications, including all of the Foundational, Associate, and Professional level certifications. He works at Modus Create, Inc. as director of engineering. You can find him on Twitter and GitHub at @obscurerichard. Richard lives in Arlington, VA, with his wife and four children.

I want to thank my wonderful wife, Patricia, and my children, for giving me the space and support I've needed to write this book, even while the COVID-19 global pandemic was raging around us. I'd also like to thank Jay Garcia for suggesting that I join this effort. The whole Packt editing team has helped this first-time book author immensely, but I'd like to give special thanks to Romy Dias who edited most of my work.

Andrew K. Dennis is a full stack and cybersecurity architect with over 17 years' experience who currently works for Modus Create in Reston, VA. He holds two undergraduate degrees in software engineering and creative computing and a master's degree in information security. Andy has worked in the US, Canada, and the UK in software engineering, e-learning, data science, and cybersecurity across his career, and has written four books on IoT, the Raspberry Pi, and supercomputing. His interests range from the application of pataphysics in computing to security threat modeling. Andy lives in New England and is an organizer of Security BSides CT.

I want to thank my wife, Megen, for her support during the writing of this book; the other authors for their collaboration and hard work; Modus Create for aiding me: and the other authors as well for helping to initiate the project; my parents for all their support over the years as my career in technology grew; and finally, a thank you to the Packt team for their edits and insights.

Michael Schwartz is a full stack software engineer, architect, and embedded engineer for Modus Create, with over 45 years' experience as a professional. He founded one of the first public ISPs in the SF Bay Area, Best Internet Communications, and an early internet advertising agency, MediaPlex. He was one of the early developers of video games, including the upright coin-operated machines and consoles. His most recent project is RoboDomo, a home automation system built around Node.js, Docker containers, MQTT, and React.js. Originally from Chicago, IL, Mike resides in the Palm Springs area of California.

I want to thank Jesus Garcia and Pat Sheridan for throwing the support of Modus Create behind this book project. I'd also like to thank my co-authors, Andy and Richard, who've made this the definitive book on Docker at this time.

About the reviewer

Sreenivas Makam is a customer engineer and application modernization specialist at Google Cloud, Bangalore. He has a master's in electrical engineering and around 20 years' experience in the public/private cloud and networking industry. Prior to Google, Sreenivas worked at Cisco Systems and a few start-ups. His interests include hybrid cloud technologies, SDN, and DevOps. He also likes to try out and follow open source projects in these areas. Sreenivas was also a Docker captain for 2 years, promoting Docker technologies. He is pretty active in cloud technology forums and meetup groups. He can be reached on Twitter at @srmakam.

I would like to thank my family for giving me extra time during the weekend to do the book reviews. Thanks to my daughters, Sasha and Masha, for keeping me energetic.

Packt is searching for authors like you

If you're interested in becoming an author for Packt, please visit authors. packtpub.com and apply today. We have worked with thousands of developers and tech professionals, just like you, to help them share their insight with the global tech community. You can make a general application, apply for a specific hot topic that we are recruiting an author for, or submit your own idea.

Table of Contents

3
Sharing Containers Using Docker Hub

4
Composing Systems Using Containers

Section 2: Running Docker in Production

5

Alternatives for Deploying and Running Containers in Production

6

Deploying Applications with Docker Compose

7

Continuous Deployment with Jenkins

8

Deploying Docker Apps to Kubernetes

9
Cloud-Native Continuous Deployment Using Spinnaker

10

Monitoring Docker Using Prometheus, Grafana, and Jaeger

11
Scaling and Load Testing Docker Applications

Section 3: Docker Security – Securing Your Containers

12
Introduction to Container Security

13
Docker Security Fundamentals and Best Practices

14
Advanced Docker Security – Secrets, Secret Commands, Tagging, and Labels

15
Scanning, Monitoring, and Using Third-Party Tools

16

Conclusion – End of the Road, but not the Journey

Other Books You May Enjoy

Index

Preface

Software engineering teams are rapidly adopting containers to package and deploy their software. Providing a platform-agnostic experience, containers allow you to run applications with a variety of operating system images and to deploy on-premises, in data centers, and in the cloud. In order to support container-based applications, vendors have developed a wide variety of tools, ranging from Docker and Google's Kubernetes project to Lyft's Envoy service mesh and Netflix's Spinnaker. Whether you are working on the software development side of the house, hosting, and infrastructure, or constructing DevOps pipelines, you need both a broad and in-depth understanding of many concepts in order to manage container-based environments.

In *Docker for Developers*, we will start with a walk-through of the basics of developing with containers locally using Docker, and then move on to deploying production-ready, cloud-hosted systems with AWS. If you are interested in learning about container orchestration, deployment, monitoring, and security, then we think you will enjoy this book.

Who this book is for

Docker for Developers is geared toward engineers and DevOps personnel who want to learn the basics of containers and then build upon this knowledge to understand how to use containers in production, through a set of successively more sophisticated deployments. We will demonstrate how Docker applications can be deployed via CI/CD pipelines and managed in a production-grade, cloud-hosted environment. A basic understanding of containers would be helpful when tackling the book's subject matter, but this is not essential. It is assumed that readers of this book are familiar with Linux, the use of command-line tools, and basic software engineering concepts, such as version control and using Git.

What this book covers

Chapter 1, Introduction to Docker, provides some background on Docker, a walk-through of containers and their purpose, and presents the reader with an introduction to the topics that will be discussed in the book.

Chapter 2, Using VirtualBox and Docker Containers for Development, guides the reader through using a virtual machine locally for development and then compares this to how Docker can be used for containerized development projects.

Chapter 3, Sharing Containers Using Docker Hub, introduces the reader to Docker Hub and pre-built containers. Next, we explore the process of building specialized containers.

Chapter 4, Composing Systems Using Containers, investigates more complex situations where multiple containers need to work together as a complete system. Additionally, we give the reader an overview of Docker Compose.

Chapter 5, Alternatives for Deploying and Running Containers in Production, helps the reader understand the spectrum of choices when it comes to running containers in a production environment, including cloud options, on-premises and hybrid solutions.

Chapter 6, Deploying Applications with Docker Compose, discusses how to deploy a production application on a single host with Docker Compose and how to deal with logging and monitoring, along with the pros and cons of this simple setup.

Chapter 7, Continuous Deployment with Jenkins, shows how to use Jenkins for **continuous integration (CI)** and **continuous deployment (CD)** for containers, using a Jenkinsfile and multiple development branches.

Chapter 8, Deploying Docker Apps to Kubernetes, explores Kubernetes concepts, cloud distribution options, and shows how to create an Amazon Web Services **Elastic Kubernetes Service (EKS)** cluster for deploying Docker applications to Kubernetes.

Chapter 9, Cloud-Native Continuous Deployment Using Spinnaker, builds upon the skills we developed around CI/CD by integrating Netflix's Spinnaker with Kubernetes and looking at automated tests.

Chapter 10, Monitoring Docker Using Prometheus, Grafana, and Jaeger, explains how to monitor container-based applications using AWS CloudWatch, Prometheus, and Grafana. We introduce the OpenTracing API and implement it using Jaeger.

Chapter 11, Scaling and Load Testing Docker Applications, explores how to scale a Docker-based application through Kubernetes. It introduces the concept of a service mesh and shows a simple implementation using Envoy, integrating load balancing and advanced traffic routing and filtering, including utilization of the circuit breaker pattern. Finally, we show how to use k6.io to perform load testing to demonstrate that our application can scale out.

Chapter 12, Introduction to Container Security, walks the reader through basic container security concepts, including how virtualization and hypervisor security models work.

Chapter 13, Docker Security Fundamentals and Best Practices, builds upon the previous chapter's introduction and delves deeper into Docker and security components. This includes a comparison of Docker commands and their security implications.

Chapter 14, Advanced Docker Security – Secrets, Secret Commands, Tagging, and Labels, covers the topics of secrets, including passwords, and how they can be used securely with container-based environments. The reader is also introduced to the use of tagging and labeling best practices.

Chapter 15, Scanning, Monitoring, and Using Third-Party Tools, expands upon our logging and monitoring skills acquired from other chapters by refocusing on these elements from a security focus. Here, we also look at what options are available for users of AWS, Azure, and GCP and how we can scan containers for security issues using Anchore.

Chapter 16, Conclusion – End of the Road, but not the Journey, wraps the book up by revisiting what we have learned so far. Finally, we provide some ideas for where the reader can go next in exploring container-based projects. This ranges from adding Netflix Chaos Monkey to their CI/CD pipeline, to running Metasploit in a container.

To get the most out of this book

You will need a Windows, Mac, or Linux workstation that can run Docker. You should use the latest version if possible. Additionally, in order to complete any of the cloud-based projects, you will need to set up a cloud provider account. The examples use **Amazon Web Services (AWS)**, although you could adapt much of the content to services hosted by another cloud provider:

Software and systems covered in the book	OS requirements and hosting environment
Docker v2.3	Windows, macOS X, and Linux (any)
Jenkins v2.25	Windows, macOS X, and Linux (any)
Kubernetes v1.15	Docker Desktop or MiniKube (Windows, macOS X, and Linux)
Elastic Container Registry (ECR) and Elastic Kubernetes Service (EKS)	AWS account
Spinnaker v1.23	AWS or another cloud account with a working Kubernetes cluster
Prometheus	AWS or another cloud account with a working Kubernetes cluster

Software and systems covered in the book	OS requirements and hosting environment
Grafana	AWS or another cloud account with a working Kubernetes cluster
Jaeger	AWS or another cloud account with a working Kubernetes cluster
Envoy	AWS or another cloud account with a working Kubernetes cluster
GitHub	GitHub account (public cloud)
Docker Hub	Docker account (public cloud)
Anchore	Docker
Datadog	Docker AWS or another cloud account with a working Kubernetes cluster

While we do not explicitly demonstrate how to deploy the projects listed in this book to Microsoft Azure or the Google Cloud Platform, if you wish to explore some of the security features available on those cloud platforms, or try out the existing projects in them, you will need to create an account for each provider.

If you are using the digital version of this book, we advise you to type the code yourself or access the code via the GitHub repository (link available in the next section). Doing so will help you avoid any potential errors related to the copying and pasting of code.

Download the example code files

You can download the example code files for this book from your account at www.packt.com. If you purchased this book elsewhere, you can visit www.packtpub.com/support and register to have the files emailed directly to you.

You can download the code files by following these steps:

1. Log in or register at www.packt.com.
2. Select the **Support** tab.
3. Click on **Code Downloads**.
4. Enter the name of the book in the **Search** box and follow the onscreen instructions.

Once the file is downloaded, please make sure that you unzip or extract the folder using the latest version of:

- WinRAR/7-Zip for Windows
- Zipeg/iZip/UnRarX for Mac
- 7-Zip/PeaZip for Linux

The code bundle for the book is also hosted on GitHub at `https://github.com/PacktPublishing/Docker-for-Developers`. In case there's an update to the code, it will be updated on the existing GitHub repository.

We also have other code bundles from our rich catalog of books and videos available at `https://github.com/PacktPublishing/`. Check them out!

Code in Action

Code in Action videos for this book can be viewed at `https://bit.ly/3kDmrtq`.

Download the color images

We also provide a PDF file that has color images of the screenshots/diagrams used in this book. You can download it here: `http://www.packtpub.com/sites/default/files/downloads/9781789536058_ColorImages.pdf`.

Conventions used

There are a number of text conventions used throughout this book.

`Code in text`: Indicates code words in text, container names, folder names, filenames, file extensions, pathnames, dummy URLs, and user input. Here is an example: "This file needs to be added to the `conf.d` directory on the host."

A block of code or `Dockerfile` is set as follows:

```
FROM ubuntu:bionic
RUN apt-get -qq update && \
    apt-get -qq install -y nodejs npm > /dev/null
RUN mkdir -p /app/public /app/server
COPY src/package.json* /app
WORKDIR /app
RUN npm -s install
```

When we wish to draw your attention to a particular part of a code block, the relevant lines or items are set in bold:

```
FROM alpine:20191114
RUN apk update && \
apk add nodejs nodejs-npm
RUN addgroup -S app && adduser -S -G app app
RUN mkdir -p /app/public /app/server
ADD src/package.json* /app/
```

Any command-line input or output is written as follows:

```
$ cp docker_daemon.yaml  /path/to/conf.d/
$ vim /path/to/conf.d/conf.yaml
```

Bold: Indicates a new term, an important word, or words that you see on screen. For example, words in menus or dialog boxes appear in the text like this. Here is an example: "You can do this by clicking the **Get It Now** button on the Azure Marketplace website."

> **Tips or important notes**
> Appear like this.

Get in touch

Feedback from our readers is always welcome.

General feedback: If you have questions about any aspect of this book, mention the book title in the subject of your message and email us at customercare@packtpub.com.

Errata: Although we have taken every care to ensure the accuracy of our content, mistakes do happen. If you have found a mistake in this book, we would be grateful if you would report this to us. Please visit www.packtpub.com/support/errata, selecting your book, clicking on the Errata Submission Form link, and entering the details.

Piracy: If you come across any illegal copies of our works in any form on the internet, we would be grateful if you would provide us with the location address or website name. Please contact us at copyright@packt.com with a link to the material.

If you are interested in becoming an author: If there is a topic that you have expertise in, and you are interested in either writing or contributing to a book, please visit authors.packtpub.com.

Reviews

Please leave a review. Once you have read and used this book, why not leave a review on the site that you purchased it from? Potential readers can then see and use your unbiased opinion to make purchase decisions, we at Packt can understand what you think about our products, and our authors can see your feedback on their book. Thank you!

For more information about Packt, please visit `packt.com`.

Section 1:
An Introduction
to Docker –
Containers and
Local Development

In this section, we introduce the reader to the technologies, skills, and steps involved in developing applications using Docker Containers. We begin by tracing the history of hosting and why we need Docker in the first place. We then demonstrate the differences between virtualization and containerization, using VirtualBox to create simple virtual machines and using Docker to create a simple PHP application with state. We discuss how applications involving multiple containers working together (microservices) are the ultimate way to use containers, and present a simple CRUD demo involving several containers, including some prepared by third parties and shared with us on Docker Hub. Finally, we present the Docker Compose tool as a means to orchestrate complete applications made up of multiple containers, while providing private access between the containers.

This section comprises the following chapters:

1
Introduction to Docker

Docker is a technology that allows entire applications and their environments to be encapsulated within individual containers. When multiple versions of these containers are run on a single machine, they are sandboxed from one another as if running on their own dedicated machines.

Docker is open source, which fits well with running Linux in containers, as well as numerous available open source components that help build complex systems. It is the logical progression of technologies used for hosting and backend development over the past decade or longer. This progression has moved from a physical kind of hosting to a logical one and has been driven by several requirements. These requirements include reliability, reachability, scalability, and security.

This book is divided into three sections. The first is an introduction to Docker, focusing on local development. The second describes the methodology for testing, deploying, and scaling applications. The third goes into detail about security when using a container-based design.

In this chapter, we will review the history of hosting and backend solutions with a focus on how Docker came to be a widely used technology.

The following topics will be covered in this chapter:

- Origins of hosting services
- Types of hosting services – co-location
- Types of hosting services – self-hosting
- The benefits of data centers
- How virtualization works
- The power requirements at data centers
- How virtualization is a solution for data centers and the invention of the cloud
- How containers are a bigger win for data centers and hosting

The drivers for Docker

The range of hosting services was originally limited to self-hosted servers, co-located server hosting, and shared hosting. In 1994 and 1995, Best Internet Communications rose from nothing to hosting 18,000+ websites on a pair of Pentium servers, which were the most powerful servers of the time. Best also offered dedicated server-hosting through co-location, dedicated broadband connectivity, and upscale premium services.

Most of the websites hosted by Best were of the shared-hosting variety. All of these sites shared the same server, the same hard drives, the same filesystem, the same RAM, the same CPUs, the same network connections, and so on.

It was not uncommon for any one of these websites to be slashdotted, or containing a link to the site from a very popular site to the hosted site. This would cause a large spike in traffic to the one out of the approximately 18,000 sites, and a performance hit to the others. As the quality of the sites grew and demanded more resources, their administrators would move to dedicated co-located hosting or self-hosting.

Co-located hosting

With co-located hosting, the customer rents a secure cage within a larger hosting facility (data center):

Figure 1.1 – A typical server rack, commonly seen in colocation

The customer can install and manage the machines of their choice. Some co-location facilities offer, for additional fees, remote hands service, where the customer can call the hosting company and one of their engineers does whatever the customer requires to the hosted servers. The cages are locked so that other customers can't gain access to other customers' equipment.

Self-hosting

With self-hosting, the customer buys a full-time dedicated broadband-style connection in a physical location of their choosing:

Figure 1.2 – Indian Railway 139 server room (self-hosting)

The customer ends up building their own kind of data center and installs and manages servers and other equipment on-premises.

Data centers

The benefits of a professional data center are numerous, and ultimately, the trend became that just a few companies, relative to all the companies with an internet presence, provided data centers, and the remaining companies paid rent for dedicated, shared, or premium hosting. A professional data center provides rich internet connectivity (more than one provider, faster connections), clean power, battery-backed-up power for 24/7/365 uptime, back-up generator-backed-up power for longer brownouts or blackouts, fire-suppression systems, a controlled climate suitable for keeping equipment at the proper operating temperatures, multiple physical locations, a professionally managed **Network Operations Center (NOC)** and technical support, and security in the form of guards, cameras, and fingerprint, handprint, and/or retina scanners:

Figure 1.3 – A server room at CERN (Switzerland)

The companies that ended up building and running the majority of data centers are Google (Google Cloud Platform), Microsoft (Azure), Amazon (**Amazon Web Services (AWS)**), Yahoo! (once upon a time), and lesser players, which include boutique hosting companies, regional hosting companies, and companies that require security beyond what a hosting company can provide (for example, banks and financial institutions, governments, and so on).

Amazon had a unique need for data centers. They are one of the largest online retailers in the world, as well as the largest data center developer/owner. The number of servers, the uptime, the security, and the reach that they require drove them to build data centers throughout the country and then the world.

Google has a unique need for data centers as well. They are the largest search engine and advertising company in the world. In order to be reachable, Google needs servers in as many physical places as possible. In order to be fast, Google needs many servers—at least enough servers for distributed search index processing in each of its geo-locations.

Companies such as RackSpace and Level 3 were originally built as data center providers. Their specialties included co-location facilities, dedicated server hosting, remote hands, NOCs, nationwide-dedicated fiber-optic backbones, clean and blackout resistant power, and very rich connectivity to various other networks, including AT&T, Verizon, and Comcast. They found themselves with the infrastructure to follow the trend toward virtualization and began to offer these cloud services.

The highest cost of providing data center services, and this passed on to the customer, was initially bandwidth. The providers paid for bandwidth by the megabit, plus a monthly cost of maintaining the physical connections that carried this bandwidth. As the providers built their own private infrastructure to carry data between their own data centers around the world, the cost became a flat rate, or a fixed cost, for a significant amount of the total bandwidth used. This allowed the price of bandwidth to decline to the point where it became a minimal consideration for hosting.

These companies ended up building a comprehensive infrastructure for dedicated hosting. It turns out that this infrastructure is ideally suited for virtualized product offerings, too.

Using virtualization to economize resource usage

Virtualization is the process of exposing a portion of a physical machine as a logical or virtual machine that acts enough like a real machine that it supports the installation of whole operating systems, their filesystems, and the software that runs on the operating system. For example, a machine with 64 GB of RAM and 4 CPUs could run virtualization software that masquerades as four 16 GB RAM machines with 1 CPU each. This machine could run four instances of Linux.

Virtualization is not a new concept, having been implemented by IBM in the early 1960s. It likely gained in overall popularity during the 1980s when it was used to run MS-DOS, and then Windows by computer systems such as the original Apple **Macintosh** (**Mac**) and Unix computers such as the Sun and Silicon Graphics workstations.

Initial virtualization software used what features were available on CPUs of the time, but often simply emulated the instruction set of the x86 on the 68000 family or custom CPUs of the professional Unix workstations. SoftPC was one of the most popular offerings in the 1980s.

SoftPC was quite slow, but the ability to run Windows or MS-DOS applications on a Mac computer allowed the use of these machines in business and education environments. Instead of adding Microsoft Office compatibility to all the programs on the Mac to support exchanging files between Windows/MS-DOS users and Mac users, users could run Microsoft Office.

People saw it in action and saw the value in it. Windows was the dominant operating system for home and business, and to fit in with Windows in the corporate environment, something like SoftPC was needed. The problem with SoftPC is that it was pure software emulation, which was quite slow in actual use. Virtualization is superior to emulation in terms of performance!

Entire companies were founded around providing consumer or business virtualization solutions. VMWare, founded in 1998, was one of the first of these companies.

Innotek developed VirtualBox and released it as open source in 2007, and was then acquired by Sun Microsystems in 2008. Then, Sun was acquired by Oracle in 2010. Parallels, a virtualization solution for Mac, was developed in 2004 and became mainstream in 2006.

The value of virtualization encouraged chip makers to gradually add CPU support for virtualization. With CPU support, an x86-based system could run virtualized machines or software at close enough to native speed to be much more tolerable. This, in turn, led the workstation companies (such as Apple, Sun, and Silicon Graphics) to move to x86 CPUs.

A key component of virtualization software is the hypervisor. The hypervisor presents the virtual machine to the chosen operating system and then manages the resources and execution of the virtual machines over time. The virtual machines themselves are configurable, at least regarding the amount of RAM, the number of logical CPU cores, graphics card memory, the host operating system disk files to act as virtual disk drives in the virtual machine, the mounting and unmounting of CD-ROM in the virtual CD-ROM drive, and so on. The hypervisor assures that these resources are truly available and that no virtual machine starves the other virtual machines for the host machine's resources.

For the enterprise, the requirements were somewhat different. Instead of providing virtual machines via a general-purpose host operating system such as Linux, the entire operating system itself could be optimized just for being the hypervisor. VMWare offered its **Elastic Sky X Integrated (ESXi)** operating system in 2004. The University of Cambridge computer laboratory developed the Xen hypervisor in the late 1990s, and the first stable version was released in 2003. Xen was originally the hypervisor used by Amazon for its Elastic Compute Cloud offering, before moving to KVM.

KVM is a virtualization solution supported directly by the Linux kernel. The kernel can act as the hypervisor under KVM. KVM can additionally emulate processors other than the host's native CPU, which is typically x86. This allows KVM to be used to emulate targets such as the Raspberry Pi.

Scaling a dedicated hosted website can be problematic. It's possible to simply upgrade to a larger and more powerful server to handle growing traffic and services. At some point, however, there is no server that is large and powerful! To scale up from that point requires distributing services across multiple servers.

Addressing the increasing power requirements

The trend toward virtualization created a demand for a new breed of servers to be housed at the data centers. Where a customer might have rented or installed their own dedicated server with 16 GB of RAM, the virtual server provider could rent a portion of a 128 GB RAM server and share that server with multiple customers. These bigger servers required more CPU cores, so the virtual servers could have reasonable computing capabilities.

Fitting these specialized servers into the same space as the smaller and less capable dedicated servers created a new challenge: power. Instead of using 400 watts of power for the dedicated server, the cloud servers might use 1,600 watts; the power requirements would be four times more. In addition to the power requirements of the machines themselves, it took more power to run the air conditioners to cool the machines.

The power cost requirements changed the equation for dedicated hosting, so bandwidth pricing was virtually free, while the power requirements of the servers were charged at a very high price.

To help mitigate the cost of power, data centers have been built to provide some of their own power. Solar panels, building near a river that can drive turbines, wind turbines, and building in places with cool or cold climates are among some of the techniques used. Data centers do use batteries for back-up power, and diesel-powered generators as well.

Energy efficiency is another way to mitigate power costs. The use of lower-powered CPUs and other computer parts is one means to this end. The CPU manufacturers have had a heavy focus on producing lower-powered CPUs for both data center and laptop use.

The hosting companies would supply a 60 watt power supply for each co-location cage. If you needed more than 60 watts, you could pay extra to have additional 60 watt lines for your cage. You'd pay for the construction and then the monthly power usage.

Hosting at one of these facilities was problematic for most customers. It required purchasing physical machines and other hardware, designing the infrastructure required for the services to be provided, physical access to the cage and hardware from time to time, and potential failures, which meant downtime.

The growth and popularity of services require scalability or more and bigger machines. You could repurpose old machines, but they take up space and power. Customer costs soared when the current cage filled up and more presence was required.

The next step, and the solution to these hassles, is virtualization and running your servers and services within the cloud.

Virtualization and cloud computing

Most customers don't need dedicated servers. What they really need is the security of a filesystem that only their software can read and write to, that the CPU is guaranteed to be dedicated to their purpose, and that the throughput and computing power is identifiable and delivered as expected.

The appeal of virtual servers offered by companies such as AWS drove many administrators to move away from dedicated and self-hosting. AWS grows its offerings to add more value to virtual hosting, so their customers get the benefit of Amazon's developers efforts.

It's relatively cheap to duplicate the customer-designed infrastructure to create a testing environment that is separate from the live/deployed applications. It's easy to scale services that grow with popularity, or when the services are **slashdotted**. This is a term that describes what happens when a very popular site adds a link to another site, driving a lot more traffic to that site—perhaps more traffic than the site was designed to handle.

The design and deployment of a virtualized infrastructure can be done from the comfort of your office. There is no need to physically visit a data center. If you need to scale horizontally, you only need to spin up additional virtual machine instances. If you need to scale vertically, you only need to spin up a more powerful virtual machine and substitute it for the one that is too slow or too small.

If hardware fails at a cloud-hosting facility, the hosting company's employees install new hardware. This is done in complete transparency with you, the customer. A feature known as **Teleport** allows the hosting company to move a running virtual machine to a different physical machine, without the interruption of service.

Along with virtual servers, hosting companies can also offer virtual disks, elastic IPs, load balancers, DNS, backup solutions, and so on. Virtual disks are handy because you can back them up by simply copying the file that is the image. You can also boot new instances from an existing virtual disk, saving the time required to install a whole operating system on a virtual machine.

The ability to use elastic IPs and virtual load balancers allows a scalability that is as easy as the click of a mouse.

You can assign an elastic IP to any virtual instance or load balancer. If the instance is stopped, you can reassign that IP to another instance. If this were handled only with DNS, there could be days' worth of delays for the DNS to propagate through the many DNS servers at the ISPs. The load balancer allows you to create virtual server farms and balance incoming requests between the virtual servers in the farm. You can trivially spin up and add additional virtual servers to the load balancer as you need to scale. The hosting companies can even provide software triggers that will automatically spin up and add new servers when traffic increases, and then spin them down and remove them when traffic is reduced:

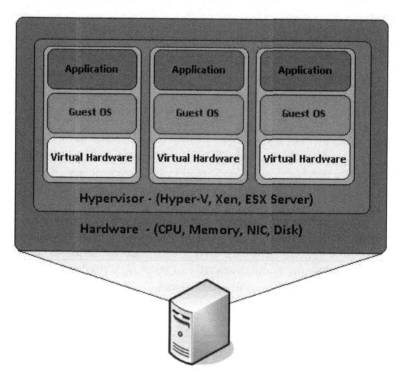

Figure 1.4 – Hardware virtualization

A popular stack technology at the time that AWS was made available to the public was **LAMP**, which is short for **Linux, Apache, MySQL, and PHP**. A typical setup would be to install these four software packages on a dedicated Linux server. AWS offered RDS, or a MySQL equivalent dedicated virtual server, which allowed the offloading and scaling of the LAMP application. AWS offered virtual load balancers, which are logical Ethernet switches that load balance traffic among two or more web servers. They offered domain name-hosting and elastic IPs, so a site's uptime could be almost infinite. AWS continues to develop new software and services to benefit its customers.

AWS and its competitors allow a cost-effective and dynamic way to grow an internet presence as it gains popularity. The price structure is common among most providers. The cost is based on the number of elastic load balancers, the number of virtual server instances, the amount of RAM, the number of virtual CPUs, the size of persistent storage, and the bandwidth. There are also optional additional services that can increase the price.

Virtual servers provide the benefits of a physical one, but it comes at the cost of the dedication of physical RAM on the host machine and the power required to run the machine. A host machine might have 64 GB of RAM; it can run some combination of virtual machines that, combined, use up that RAM—for example, four 16 GB virtual machines, two 32 GB virtual machines, two 16 gigabytes and one 32 GB virtual machine, and so on.

A risk of virtual machines is that when the host machine is rebooted or fails, all the virtual machines hosted on it will go off air.

The features that enable virtualization and the limitations of virtualization when applied at data centers make containerization a viable and preferred alternative.

Using containers to further optimize data center resources

Docker is a clever use of OS-level virtualization support that allows multiple Docker containers to execute on a single machine. A container is a running instance of a container image. The containers are, by default, isolated from the host machine, as well as from one another.

They can be configured to expose resources, such as networking ports, to the host network (for example, the internet) or to one another. The following diagram illustrates the basic structure of containers on a host:

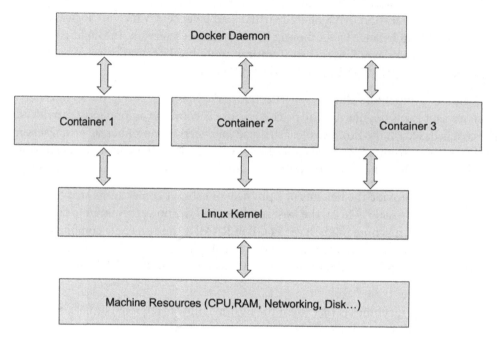

Figure 1.5 – Docker containerization

Containers share their Linux kernel with the host, so you do not need to install complete operating systems within the container as you do with virtual machines. The containers are managed by the Docker daemon, which handles the management of the containers and resources they use, as well as the images, networks, volumes, and so on.

An important distinction between virtual servers and containers is that containers share the resources, directly, of the host, whereas virtual servers require duplicate resources. For example, two identical containers use the host's RAM, rather than a block of RAM configured before booting the virtual machine. If you need to constrain the resources (the CPU, memory, swap, and so on) of a container, you can do so, but the default is to have no resource constraints on any container.

Unlike with virtual servers, you deal with an application image, rather than a virtual disk. You can copy the image to back it up, but there is no virtual disk file to copy. These application images are progressively built on top of other containers. When you build a container, only the bits of the application image that change need to be dealt with.

When designing services that use containers, you will not likely install many components within any one container. For a virtual machine running a LAMP application, you might install Apache, MySQL, and PHP all within one virtual machine. When designing the same LAMP application for containers, you might configure one container just for MySQL and another for Apache and PHP. You can then scale your application by running additional Apache and PHP containers and additional MySQL instances in a cluster configuration.

If we consider the use of containers for the LAMP application discussed earlier, we can implement MySQL in a dedicated container, and Apache and PHP in another; all this running on top of the host's Linux kernel. To scale the LAMP application, a second, third, fourth, and so on instance of the Apache/PHP container can be spun up, and the same is true for the MySQL container. MySQL containers can be configured for master-subordinate operations.

If the host operating system is not Linux kernel-based, there are two options. The first option is to run host OS native containers (for example, Windows containers on a Windows host). The second option is to run a Linux virtual machine on the host and run the containers within that virtual machine.

Containerization is a boon for hosting companies and their customers. No longer is it required to dedicate a fixed amount of RAM per container as is required with virtual machines. A physical machine is limited only by its resources when it comes to the number of containers it can run concurrently. The pricing model for containers can save customers on monthly costs. Thus, containerization is a big win.

In the next chapter, we'll look at how to use virtual machines and Docker to develop applications locally. Later in this book, we'll look at how to deploy our locally developed software to publicly accessible internet/cloud infrastructure.

Summary

In this chapter, we saw how Docker and containerization was a natural result of the progression of hosting requirements since the start of the commercial internet. We reviewed the history of hosting and how we got to today's hosting configurations. You should now have a decent understanding of the difference between virtualization and containerization.

In the next chapter, we'll look at VirtualBox and Docker. This is a good way to explore the differences between virtual machines and Docker containers.

Further reading

If you would like to look into some of the subjects discussed so far in-depth, refer to the following links:

- This link partially describes how Google's search algorithm is implemented: `https://www.google.com/search/howsearchworks/`

- This link describes Google's search infrastructure: `https://netvantagemarketing.com/blog/how-does-google-return-results-so-damn-fast/`

- This link also describes Google's search infrastructure: `https://www.ctl.io/centurylink-public-cloud/servers/`

- This link describes IBM's early technology to support virtualization: `https://en.wikipedia.org/wiki/IBM_CP-40`

- This link describes an old program that emulates a PC to run Windows on a non-Windows host: `https://en.wikipedia.org/wiki/SoftPC`

- This link provides an introduction to the VMWare company: `https://en.wikipedia.org/wiki/VMware`

- This link describes Oracle's VirtualBox: `https://en.wikipedia.org/wiki/VirtualBox`

- This link introduces Parallels: `https://en.wikipedia.org/wiki/Parallels_(company)`

- This link discusses the role of the Hypervisor in virtualization and containerization: `https://en.wikipedia.org/wiki/Hypervisor`

- This link describes VMWare's standalone operating system designed specifically to run virtual machines: `https://en.wikipedia.org/wiki/VMware_ESXi`

- This link describes the Xen hypervisor: `https://15anniversary.xenproject.org/#Intro`

- This link describes Amazon's AWS virtual machines: `https://en.wikipedia.org/wiki/Amazon_Elastic_Compute_Cloud`

- This link describes kernel features to support virtualization and containerization: `https://en.wikipedia.org/wiki/Kernel-based_Virtual_Machine`

- This link describes using QEMU to emulate Raspberry Pi on a workstation: `https://azeria-labs.com/emulate-raspberry-pi-with-qemu/`

2
Using VirtualBox and Docker Containers for Development

In the previous chapter, we introduced virtualization and containerization. In this chapter, we'll demonstrate how you can use software such as VirtualBox to create virtual machines and we'll use Docker to create containers. The focus of this chapter will be on using these technologies for development on your workstation.

A common problem among developers who work on multiple projects is that, over time, they end up with a lot of software installed on their workstations that they don't currently use. This can be so problematic that the developer might reformat their workstation's hard drive and reinstall the operating system.

Both VirtualBox and Docker containers can be used to resolve this problem. The software you install stays within either the **virtual machine's** or the container's filesystem and is separate from the workstation's native filesystem. If you delete a virtual machine or container, all the files installed therein are removed – including any applications or development software that was installed.

Another problem that arises for developers is the version of software required to work on a specific project. If the developer is working on one project that uses Node.js v12 and another that uses Node.js v10, they can't really run both projects on the workstation at the same time and switching between versions of Node.js is doable, but ugly. This is a non-issue with virtual machines or containers – you can have one virtual machine with Node.js v12 and another with Node.js v10 and run both virtual machines at the same time. It is similar with two containers, one for each version of Node.js.

Virtualization is very useful when you need to model an entire machine. If your production systems are virtual machines or physical machines, a virtual machine is a good way to emulate that environment. Virtualization is terrific for running a complete alternate operating system on the workstation; that is, you can run Windows 10 in a virtual machine on a macOS or Linux workstation.

In this chapter, we will cover the following topics:

- Host filesystem pollution problem
- Using VirtualBox for virtual machines
- Using Docker containers

Technical requirements

The code for this chapter can be downloaded from: `https://github.com/PacktPublishing/Docker-for-Developers/tree/master/chapter2`

Check out the following video to see the Code in Action:

`https://bit.ly/3gX9dFE`

Host filesystem pollution problem

Both virtualization and containerization solve certain problems developers face. There's no real point in installing server-style software systems on your workstation – that kind of software can be installed in a virtual machine or a Docker container. Using this strategy means you don't have to pollute your workstation's filesystem, you won't have software version conflicts, and you can run a different operating system than the one your workstation runs.

The pollution problem is a real concern for developers – they end up with a lot of cruft, or installed software, that they don't use day to day, but that take up system resources. We will learn to use virtualization or containerization to install that software in a way that isn't installed on your host's filesystem.

Using VirtualBox for virtual machines

There are several options for running virtual machines on your workstation. These include Parallels (for macOS), KVM/QEMU (for Linux), VMware (commercial for several host operating systems), and VirtualBox (an Oracle product). We'll use VirtualBox because it is open source and free to use. It's also portable in the sense that you can run VirtualBox and your virtual machines on Linux, Windows, macOS, and other host operating systems.

Introduction to virtualization

Virtualization uses special instructions and features of your workstation's CPU to run a generic pseudo-computer system (virtual machine) on your host. Within this virtual machine, you can install a wide range of operating systems, including various versions of Windows Server, Linux, BSD, and so on. The operating system running in a virtual machine is called the guest operating system; the operating system running on your workstation is called the host operating system.

As the guest operating system executes code, it will be required to perform disk and network access, execute privileged CPU instructions, and otherwise access shared resources with the host. The virtualization software effectively traps these guest operating system accesses and translates them into host operating system calls. Thus, code running in the virtual machine is mostly running at full native CPU speed until these shared access traps are executed – then there is some overhead for the translation to host accesses.

The guest virtual machines may be configured before you install an operating system within. You can set how much RAM to use, one or more virtual disks, one or more Ethernet controllers, a graphics card, an ISO file (installation media) to insert in the virtual CD-ROM drive, and so on.

You typically set RAM, disk space, and the number of virtual CPU cores to appropriate values for your guest operating system and the apps you intend to use within the guest. For example, if you are going to run Windows in a virtual machine, you might want to give it at least 2 virtual CPU cores and 8 gigabytes of RAM and 32 gigabytes of disk space. If you are going to run an application in the virtual machine that needs more than 8 gigabytes of memory, you would want to assign more RAM; if the app needs a lot of disk space, you would assign more disk space.

Creating a virtual machine

To boot the virtual machine, use the VirtualBox program (user interface). When the virtual machine boots, it acts just like a physical PC – as far as the installer on the installation media is concerned, it is a physical PC. The installer will work as if you were installing on a new PC or reinstalling on your PC.

A virtual machine may present its console or desktop within a window on your workstation's desktop, or it can be **headless**. A headless virtual machine is similar to a server machine – you access it via FTP, SSH, and so on. You would use a headless virtual machine when you have no use for the operating system console or graphical interface. The headless machine provides all the services of a server you would remotely access.

You start a headless virtual machine from the command line instead of the VirtualBox user interface program. This is done via the VBoxManage command, which is documented here: https://www.virtualbox.org/manual/ch08.html. It is more likely that you will be using a guest operating system with a graphical user interface, though.

A typical headless virtual machine might be used to run a **LAMP** application—**Linux, Apache, MySQL, and PHP** all contained neatly within the virtual machine and not within the filesystem of your workstation. You can model a scalable LAMP application by starting a headless virtual machine that runs MySQL and two headless virtual machines that run the HTTP server and the PHP code.

A typical graphics/desktop virtual machine might be used to run Windows in a window on your Mac computer, to run Linux in a window on your Mac computer, to run Linux in a window on your Windows machine, and so on. If you like to use Linux, but you need to run Windows programs, doing it in a virtual machine is a good way to go.

A non-headless install will have a few display options. The entire desktop can be displayed in a window on your host's desktop. This is the default display mode. The window can be resized like any other window on the desktop. However, within the interior of the window, the guest's desktop will not resize to fit until you install the VirtualBox guest additions in the guest.

The guest window can be made full screen. This makes the guest look like it's the operating system running native on the workstation. If you are running macOS, you can switch desktops using the macOS gestures and go back and forth between full-screen Windows and full-screen macOS desktops.

For some host operating systems, the guest can be put into seamless mode, where the desktop is not displayed at all, but any applications running in the virtual machine render their windows on top of the host desktop.

The result is a mixture of virtual machine application windows and your host operating system application menus on your desktop, as shown in the following screenshot:

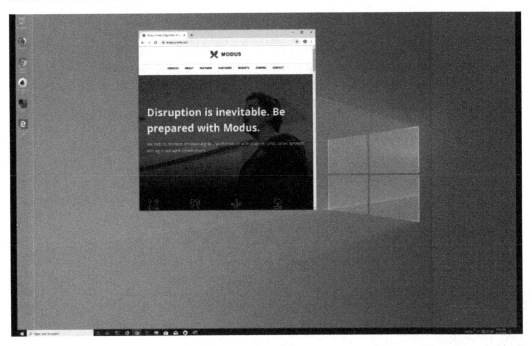

Figure 2.1 – Microsoft Windows 10 running fullscreen in VirtualBox on a Linux host

As you can see, you may run and manage a full Windows installation on your workstation within a virtual machine. You can access the files and directories on your host if you set up Samba for file sharing on the host.

Incidentally, portions of this book were written using Microsoft Word 365, running in a Windows 10 virtual machine on a Linux host. The Docker examples that follow were executed on the Linux host. This is a great example of why you would run a virtual machine.

> **Note:**
>
> Microsoft allows you to buy a Windows 10 license and use it to activate Windows 10 within a virtual machine.
>
> Apple only allows macOS to be run in a virtual machine on Apple hardware. It is a violation of their licensing terms to run macOS within a virtual machine on a PC running Windows or Linux.
>
> Linux and most BSD variants are generally free to use on a PC or within a virtual machine on a PC.

Guest additions

For Windows and Linux guest operating systems, you can install drivers that fully integrate the guest and host operating systems. These drivers are known as guest additions and you can download these from the VirtualBox site: `https://virtualbox.org`. They are installed within the virtual machine as any program you install for Windows or Linux. The integration with the host is quite useful.

The guest additions display drivers that allow you to use the full resolution of the host's screen and, if you're running in windowed mode (guest desktop in a host desktop window), resizing the window will cause the guest desktop to resize to fit the new window size. If you want to use the seamless windows feature, you are required to install the guest display drivers.

The additions provide mouse pointer integration. This allows you to freely move the cursor between physical screens, from guest windows to host windows. Otherwise, the mouse would be captured by the virtual machine so that it can manage pointer events.

The guest additions also share the host and guest clipboards as if they were one clipboard. You can select and copy text in a macOS host application and then paste that copied text into a Windows application running in the virtual machine.

For Linux guests, the additions allow you to share host filesystem directories and files. This is particularly useful because you can use the host operating system tools and software to develop files seen by the host. For example, you create a shared folder on your macOS machine for your project's working directory. You can use your macOS editors to edit files in the project and, in the virtual machine, you can run Linux native compilers or tools to execute your project. Let's now begin by installing VirtualBox.

Installing VirtualBox

The URL for VirtualBox is `https://www.virtualbox.org/`. There, you can find documentation and downloads for the various host platforms (workstation operating systems), add-ons, see screenshots, see recommended third-party software that works with VirtualBox, and so on.

Windows installation instructions

To install the Windows installation, go to the downloads page at the VirtualBox site, download the installer for the latest version, and then, when the download is complete, double-click on it. Then, follow the onscreen instructions.

macOS installation instructions

For macOS installation, you can use Homebrew or download the installer .dmg file from the VirtualBox site and install from that. To use Homebrew, you only need to enter one command:

```
$ brew cask install virtualbox
```

Homebrew (https://brew.sh/) is the missing package manager for macOS. It is a command-line system for installing software from Homebrew's repositories. It is a terrific tool for augmenting the software shipped with macOS. The software in those repositories is updated far more frequently than the Apple software updates.

Linux installation instructions

The installation instructions for VirtualBox on Linux varies depending on the Linux distribution that you use on your workstation. Since there are so many different distributions, we'll cover Ubuntu to give you an idea of what to do and provide you with helpful pointers for installing VirtualBox on other distributions (Arch Linux, Fedora, and suchlike).

For Ubuntu, you can install VirtualBox from the Ubuntu Software Center, download a .deb file from the VirtualBox site, or use apt:

```
$ sudo apt install virtualbox
```

For Arch Linux and its variants, you can follow the instructions on the terrific Arch wiki at https://wiki.archlinux.org/index.php/VirtualBox.

For Fedora or other RPM-based Linux distributions, follow the instructions at the VirtualBox site: https://virtualbox.org. Let's now learn how to use Docker containers.

Using Docker containers

Docker is generally used to create containers, which run your application as if in a headless virtual machine. In fact, on host operating systems that are not Linux-based, Docker effectively runs Linux in a virtual machine and runs your containers within that virtual machine. This is done transparently.

> **Note:**
> You don't have to install VirtualBox yourself. Docker is packaged in such a way that it will install or use any already-existing virtualization technology (for example, a hypervisor) for your operating system.

Introduction to containers

Earlier versions of Docker installed VirtualBox to create its virtual machine, but more recent virtualization technology implemented within the operating systems allows Docker to use those technologies instead.

Docker for Linux containers expects the host operating system or the virtual machine to be running Linux. The containers share the Linux kernel with the host. Docker can be used to run Windows native containers, in a similar manner to Linux containers. The Windows kernel is shared among the host and guests. For discussion purposes, we'll focus on the Linux host and guests.

Docker containers are typically used to implement something like headless virtual machines. The use of virtual machines for each application you might create a container for is expensive – you must reserve a fixed amount of RAM and disk space for the virtual machine. On a 16 gigabyte RAM MacBook Pro, you can roughly fit three 4 gigabyte RAM virtual machines running at the same time. You do need to have some RAM for the host operating system to run. Starving the host or guest virtual machines of RAM will cause them to swap, which crushes performance:

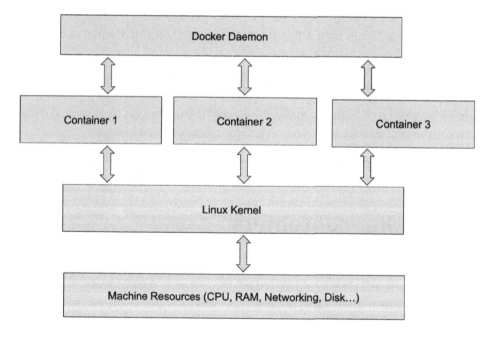

Figure 2.2 – Docker containers illustrated

Containers are separated from the host operating system using host operating system features. The containers use the Linux kernel's namespaces feature (`https://manpages.debian.org/stretch/manpages/namespaces.7.en.html`) to separate the code running in containers from one another, and cgroups (see `https://manpages.debian.org/stretch/manpages/cgroups.7.en.html`) to limit the resources that a container may use (including RAM and CPU). Containers also use the Linux `unionfs` (`https://manpages.debian.org/buster/unionfs-fuse/unionfs.8.en.html`) filesystem to implement the layered filesystem our containers see when running under Docker.

From the applications running within the container's point of view, the container is a whole and dedicated computer; there is no direct communication with the host operating system.

Containers do not require the number of virtual CPUs or a dedicated block of RAM per container.

You are only limited by how much RAM the containers need and how much RAM the host has.

Containers share the host's Linux kernel, while virtual machines must have a whole operating system installed!

You may choose to limit the resources used by a container instance, but this is not required.

Host resources may be shared with the guest containers. The host's networking can be shared with any container, but this is only really needed for containers running applications that require this. For example, to use the host's Bonjour networking functionality, the guest would use the host's networking.

The guest containers may expose ports to the host and any computers that can access the host. For example, a container running an HTTP server might expose port 80 and, when the host is accessed at port 80, the container responds.

Containers have driven the concept of microservices. An application using microservice architecture implements a collection of services that communicate among themselves and the host. These services are meant to be trivial to implement – only the specific code required to support the service needs to be included in the program. It's not uncommon for microservices to be implemented in a single source code file with just a few lines of code.

Container architecture is quite scalable. You can run multiple containers running the same application (horizontal scaling) and you can dedicate more host resources to the container system (vertical scaling). For example, you might create a container running an HTTP server; you can create a server farm by instantiating as many of these containers as you desire.

Using Docker for development

A great reason to use Docker for development is that you don't have to install any programs, other than Docker itself, on your host to enable development. For example, you can run Apache in a container without installing it on your workstation.

You can also mix and match software versions within your containers. A microservices architecture might require one container to use Node.js version 8 and another container to use Node.js version 10. This is obviously problematic on a single host, but is straightforward when using Docker. One container installs and runs version 8, and another container installs and runs version 10.

During development, you can share your project's development files with the container so that when you edit these files, the container sees that the files have changed.

Each container has its own set of global environment variables. It's typical to configure the application using environment variables, rather than in source code or configuration files within the container.

When you are ready to deploy or publish a container, you can push it to a container hosting service, such as Docker Hub. In fact, Docker Hub is a terrific source for already-existing containers that may aid you in your project development. There are pre-made container images for MongoDB, Node.js (various versions), Apache, and so on.

Container construction is effectively object-oriented. You inherit from a base container and add the functionality you need to that. You can create a Node.js application in a container that starts with a ready-made Node.js container, install npm packages in the container, and run your custom code in the container.

You can always develop your own base containers. For these, you can start with ready-made packages for a flavor of Linux. The Alpine Linux base container is popular because it is one of the most lightweight images to start from. There are base containers for Fedora, Ubuntu, Arch Linux, and more. Whichever of these Linux containers you start from, you can use that operating system's installation tools to add packages from the official repositories for that operating system; that is, apt for Ubuntu, yum for Fedora, and so on.

It's a good idea to Dockerize an existing application that wasn't designed to run in a container. You can choose a flavor and version of Linux for the container that is compatible with the application, and you can split up the application into multiple container images to afford future scalability.

For example, you might have an older LAMP application that requires specific versions of PHP, MySQL, and Apache, as well as an older version of Ubuntu. You would break this up into a distinct MySQL container, and a distinct Apache plus PHP container. You would want your Apache+PHP containers to use a shared volume so that they're all running the same and latest PHP source code. You can set up the MySQL container to use master-slave replication. You can set up a load balancer in another container that balances between as many Apache and PHP container instances as you choose.

Time for a hands-on example, using Docker for development.

Getting started with Docker

We have created a GitHub repository to share code examples for this book. The repository can be found at `https://github.com/PacktPublishing/Docker-for-Developers`. You should fork this repository, and then clone it to your host. Creating the fork means you can manage your copy of the repository as you see fit without requiring permissions. The code of interest for this section is in the `chapter2/` directory. The code here implements a small Apache+PHP application that is designed to run in a container. There are `sh` scripts to perform the Docker command lines, so you don't have to keep typing in a long string of command-line arguments.

Before we get into the code, let's make sure that Docker is installed properly. The `docker ps` command prints a list of all running Docker containers. We can see we have no containers running and there is an actual `docker` command:

```
% docker ps
CONTAINER ID          IMAGE              COMMAND
CREATED               STATUS             PORTS
NAMES
%
```

A Dockerfile is a text file that defines how to build a Docker container image. The container is not started; it is just created on disk. Once built, you can start as many instances as you wish.

Automating Docker commands via sh scripts

We're going to make heavy use of the `docker cli` command and `sh` scripts to automate command-line use. The use of `sh` script files has a few advantages. Once the script file is created, you don't have to remember what all the command-line switches to the command are. Once the script is correct, you won't have any issues due to typos or improper command-line switches. Typing the script filename is much shorter and your shell should autocomplete it when you type the first few characters of the name and hit the *Tab* key. Finally, the names of the scripts are mnemonic: `build.sh` means build the container, `run.sh` means run the container, and so on.

The `sh` scripts we provide are as follows:

- `./build.sh`: This builds the container from the Dockerfile. You will want to run this script whenever you edit the Dockerfile, or if the container otherwise needs to be built.

- `./debug.sh`: This runs the container in debug mode. In debug mode, Apache is run in foreground mode and you can hit `^C` to stop the container.

- `./run.sh`: This runs the container as a daemon. Unlike the `./debug.sh` script, you will be returned to the command-line prompt, with the container running in Docker. You will use this script to run the container locally, as if in production, so that you can test production behavior.

- `./stop.sh`: When you have your container running in the background, this script can be used to stop it.

- `./shell.sh`: Sometimes, when creating your container and editing the Dockerfile, things do not work as expected. You can use this script to get a Bash command line running within the container. From this command line, you can inspect and diagnose the problems.

- `./persist.sh`: This script demonstrates using a named volume to persist the application state within the container. That is, with a named volume, you can stop and restart the container and the contents of the volume are persisted. The volume is mounted in the container as if it were a disk.

To demonstrate how building a container using a Dockerfile works, we've created one in the GitHub repository, in the `chapter2/` directory (file named `Dockerfile`):

```
# we will inherit from the Debian image on DockerHub
FROM debian

# set timezone so files' timestamps are correct
ENV TZ=America/Los_Angeles
```

```
# install apache and php 7.3
# we include procps and telnet so you can use these with shell.
sh prompt
RUN apt-get update && apt-get install -y procps telnet apache2
php7.3

# add a user - this user will own the files in /home/app
RUN useradd --user-group --create-home --shell /bin/false app

# set up and copy files to /home/app
ENV HOME=/usr/app
WORKDIR /home/app
COPY . /home/app

# The PHP app is going to save its state in /data so we make a
/data inside the container
RUN mkdir /data && chown -R app /data && chmod 777 /data
```

```
# we need custom php configuration file to enable userdirs
COPY php.conf /etc/apache2/mods-available/php7.3.conf

# enable userdir and php
RUN a2enmod userdir && a2enmod php7.3

# we run a script to stat the server; the array syntax makes it
so ^C will work as we want
CMD ["./entrypoint.sh"]
```

Let's look at what the Dockerfile does, step by step:

1. The Dockerfile inherits from the Debian image on Docker Hub.

2. We set the time zone for the container to match the time zone of the host; in other words, ensure that the timestamps of files inside the container and on the host match. This is important when mapping host directories to the container's filesystem.

3. We then install Apache and PHP 7.3. These are installed in the container's filesystem and not on the host's filesystem. We have avoided the pollution problem of having a version of both installed on the host that later become unused when not working on this project.

4. We also installed some command-line utilities that allow us to examine the state of the built container from a Bash shell running within the container.

5. By default, the user and group that will be running the project in the container is
    `root`. In order to provide some typical Unix/Linux security, we want to run as an
    actual user; in our case, the username is `app`. So we add the user to the container's
    environment with `useradd`.

6. We are going to put our PHP scripts in `/home/app`, with the ability to map our
    working directory with our PHP scripts on the host over `/home/app`.

7. Our demo app writes its state to `/data`, so we need to create it and ensure that the
    PHP script running as a user app can read and write files there.

8. We created a custom PHP configuration file that we want to use within the
    container, so we copy it to the container in the correct location in the filesystem.

9. We need to enable the `userdir` and `php7.3` modules. This allows us to run PHP
    scripts from Apache as well as have our PHP scripts in `/home/app/public_`
    `html` accessed via a URL such as `http://localhost/~app/index.php`.

10. When the container is started, it needs to run some program or script within
    the container. We use an `sh` script named `entrypoint.sh` in the `/home/app`
    directory to start the application. We can edit this file to suit our needs
    during development.

We could have chosen from a variety of Linux flavors from which to start. We chose
Debian here because the configuration commands should be familiar to most readers.
If you install Debian in a virtual machine, you'd use the same commands to install and
maintain your system. Debian isn't the smallest or most lightweight of Linux images
to start from; Alpine is a great choice if you want to make your container use fewer
resources. If you choose to use Alpine, be sure to read up on how to install packages
and maintain the system using Alpine.

Note that whichever Linux image you start from, it's sharing the Linux kernel with your
host machine. Only within the container is it Debian – your host operating system can be
some other Linux distribution. What you install inside the container is not installed on
your workstation, only within the container. Obviously, you shouldn't mix, say, Debian
commands and installed packages directly on an Arch Linux workstation.

When you install Apache on an actual host or virtual machine, you configure it by using
the `a2enmod` and `a2dismod` commands, as well as by editing the various configuration
files in `/etc/apache2`. What we do here is edit the configuration file locally on our
workstation, and then we copy that configuration file to the container.

The Dockerfile installs a few Debian applications within the container using apt-get. The RUN command that spawns apt-get within the container uses the -y switch to answer yes to any questions apt-get might ask, the -qq switch to make the apt-get command less verbose, and the >/dev/null redirection of stdio to make the Docker build (build.sh) output compact. Without the -qq and stdout redirection, the build output would contain every package and dependency downloaded, along with all the installation commands for all these packages.

Note that the final line in the Dockerfile is a CMD, the command to run when the container is instantiated. In our case, we use an array with one item, entrypoint.sh. The array makes it so that you can hit *Ctrl* + *C* to stop the container. The entrypoint.sh script runs Apache in the container after performing the necessary initialization. Also note that we enabled both the userdir and php7.3 modules in the Dockerfile.

Now that we have a Dockerfile, we need to be able to build the container so that we can then use it. This is where the first of our .sh scripts comes into play.

Understanding build.sh

The build.sh script is used to build the container. You will need to build the container at least once so that we can edit files on the host and see the changes in action within the container. You will need to rebuild the container each time you want to try the container in production mode and have the latest versions of the files:

```
#!/bin/sh

# build.sh

# we use the "docker build" command to build a container named
"chapter2" from . (current directory)
# Dockerfile is found in the current directory, and determines
how the conatiner is built.

docker build -t chapter2 .
```

The -t flag says to name the container chapter 2. The Dockerfile is found in the current directory. The output of the build.sh script is lengthy, so it is omitted here.

You can see that each step printed in the output while building the container corresponds
to a line in the Dockerfile:

```
Sending build context to Docker daemon  15.87kB
Step 1/11 : FROM debian
 ---> 67e34c1c9477
Step 2/11 : ENV TZ=America/Los_Angeles
 ---> Using cache
 ---> 7bfa02a200a8
Step 3/11 : RUN apt-get update -qq >/dev/null && apt-get
install -y -qq procps telnet apache2 php7.3 -qq >/dev/null
 ---> Running in 98a4e3192e22
debconf: delaying package configuration, since apt-utils is not
installed
Removing intermediate container 98a4e3192e22
 ---> 86aa2b03b3b1
Step 4/11 : RUN useradd --user-group --create-home --shell /
bin/false app
 ---> Running in 917b16b86dc5
Removing intermediate container 917b16b86dc5
 ---> ef96ff367f1f
Step 5/11 : ENV HOME=/usr/app
 ---> Running in c9706abf0afd
Removing intermediate container c9706abf0afd
 ---> 4cc08031746b
Step 6/11 : WORKDIR /home/app
 ---> Running in 08c2b9c79204
Removing intermediate container 08c2b9c79204
 ---> 9b68722d6776
Step 7/11 : COPY . /home/app
 ---> d6a7b4a1a4f3
Step 8/11 : RUN mkdir /data && chown -R app /data && chmod 777
/data
 ---> Running in fe824496056c
Removing intermediate container fe824496056c
 ---> 75996f4d08bc
Step 9/11 : COPY php.conf /etc/apache2/mods-available/
php7.3.conf
 ---> c6a3b094a041
Step 10/11 : RUN a2enmod userdir && a2enmod php7.3
 ---> Running in 1899c1d01a2e
Removing intermediate container 1899c1d01a2e
 ---> ae6ddd93786c
Step 11/11 : CMD ["./entrypoint.sh"]
 ---> Running in cb0ffeaefca6
```

```
Removing intermediate container cb0ffeaefca6
 ---> 9c64d1cb6bd3
Successfully built 9c64d1cb6bd3
Successfully tagged chapter2:latest
```

The container is incrementally built, as described by the Dockerfile. Each step is built in an image layer denoted with a hash value – those are the hex hash values printed. When you build the container again, Docker can start from the state of any of those layers' / hash values, reducing the need to constantly rebuild the container from scratch. Each layer is simply a diff (difference) between the current layer's requirements and the state of the previous layer.

The first layer is the Debian image. The next layer is an intermediate image, the diff between the result of the ENV command in the Dockerfile and the original Debian image. The next layer is the diff between this previous intermediate image and the result of the apt-get installed packages. Note that we use && to pack a few apt-get commands into one layer in the container. This greatly speeds up the build process. The layering continues as each command in the Dockerfile is processed by the Docker build command.

Docker is smart about how it caches and works with the layers. It doesn't have to download the Debian image each time you build; it can start building from a previous intermediate stage if it knows the previous steps have not changed the state of the container to that point.

Whenever we need to build the container, because we've made changes to the Dockerfile, we use the build.sh script. Once we have the container built, we have a few ways to use it. The debug.sh script is probably the most common script you'll use during development.

Understanding debug.sh

The debug.sh script runs the container image that is not in daemon mode. You can hit *Ctrl + C* to stop the program:

```
#!/usr/bin/env bash

# debug.sh

# run container without making it a daemon - useful to see
logging output

docker run \
    --rm \
    -p8086:80 \
```

```
--name="chapter2" \
-v `pwd`:/home/app \
chapter2
```

The `docker run` command takes many optional arguments that are too numerous to detail here. For more complete information on all of the possible command-line arguments to `docker run`, refer to the `docker run` documentation on the Docker site: `https://docs.docker.com/engine/reference/run/`. We'll only cover the ones used in our scripts:

- Here, we use `-rm`, which tells Docker to clean up when the container exits, removing the container and filesystem for the container.

- The `-p` flag tells Docker to map port `80` from the container (HTTP) to port `8086` on the host; you can access the HTTP server in the container by using port `8086` on the host.

- The `-name` argument names the running container; if you don't provide a name, you'll have to use `docker ps` to get the hash that identifies the container to stop it using `docker stop`.

- The `-v` switch mounts volumes in the container. A volume can be a directory of a file on the host, a named volume that Docker manages for you. If you want to stop and restart the container and retain data that is written to the filesystem by the container, you must mount a volume and the container must write to this volume. You can mount multiple volumes, if you like. In our `debug.sh` script, we mount the current directory with the sources over `/home/app`, so we can modify the sources and the container programs see that the files are changed (because the file timestamps are newer) as if they were inside the container, too. For this demo, you can edit the `index.php` script and reload the page, and you'll see the change in action. If you don't mount this volume, then the container will access the files copied to `/home/app` by the Dockerfile and the `build.sh` script; this is what you want for production.

- The last argument to `docker run` is the name of the container to start – in our case, it's `chapter2`, the container image we created using the `build.sh` script.

> **Note:**
> We do not persist `/data` in the container. We can do this by adding the `-v` switch to map a Docker volume to `/data`, which we will do in the `persist.sh` script.

Running our chapter2 container with debug.sh

Let's see the container in action. We run the `build.sh` script and see that it succeeds. Then, we use the `debug.sh` script to launch the container in `debug/foreground` mode. Note that we did not do any configuration of the hostname for the container, so there is a warning message printed by Apache:

```
%  ./debug.sh
entrypoint.sh
----> Point your browser at http://localhost:8086/~app/index.
php
AH00558: apache2: Could not reliably determine the server's
fully qualified domain name, using 172.17.0.5. Set the
'ServerName' directive globally to suppress this message
```

On the host, we can use a browser to fetch `http://localhost:8086/~app/index.php`.

Remember, we mapped port `8086` to port `80` of the container, we enabled the `userdir` module, and, in the Dockerfile, we copied the `index.php` script to `/home/app/public_html` (the `userdir` module).

We could have configured Apache with a default host and copied our files to `/var/www` in the Dockerfile and build process. This would have given us a cleaner URL, and this is what you would want to do for an actual production site. For our purposes, it's good to see the Apache modules enabled and working within the container:

```
Hello, world
Counterx: 1
```

Figure 2.3 – Browser showing the output of our program

When we reload the page in the browser a few times, we can see that the counter is being properly maintained:

```
Hello, world
Counterx: 5
```

Figure 2.4 – Page after we reload

Note that we aren't generating any HTML (yet). If you're trying this yourself, you can now edit the `index.php` file, change `Counterx:` to `Counter:` and reload the page, and you will see that the page prints `Counter:` now.

We are now set up for PHP development.

If we want to add, say, MySQL support, we'll have to modify the Dockerfile to install the PHP MySQL module, and enable it as we did with `userdir` and `php`. If we want to add a PHP framework, we either need to install it within the container via the Dockerfile, or add it to the `chapter2/` directory that is copied to the container's `/home/app` directory and, for development, mounted/bound in the container by replacing `/home/app`.

We can check to see that the container is running by using the `docker ps` command:

```
% docker ps
```

CONTAINER ID CREATED NAMES	IMAGE STATUS	COMMAND PORTS
54925e51e404 seconds ago chapter2	chapter2 Up 1 second	"./entrypoint.sh" 2 0.0.0.0:8086->80/tcp

We can exit or kill the container by pressing *Ctrl + C* in the window where we started it with `debug.sh`.

When we run the container with the `run.sh` script, we don't see any output from the container, not even the Apache warning:

```
% ./run.sh
1707b1ff84fabed4d9696aadbcd597cee08063eaa7ad22bfe572c922df
43997e
```

Again, we use `docker ps` to see that it is running:

```
% docker ps
```

CONTAINER ID CREATED NAMES	IMAGE STATUS	COMMAND PORTS

```
1707b1ff84fa            chapter2                "./entrypoint.sh"    41
seconds ago          Up 39 seconds         0.0.0.0:8086->80/tcp
chapter2
```

Loading the same URL in the browser, we see that the counter is again 1. Reloading a few times, we see the counter increments as we designed.

We can restart the container using `docker restart`. Note that the container was first instantiated 3 minutes ago, but since we restarted it, the status is `Up 1 second`:

```
% docker ps
CONTAINER ID          IMAGE                 COMMAND
CREATED               STATUS                PORTS
NAMES
1707b1ff84fa          chapter2              "./entrypoint.sh"
About a minute ago    Up 1 second           0.0.0.0:8086->80/tcp
chapter2
```

Since the container was only restarted, its filesystem remains intact. Reloading the URL in our browser, we see that the counter continues to increment. We can stop the container using `docker stop`, or the `stop.sh` script. The `docker ps` command shows no containers running. Then we start it up again:

```
% docker ps
CONTAINER ID          IMAGE                 COMMAND
CREATED               STATUS                PORTS
NAMES
```

Now, when we reload in our browser, the counter is reset to 1. This is because we are writing to the container's filesystem. The filesystem goes away when the container exits.

If we want the counter to persist between container start/restart, we'd have to write it to a volume that is mounted on the container.

We write to `/data/container.txt`, so we can do the following:

- Mount our own `container.txt` on the host to `/data/container.txt` on the guest.

- Mount a directory on the host as `/data` on the guest.

- Have Docker create and maintain a named or anonymous volume for us.

Since the advent of named volumes, they are the better choice. A named volume is created and maintained using the -v switch to docker run with just the name of the directory on the guest; for example, -v name:/data. We have a script, persist.sh, designed to make using the named volume easy.

persist.sh

The persist.sh script does the same thing as the debug.sh script, except that it adds the -v name:/data switch to the docker run command:

```
#!/usr/bin/env bash


# run container without making it a daemon - useful to see
logging output
# we are adding an anonymous volume for /data in the container
so the
# counter persists between runs.


docker run \
    --rm \
    -p8086:80 \
    --name="chapter2" \
    -v `pwd`:/home/app \
    -v name:/data \
    chapter2
```

When we run it and point our browser at http://localhost:8086/~app/index.php, we see that the counter works, even if we stop and restart the container.

run.sh

The run.sh script runs the container in daemon mode – you won't be able to see the application's output without using the docker log command. It also does not mount the host directory as a volume in the container. This simulates the production environment:

```
#!/usr/bin/env bash

# run.sh


# run the container in the background
# /data is persisted using a named container
```

```
docker run \
    --detach \
    --rm \
    --restart always \
    -p8086:80 \
    -v name:/data \
    --name="chapter2" \
    chapter2
```

We are using the `docker run` command, once again, but with slightly different arguments:

- The `-detach` flag to Docker Run is what causes the container to run in the background.

- The named volume is used, so the data is persisted between starting and stopping the container.

- The development working directory is mounted on `/home/app` within the container.

- The `-restart` switch always tells Docker to restart the container when the system is rebooted. This is handy since you won't have to figure out some way to automatically start your container(s) when the operating system starts.

The container is only able to run using the files copied to it using the Dockerfile and `build.sh`. If you edit files on your host, you will not see the changes within the running container, as with `persist.sh`. You will need to run the `build.sh` script every time you edit files and want them changed within the container for the purposes of `run.sh`.

We'll need a way to stop our running container. This is where `stop.sh` comes in.

stop.sh

The `stop.sh` script will stop your `chapter2` container. This is particularly useful when you've used the `run.sh` script to launch your container in the background:

```
#!/bin/sh

# stop.sh

# stop running container - typing stop.sh is easier than the
whole docker command

docker stop chapter2
```

Let's see `run.sh` and `stop.sh` in action:

```
build.sh  debug.sh  Dockerfile  entrypoint.sh  install-
virtualbox-macos.sh  persist.sh  php.conf  public_html  README.
md  run.sh  shell.sh  stop.sh
 % docker ps
CONTAINER ID             IMAGE                  COMMAND
CREATED                  STATUS                 PORTS
NAMES
 % ./run.sh
7d6bc5195a583b3979a2533b50708978d96981d3d9ac59b266055246b6
fad329
 % docker ps
CONTAINER ID             IMAGE                  COMMAND
CREATED                  STATUS                 PORTS
NAMES
7d6bc5195a58            chapter2               "./entrypoint.sh"    2
seconds ago     Up 1 second          0.0.0.0:8086->80/tcp
chapter2
 % ./stop.sh
chapter2
 % docker ps
CONTAINER ID             IMAGE                  COMMAND
CREATED                  STATUS                 PORTS
NAMES
%
```

The `shell.sh` script runs the container and starts the Bash shell so that you can use command-line programs to diagnose issues with the container as it's built:

```
#!/usr/bin/env bash

# shell.sh

# This script starts a shell in an already built container.
Sometimes you need to poke around using the shell
# to diagnose problems.

# stop any existing running container
./stop.sh

# fire up the container with shell (/bin/bash)
docker run -it --rm --name chapter2 chapter2 /bin/bash
```

The following code snippet shows the `shell.sh` script in action:

```
% ./shell.sh
Error response from daemon: No such container: chapter2
root@f10092244abe:/home/app# ls -l
total 44
-rw-r--r-- 1 root root 871 Dec 13 10:28 Dockerfile
-rw-r--r-- 1 root root 808 Dec  5 14:56 README.md
-rwxr-xr-x 1 root root  38 Dec  4 12:15 build.sh
-rwxr-xr-x 1 root root 197 Dec  4 16:12 debug.sh
-rwxr-xr-x 1 root root 411 Dec 13 10:28 entrypoint.sh
-rw-r--r-- 1 root root  75 Dec  2 17:31 install-virtualbox-
macos.sh
-rwxr-xr-x 1 root root 315 Dec 13 10:26 persist.sh
-rw-r--r-- 1 root root 860 Dec  4 16:24 php.conf
drwxr-xr-x 1 root root  18 Dec 13 10:27 public_html
-rwxr-xr-x 1 root root 152 Dec  5 13:01 run.sh
-rwxr-xr-x 1 root root 308 Dec  4 17:40 shell.sh
-rwxr-xr-x 1 root root 115 Dec  4 17:41 stop.sh
root@f10092244abe:/home/app# ls -ldg /data
drwxrwxrwx 1 root 0 Dec 13 10:28 /data
root@f10092244abe:/home/app# exit
%
```

We can see that `/data` was created and has world write permissions.

These few `sh` scripts are enough to get you developing and using your own containers. As you work with Docker, you'll likely come up with additional scripts of your own! However, we will see in *Chapter 4, Composing Systems Using Containers*, a way to work with Docker without the `sh` scripts.

Summary

In this chapter, we have learned about how VirtualBox can be used to create virtual machines on your workstation and how you can use it to run Windows (or Linux or other operating systems) in a virtual machine. We also learned enough about Docker to use it to build our first application.

This chapter was written using Windows 10 running within a VirtualBox virtual machine, running on an Arch Linux host. Microsoft Word was used within Windows, while the Docker commands and scripts were run and edited on the Arch Linux host.

We demonstrated how we can build a LAMP-style application, without MySQL, and containerize it. We can mount our source code directory from the host to the container so that we can edit files and see the changes immediately in the container. We learned how to persist data, meaning that stopping and starting the container would retain important files and state.

In the next chapter, we'll explore Docker Hub and build a more complex application that requires more than one container.

Further reading

- This URL is for the official Docker documentation:
  `https://docs.docker.com`

- This URL is for the Dockerfile reference:
  `https://docs.docker.com/engine/reference/builder/`

- This URL is for the documentation for the Docker `ps` command:
  `https://docs.docker.com/engine/reference/commandline/ps/`

- This URL is for the documentation pertaining to volumes and storage in Docker:
  `https://docs.docker.com/storage`

- This URL is for the documentation pertaining to the Docker `run` command:
  `https://docs.docker.com/engine/reference/run/`

- This URL is for the documentation pertaining to the Docker `restart` command:
  `https://docs.docker.com/engine/reference/commandline/restart/`

- This URL is for the documentation pertaining to the Docker `stop` command:
  `https://docs.docker.com/engine/reference/commandline/stop/`

3

Sharing Containers Using Docker Hub

In the previous chapter, we learned how to build a container and run it on our workstation using Docker. We used a Debian image as our starting point, but where did that image come from? The answer is that it came from Docker Hub. Docker Hub is the official container image library for Docker, run by the same folk who brought us Docker itself.

The container library contains the official images for numerous programs, servers, services, and so on that you might install within your own containers. For example, there are official images for various Linux distributions, versions of Node.js, versions of MySQL and MongoDB, and so on.

You can think of Docker Hub as being like GitHub. You can explore existing organizations and pre-made containers, as well as upload your own containers and create your own organizations.

We will demonstrate how to use the Docker Hub website to search and get information for third-party containers that you can use in your applications. We will also demonstrate how to use third-party containers from Docker Hub using the command line. We will use the official MongoDB container from Docker Hub, which is published by MongoDB, Inc.

Entire backend applications can be implemented as a combination of multiple Docker containers working together. This application structure allows each of our custom container implementations to be simple and minimal. We'll apply microservices architecture to build a simple application. This demonstrates how containers can work together to create a complete working application. Lastly, we'll see how you can share your ready-for-production containers with third parties and your development team using Docker Hub.

In this chapter, we will cover the following topics:

- Introducing Docker Hub

- Implementing a MongoDB container for our application

- Introducing the microservices architecture

- Implementing a sample microservices application

- Sharing your containers on Docker Hub

Technical requirements

The only technical requirements are to have Docker installed on your host, and a browser, such as Google Chrome, Firefox, or Microsoft Edge. This is one of the best parts of Docker—you don't have to install the complex servers/services on your host; we install them in Docker containers.

We have prepared examples that you can use directly without modification in a public GitHub repository, which can be found at `https://github.com/PacktPublishing/Docker-for-Developers`.

Check out the following video to see the Code in Action:

`https://bit.ly/2PTADjH`

Introducing Docker Hub

You will typically interact with Docker Hub from the command line or in Dockerfiles, but you can use the Docker Hub website (`https://hub.docker.com`) to search for any pre-built containers that you know you want to use. You can also use the website to discover pre-built containers that might be of interest to you.

In general, you will inherit from some pre-built Docker containers on Docker Hub to create your own custom containers. For example, you might inherit from a Linux distribution container and install the software you want for your project within that inherited/custom container.

When you inherit from the Linux distribution, some of that distribution's base software packages are installed. If you inherit from a Debian-flavor Linux container, you will be able to use the `apt` package manager within the container to install software as if you were running that Debian-flavor Linux container on a dedicated or virtual machine.

Some pre-built containers inherit from a Linux flavor and provide pre-installed packages that are specific to the offering. When you inherit from a Node.js container, that Node.js container might inherit from a Linux distribution container and will have Node.js, npm, and `yarn` already installed.

Interacting with Docker Hub from the command line

The easiest way to see Docker Hub and Docker working together is to run the official `hello-world` container. The command to run a container from Docker Hub is `docker run name-of-container`; we'll type `docker run hello-world`:

```
# docker run hello-world
Unable to find image 'hello-world:latest' locally
latest: Pulling from library/hello-world
1b930d010525: Pull complete
Digest: sha256:4fe721ccc2e8dc7362278a29dc660d833570ec2682f4e
4194f4ee23e415e1064
Status: Downloaded newer image for hello-world:latest


Hello from Docker!
This message shows that your installation appears to be working
correctly.


To generate this message, Docker took the following steps:
 1. The Docker client contacted the Docker daemon.
 2. The Docker daemon pulled the "hello-world" image from the
Docker Hub.
    (amd64)
 3. The Docker daemon created a new container from that image
which runs the
    executable that produces the output you are currently
reading.
 4. The Docker daemon streamed that output to the Docker
client, which sent it
    to your terminal.
```

```
To try something more ambitious, you can run an Ubuntu
container with:

 $ docker run -it ubuntu bash


Share images, automate workflows, and more with a free Docker
ID:

 https://hub.docker.com/


For more examples and ideas, visit:

 https://docs.docker.com/get-started/
```

Docker did not find the container in its local container cache, so it automatically downloaded it and then ran it within the Docker engine. This code in the container is simple—it just prints the preceding messages.

> **Note**
>
> You can run any container you find on the Docker Hub website in the same way!

If your output does not resemble the preceding output, you either have an issue with your Docker installation or the Docker Hub servers are not accessible from your host. One possible problem may be that your installation of Docker requires you to run the `docker` commands as root or an administrator.

The installation instructions can be found at `https://docs.docker.com/install/`, while the post-installation instructions for Docker can be found at `https://docs.docker.com/install/linux/linux-postinstall/`. These post-installation instructions explain how to set up Docker so that you can manage it as a non-root user.

Using the Docker Hub website

Let's go find the `hello-world` container page in Docker Hub—`https://hub.docker.com/_/hello-world`. The page will look something like this:

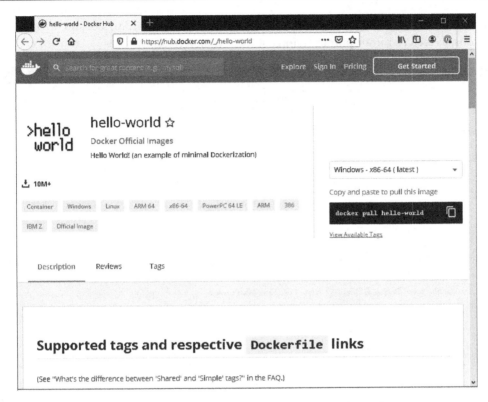

Figure 3.1 – The hello-world image page on Docker Hub

This is typical of what you'll see for most containers shared on Docker Hub. Specific software packages encapsulated in a container, such as MongoDB, offer official images for various versions of the software. This allows you to deal with software that depends on a specific version of a Docker Hub package.

The MongoDB page on Docker Hub is `https://hub.docker.com/_/mongo`. To find it, simply type `mongodb` into the search box at the top of the **hello-world** (or any other package) page and select it from the search results page. You can use the search box to find any shared images for whatever software you might want.

Of interest are the **Simple Tags** and **Shared Tags** sections of the page. The various version images of MongoDB are tagged with simple tags and shared tags.

For example, the **3.4-xenial** simple tag means there is an image for version 3.4 of MongoDB running in an Ubuntu Xenial container.

The **3.4** shared tag means there are images of version 3.4 of MongoDB that run on more than one host operating system—typically, Windows Server, Linux, or macOS. The Docker daemon will choose the appropriate image for the host operating system.

As of the time of writing, there are images for the MongoDB 3.4, 3.6, 4.0, and 4.2 major versions, as well as minor point versions of these major versions:

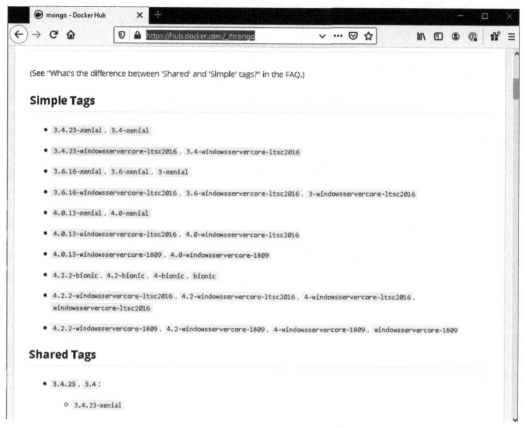

Figure 3.2 – Simple tags and shared tags for hello-world

The process for finding the available pre-built third-party containers is the same. You can search for Redis, for example, and you will get a similar page with details about the available Redis containers.

Implementing a MongoDB container for our application

We can explore using pre-built containers from Docker Hub by implementing a MongoDB container. We'll use this container later as part of a demo application that is made up of several containers that work together.

We will use the official Docker image for MongoDB, found on the Docker Hub website at `https://hub.docker.com/_/mongo`. We will create a `.sh` script to start running our image within Docker so that the startup process is easy and repeatable.

We learned in *Chapter 2, Using VirtualBox and Docker Containers for Development*, that we can expose a container's network ports to the host. That means we can run this MongoDB container image in Docker and access the running MongoDB server within that container by accessing the MongoDB port on the host.

In the GitHub repository (`https://github.com/PacktPublishing/Docker-for-Developers`) for this book, there is a `chapter3/` directory, which is a companion for this chapter. Within that directory is a shell script, `start-mongodb.sh`. This script is a bit more elaborate than the simple ones we used in the previous chapter. We're going to use environment variables to configure MongoDB, and we're going to use a directory on the host for MongoDB's data files—this makes backing up the data as easy as copying those files to back-up media:

```
#!/bin/bash
# start-mongodb.sh
SERVICE=mongodb # name of the service
# You can set these in this script (uncomment and edit the
lines) or set them in your .zshrc/.bashrc/etc.
# Change this to an EXISTING directory on the HOST where the
mongodb database files will be created #!/bin/bash
# start-mongodb.sh
SERVICE=mongodb # name of the service
# Change this to an EXISTING directory on the HOST where the
mongodb database files will be created and maintained.
#MONGO_DATADIR="$HOME/data"
# Stop any running MongoDB container, remove previous
container, pull newer version
docker stop $SERVICE
docker rm $SERVICE
docker pull mongo:3.4
# Now we run it!
docker run …
```

You do need a Dockerfile to create a container image. However, if you are using a pre-made container image from Docker Hub that is standalone, such as MongoDB, you won't need one. The developers at MongoDB use Dockerfiles to generate the images before uploading them to Docker Hub.

In fact, you can see from the **Supported tags** section of the MongoDB page in Docker Hub that they produce and support quite a few images, including different versions—some for Windows OS, some for Linux, and so on. The MongoDB developers must have quite a few Dockerfiles—one for each image!

We must provide one environment variable to `start-mongodb.sh`: `MONGO_DATADIR`, which is an existing directory on your workstation where you want MongoDB in the container to store its data files. There are a few ways to set this variable:

- You can add `export MONGODB_DATADIR=/path/to/data/dir` to your shell startup file (`.zshrc`, `.bashrc`, and so on).

- You can do the `export` (environment variable) operation by hand in the shell before running the script.

- You can set the value of the environment variable when using the command line to run the `start-mongodb.sh` script:
  `# MONGODB_DATADIR=~/data ./start-mongodb.sh`.

- You can uncomment the line that sets `MONGO_DATADIR` in the `start-mongodb.sh` script file and edit it to set it to your desired data directory each time you run the script.

The last line in the `start-mongodb.sh` script is a single command line. The backslash (\) character at the end of the line signifies that the line is being continued or joined with the next line. This command is the one that starts the container. As you can imagine, if you had to type in this long command every time to start your MongoDB container, it would be painful. The `.sh` script makes it rather painless:

```
docker run \
  --name $SERVICE \
  -d \
  --restart always \
  -e TITLE=$SERVICE \
  -p 27017:27017 \
  -v "$MONGO_DATADIR":/data/db \
  mongo:3.4
```

Let's take a look at the different parts of the preceding command:

- The `docker run` command names the `mongodb` running container.

- The `-d` switch runs the container in detached mode. The container will automatically start when your workstation is rebooted.

- The -e switch allows you to pass environment variables to the container; in this case, we pass the TITLE=mongodb environment variable. You can have multiple -e switches if you want to pass more than one variable.

- The -p switch exposes port 27017 in the container to port 27017 on the host. You can remap an exposed port in the container to a different port number on the host. You would do this if you have a MongoDB server already running in a container or on your host. However, Docker provides us the flexibility to always run MongoDB within a container, so we'll never have to install it on our host.

  We might want to install MongoDB client programs on the host so that we can access MongoDB using the MongoDB REPL/shell. Once port 27017 is exposed on the host, any program can access the MongoDB database, using it as if it were running on the host.

- The -v switch maps a directory on the host to the directory in the container where MongoDB will manage its database and other files.

- We choose to download and run mongo:3.4 (tag/version 3.4) from Docker Hub.

> **Note**
> The docker run command only downloads the container from Docker Hub if it doesn't exist on your workstation yet or if the container image on Docker Hub is newer.

You can run any container you find on Docker Hub in the same way!

Let's run the script by using the following commands:

```
# mkdir -p ~/mongodb
# MONGO_DATADIR=~/mongodb ./start-mongodb.sh
```

The following output contains a few warnings about not being able to stop an already-running container named mongodb (this is expected):

```
# mkdir -p ~/mongodb && MONGO_DATADIR=~/mongodb ./start-mongodb.sh
stopping mongodb
Error response from daemon: No such container: mongodb
removing old mongodb
Error: No such container: mongodb
pulling mongodb
3.4: Pulling from library/mongo
976a760c94fc: Pull complete
```

```
c58992f3c37b: Pull complete
0ca0e5e7f12e: Pull complete
...

3757d63ce2b9: Pull complete
Digest: sha256:4c7003e140fc7dce5f12817d510b5a9bd265f2
c3bbd6f81d50a60cc11f6395d9
Status: Downloaded newer image for mongo:3.4
docker.io/library/mongo:3.4
e3854f6931e1aa4b64557d5a54e652653123f84a
544fedf39a5cf68d2ee9d0af
 # docker ps
CONTAINER ID          IMAGE               COMMAND
CREATED               STATUS              PORTS
NAMES
e3854f6931e1           mongo:3.4           "docker-entrypoint.s…"
5 seconds ago         Up 3 seconds        0.0.0.0:27017->27017/
tcp    mongodb
 #
```

Docker pulled the proper MongoDB image and ran it in the background in the Docker engine. You can observe the following:

- The MongoDB image consists of several layers that were downloaded (`Pull complete`).

- There was already an existing (but older) image on the workstation (`Downloaded newer image...`).

- The container is running via the `docker ps` command.

If the container encounters errors, it may exit and print diagnostic messages in the output. You can run a shell in the container to perform forensic diagnosis.

Running a shell within a container

Generally, you would run a shell within the container so that you can discover more about the container's environment. For example, you may have a bug in your Dockerfile—such as forgetting to copy a file into the container. You can run a shell in the container and list directories and you will see that the file is missing.

In the case of the MongoDB container, you might want to run the MongoDB client commands from within the container. The Docker Hub page for the MongoDB container says we can run the client commands by simply attaching to the running container (`https://hub.docker.com/_/mongo`). The command from the MongoDB Docker Hub page is as follows:

```
docker exec -it mongodb bash
```

The different parts of this command are as follows:

- `docker exec` runs a command in a running container (`https://docs.docker.com/engine/reference/commandline/exec/`).
- The `-it` switches specify that Docker is to run the container interactively—this means it gets input from the keyboard and sends output to the Terminal window.

Within the container, we can list directories using the `ls` command:

```
# docker exec -it mongodb bash
root@e3854f6931e1:/# ls
bin   data docker-entrypoint-initdb.d etc   js-yaml.js  lib64
mnt   proc run   srv   tmp   var
boot  dev   entrypoint.sh               home  lib         media
opt   root  sbin  sys   usr
```

We can see that the Docker containers are running using the `ps` command within the container:

```
root@e3854f6931e1:/# ps -aux
USER          PID %CPU %MEM    VSZ    RSS TTY       STAT START
TIME COMMAND
mongodb         1  0.7  0.0 954676 62028 ?         Ssl  22:37
0:02 mongod
root           40  2.8  0.0  18240  3248 pts/0     Ss   22:41
0:00 bash
root           51  0.0  0.0  34420  2848 pts/0     R+   22:41
0:00 ps -aux
root@e3854f6931e1:/#
```

We can run the command-line MongoDB tools inside the container. We did not have to install these on our workstation! Here, we run the MongoDB command and then run the `show collections` and `show databases` commands within the Mongo REPL:

```
root@e3854f6931e1:/# mongo
MongoDB shell version v3.4.23
```

```
connecting to: mongodb://127.0.0.1:27017
MongoDB server version: 3.4.23
Welcome to the MongoDB shell.
For interactive help, type "help".
For more comprehensive documentation, see
        http://docs.mongodb.org/
Questions? Try the support group
        http://groups.google.com/group/mongodb-user
Server has startup warnings:
2019-12-13T22:37:12.342+0000 I CONTROL   [initandlisten]
2019-12-13T22:37:12.342+0000 I CONTROL   [initandlisten] **
WARNING: Access control is not enabled for the database.
2019-12-13T22:37:12.342+0000 I CONTROL   [initandlisten]
**            Read and write access to data and configuration is
unrestricted.
2019-12-13T22:37:12.342+0000 I CONTROL   [initandlisten]
> show collections
> show databases
admin   0.000GB
local   0.000GB
>root@e3854f6931e1:/# exit
```

We're all set to go—MongoDB is running and we were able to use the REPL. The show
collections command returned no collections because we haven't created any. The
show databases command shows that MongoDB has, by default, two databases:
admin and local.

The docker logs command shows us the stdout and stderr output of the container:

```
# docker logs mongodb
2019-12-13T22:37:09.161+0000 I CONTROL   [initandlisten]
MongoDB starting : pid=1 port=27017 dbpath=/data/db 64-bit
host=e3854f6931e1
2019-12-13T22:37:09.162+0000 I CONTROL   [initandlisten] db
version v3.4.23
2019-12-13T22:37:09.162+0000 I CONTROL   [initandlisten] git
version: 324017ede1dbb1c9554dd2dceb15f8da3c59d0e8
2019-12-13T22:37:09.162+0000 I CONTROL   [initandlisten] OpenSSL
version: OpenSSL 1.0.2g  1 Mar 2016
2019-12-13T22:37:09.162+0000 I CONTROL   [initandlisten]
allocator: tcmalloc
2019-12-13T22:37:09.162+0000 I CONTROL   [initandlisten]
modules: none
2019-12-13T22:37:09.162+0000 I CONTROL   [initandlisten] build
environment:
```

```
2019-12-13T22:37:09.162+0000 I CONTROL  [initandlisten]
distmod: ubuntu1604
2019-12-13T22:37:09.162+0000 I CONTROL  [initandlisten]
distarch: x86_64
2019-12-13T22:37:09.162+0000 I CONTROL  [initandlisten]
target_arch: x86_64
2019-12-13T22:37:09.162+0000 I CONTROL  [initandlisten]
options: {}
2019-12-13T22:37:09.165+0000 I STORAGE  [initandlisten]
wiredtiger_open config: create,cache_size=31491M,session_
max=20000,eviction=(threads_min=4,threads_m
ax=4),config_base=false,statistics=(fast),log=(enabled=true,
archive=true,path=journal,compressor=snappy),file_
manager=(close_idle_time=100000),checkpoint=(w
ait=60,log_size=2GB),statistics_log=(wait=0),verbose=(recovery_
progress),
2019-12-13T22:37:14.335+0000 I INDEX    [initandlisten]
building index using bulk method; build may temporarily use up
to 500 megabytes of RAM
2019-12-13T22:37:14.342+0000 I INDEX    [initandlisten] build
index done.  scanned 0 total records. 0 secs
2019-12-13T22:37:14.344+0000 I COMMAND  [initandlisten] setting
featureCompatibilityVersion to 3.4 (
...
```

You will likely use the docker logs command to see the debugging output from your containers.

What we see in our preceding logs is that MongoDB seems to be running just fine within the container. There are no error messages printed.

You can have the docker logs command follow the log file using the -f command-line switch. When the command is in follow mode, any new lines written to the log as the application is running will be appended to the display on the screen.

Up to point, we have explored using Docker to run a complex server application (MongoDB) without having to install MongoDB on our workstation. Using Docker, we have access to MongoDB.

We can start MongoDB using our .sh script, and we can also stop it—we can do this at will so that we don't have to always have MongoDB running in the background.

Now that we know how to run a Docker container, let's have a look at how to work with multiple containers that work together.

Introducing the microservices architecture

Docker and Docker Hub enable development using the microservices architecture. This architecture emphasizes building and running containers that focus on a single aspect of the overall application. When all the containers are running, you have your complete backend application. The containers can be complex, such as a full-blown database server, or simple, such as a short shell script. Ideally, the containers you implement for your application will be simple, short, and focused. Each microservice you write should be simple to debug since you don't need many lines of code.

Suppose we want to develop a backend application that uses MongoDB and Redis and whose application code is written using Node.js. We have the option to create a Dockerfile and start with the MongoDB image. We would then add Redis by installing it using apt, and then add our program to it as we did with the Debian image in *Chapter 2, Using VirtualBox and Docker Containers for Development*. The problem with creating the application using this method is that when you stop the container for development reasons, you're also stopping the running MongoDB and Redis servers.

Instead of a monolithic container with everything installed, you can run MongoDB, Redis, and your custom application containers separately. You can even divide your custom application into multiple containers. All you need is a mechanism to communicate between your application containers.

> **Note**
> It is far better to avoid using monolithic containers in your design! While it might seem that a large and complex program such as MongoDB is a monolithic sort of thing, it's just one dedicated service you can use as a microservice.

Now that we have a brief understanding of microservices architecture, we can examine some of the benefits and requirements of containers as microservices.

Scalability

Scalability is almost always a huge consideration for backend implementations. For example, a simple HTTP/WWW (web page) server can grind to a halt if enough people are trying to fetch our pages from it at the same time. For this reason, server farms exist so that you can deploy two or more of these HTTP/WWW servers that duplicate the functionality of serving our pages. For a two-server farm, you basically get double the number of people fetching your pages from it than for a single server. As traffic grows—for example, if the site gains in popularity—you can add a third server, then a fourth server, and so on. The capability of the backend to serve pages grows as you need it.

In a microservices architecture, we achieve a similar means of scalability. We can run multiple instances of our MongoDB container to achieve more capacity for database operations. The only trick is to configure MongoDB as a cluster or as shards and the application containers to use this database setup.

Inter-container communication

Inter-container communication usually involves some technology that allows messages to be sent from one container to another and for responses or statuses to be sent in return. Being able to communicate between running containers can be done via a few technologies, including the following:

- Sockets
- The filesystem
- Database records
- HTTP
- MQTT

Let's discuss each of them now.

Using sockets

Using sockets is a non-trivial way to communicate between containers. If you have five containers, you might have five sockets per container to provide communication paths between them all. As you scale, more sockets need to be created in each container, and you really want to automate this. There's quite a bit of business logic involved.

Using the filesystem

Using the filesystem involves sharing something such as a network drive among all the containers. To send a message, a container writes to a file in the filesystem. To receive a message, the container reads from a file in the filesystem. The receiver needs to poll, or repeatedly check, the filesystem to detect when the file is written to. This is not ideal because we don't really want to share a network drive like this—the performance is going to be on the slow side.

> **Note**
> Polling is a programming technique where you continuously check the status of a machine state (such as whether a file has changed).

Using database records

Using database records is similar to the filesystem method, except the messages to be sent are simply written to records in the database and the receivers only need to poll the database records for changes. Some databases provide a notification mechanism to tell a client (receiver) that the database has changed.

Both filesystem and database schemes require a good amount of business logic and debugging. You have to consider the order of messages sent and received and avoid missing a message because an older message is overwritten in the database or filesystem.

Using HTTP

HTTP is a stateless protocol, so you don't have to maintain a mesh of open sockets for communication. The protocol is well-defined and human-readable (for example, in text). To send a message, you send an HTTP request to the container you want to communicate with and wait for the response. You can close or persist the connection (keep it alive) as the HTTP protocol permits. Additionally, to avoid having to poll for messages or state change via HTTP, you can use WebSockets.

Using MQTT

MQTT is a well-designed message bus. It works much like IRC or Slack in that you have rooms (topics) and people in rooms (subscribers). Messages sent to a room (topic) are received by the people (subscribers). The people (subscribers) can join multiple rooms (topics) and they receive the messages for those rooms (topics).

For an MQTT application, there must be one MQTT server (broker) container that is accessible from the other containers. The other containers do not have to know about one another, only the address of the MQTT broker.

The MQTT broker accepts connections from one or more clients. The clients can subscribe to one or more topics. The topics are as arbitrary as the channel/room names are in IRC or Slack; they are typically strings. When a message is sent to the MQTT broker for a specific topic, the broker sends the message to all the clients who are subscribed to that topic.

Mosca (`https://hub.docker.com/r/matteocollina/mosca`) is an MQTT broker written in JavaScript. You can run it in a container, as you do with MongoDB or Redis.

There are several other MQTT brokers to choose from, as well—you can find them on Docker Hub.

HTTP versus MQTT

MQTT is a protocol specifically designed for passing messages of key/value pairs. Its strength is in its broadcast capability. Each client is responsible for asking for modifications to values based on the specific keys it cares about. Each client can be assured that their updates are received by any and all other interested clients. MQTT also has the capability to retain specific key/value pairs, so when a new client subscribes, it can be notified of the current key/value pair (the most recently sent one).

MQTT does not provide a request/response protocol, although it is simple to implement one. The downside of using MQTT for request/response-type transactions is that the response is not guaranteed to happen as soon as possible.

HTTP requires custom programming to provide the message-passing services that MQTT provides. You could implement a message bus sort of system that mimics MQTT's functionality, but that means more programming work for you and additional maintenance costs down the line. HTTP's strength is that it is a request/response protocol, so you can typically expect a response right away. The downside is that if the server is maintaining a set of key/value pairs, you would be required to poll the server from the clients to see whether the values have changed and post to the server to update the values. Polling causes the server to burn CPU, even when values haven't changed, and this can add up in a way that grinds your server to a halt if enough clients are polling frequently enough. You could use WebSockets, but in the end, you've reinvented MQTT.

HTTP is a good choice if you need more than what MQTT provides. Certainly, HTTP supports PHP or Node.js (and others) backend services.

It's possible to combine HTTP and MQTT. Use HTTP for request/response-type transactions and MQTT for state updates.

MQTT is a good choice for our purposes.

The `chapter3/` directory in the companion GitHub repository contains a simple microservices-based backend demonstration application. It uses MongoDB, Redis, and MQTT, along with some publisher and subscriber applications that you can find in the GitHub repository for this book (`https://github.com/PacktPublishing/Docker-for-Developers`). Later in this chapter, we'll learn how to share our subscriber and publisher containers via Docker Hub.

Implementing a sample microservices application

We can use the Mosca, MongoDB, and Redis containers, along with a couple of custom containers, to implement a simple but complete application:

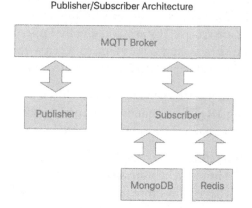

Figure 3.3 – Diagram of our sample microservices application

The publisher and subscriber will communicate with each other using MQTT. The subscriber will listen for a handful of MQTT topics that direct it to operate on or retrieve information from the MongoDB and Redis databases. The publisher will send these MQTT topics and print the responses.

The publisher will be based on Node.js version 11 and the subscriber will be based on Node.js version 12. Without Docker or a virtual machine, running two Node.js versions on the same machine concurrently requires the use of **Node Version Manager (nvm)** and having multiple versions of Node.js installed on your workstation. Docker containers make it simple to use as many versions as you need and to package the version, along with the app that uses it, in a nice package (a container).

The publisher and subscriber apps are in their own `publisher/` and `subscriber/` subdirectories of `chapter3/` in the companion repository. These programs each need their own Dockerfile so that we can build the two separate containers. They also have their own helper `.sh` scripts (`debug.sh`, `run.sh`, `build.sh`, and so on). The publisher app only needs to have an MQTT library. The subscriber app needs the MQTT library and a MongoDB library and a Redis library. These libraries will be installed using npm (the Node.js package manager) within the containers.

The publisher and subscriber apps demonstrate how a microservices architecture works, using multiple Docker containers.

The subscriber connects to the MongoDB and Redis containers using Node.js packages/libraries, which are installed in the container with npm. The subscriber provides basic **Create, Read, Update, and Delete (CRUD)** functions for adding, listing, removing, and retrieving count of records in each of the MongoDB and Redis databases. The publisher sends MQTT messages to the subscriber to invoke this functionality.

Our topics are strings that are derived from a pattern: container/command. If we want to communicate with the subscriber, the pattern is subscriber/command. If we want to communicate with the publisher, the pattern is publisher/command. This convention makes it obvious which topics each microservice would want to subscribe or publish to.

The MQTT topics and messages are as follows:

- `subscriber/mongo-count`: Responds with the count of records in the MongoDB database.

- `subscriber/mongo-add`: Adds the message content to the MongoDB database.

- `subscriber/mongo-list`: Returns a JSON object that contains a list of records in the MongoDB database. If the message is a non-zero length string, it is used to filter the list of records returned.

- `subscriber/mongo-remove`: Removes a record from the MongoDB database. The message may contain a string or an object (JSON) suitable for passing to MongoDB's `collection.deleteOne()` method.

- `subscriber/mongo-removeall`: Deletes all records from the MongoDB database.

- `subscriber/redis-count`: Responds with the count of records in the Redis database.

- `subscriber/redis-flushall`: Removes all the records from the Redis database.

- `subscriber/redis-set`: Adds a record to the Redis database; the message is of the `key=value` form.

- `subscriber/redis-list`: Lists all the records in the Redis database and returns a JSON array of records.

- `subscriber/redis-del`: Deletes a record from the Redis database.

- `subscriber/commands`: Returns a list of available commands (MQTT topics).

There are shell scripts in the root of the `chapter3/` directory that individually start Redis (`start-redis.sh`), MongoDB (`start-mongodb.sh`), and the Mosca MQTT broker (`start-mosca.sh`), as well as a script, `start-all.sh` that starts all three.

We've already detailed the workings of the `start-mongodb.sh` script earlier. The `start-redis.sh` and `start-mosca.sh` scripts are roughly the same; just the names of the programs that are started (Redis and Mosca) are changed.

It is important to note that the `start-mongodb.sh` script connects the host's port 27017 to the container's port 27017. This is so that other containers can reach MongoDB via the default port. The `start-mosca.sh` script connects ports 1883 and 80 to the host so that MQTT and MQTT, over WebSocket, can be used from any of the containers. The `start-redis.sh` script connects port 6379 to the host so that Redis can be accessed from the containers via the default Redis port. Of course, the host can access any of the containers as well.

The `subscriber/start-subscriber.sh` and `publisher-start-publisher.sh` scripts both run the applications locally on the host, not in containers. This allows host native debugging functionality, using WebStorm or another IDE or Node.js debugger. Developing and debugging our publisher and subscriber entirely within Docker containers is covered in the next chapter.

Note

To use the `start-subscriber.sh` and `start-publisher.sh` scripts, you will need to install Node.js and `yarn` on your development workstation. Ensure that you run `yarn install` in both `subscriber/` and `publisher/` directories.

This is what `start-subscriber.sh` looks like:

```
#!/bin/sh
# start-subscriber.sh
yarn start
```

The `start-publisher.sh` script is identical to the `start-subscriber.sh` script. The `package.json` file in the publisher directory signals `yarn start` to launch the publisher program.

The HOSTIP variable must be set to your host machine's IP, available to our publisher and subscriber, and is used by our Node.js programs to address the MQTT broker, MongoDB server, and Redis server when connecting.

To find your IP on macOS (assuming you use 192.168.*.* as your home network IP address range):

```
# ifconfig | grep 192
inet 192.168.0.19 netmask 0xffff0000 broadcast 192.168.255.255
```

The IP of the host is 192.168.0.19.

To find your IP on Linux, use the following command:

```
$ ip address | grep 192
inet 192.168.0.21/16 brd 192.168.255.255 scope global dynamic
enp0s31f6
```

The IP of this host is 192.168.0.21.

You will run the start-publisher.sh script using the following command:

```
HOSTIP=192.168.0.19 ./start-publisher.sh
```

To run the start-subscriber.sh script use the following command:

```
HOSTIP=192.168.0.19 ./start-subscriber.sh
```

The publisher program is relatively simple. It connects to the MQTT broker and listens for topics starting with publisher/. The topics and messages received are then converted into the subscriber/ format topics and published to MQTT. The subscriber responds with the publisher topic and the response message.

With both the publisher and subscriber running, we use the MQTT command-line tool to send messages to the publisher. In the following screenshot, you can see how we exercise a few of the subscriber commands.

These two scripts assume that we have Mosca installed on our host. We don't need to install it for the MQTT broker, but for the command-line tools. Being able to send MQTT topics/commands from the command line on the host, in .sh scripts on the host, and in crontabs on the host is very useful. You can also use Mosca as a library to implement a broker in your own Node.js code.

> **Note**
>
> For curious readers, the screenshot is of a Terminal window running tmux with three panes. **tmux** is a **terminal multiplexer**: it enables several terminals to be created, accessed, and controlled from a single screen. The tmux GitHub repository can be found at `https://github.com/tmux/tmux`.

In the following screenshot, you can see how we exercise a few of the subscriber commands:

Figure 3.4 – Three shells demonstrating the publisher and subscriber working together

As we can see, the publisher and subscriber work as expected, as do the database queries between containers and the host. We can edit and debug the publisher and subscriber programs to get them working to our satisfaction.

Now that we have these working publisher and subscriber containers, we want to share them with the rest of the development team.

Sharing your containers on Docker Hub

To share our containers, we'll use Docker Hub and publish the two containers. The rest of the team can pull the pre-built containers from Docker Hub and use them without having to deal with the source code repository at all. They are just microservices to them, just as we don't need the source to Mosca, MongoDB, or Redis with those containers.

Of course, the development team is going to have to run them.

We have created an organization on Docker Hub, `dockerfordevelopers`, which we will use to publish the containers for this book. You won't be able to push to it, but we can. In order to publish to Docker Hub, you will need to use the `docker login` command, and you must have already created an account on `https://hub.docker.com/`.

You can also create your own organization on Docker Hub where you can share your own containers. If you want to use the examples in the GitHub repository for this chapter, you will have to edit the scripts to replace `dockerfordevelopers` with your own organization name.

Since we are creating our own custom containers, we will need some `.sh` scripts for each container, as explained in the previous chapter. There are a set of `.sh` scripts for the publisher and the subscriber.

The Dockerfile used to build the container for the publisher is almost identical to the one used in the previous chapter:

```
# we will inherit from the NodeJS v12 image on Docker Hub
FROM node:12
# set time zone so files' timestamps are correct
ENV TZ=America/Los_Angeles
# we include procps and telnet so you can use these with
shell.sh prompt
RUN apt-get update -qq >/dev/null && apt-get install -y -qq
curl procps telnet >/dev/null
# add a user - this user will own the files in /home/app
RUN useradd --user-group --create-home --shell /bin/false app
# set up and copy files to /home/app
ENV HOME=/usr/app
WORKDIR /home/app
COPY . /home/app
# install our NodeJS packages (from package.json)
```

```
RUN yarn install
# we run a script to stat the server; the array syntax makes it
so ^C will work as we want
CMD  ["yarn", "start"]
```

The major difference in this Dockerfile and the one in the previous chapter is that we are not installing Apache and PHP, but we are inheriting from node:12 and installing our Node.js program's required packages.

We are inheriting from node:12 in this Dockerfile for the publisher. The Dockerfile for the subscriber is identical, except that it inherits from node:13. This illustrates how you can have containers with different base software versions on the same host; this would be unpleasant to deal with on a host without containers.

> **Note**
>
> The node:12 and node:13 containers are pulled from Docker Hub and updated each time we build the containers.

The following is the build.sh script that is used to build the publisher:

```
#!/bin/sh
# build.sh
# we use the "docker build" command to build a container named
"dockerfordevelopers/publisher" from . (current directory)
# Dockerfile is found in the current directory, and determines
how the container is built.
docker build -t dockerfordevelopers/publisher .
```

The build.sh script is very short and only really consists of the line, a single command. It is easier to type ./build.sh instead of the whole docker build -t dockerfordevelopers/publisher . command. This also makes the process less error-prone and you don't have to memorize the command-line switches and format.

There is a nearly identical build.sh script for the subscriber, too. Only the name of the container built is different: dockerfordevelopers/subscriber.

The output of the `build.sh` script for the publisher is as follows:

```
# ./build.sh
Sending build context to Docker daemon  4.902MB
Step 1/9 : FROM node:12
Step 2/9 : ENV TZ=America/Los_Angeles
Step 3/9 : RUN apt-get update -qq >/dev/null && apt-get install
-y -qq curl procps telnet >/dev/null
Step 4/9 : RUN useradd --user-group --create-home --shell /bin/
false app
Step 5/9 : ENV HOME=/usr/app
Step 6/9 : WORKDIR /home/app
Step 7/9 : COPY . /home/app
Step 8/9 : RUN yarn install
yarn install v1.16.0
[1/4] Resolving packages...
[2/4] Fetching packages...
[3/4] Linking dependencies...
[4/4] Building fresh packages...
Done in 1.55s.
Step 9/9 : CMD  ["yarn", "start"]
 ---> Running in f882d870bc6a
Removing intermediate container f882d870bc6a
 ---> b8f9439e36fa
Successfully built b8f9439e36fa
Successfully tagged dockerfordevelopers/publisher:latest
```

You can see that the 1/9, 2/9, 3/9, and so on steps map one to one to the lines in our Dockerfile. The first line in our Dockerfile reads From Node:12 and the Step 1/1 line reads From Node:12. Similarly, Step 2/2 is the second line in the Dockerfile. The build process follows the Dockerfile as a series of steps to build the final container image.

The last line in the output tells us that the name of the container is dockerfordevelopers/publisher:latest. We use this name to push our build container to Docker Hub.

We use the push.sh script to perform the commands to push the publisher container to the organization on Docker Hub:

```
#!/bin/sh
# push.sh
docker push dockerfordevelopers/publisher
```

This is another one-line .sh script for our convenience.

The following is the output of the push.sh script for the publisher:

```
# ./push.sh
The push refers to repository [docker.io/dockerfordevelopers/
publisher]
9502c45a0d0e: Pushed
79b7f0047832: Pushed
bca5484440a2: Pushed
...
6a335755bda7: Pushed
latest: digest: sha256:e408ae01416511ad8451c31e532e3c2c6eb3324
ad43834a966ff161f9062e9ad size: 3056
#
```

We have a sort of template or pattern for working with custom containers in our microservices architecture project:

1. We edit and debug the code for our container.
2. We run the build.sh script to build a container image.
3. We run the push.sh script to push the container to Docker Hub.

Your fellow developers can now run the publisher image. This is run on a second machine, such as a developer's workstation:

```
# docker run --rm dockerfordevelopers/publisher
Unable to find image 'dockerfordevelopers/publisher:latest'
locally
latest: Pulling from dockerfordevelopers/publisher
c5e155d5a1d1: Pull complete
221d80d00ae9: Pull complete
```

```
4250b3117dca: Pull complete

69df12c70287: Pull complete

...

Digest: sha256:e408ae01416511ad8451c31e532e3c2c6eb3324ad
43834a966ff161f9062e9ad

Status: Downloaded newer image for dockerfordevelopers/
publisher:latest

yarn run v1.16.0

$ node ./index.js
```

Of course, on this second machine, the developer has installed and run the required microservices: Mosca, MongoDB, and Redis. The application will not run without all the microservices running within Docker.

Pushing to Docker Hub on your development host and pulling from Docker Hub on a production host is a simple way to deploy containers for production. It is not very robust, however. We will cover better schemes for deployment in later chapters.

Summary

In this chapter, we learned how to break up an application that would normally be run in a virtual machine with multiple services (MongoDB, Redis, and Mosca) into a microservices-based architecture run as containers within Docker.

We learned how to navigate the Docker Hub website and find useful pre-made Docker containers that you simply download and run.

We also learned how to package our own microservices as Docker containers and how we can push them to Docker Hub for the public or development team members to use.

Several containers were used to launch the complete application as microservices communicated through ports mapped to the host's ports. This is not ideal, especially if you already have a WWW server running on port 80; Mosca uses port 80, too.

In the next chapter, we will discuss how we can use the Docker Compose tool to design complete microservice architecture applications and run them so that they have a private internal network and so host ports are not required.

Further reading

You can refer to the following links for more information on the topics covered in this chapter:

- The official Docker documentation: `https://docs.docker.com`

- The Dockerfile reference: `https://docs.docker.com/engine/reference/builder/`

- The Docker Hub site: `https://hub.docker.com/`

- The documentation for Docker Hub: `https://docs.docker.com/docker-hub/`

- The documentation for the Node.js containers on Docker Hub: `https://hub.docker.com/_/node`

- The documentation for the Redis containers on Docker Hub: `https://hub.docker.com/_/redis`

- The documentation for the MongoDB containers on Docker Hub: `https://hub.docker.com/_/mongo`

- The documentation for the Mosca containers on Docker Hub: `https://hub.docker.com/r/matteocollina/mosca`

4

Composing Systems Using Containers

In the previous chapter, we created a server-side application using microservices architecture. The application was made up of five separate containers: three official images and two custom images. The official images were for MongoDB, Redis, and Mosca (MQTT).

For the most part, communication between containers is done via MQTT message passing. The subscriber container carries out the database **Create, Read, Update, and Delete (CRUD)** operations via the Node.js API for MongoDB and Redis. All of the relevant network ports are exposed on the development host, enabling the subscriber program to access the database servers at `localhost` (`127.0.0.1`) and both subscriber and publisher programs to access Mosca/MQTT at `localhost`, too.

In this chapter, we are going to discuss composing systems—specifically, Docker Compose. We are also going to learn how to keep network access private so that services can be accessed from within our containers but not be accessible from the host. We will learn how we can share volumes in the filesystem between containers. There are alternatives to Docker Compose, and we will look at some of them.

We will cover the following topics in this chapter:

- Introduction to Docker Compose

- Using Docker local networking

- Local volumes

- Other composition tools

To recap, we have three official image containers for MongoDB, Mosca, and Redis. We have an additional two containers created for this book—publisher and subscriber microservices.

The publisher microservice has been modified to present a form in a web browser. The fields in the form and the submit buttons allow us to exercise the various operations supported by the subscriber microservice:

Figure 4.1 – The form generated by our updated publisher program

You can choose which database to perform CRUD operations on. You can also set a value that is to be used for the **List**, **Count**, **Add**, and **Remove** operations. There is a button for each of the CRUD operations, as well as a **Flush** button, which removes all the records from the selected database. The return value/result of the operation is shown beneath the form under the **Result** heading.

Technical requirements

The prerequisite software for this chapter includes Docker, Docker Compose (see https://docs.docker.com/compose/install/), Git, and a web browser, such as Google Chrome or Safari.

The Docker and Docker Compose documentation use the term *service*, whereas we use the term *microservice*. For the purposes of this chapter, the terms are interchangeable.

In the GitHub repository (`https://github.com/PacktPublishing/Docker-for-Developers`), there is a `chapter4/` directory that accompanies this chapter. It contains a modified version of the microservices architecture code used in the previous chapter.

Check out the following video to see the Code in Action:

`https://bit.ly/3iRWqoH`

Introduction to Docker Compose

A composing system for containers is a tool that allows us to describe the whole microservices architecture program in a configuration file and then perform operations on the system described. Docker Compose is one such tool. Before we get into what Docker Compose is and does, let's look at the reason why we need a tool like this.

The problem with .sh scripts

So far, we've been using `.sh` scripts to make working with our microservices application easy. We have used the following scripts:

- `start-mongodb.sh`
- `start-redis.sh`
- `start-mosca.sh`
- `subscriber/start-subscriber.sh`
- `publisher/start-publisher.sh`
- `subscriber/build.sh`
- `publisher/build.sh`
- `subscriber/push.sh`
- `publisher/push.sh`

Instead of having to invoke each of these as separate commands, we can make a single `start-all.sh` script that invokes them all:

```
#!/bin/sh


./start-mosca.sh
./start-mongodb.sh
./start-redis.sh
```

```
cd subscriber && ./start-subscriber.sh & cd ..
cd publisher && ./start-publisher.sh & cd ..
```

> **Note**
>
> The `start-all.sh` script is presented for informational purposes. We will not be using it going forward!

This approach works, but the information about what ports are open and other container-specific access information is hidden within those `.sh` scripts. For example, the `mongodb.sh` script starts MongoDB and binds port `27017` of the container to port `27017` of the host.

Making changes to the configuration may require editing each of those `.sh` scripts, and maybe even the `start-all.sh` script itself, as well as its counterpart, `stop-sll.sh`. We have several additional scripts as well for building and publishing the containers and to perform other housekeeping tasks. This approach is both inconvenient and error-prone.

The Docker Compose tool solves most of the issues with `.sh` scripts, although we might still want to use `.sh` scripts to invoke the `docker-compose` command with its various command-line arguments.

Docker Compose configuration files

Configuration for Docker Compose is done via `.yml` files, the contents of which are YAML. YAML is a markup language that allows data serialization. It is similar to JSON format but is much more human-friendly in its syntax.

A file named `docker-compose.yml` is Docker Compose's default configuration file. You may have multiple configuration files, and you can tell Docker Compose which configuration files to use via a command-line switch.

Let's look at the `docker-compose-example.yml` file in the `chapter4/` directory in the repository. The Docker Compose tool can replace the shell script methodology we've used so far:

```
# Example Docker Compose file for our chapter 4 application
version: '3'
services:
```

Docker Compose supports different versions of the `docker-compose.yml` format. Newer versions have higher version numbers and add additional `docker-compose` features. In the `services` section, we describe each of the containers that are to be built and run.

We have our `redis` container under the `services` section. The `image` field specifies that we will be using the `redis` image from Docker Hub. We persist the database in `/tmp/redis` so that the data is not lost when the container is stopped and restarted:

```
redis:
    image: redis
    volumes:
        - /tmp/redis:/data
    ports:
        - 6379:6379
```

We expose port `6379`, the default Redis port, on the host. Exposing this port allows the host and other containers to access the Redis server.

After Redis, we have our MongoDB container. We are going to use the `mongo` image from Docker Hub. We persist the data in the host's `/tmp/mongo` directory so that the database's contents are retained between stopping and restarting the container:

```
mongodb:
    image: mongo
    volumes:
        - /tmp/mongo:/data/db
    ports:
        - 27017:27017
```

The default TCP port for MongoDB is `27017`, and we expose it to map port `27017` in the container to port `27017` on the host. Tools on the host and within our containers can access MongoDB via `localhost`, and we don't need to specify a port on the command lines since the default is configured.

Next is the Mosca container. We are using the `matteocollina/mosca` image from Docker Hub. We set the `/db` volume in the container to `/tmp/mosca` on the host to persist Mosca's state:

```
mosca:
    image: matteocollina/mosca
    volumes:
        - /tmp/mosca:/db
    ports:
        - 1883:1883
        - 80:80
```

We expose ports 1883 and 80 as the same ports on the host. Port 1883 is the default MQTT port. Port 80 is provided to support MQTT over WebSocket, so you can use MQTT in JavaScript programs in the browser.

In our publisher container, the build: line tells docker-compose that we need to build the container specified in the publisher/ directory. The Dockerfile in the publisher directory is used to define how the container is to be built:

```
publisher:
  build: publisher
  environment:
  - MQTT_HOST=${HOSTIP}
  - REDIS_HOST=${HOSTIP}
  - MONGO_HOST=${HOSTIP}
  ports:
  - 3000:3000
```

We expose port 3000 so that we can access the web server that is running in the container using a web browser on the host.

In our subscriber container, the build: line tells docker-compose that we need to build the container specified in the subscriber/ directory. The Dockerfile in the subscriber directory is used to define how the container is to be built:

```
subscriber:
  build: subscriber
  environment:
  - MQTT_HOST=${HOSTIP}
  - REDIS_HOST=${HOSTIP}
  - MONGO_HOST=${HOSTIP}
```

We don't expose anything—the subscriber performs all of its I/O operations via direct API calls for MongoDB and Redis, as well as accepting commands and reporting status via MQTT.

Some things to note are as follows:

- All the containers are described neatly within the single configuration file.
- The containers still expose the same ports on the host as with the .sh scripts.

- The containers must still find the database and MQTT broker containers via the `HOSTIP` environment variable. This variable must still be set as explained in the previous chapter.

To use our `docker-compose-example.yml` script to bring up all five microservices, we use the `docker-compose up` command. The `-f` switch tells `docker-compose` which Docker Compose `.yml` file to use:

```
% docker-compose -f docker-compose-example.yml up
```

By default, `docker-compose` runs all the containers in the configuration file in debug mode. They will print their output to the Terminal/console in the order that the lines are printed. You may see lines printed by the subscriber, then lines printed by the publisher, then lines printed by subscriber again. If you hit *Ctrl + C*, it will terminate all of the containers and return you to Command Prompt.

If you want the containers to run in detached or daemon mode, use the `-d` switch:

```
% docker-compose -f docker-compose-example.yml up -d
```

In detached or daemon mode, the containers will not print output to the Terminal/console and you will be returned to the prompt right away.

To stop all five microservices, we use a similar `docker-compose` command:

```
% docker-compose -f docker-compose-example.yml down
```

If we do not specify the Docker Compose configuration file to use (`-f docker-compose-example.yml`), then the `docker-compose` command will look for and use a file named `docker-compose.yml` instead.

The `docker-compose up/down` commands allow us to start and stop one or more of our services as well. For example, we can start only the `mongodb` and `redis` containers:

```
% docker-compose -f docker-compose-example.yml up mongodb redis
```

The existing `mongodb` and/or `redis` containers will be stopped and new ones started. It is up to your programs to detect whether the connections to these services were stopped and to handle the error accordingly.

We can build any or all of our services using `docker-compose`:

```
% docker-compose -f docker-compose-example.yml build publisher
```

This command builds our publisher container but does not start any containers.

The key takeaway from the ability to specify none (none means *all*) or one or more of our containers (by name) replaces several of our old `.sh` scripts. We don't need start scripts anymore because we can use `docker-compose up`; we don't need stop scripts because we can use `docker-compose down`; we don't need build scripts because we can use `docker-compose build`; and more! See `https://docs.docker.com/compose/reference/` for details on other `docker-compose` command functionality.

We are likely to have different setups for development and production, if not additional scenarios. With `.sh` scripts, we have a `debug.sh` and `run.sh` script for development and production. The problem with this `.sh` file scheme is that we have almost identical `docker run` commands in each, with only minor differences.

Docker Compose has an inheritance feature where multiple configuration files can be specified on the `docker-compose` command line.

Inheritance using multiple configuration files

We can implement a base `docker-compose.yml` file and then override the settings in that file with our own override configuration files. This feature is called **inheritance**—we will inherit the base settings from the `docker-compose` file and override the settings for our purposes.

Docker Compose starts with the first configuration file on the command line, then merges the second one into it, then merges the third (if there is one), and so on. To merge means to apply settings in the second (or third) configuration file to the current state of the configuration, which will ultimately be used. Any settings in the second configuration file will replace the ones in the first configuration file, if they exist, or will add new services or settings if they don't already exist.

Let's look at the `docker-compose.yml` base file, which we'll use from now on:

```
version: '3'
services:
  redis:
    image: redis
  mongodb:
    image: mongo
    volumes:
      - /tmp/mongo:/data/db
  mosca:
    image: matteocollina/mosca
```

```
      volumes:
        - /tmp/mosca:/db
  publisher:
    build: publisher

    depends_on:
      - "mosca"
      - "subscriber"
  subscriber:
    build: subscriber
    depends_on:
      - "redis"
      - "mongodb"
      - "mosca"
```

This looks like the `docker-compose-example.yml` file from the previous section, but you may notice a couple of differences:

- There are two `depends_on` options—one for the publisher and one for the subscriber.

- We are no longer exposing or binding the container's ports to the host's ports.

Let's take a look at them in detail in the following sections.

The depends_on option

The `depends_on` option allows us to control the start-up order of the containers (refer to `https://docs.docker.com/compose/startup-order/`). Additionally, `depends_on` expresses an interdependency between containers. Refer to `https://docs.docker.com/compose/compose-file/#depends-on#depends_on` for more information about the `depends_on` option.

Service dependencies cause the following behaviors:

- `docker-compose up` starts services in dependency order. In our example, `redis`, `mongo`, and the `mosca` services are started before the `subscriber` container, and both `mosca` and `subscriber` are started before `publisher`.

- `docker-compose up SERVICE` automatically includes dependencies under `SERVICE`.

docker-compose stop stops services in dependency order (mosca, then mongodb, then redis in our docker-compose.yml file).

The order in which the services are started is important because if we start publisher before mosca is running, the logic to connect to the MQTT broker in the publisher program will fail. Similarly, starting subscriber before the database and MQTT broker services would likely cause the logic in subscriber to connect to the databases and the MQTT broker to fail. It doesn't make sense to start publisher before subscriber is running because anything publisher sends via MQTT will fall on deaf ears, so to speak.

Even though a container has started, there is no guarantee that the container's program will have completed its initialization by the time the microservices that use them try to connect. In our publisher and subscriber code, we created a wait_for_services() method that ensures that we can connect to the services only when they are up and ready.

We call wait_for_services() first thing in our publisher and subscriber programs to ensure we have waited just long enough for the dependent services to be up and ready.

The wait_for_services() method in publisher/index.js is as follows:

```
/**
 * wait_for_services
 *
 * This method is called at startup to wait for any dependent
 containers to be running.
 */
const waitOn = require("wait-on"),
  wait_for_services = async () => {
    try {
      await waitOn({ resources: [`tcp:${mqtt_host}:${mqtt_port}`]
});
    } catch (e) {
      debug("waitOn exception", e.stack);
    }
};
```

Our publisher microservice only connects to the MQTT broker, so the wait_for_services() method only waits for our MQTT broker's TCP port to be accessible.

The `wait_for_services()` method in `subscriber/index.js` is a bit more complicated:

```
/**
 * wait_for_services
 *
 * This method is called at startup to wait for any dependent
 * containers to be running.
 */
const waitOn = require("wait-on"),
  wait_for_services = async () => {
   try {
     debug(`waiting for mqtt (${mqtt_host}:${mqtt_port})`);
     await waitOn({ resources: [`tcp:${mqtt_host}:${mqtt_port}`]
});
     debug(`waiting for redis (${redis_host}:${redis_port})`);
     await waitOn({ resources: [`tcp:${redis_host}:${redis_
port}`] });
     debug(`waiting for mongo (${mongo_host}:${mongo_port})`);
     await waitOn({ resources: [`tcp:${mongo_host}:${mongo_
port}`] });
   } catch (e) {
     debug("***** exception ", e.stack);
   }
 };
```

The `subscriber` microservice needs to connect to the MQTT broker, the `redis` server, and the `mongo` server. We wait for the TCP ports of those servers to be accessible.

There are other ways to wait for services to be available that involve installing command-line programs/scripts in the container and running them before starting our publisher or subscriber service. For example, you might use this handy `wait-for-it.sh` script, which can be found at `https://github.com/vishnubob/wait-for-it`.

The lack of options in the `docker-compose.yml` file to expose container ports is not an oversight. We are fully able to specify those options in an override file that can provide options to existing containers.

Adding port bindings using overrides

In the chapter4/ directory in the code repository, we have a docker-compose-simple.yml file that is an example of an override file:

```
version: '3'
services:
  redis:
    ports:
      - 6379:6379
  mongodb:
    ports:
      - 27017:27017
  mosca:
    ports:
      - 1883:1883
      - 80:80
  publisher:
    environment:
      - MQTT_HOST=${HOSTIP}
      - REDIS_HOST=${HOSTIP}
      - MONGO_HOST=${HOSTIP}
    ports:
      - 3000:3000
  subscriber:
    environment:
      - MQTT_HOST=${HOSTIP}
      - REDIS_HOST=${HOSTIP}
      - MONGO_HOST=${HOSTIP}
```

Here, we specify the ports for each container. We are inheriting the options from our docker-compose.yml file and adding options to expose the ports for each of our containers.

We don't expose any ports for the subscriber microservice because it never exposes any ports to the host's ports.

We also define three environment variables to be used by the publisher and subscriber containers to access the MQTT_HOST (mosca), REDIS_HOST (redis), and MONGO_HOST (mongodb) services.

The docker-compose command to bring up our services using the two configuration files (inheritance) is as follows:

```
% HOSTIP=192.168.0.21 docker-compose -f docker-compose.yml -f
docker-compose-simple.yml up
```

Since we are not using the -d switch, our containers are not detached but print their console/debug output to the Terminal. You cannot enter more commands until you hit *Ctrl+ C*. Doing this will stop all the containers in reverse depends_on order and return you to Command Prompt:

```
% HOSTIP=192.168.0.21 docker-compose -f docker-compose.yml -f
docker-compose-simply.yml up -d
```

Adding the -d switch causes all the containers to be started in daemon mode. They run in the background and you immediately get a command-line prompt. No further output is sent to the Terminal.

If containers are running in daemon mode, you can stop them using the docker-compose down command:

```
% HOSTIP=192.168.0.21 docker-compose -f docker-compose.yml -f
docker-compose-simple.yml down
```

We can use three or more configuration files as well. Each additional file specified on the command line further extends the containers and options specified within.

What we have so far is effectively a production that is set up using inheritance. Debugging using this is particularly painful because your only means of diagnosing errors is to add debug() calls to the publisher and/or subscriber, then rebuilding the container(s), and then rerunning the whole application.

To improve our development and debugging cycles, we can bind/mount our publisher/ and subscriber/ directories to the /home/app directory in the containers. The Dockerfiles for both containers use the nodemon (https://nodemon.io/) utility to start the application within the container.

The nodemon utility does a bit more than just starting our program:

- It also monitors the state of the program, and if it stops, nodemon will restart it. This is useful because our Node.js programs might detect an error from which they cannot easily be recovered, so they just exit and allow nodemon to restart them.
- For development, nodemon also monitors the timestamps of the files in the code directory and will restart the program if any of the files change.

Since we can bind/mount our source code directly in the container, any changes we make to the files using our editor or IDE on the host will immediately affect the changes in the container.

We can create a `docker-compose-simple-dev.yml` file, which adds our bind/mounts to publisher and subscriber:

```
version: '3'
services:
  publisher:
    volumes:
      - ./publisher:/home/app
  subscriber:
    volumes:
      - ./subscriber:/home/app
```

We run this using the `docker-compose up` command:

```
% HOSTIP=192.168.0.21 docker-compose -f docker-compose.yml -f
docker-compose-simple.yml -f dockercompose-simple-dev.yml up -d
```

If we edit, say, the `publisher/index.js` file on the host, we can see that nodemon sees the change and restarts the publisher program:

```
publisher_1   | [nodemon] restarting due to changes...
publisher_1   | [nodemon] starting `node ./index.js`
publisher_1   | 2020-03-30T18:03:39.537Z publisher publisher
microservice, about to wait for MQTT host(192.168.0.21, 1883
publisher_1   | 2020-03-30T18:03:39.546Z publisher ---> wait
succeeded
publisher_1   | 2020-03-30T18:03:39.587Z publisher publisher
connecting to MQTT mqtt://192.168.0.21
publisher_1   | 2020-03-30T18:03:39.591Z publisher connected to
192.168.0.21 port 1883
publisher_1   | 2020-03-30T18:03:39.638Z publisher listening on
port  3000
```

We now have a good handle on `docker-compose`, but we are binding ports from our containers to the host's ports. This is problematic if you have a container that wants to bind to port 80 on the host but the host is running a web server or another container for another project that also wants to bind to port 80.

Fortunately, Docker provides a facility to only expose our ports to our containers!

Using Docker local networking

Both Docker and Docker Compose have command-line options to specify a Docker local network that the application will use. Using this Docker local network allows our containers to access another container's ports without having to bind/expose these ports to the host's ports.

Networking using .sh scripts

You use the `docker network create` command to create a named network that your containers can use to privately communicate with one another. You can have as many of these private networks defined as you like—you might want to work on multiple unrelated projects simultaneously and each needs its own network:

```
% docker network create chapter4
```

This command creates a network named `chapter4` that we can use for our microservices example programs. We can destroy networks we have created using the `docker network rm` command:

```
% docker network rm chapter4
```

This command removes our `chapter4` network from the system.

The `start-mongodb.sh`, `start-redis.sh`, `start-mosca.sh`, `publisher/run.sh`, and `subscriber/run.sh` scripts are used by the `up.sh` script to bring up our application's containers using the `docker run` command.

Let's examine our `up.sh` script:

```
#!/bin/sh
./stop-all.sh
```

We run the `docker network create` command to create our `chapter4` network:

```
docker network create chapter4
```

We start our three servers:

```
./start-mosca.sh
./start-mongodb.sh
```

We also run `./start-redis.sh`:

```
###### SUBSCRIBER
cd subscriber
./run.sh
```

Finally, we start the publisher:

```
###### PUBLISHER
# publisher needs to expose port 3000
# so we can access the WWW interface
cd ../publisher
./run.sh
```

The `start-mongodb.sh` and `start-redis.sh` scripts are roughly the same as the `start-mosca.sh` script. The relevant lines in the `start-mosca.sh` script are the ones for the `docker run` command:

```
docker run \
  --name $SERVICE \
  -d \
  --restart always \
  -e TITLE=$SERVICE \
  --network chapter4 \
  -v /tmp/mosca:/db \
  matteocollina/mosca
```

Only the service name, which third-party/Docker Hub container to use, and any container to host directory bindings are specific to mongodb, mosca, or redis. They all share the chapter4 network.

The `docker run` command in the `subscriber/run.sh` script looks as follows:

```
docker run \
  --name $SERVICE \
  -d \
```

```
--restart always \
-e TITLE=$SERVICE \
--network chapter4 \
dockerfordevelopers/$SERVICE
```

We are no longer defining the HOSTIP environment variable because the Docker local networking system provides a DNS function that allows the programs in our containers to look up the other containers by name. The name is the name of the container, which is specified in the docker run commands scripts with the –name command-line option.

The relevant lines in subscriber/index.js are as follows:

```
const debug = require("debug")("subscriber"),
    mongo_host = process.env.MONGO_HOST || "mongodb",
    mongo_port = 27017,
    mongoUrl = `mongodb://${mongo_host}:${mongo_port}`,
    mqtt_host = process.env.MQTT_HOST || "mosca",
    mqtt_port = 1883,
    mqttUrl = `mqtt://${mqtt_host}`,
    redis_host = process.env.REDIS_HOST || "redis",
    redis_port = 6379,
    redisUrl = `redis://${redis_host}`;
```

The code is designed to accept the MONGO_HOST environment variable; otherwise, it will use the mongodb container name. The same is the case for MQTT_HOST/mosca and REDIS_HOST/redis.

> **Note**
>
> We have been defining the HOSTIP, MONGO_HOST, MQTT_HOST, and REDIS_HOST environment variables, especially in the .sh script examples. Since we've been naming our containers using the --name switch on our docker run commands, Docker's local DNS will work with .sh scripts. That is, we don't need to define those environment variables if we name our containers. We still need to bind container ports to the host's ports, unless we also add the --network switch and docker network create to the Docker local network.

The down.sh script stops all the containers and removes the chapter4 network:

```sh
#!/bin/sh
docker stop publisher
docker stop subscriber
docker stop redis
docker stop mongodb
docker stop mosca
docker network rm chapter4
```

We can use these .sh scripts, but we've already learned that Docker Compose is the superior method for managing our microservices.

Networking with Docker Compose

The docker-compose.yml configuration file that we created is still enough to use as the base for using the docker-compose commands to manage our containers. However, we no longer need to expose or bind container ports to the host's ports; the only exception is we'll continue to bind port 3000 so that we can access the publisher web pages using our browser on the host. The base docker-compose.yml file does not bind port 3000, so we will continue to bind ports using the override file.

By default, if you specify no configuration files on the command line, docker-compose looks for docker-compose.yml and uses it, and then looks for docker-compose.override.yml and uses that.

If you need to specify a third configuration file, you must use the -f command-line switch for each configuration file.

Our docker-compose.override.yml file handles our production case:

```yaml
version: '3'
services:
  redis:
    networks:
      - chapter4
  mongodb:
    networks:
      - chapter4
  mosca:
    networks:
```

```
        - chapter4
  publisher:
    ports:
      - 3000:3000
    networks:
      - chapter4
  subscriber:
    networks:
      - chapter4
networks:
  chapter4:
```

This file adds the `chapter4` network, assigns it to each of the containers, and binds port `3000` in the publisher container to port `3000` on the host.

All we need to do to use `docker-compose.yml` and `docker-compose.override.yml` is run a simple `docker-compose` command:

```
% docker-compose up
```

After a few seconds, our five containers are up and running and we can access the application with our browser on the host. We can see it is all working. We can also do the following:

- Use the `-d` switch to run the containers in detached/daemon mode.
- Use `docker-compose` to stop and start any one or more containers.
- Use `docker-compose` to build any one or more containers.
- Use `docker-compose logs` to show the logs of any of our containers running in daemon mode.

What we now have is a pair of configuration files that work for production mode. We now need a way to work in development mode by binding our source code to the container's home directory.

Binding a host filesystem within containers

Previously, we used a third `docker-compose` configuration file to specify bindings so that our source code directory would be overlaid within the container (in place of the app's home directory). We will do the same for the latest incarnation of our Docker Compose setup.

We first create a `docker-compose-dev.yml` file:

```
version: '3'
services:

  publisher:
    volumes:
      - ./publisher:/home/app

  subscriber:
    volumes:
      - ./subscriber:/home/app
```

This override file simply maps the publisher and subscriber source code directory over /home/app in the related container. Now, we can freely edit sources on the host and, thanks to nodemon, our changes will take effect almost immediately within the running containers. There is no need to stop, rebuild, or restart any containers.

Unfortunately, `docker-compose` has no facility to remove options using inheritance; we can only modify existing ones or add new ones. If we could remove options, we would bind the source in our `docker-compose.override.yml` file and remove them in a `docker-compose-production.yml` file. This would allow us to use the short `docker-compose` up form for development and to use a command line with three `-f` switches for production. This would be handy because we would use development most of the time and rarely use production.

As it is, we must specify the three `-f` switches:

```
% docker-compose -f docker-compose.yml -f docker-compose.
override.yml -f docker-compose-dev.yml up
```

There are other uses for volumes, which we will explore.

Optimizing our container size

We can examine our container images using the `docker images` command:

```
% docker images | grep pub
chapter4_publisher                    latest
15f3a84d348d        24 minutes ago        987MB
```

As you can see, our publisher image is `987` megabytes! All that for an almost-250-line JavaScript program. We can try to shrink this size by moving our `node_modules` directory out of the container and into a named volume. This will also speed up the building of our container since `node_modules` will be persisted in this named volume from build to build, and using the `yarn` command to install the modules will only install anything that is new.

> **Note**
>
> We renamed the Dockerfile to `Dockerfile.chapter3` in the `publisher/` directory. The new Dockerfile has been modified to build a very small image.

A smaller image can be created by optimizing our Dockerfile. What we're going to do is build a base image and our result image. The base image will have `node_modules` installed. The base image is only rebuilt when something changes that requires one of its layers to be rebuilt.

Let's look at an optimized Dockerfile for the publisher:

```
FROM node:12-alpine
```

We inherit from the alpine OS node v12 image. This image is much lighter than the Debian flavor default node container:

```
ENV TZ=America/Los_Angeles
WORKDIR /home/app
# add a user - this user will own the files in /home/app
RUN adduser -S app
ENV HOME=/home/app
COPY . /home/app
```

The resulting image is built without installing or updating `node_modules`. We will install the modules in another step. This saves us from having to use `yarn` install every time we build our container:

```
CMD    ["yarn", "start"]
```

We use `yarn start` to launch our publisher app.

After we run `docker-compose build publisher`, we can see we have greatly reduced the size of our container!

Before our optimizations, the container was `987` megabytes. After the optimizations, `89.5` megabytes, which is almost a 900-megabyte reduction:

```
# docker images | grep pub
chapter4_publisher                       latest
080efb97e0d3        About a minute ago    89.5MB
```

We still need to install our `node_modules/` modules, which will be done within a named volume and defined in the `docker-compose-overrides.yml` file. This is done once, and then again only if you add packages to the `packages.json` file in the `publisher/` directory:

```
# docker-compose run publisher yarn install
```

This command installs the `node_modules/` packages using `yarn install` within the publisher container. The named volume is mounted correctly because it is specified within the `docker-compose` configuration (`.yml`) files.

> **Note**
> We did not optimize the subscriber build.

We can verify that the volume was created and does contain the installed `node_modules` modules by examining the `_data` directory of our volume, which on Linux should be in `/var/lib/docker/volumes`:

```
# cd /var/lib/docker/volumes/
# ls -1 chapter4_node_modules_publisher/_data/
abbrev
accepts
ajv
ansi-align
ansi-regex
ansi-styles
anymatch
```

The location of the volumes is significantly different for macOS. You will need to use the following command to get a shell in the Linux virtual machine that is running Docker:

```
# screen ~/Library/Containers/com.docker.docker/Data/vms/0/tty
```

You might have to hit ^C a few times to get a shell prompt. This prompt is a shell running in the virtual machine. Within the virtual machine, the volume for the node_modules/ directory in the container is at /var/lib/docker/volumes, as with Docker on Linux.

We can see the speedup of our build. The initial build of the publisher, after completely removing all of the images from the system, takes around 16 seconds:

```
# time docker-compose build publisher
Successfully built e50ec5f4d53b
Successfully tagged chapter4_publisher:latest
docker-compose build publisher  0.36s user 0.09s system 2% cpu
16.187 total
```

A subsequent build without node_modules installed takes around a half a second:

```
# time docker-compose build publisher
Successfully tagged chapter4_publisher:latest
docker-compose build publisher  0.34s user 0.08s system 74% cpu
0.568 total
```

After editing index.js and doing a rebuild, it takes less than 1 second:

```
# time docker-compose build publisher
Successfully tagged chapter4_publisher:latest
docker-compose build publisher  0.34s user 0.08s system 49% cpu
0.842 total
```

As you can see, we were able to reduce the size and build time of our containers!

Using the build.sh script

There is a build.sh script provided in the chapter4/ directory of the GitHub repository. It just contains a few lines of actual shell commands:

```
#!/bin/sh

# build.sh
```

```
# build publisher and subscriber and install node_modules in
each
```

```
docker-compose build --force-rm --no-cache
docker-compose run publisher yarn install
docker-compose run subscriber yarn install
```

The build.sh script builds all five containers and runs yarn install in both the publisher and subscriber containers to install the node_modules modules in their respective named volumes. The command-line switches to the docker-compose build command are as follows:

- --force-rm: Forces Docker to remove all the intermediate container images as it builds

- --no-cache: Forces Docker to use no cached/downloaded/built versions of anything

You can drop these two switches to greatly improve the build speed. They are provided here to demonstrate a way of forcibly rebuilding everything from scratch.

That's a decent overview of Docker Compose. It is one of the first, if not the first, composition tools for describing, building, and running Docker applications. But there are also other alternatives out there.

Other composition tools

We have already seen how we can compose and build a multiple service application using docker-compose and .sh scripts. But there are some other options that you may want to consider.

Docker Swarm

Docker Swarm is a cluster management system. It allows you to deploy containers that are defined with docker-compose to a cluster of nodes or servers. There are some limitations to what you can do with docker-compose.yml if you want to use Docker Swarm. For example, you cannot use volumes with Docker Swarm, and binding container ports to the host should be carefully planned.

Kubernetes

Kubernetes is a feature-rich alternative to `docker-compose`. It allows containers to be deployed to a cluster of Docker container servers and uses a configuration file format similar to `docker-compose.yml`.

Packer

Packer is a tool that generates several output formats, including Docker containers. You define your containers using JSON files and the tool reads from them. Packer uses builders to generate output files. The output can be (but is not limited to) the following:

- Azure machine images
- DigitalOcean machine images
- Docker container images
- Google cloud images
- Parallels (for macOS) images
- VirtualBox images
- VMware images

The composition tool that you choose should make your job easier. Be sure to choose one that truly suits your needs. Docker Compose is the official Docker composition tool. The others may be more modern and solve additional problems that Docker Compose does not.

Summary

In this chapter, we introduced Docker Compose as a superior management tool for managing and running a complex system of containers. We described several useful `docker-compose` configuration file options that allow us to specify ports to expose, local networking, and local volumes. We exploited the `docker-compose` tool's inheritance capabilities as well.

A critical part of using Docker is the development cycle. We typically edit, build, run, and test each cycle—then repeat. The size of images, as well as the time spent building, publishing, and downloading them, can be strategically reduced.

We also explored some alternatives to using `.sh` scripts and `docker-compose`. These are a natural next step in your Docker education as they provide facilities for deploying your orchestrations to swarms or clusters of servers in production or for testing.

The next few chapters go into detail about how to deploy your applications and how to implement continuous integration and automated testing. After that, we will cover security considerations for containerized applications.

Further reading

You can refer to the following URLs for more information on the topics covered in this chapter:

- The official Docker documentation:
  `https://docs.docker.com`

- The official Docker Compose documentation:
  `https://docs.docker.com/compose/`

- The Dockerfile reference:
  `https://docs.docker.com/engine/reference/builder/`

- The Docker Hub site:
  `https://hub.docker.com/`

- The documentation for Docker Hub:
  `https://docs.docker.com/docker-hub/`

- The documentation for the `Node.js` containers on Docker Hub:
  `https://hub.docker.com/_/node`

- The documentation for the Redis containers on Docker Hub:
  `https://hub.docker.com/_/redis`

- The documentation for the MongoDB containers on Docker Hub:
  `https://hub.docker.com/_/mongo`

- The documentation for the Mosca containers on Docker Hub:
  `https://hub.docker.com/r/matteocollina/mosca`

Section 2:
Running Docker
in Production

In this section, you will learn how to choose between the different alternatives for running Docker applications in production, ranging from single-host configurations to sophisticated clusters of servers in the cloud that can scale out to handle heavy loads. You will learn how to deploy systems first using Docker Compose, and how to automate building and deploying a simple setup using Jenkins. We will then explore a more sophisticated setup in *Chapter 8*, *Deploying Docker Apps to Kubernetes* through *Chapter 11*, *Scaling and Load Testing Docker Applications*, centering around the use of Kubernetes and Amazon Web Services. You will learn how to deploy applications both manually and using the Spinnaker continuous deployment system, and how to use a variety of tools to monitor applications. Finally, we will learn how to scale Docker applications using Kubernetes, using tools such as the Envoy service mesh and k6 for load testing. We will use a sample application, a game called ShipIt Clicker, to demonstrate each of these concepts in turn.

This section comprises the following chapters:

- *Chapter 5, Alternatives for Deploying and Running Containers to Production*
- *Chapter 6, Deploying Applications with Docker Compose*
- *Chapter 7, Continuous Deployment with Jenkins*
- *Chapter 8, Deploying Docker Apps to Kubernetes*
- *Chapter 9, Cloud-Native Continuous Deployment Using Spinnaker*
- *Chapter 10, Monitoring Docker Using Prometheus, Grafana, and Jaeger*
- *Chapter 11, Scaling and Load Testing Docker Applications*

5

Alternatives for Deploying and Running Containers in Production

As container technology and cloud computing mature, the number of ways in which you can deploy your Docker containers has exploded. Some of the options are as simple as running Docker on a single host, and others feature advanced features such as autoscaling, multi-cloud support, and more. You could even run your Docker containers on-premises on bare-metal servers or adopt a hybrid cloud solution.

After reading this chapter, you will understand that the many choices available offer different trade-offs. You will learn how to build the smallest viable production environment. You will be able to choose between different cloud providers and their managed container runtimes, as well as articulate the benefits of running Docker either on-premises or in a hybrid cloud. Most importantly, you will be able to make an informed decision about choosing a production path for deploying Docker containers given competing objectives.

Understanding the spectrum of choices will help guide you toward making better decisions.

In this chapter, we are going to cover the following main topics:

- Running Docker in production – many paths, choose wisely
- What is the minimum realistic production environment?
- Managed cloud services
- Running your own Kubernetes cluster – from bare-metal servers to OpenStack
- Deciding on the right Docker production setup

Technical requirements

To complete the exercises in this chapter, you'll need Git and Docker on your local workstation. For Mac and Windows users, please install Docker Desktop (https://www.docker.com/products/docker-desktop) as this is how most people using Docker use it on their local workstations. You need to learn more about the options before you choose a production deployment tool.

Depending on what avenues you explore, you may also want to establish accounts with Amazon Web Services, Google Cloud, Microsoft Azure, or Digital Ocean. Most of these services have fairly generous free tiers that may allow you to experiment without spending much money, especially if you only use the services for a short duration. When considering what sort of environment might be suitable for your application, it helps to have multiple options. If you do create resources in the cloud, don't forget to terminate resources that you are done with or are not planning to keep, or you could receive a nasty surprise when you see the bill. Most cloud providers have a billing alert system. Please consider setting up an alarm that will notify you if your spending exceeds your budget.

If you want to explore hosting a more complex on-premises setup, or use a bare-metal hosting service such as Packet (https://www.packet.com/), you may need one or more server computers that meet the specifications for running Docker or OpenStack on bare-metal computer hardware.

The GitHub repository for this chapter is https://github.com/Packt-Publishing/Docker-for-Developers – please see the chapter5 folder inside.

Check out the following video to see the Code in Action:

https://bit.ly/2DYMria

Example application – ShipIt Clicker

The linked GitHub repository for this chapter has code for a prototype for an online game – called ShipIt Clicker. In this game, a fedora-clad squirrel urges you to deploy containers to production; the faster you click, the faster you accumulate **Squirrel Dollars (SQ\$)**, which you can use in the ShipIt Store to purchase upgrades that either increase how many containers you deploy per click, or allow you to deploy containers even if you are not clicking. The prototype version of this game has a simple HTML interface, with a RESTful API that talks to a Redis database to keep score. The version of ShipIt Clicker included in this chapter is a bare-bones prototype that has only a fraction of the full features of the game. However, it has many of the characteristics of an early-stage production application and is ready for its first production deployment. It features a setup using `docker-compose` to run multiple containers. The game features communications between a web browser game client, a Node.js server using Express and a Swagger-driven API, and a Redis NoSQL database used to track scores and other game information.

You can experiment with ShipIt Clicker to get familiar with more elaborate applications than previous chapters explored. Feel free to adapt and improve both the configuration files and the code in conjunction with a variety of tools and services in order to learn more about deploying to production. In subsequent chapters, we will learn how to deploy this application to production in several different ways, each offering progressively more capabilities, but different trade-offs in terms of cost, complexity, and availability. Before we do that, let's learn more about these alternatives.

Running Docker in production – many paths, choose wisely

If you thought running Docker on your local workstation offered many choices, buckle up as the variety available to developers and system administrators in deploying an application built using Docker in a robust way makes the local development environment look simple by comparison. Some of the largest information technology companies in the world use Docker (or equivalent container technologies) to run at a massive scale, and container orchestration makes that possible. The promise of having a self-healing cluster that can continue to run applications in the face of network partitions and hardware failure has lured many into the Docker arena. Many people see their enthusiasm wane when the complexity of running a fault-tolerant cluster becomes evident.

However, you don't have to do it all yourself. Multiple cloud providers offer services that make running applications with Docker more manageable. The solution larger organizations are gravitating toward is Kubernetes, a project sponsored by Google as a public and community-supported alternative to proprietary container orchestration tools. Kubernetes takes the lessons that Google learned from building and operating Borg, their internal container orchestration tool, and makes them available to the public.

Or maybe you just need to run a simple dynamic website on as small a setup as possible – you don't have to learn cloud orchestration to do that if you have access to an internet-connected server that itself can run Docker.

What is the minimum realistic production environment?

Docker can run on a wide variety of hardware and software, but the level of support you will receive from either Docker itself or from a third party, such as an operating system distribution that bundles Docker, may vary significantly. Docker can run on a wide variety of operating systems: Linux, Apple macOS, Microsoft Windows, and even IBM S/390x.

Bare minimum – run Docker and Docker Compose on one host

Given the wide distribution of Docker on different environments, the minimum production environment for a Docker-hosted application is a single host, whether it is physical or virtual, running an operating system that supports Docker and Docker Compose. Many popular mainstream operating systems and distributions have some version of Docker built in, including the current **Long-Term Support (LTS)** versions of Ubuntu (16.04, 18.04, and 20.04) and CentOS (7 and 8). Other more specialized operating systems, such as CoreOS and Container Linux, focus exclusively on running containers and may be good choices, albeit with a learning curve for people used to more mainstream systems.

You could even run Docker on Windows or macOS for a production system. You might be more comfortable running Docker on a platform that has support, depending on your risk tolerance and needs. Trade-offs abound!

Docker support

The community edition of Docker receives support from the parent company for a very limited time – the developer-focused Docker Inc. company (`https://www.docker.com`) produces quarterly releases of the **Community Edition (CE)** Docker toolchain with a 4-month rolling support window. As of November 13, 2019, the **Enterprise Edition (EE)** of Docker is a Mirantis product; see `https://www.mirantis.com/company/press-center/company-news/mirantis-acquires-docker-enterprise/` for more details. The EE version of Docker features longer support horizons; support for a variety of Linux, Windows, and macOS operating systems; and an expanded set of supported orchestration systems; see `https://docs.docker.com/ee/` for more information on Docker EE. Mirantis announced that it would end support for the Docker Swarm container orchestrator, a part of Docker EE, in November 2021, but retracted the retirement announcement in February 2020. See `https://devclass.com/2020/02/25/mirantis-to-keep-docker-swarm-buzzing-around-pledges-new-features/` for more details.

Kubernetes appears to be the winner of the Docker container orchestration wars, given this news, although Mirantis is still supporting Docker Swarm.

Problems with single-host deployment

Running Docker on a single host has major drawbacks, however. If that host suffers a major hardware or software failure or has impaired internet connectivity, your application will suffer decreased availability. Computers are fundamentally unreliable and even systems that have enterprise availability features, such as redundant disks, power supplies, and cooling features, can suffer failures due to environmental factors. If you do go down this route, it would be prudent to add some sort of external monitoring and ensure you have a reliable backup and restore routine to mitigate these risks. In order to avoid these risks, we need to consider more sophisticated approaches, such as relying on more container orchestration systems that a third party runs.

Managed cloud services

In order to overcome the limitations of deploying applications on a single host, the easiest option to choose is to consider running your application using a managed cloud service that provides a container orchestration solution. Some of the most popular solutions include the following:

- **Google Kubernetes Engine (GKE)**
- Amazon Web Services **Elastic Beanstalk (EB)**

- Amazon Web Services **Elastic Container Service (ECS)**

- Amazon Web Services **Elastic Kubernetes Service (EKS)**

- Microsoft **Azure Kubernetes Service (AKS)**

- DigitalOcean Docker Swarm

Most of these services support running a set of Docker containers through Kubernetes (`https://kubernetes.io/`), a project initiated by Google. For many years, Google has run a container orchestration system called Borg (`https://ai.google/research/pubs/pub43438`), and Google used that as inspiration to create a container orchestration system suitable for external use, which got named Kubernetes.

Some managed cloud services support Docker Swarm, while others (including AWS Elastic Beanstalk and AWS ECS) have their own custom orchestration systems.

All of the container orchestration systems allow software developers and system administrators to run a fleet of servers that execute multiple containers simultaneously, with policy-based mechanisms for distributing multiple container instances among the cluster. The container orchestrators are responsible for starting, monitoring, and moving container workloads from host to host as health checks and scaling constraints dictate. Since Google popularized running these container orchestration systems, many vendors have devised managed service offerings, including Google, Microsoft, Amazon Web Services, Digital Ocean, and others, as we will discuss in the following subsections.

Google Kubernetes Engine

Google offers a system called **Google Kubernetes Engine (GKE)** (`https://cloud.google.com/kubernetes-engine/`), which offers a supported Kubernetes cluster running within the Google Cloud. If you use this service, you don't have to operate and upgrade the Kubernetes cluster master nodes yourself; you won't see the master nodes in the cloud console at all, as Google operates them directly. Furthermore, Google does not charge customers for running those Kubernetes master nodes. This option is appealing to developers because it has a way to run low-cost Kubernetes clusters. Having the support directly from Google to run Kubernetes workloads gives some customers additional confidence with this system.

However, Google Cloud is not the first or even the second biggest cloud provider, and the rest of the services available from Google Cloud are not as varied as the services that Azure, AWS, or other cloud providers such as AliBaba offer.

If you are invested in Google Cloud, or you want a low-cost environment to experiment with Kubernetes or take it to production and you are not tied to cloud services from other providers, evaluate GKE for running Docker and Kubernetes loads.

AWS Elastic Beanstalk

Amazon Web Services offers a way to run Docker applications through its platform-as-a-service offering, Elastic Beanstalk (`https://aws.amazon.com/elasticbeanstalk/`). You can run either single Docker containers or a setup that supports multiple Docker containers. Under the covers, Elastic Beanstalk uses ECS if you select multiple containers. With Elastic Beanstalk, developers use a command-line interface tool that simplifies deployment to multiple environments, in conjunction with some concise configuration files that hide some of the complexity of running an autoscaling cluster.

It is easier to set up Elastic Beanstalk than it is to set up either ECS or EKS, and developers needing an easy on-ramp to get to production with low overhead and minimal setup might consider using Elastic Beanstalk.

AWS ECS and Fargate

AWS also offers a container orchestration system called ECS (`https://aws.amazon.com/ecs/`). ECS has two basic modalities: one where containers run on a fleet of EC2 instances managed directly by the account owner, and one where AWS manages the nodes that containers run on, called Fargate (`https://aws.amazon.com/fargate/`).

Using ECS with either EC2 or Fargate can make sense if you are invested in AWS. While this path allows you to deploy containers without having to deal with Kubernetes or Docker Swarm, however, it is a proprietary system that only AWS supports, so you would have to do extra work to move your systems away from it compared to using Kubernetes or Docker Swarm as an orchestrator. It has its own learning curve and requires that you commit to running your Docker workloads on AWS because these interfaces are AWS-specific.

AWS EKS

Amazon Web Services (AWS) offers EKS, a managed Kubernetes service that offloads the maintenance and configuration of the Kubernetes master servers to AWS. EKS is the AWS equivalent of Google's GKE. It offers robust integration with the rest of the AWS services, and even though it is not as economical as the GKE service with respect to running the Kubernetes masters, the baseline costs are modest compared with the cost of running a busy application. AWS has generally had support available for Kubernetes through EKS since 2018 and has fixed enough of the initial rough spots that surfaced after its launch (such as a lack of support for some common autoscaling strategies) to make EKS a formidable Kubernetes distribution. In December 2019, AWS announced support for running Kubernetes containers managed by EKS through Fargate, melding the support AWS has for EKS with the managed container runtime and elastic and transparent provisioning that AWS provides.

AWS has the largest and most comprehensive set of services available from a cloud provider as of early 2020. If you have an investment in AWS, and you want a well-trod path that many people have traveled, consider using AWS EKS as your Kubernetes master environment.

Microsoft Azure Kubernetes Service

Microsoft Azure provides a robust container deployment service in **Azure Kubernetes Service (AKS)**. This option may be particularly appealing if you or your company have a large investment in Microsoft platform tooling, including Windows, Visual Studio Code, or Active Directory. Microsoft claims to have robust support for all these concerns. The developer tooling from Microsoft also tends to have a gentler learning curve than the tools from some other organizations. However, if you rely really heavily on elements of the Microsoft stack, it may be more difficult to migrate to other solutions.

If you are working for a Microsoft shop, or you want an easy on-ramp to Kubernetes that is tightly integrated into Visual Studio Code, consider AKS.

Digital Ocean Docker Swarm

Digital Ocean provides support for running a fleet of containers using Docker Swarm, a relatively simple container orchestration system. This technology has a reputation for being easier to deploy than deploying containers on Kubernetes or even AWS ECS. The Docker tooling has support for deploying to Docker Swarm out of the box.

However, after the Mirantis acquisition, Docker Swarm's support status was deprecated and then revived after customers demanded continuing support. Given the wavering commitment from the main vendor supporting it, you should carefully consider whether you should field new applications using Docker Swarm.

Now that we have seen what the alternatives entail for running Docker applications in production, let's examine the set of alternatives for running applications using Docker and Kubernetes.

Running your own Kubernetes cluster – from bare metal to OpenStack

If you must run your application on-premises, in a data center, or if you have the need to run across multiple cloud computing providers, you may need to run your own Kubernetes cluster. Once you learn more about the benefits and drawbacks of running Docker and Kubernetes either on-premises or in a hybrid cloud, you should be able to know when it is an appropriate solution. While these scenarios are more complex than using one of the managed services, they can provide different benefits, listed as follows:

- Upgrading cluster software (or not) on your own schedule, with full control of what versions you run today and tomorrow. Cloud vendors may lag in what versions are supported, or deprecate versions in ways that can impose operational risk.

- Using one of the many mature Kubernetes provisioning solutions, such as Kops, that facilitate setting up k8s clusters on AWS EC2.

- Operating a hybrid cloud solution across a mixture of data center and cloud computing environments. While some cloud provider solutions, such as Google Cloud Anthos or Azure Arc, can support hybrid environments, many do not.

- Running high-performance Kubernetes clusters on bare metal, without the overhead of a hypervisor.

- Running on platforms not supported by major cloud vendors, such as running Docker and Kubernetes on a cluster of Raspberry Pi computers.

- Having complete control over the supporting infrastructure of your cluster integrating with a platform that uses Kubernetes as a starting point, such as the OpenShift platform.

- Running on a private cloud solution, such as OpenStack or VMware Tanzu (formerly known as VMware Enterprise PKS).

- Running Docker containers as part of a comprehensive computing platform that has other major features and capabilities beyond vanilla Kubernetes, such as Red Hat OpenShift or Rancher.

In practice, running any of these solutions is more complex than relying on either a single-host deployment of Docker or a vendor-managed software-as-a-service Kubernetes clustering solution.

Deciding on the right Docker production setup

Because of the bewildering number of choices, picking the right path to deploy your application in production is daunting. You may need to weigh many factors, including the following:

- **Setup**: How hard is it to go from local development to production?
- **Features**: Deployment, testing, monitoring, alerting, and cost reporting.
- **Cost**: Initial and ongoing monthly charges.
- **Support**: Is support easily available either from vendors or from the community?
- **Elasticity**: Can it scale out as the load increases, with automatic or manual controls?
- **Availability**: Can the setup survive the loss of services, hosts, and networks?
- **Stickiness**: How hard will it be to change the deployment strategy?

Running Docker on a single host is inexpensive and easy to set up but has poor scaling and availability characteristics. All the major cloud orchestration services that support Kubernetes are well-balanced in terms of features and scaling and availability characteristics, but they are more complex to set up and operate. The non-Kubernetes options are stickier than the Kubernetes options. Running your own clusters either in the cloud, on bare-metal servers, or in a hybrid cloud gives you enormous flexibility at the cost of increased complexity and support burden.

Learning the relative strengths and weaknesses of these systems will help you judge the right set of technologies to use to deploy your applications. The following matrix shows my snap judgements on a scale of 1 to 5, where 5 is the best, of how well the different technology options compare.

Technology	Setup	Features	Cost	Support	Elasticity	Availability	Stickiness
Docker on a single host	5	1	5	3	1	1	5
Google Cloud GKE	4	5	3	4	5	5	3
AWS Elastic Beanstalk	5	3	3	4	5	5	3
AWS ECS	2	2	3	4	5	5	2
AWS EKS	4	5	2	5	5	5	3
Azure AKS	4	4	3	4	5	5	2

Technology	Setup	Features	Cost	Support	Elasticity	Availability	Stickiness
DigitalOcean Docker Swarm	4	2	3	1	4	4	2
Run your own k8s cluster (bare metal)	2	4	3	2	1	3	3
Run your own k8s cluster (public cloud)	3	5	2	2	5	5	2
Run your own k8s cluster (hybrid cloud)	1	5	3	2	5	5	4
OpenShift	3	4	1	5	4	4	1
OpenStack and Kubernetes	1	5	1	1	4	4	2

You can use this matrix to help rank alternative solutions. By comparing two or more of the choices, you can get a better idea of what sort of solution would be appropriate. In order to evaluate this matrix, you could build an evaluation table where you compare alternatives. If you rank the priorities with a number, where 5 is the highest priority and 1 is the lowest priority, you can multiply the priority by the scores in Table 1 in order to get a scaled score.

The following example matrix has priorities that emphasize ease of setup, minimization of cost, and minimization of stickiness, while disregarding robustness in the form of high availability or elasticity under load. That set of priorities matches up with the priorities many real-world applications have when they first launch – the struggle developers face is often to get things up and running quickly, and it is OK to compromise on the other factors. The scaled scores in the Alternative columns represent the result of multiplying the priority versus the Production Alternatives Rank table for each alternative.

Dimension	Priority	Alternative 1: Docker on a single host	Alternative 2: Google Cloud GKE
Setup	5	25	20
Features	1	1	5
Cost	5	25	15
Support	3	9	12
Elasticity	1	1	5
Availability	1	1	5
Stickiness	4	16	12
Total		78	74

In this case, alternative 1, Docker on a single host, has the highest-ranked scaled score, 78 versus 74. The factors that are important, setup, cost, and stickiness, combine with the weights to push it above the other alternative. Given this score, you should consider using that deployment alternative. Consider though that if the availability or elasticity priority was even one notch higher, the other alternative, Google Cloud GKE, would have been the higher-ranking service.

You may find that your needs are served by a hybrid solution also, where more than one of the solutions is appropriate and necessary to solve your problems. For example, you might find that your everyday demands tilt toward an on-premises cluster, but peak demand might require scaling out into the cloud.

Exercise – join the ShipIt Clicker team

Let's pretend that you have just joined the ShipIt Clicker development team. Other people on the team have created the basic design for the game (see the game design document in https://github.com/PacktPublishing/Docker-for-Developers/blob/master/chapter5/ShipIt_Clicker-spec.md) and written a prototype that has only the bare minimum required functionality to build, test, and package the application with Docker.

The rest of the team might be experts in design, or frontend or backend development, but they are not sure how they should proceed regarding deploying to production. At this point, you have more experience using Docker than any of the other developers on the team. The Dockerfile and docker-compose.yml files they have produced are functioning.

Get the ShipIt Clicker—the version made for this chapter—running on your local workstation to better understand how it is put together.

Run docker-compose up in order to start the containers on your local machine. This will allow you to evaluate the deployment alternatives and experiment with changes that will prepare the application for production use. You will see output similar to the following; we will explain in detail what each group of lines in the output means:

```
$ docker-compose up
Building shipit-clicker-web
Step 1/11 : FROM ubuntu:bionic
---> 775349758637
Step 2/11 : RUN apt-get -qq update &&        apt-get -qq install
-y nodejs npm > /dev/null
---> Using cache
---> f8a9a6eddb8e
```

The preceding output shows Docker using the `ubuntu:bionic` image, and then the installation of the operating system packages.

Steps 3-5 of the Dockerfile prepare the container image for the application installation by creating essential directories and copying the package configuration file for node modules into place:

```
Step 3/11 : RUN mkdir -p /app/public /app/server
---> Using cache
---> f7e56a628e8b
Step 4/11 : COPY src/package.json* /app
---> eede94466dc7
Step 5/11 : WORKDIR /app
---> Running in adcadb6616c2
Removing intermediate container adcadb6616c2
---> 6256f613803e
```

Next, the Dockerfile installs the node modules:

```
Step 6/11 : RUN npm install > /dev/null
---> Running in 02ae124cf711
npm WARN deprecated superagent@3.8.3: Please note that v5.0.1+
of superagent removes User-Agent header by default, therefore
you may need to add it yourself (e.g. GitHub blocks requests
without a User-Agent header).  This notice will go away with
v5.0.2+ once it is released.
npm WARN optional Skipping failed optional dependency /
chokidar/fsevents:
npm WARN notsup Not compatible with your operating system or
architecture: fsevents@1.2.11
npm WARN shipit-clicker@1.0.5 No repository field.
npm WARN shipit-clicker@1.0.5 No license field.
Removing intermediate container 02ae124cf711
---> 64ea4b348ed1
```

After this, the Dockerfile copies more configuration files into the container image, as well as copying the sources for the application itself into place within the container under /app:

```
Step 7/11 : COPY src/.babelrc        src/.env        src/.
nodemonrc.json       /app/
---> 88e88c1bc35d
Step 8/11 : COPY src/public/ /app/public/
---> c9872fccc1c9
Step 9/11 : COPY src/server/ /app/server/
---> f6e76811659a
```

Finally, the Dockerfile tells Docker what port to expose and how to run the application:

```
Step 10/11 : EXPOSE 3000
---> Running in 75fbd217ef27
Removing intermediate container 75fbd217ef27
---> 03faaa0e8030
Step 11/11 : ENTRYPOINT DEBUG='shipit-clicker:*' npm run dev
---> Running in 0a44ab13b0d3
Removing intermediate container 0a44ab13b0d3
---> ab6e4da773e7
Successfully built ab6e4da773e7
```

At this point, the Docker container is built, and Docker applies the latest tag:

```
Successfully tagged chapter5_shipit-clicker-web:latest
WARNING: Image for service shipit-clicker-web was built because
it did not already exist. To rebuild this image you must use
`docker-compose build` or `docker-compose up --build`.
```

The power of using docker-compose up is on display next, as the one command we ran at the beginning not only builds the Docker container for our application, but it also starts all the containers together. When it starts the containers, it starts both the application container, and the Redis container. The Redis container emits some detailed output as part of its startup. The output of our docker-compose up command continues with container startup messages:

```
Starting chapter5_redis_1 ... done
Creating chapter5_shipit-clicker-web_1 ... done
Attaching to chapter5_redis_1, chapter5_shipit-clicker-web_1
```

```
redis_1              | 1:C 04 Feb 2020 06:15:08.774 #
oO0OoO0OoO0Oo Redis is starting oO0OoO0OoO0Oo
```

```
redis_1              | 1:C 04 Feb 2020 06:15:08.774 # Redis
version=5.0.7, bits=64, commit=00000000, modified=0, pid=1,
just started
```

```
redis_1              | 1:C 04 Feb 2020 06:15:08.774 # Warning:
no config file specified, using the default config. In order to
specify a config file use redis-server /path/to/redis.conf
```

```
redis_1              | 1:M 04 Feb 2020 06:15:08.776 * Running
mode=standalone, port=6379.
```

```
redis_1              | 1:M 04 Feb 2020 06:15:08.776 # WARNING:
The TCP backlog setting of 511 cannot be enforced because /
proc/sys/net/core/somaxconn is set to the lower value of 128.
```

```
redis_1              | 1:M 04 Feb 2020 06:15:08.776 # Server
initialized
```

Note that Redis is not entirely happy being run as part of a Docker container that uses
a Linux kernel that is not tuned explicitly for it. This is an example where using Docker
might not yield optimal results, but results that are good enough anyway:

```
redis_1              | 1:M 04 Feb 2020 06:15:08.776 # WARNING
you have Transparent Huge Pages (THP) support enabled in your
kernel. This will create latency and memory usage issues with
Redis. To fix this issue run the command 'echo never > /sys/
kernel/mm/transparent_hugepage/enabled' as root, and add it
to your /etc/rc.local in order to retain the setting after a
reboot. Redis must be restarted after THP is disabled.
```

```
redis_1              | 1:M 04 Feb 2020 06:15:08.776 * DB
loaded from disk: 0.000 seconds
```

```
redis_1              | 1:M 04 Feb 2020 06:15:08.776 * Ready to
accept connections
```

You can see that Redis is now ready to go. Next, `docker-compose` starts up the ShipIt
Clicker container, using the command given in the preceding `ENTRYPOINT DEBUG`
output (`'shipit-clicker:*' npm run dev`):

```
shipit-clicker-web_1  |
```

```
shipit-clicker-web_1  | > shipit-clicker@1.0.5 dev /app
```

```
shipit-clicker-web_1  | > nodemon server --exec babel-node
--config .nodemonrc.json | pino-pretty
```

```
shipit-clicker-web_1  |
```

```
shipit-clicker-web_1    | [nodemon] 1.19.4

shipit-clicker-web_1    | [nodemon] to restart at any time, enter
`rs`

shipit-clicker-web_1    | [nodemon] watching dir(s): *.*

shipit-clicker-web_1    | [nodemon] watching extensions:
js,json,mjs,yaml,yml

shipit-clicker-web_1    | [nodemon] starting `babel-node server`

shipit-clicker-web_1    | [1580796912837] INFO  (shipit-
clicker/47 on 52e6d59c6121): Redis connection established

shipit-clicker-web_1    |          redis_url: "redis://redis:6379"

shipit-clicker-web_1    | [1580796913083] INFO  (shipit-
clicker/47 on 52e6d59c6121): up and running in development @:
52e6d59c6121 on port: 3000}
```

Once you have done this, you can play the game by going to `http://localhost:3005/` in a web browser. In the following figure, we see the output of the main menu of the game, with a link to the API documentation at `http://localhost:3005/api-explorer/`:

Figure 5.1 – ShipIt Clicker game main menu

Once you have the application running and have explored it, you can learn how to deploy it in different ways.

Exercise – choosing from reasonable deployment alternatives

The setup in this chapter works to get the game running on a local development environment. However, the setup has some issues that might cause problems for a production deployment.

The initial audiences for the game in this prototype stage are as follows:

- Your fellow game developers and the management team of the company

- A globally distributed team of enthusiasts who signed up for an Alpha program

- A professional cadre of testers twelve time zones away from where you live

Management wants to get the prototype available for the alpha tester volunteers and the professional testers as soon as possible, but wants to know what the options and costs will be to support a more robust deployment environment that can scale if the game goes viral or the investors approve an ad campaign to boost subscribers.

Your tasks, given what you know about Docker and the alternatives for deploying to production, are as follows:

- Advise management on what the first production deployment should be, after constructing a *Production Decision Alternatives* table.

- Advise management on what one or more reasonable alternatives to the first deployment would be, which would increase elasticity and availability.

- Build a spreadsheet model of the one-time and recurring costs incurred over the first year for each option, after consulting current price lists from vendors.

Solution

Compare your decision matrix to the preceding example in the *Deciding on the right Docker production setup* section and see whether your result differs. Show the spreadsheet model of costs and your decision matrix to a colleague and ask them what they might choose and whether they agree with your decision.

Exercise – Dockerfile and docker-compose.yml evaluation

Management wants you to stretch a little and help smooth the way for a production deployment. They want you to identify areas for improvement:

- Are the choices made in the Dockerfile and `docker-compose.yml` files reasonable for this application?

- What choices could be made to better prepare the application for a production deployment?

- What effect does the choice of a commodity operating system distribution have when choosing a container base to use in `FROM`?

Solution

Look at the versions of the Dockerfile and `docker-compose.yml` files in `https://github.com/PacktPublishing/Docker-for-Developers/tree/master/chapter6` and see how your recommendations line up. We will explore this in more detail in *Chapter 6, Deploying Applications with Docker Compose.*

Now that we have learned more about the alternatives for deploying Docker containers into production, and done some practical exercises, let's review what we have learned.

Summary

In this chapter, we learned about the alternatives for deploying your Docker-based application to production. We learned that the many choices involve trade-offs, and how to build the smallest viable production environment. We learned how to choose between different cloud providers and their managed container runtimes, and how to articulate the benefits of running Docker either on-premises or in a hybrid cloud. We also learned how to decide on a production path for deploying Docker containers given competing objectives.

Given these lessons, you can apply what you have learned to create a real production deployment. Having enough context about the technology alternatives is very important – because different strategies offer different advantages and disadvantages. Your company might need a super-robust autoscaling deployment in the future but might only need something that works today.

In the next chapter, we will show how you can create a robust single-host Docker production deployment while maintaining the ability to develop locally.

6
Deploying Applications with Docker Compose

The simplest possible practical deployment scenario of an application packaged with Docker involves running Docker Compose on a single host. Many of the commands that you use as a developer, such as `docker-compose up -d`, also apply to deploying Docker applications on a single host.

Running Docker applications on a single host is easier to understand than running them using one of the more complex container orchestration systems because many of the same techniques you might use to run a non-Docker application apply; however, it has some significant drawbacks in terms of performance and availability.

In this chapter, you will discover why this is the simplest practical option, learn how to configure Docker for production on a single host, and master some techniques for managing and monitoring a simple setup efficiently. Furthermore, you will better understand the drawbacks of running Docker on a single host, including the problems you may face.

In this chapter, we're going to cover the following main topics:

- Selecting a host and operating system for single-host deployment

- Preparing the host for Docker and Docker Compose

- Deploying using configuration files and support scripts

- Monitoring small deployments—logging and alerting

- Limitations of single-host deployment

Technical requirements

To complete the exercises in this chapter, you'll need Git and Docker on your local workstation, and you will need a single host capable of running Linux and Docker for your production server, connected to a network that you can SSH into and that your users can reach.

The GitHub repository for this chapter can be found at `https://github.com/PacktPublishing/Docker-for-Developers`—please refer to the `chapter6` folder.

Check out the following video to see the Code in Action:

`https://bit.ly/31OSi1H`

Example application – ShipIt Clicker v2

The version of ShipIt Clicker in this chapter is more polished than the one we used in *Chapter 5, Alternatives for Deploying and Running Containers in Production*. It has the following features:

- An improved Dockerfile and `docker-compose.yml` file suitable for basic production use

- Storage of game state in Redis tied to a server session, leading to distinct game states for different client devices

- Improved visual and audio assets

We will use this enhanced version of ShipIt Clicker as the application to deploy on a single host using Docker Compose.

Selecting a host and operating system for single-host deployment

Deploying your application on a single host is the simplest possible way to run an application in production. In many ways, it resembles the user experience of performing local development using Docker and Docker Compose. If you can package the parts of your application using a `docker-compose.yml` file, you are already 70 percent of the way there. If you already have basic UNIX or Linux system administration skills, this will be very easy—this strategy requires the least effort and you can master the essentials in an hour or two.

Requirements for single-host deployment

In order to proceed with deployment, you will need a computer running a modern Linux operating system of the same architecture as your development system, with enough memory and processor and storage capacity to run your application. If you are developing on a Windows 10 64-bit desktop using Docker Community Edition, you need a Linux system that also uses the x86_64 architecture. If you're using Docker on a Raspberry Pi 4 running Raspbian, you need an ARM architecture server. Really, you could use any bare metal or virtual machine server, either on-premises or in the cloud, as long as it supports Docker.

Some cloud providers, such as **Amazon Web Services** (**AWS**), offer a free tier for their smallest virtual machine deployments, at least for the first year. The example in this chapter will work on a host like this, but if you have a larger application, you may need to use a larger and more expensive system.

Production applications often must run *24*7*, and the users of these applications may have reliability concerns. While running Docker applications on a single host is possibly the least reliable way to proceed, it might be good enough for your application. All the single-host reliability measures that vendors such as HP, Dell, and IBM have built can be enough in many cases to ensure adequate reliability if your application requires that.

You will need one of the following Linux operating system distributions that support Docker:

- Red Hat Enterprise Linux (or CentOS) 7 or 8
- Ubuntu 16.04 or 18.04 or newer
- Amazon Linux 2
- Debian Stretch 9
- Buster 10

To minimize time to production and to maximize ease, pick one that you know already, or use CentOS 7, which is used in the following examples.

Only select a Docker-focused distribution, such as Container Linux or CoreOS, if you want to take a slower, more advanced path to production, as your system administration skills may be less effective in those environments. User management in CoreOS, for example, works quite differently than it does in more mainstream distributions.

Because this strategy depends only on having a host that the users of your application can reach, you have tremendous flexibility.

Preparing the host for Docker and Docker Compose

Before you configure the software on the host, you should ensure that it has a stable IP address. Sometimes these are referred to as static IP addresses, or Elastic IP addresses, in an AWS context. You may need to specially allocate these IP address through your provider, which can often be done through the provider's console, such as with the **Network** tab in AWS Lightsail, or the **Elastic IPs** settings in the AWS EC2 console.

Also, you should map an address (type **A**) record in a **Domain Name System** (**DNS**) zone that you control to the IP address so that your users can get to the application by using a short name, such as `shipitclicker.example.com` instead of a raw IP address, such as `192.2.0.10`. All public cloud systems have the ability to manage DNS entries—for example, AWS Route 53 (`https://docs.aws.amazon.com/route53/index.html`), and most virtual hosting systems have this capacity as well.

Using operating system packages to install Docker and Git

You will need to install Docker on the host. For production use, avoid the outdated Docker versions that ships with operating system distributions, and try to use the operating system packages that Docker publishes for Docker Community Edition. You can find instructions on installing Docker Community Edition on the Docker website for various operating systems, as follows:

- **CentOS**: `https://docs.docker.com/install/linux/docker-ce/centos/`
- **Debian**: `https://docs.docker.com/install/linux/docker-ce/debian/`

- **Fedora**: `https://docs.docker.com/install/linux/docker-ce/fedora/`
- **Ubuntu**: `https://docs.docker.com/install/linux/docker-ce/ubuntu/`
- **Binaries**: `https://docs.docker.com/install/linux/docker-ce/binaries/`

Use the following commands for a fresh installation of CentOS 7:

```
$ sudo yum install -y yum-utils
$ sudo yum install -y device-mapper-persistent-data lvm2

$ sudo yum-config-manager --add-repo \
https://download.docker.com/linux/centos/docker-ce.repo

$ sudo yum install -y docker-ce docker-ce-cli containerd.io
```

Add your normal, non-root user to the Docker user group, and become a member of that group for this Terminal session:

```
$ sudo usermod -aG docker $USER
$ newgrp docker
```

Make sure the Docker service is enabled so that it will start on boot, and that the Docker service is started:

```
$ sudo systemctl enable docker
$ sudo systemctl restart docker
```

Install `docker-compose` by following the directions at `https://docs.docker.com/compose/install/`. `1.25.3` is the latest version as of January 2020, but please check the version number on that page for the latest to put in the following command, which should all be one line:

```
$ sudo curl -L "https://github.com/docker/compose/releases/download/1.25.3/docker-compose-$(uname -s)-$(uname -m)" -o /usr/local/bin/docker-compose
$ sudo chmod +x /usr/local/bin/docker-compose
```

Now that you have the Docker daemon running and enabled, and you also have `docker-compose` installed, you can deploy your application.

Next, install `git` through your operating system's package manager. For Red Hat family distributions (such as RHEL, CentOS, Fedora, and Amazon Linux), use the following command:

```
$ sudo yum install -y git
```

For Debian family distributions (including Ubuntu), run the following command:

```
$ sudo apt-get update && apt-get install -y git
```

At this point, the host is ready to deploy Docker applications. In order to complete deployment, we will use a strategy that relies on shell scripts and Docker environment configuration files.

Deploying using configuration files and support scripts

To deploy our application to a production server, we will use a combination of simple commands and support scripts that start or update the running set of containers. Let's start by taking a close look at the two most important files required for deployment: `Dockerfile` and `docker-compose.yml`.

Re-examining the initial Dockerfile

The Dockerfile from *Chapter 5, Alternatives for Deploying and Running Containers in Production*, has good layering and has `package.json` and `package.json.lock` copied into the image before `RUN npm -s install` executes and before the main parts of the app are copied into the image. However, it has some rough edges, which we are going to smooth out in this chapter to prepare a solid production deployment. First, let's take a look at the initial Dockerfile:

```
FROM ubuntu:bionic
RUN apt-get -qq update && \
    apt-get -qq install -y nodejs npm > /dev/null
RUN mkdir -p /app/public /app/server
COPY src/package.json* /app
WORKDIR /app
RUN npm -s install
COPY src/.babelrc \
    src/.env \
```

```
        src/.nodemonrc.json \
        /app/
COPY src/public/ /app/public/
COPY src/server/ /app/server/
EXPOSE 3000
ENTRYPOINT DEBUG='shipit-clicker:*' npm run dev
```

The preceding Dockerfile for the ShipIt Clicker game prototype gets many things right from a local development perspective, but has some limitations, which we will address in the Dockerfile for this chapter.

Very often, developers start with a base image (such as FROM ubuntu:bionic) that mirrors what they know best: traditional Linux distributions that you might run on your workstation. This may help with debugging the Dockerfile initially, but it comes at a steep cost because both the base and generated images are large, consisting of hundreds of megabytes. Also, the package installation for Ubuntu is quite verbose, so the apt-get install command has to redirect stdout to /dev/null to prevent verbose output from taking over our Terminal (see https://askubuntu.com/a/1134785).

The rest of the initial Dockerfile has some common quirks that you should avoid for production, such as copying configuration files for all of the development tooling (see the COPY command, which copies dotfiles). The initial Dockerfile has an entry point (ENTRYPOINT) that refers to a server that is best suited for development, not production, because it was quick and easy to define that way. A real production setup requires a build step that will create a set of assets suitable for distribution, as well as a different npm command that launches the app using those assets.

The Dockerfile for this chapter has corrections for all of these issues:

```
FROM alpine:20191114
RUN apk update && \
    apk add nodejs nodejs-npm
RUN addgroup -S app && adduser -S -G app app
RUN mkdir -p /app/public /app/server
ADD src/package.json* /app/
WORKDIR /app
RUN npm -s install
COPY src/public/ /app/public/
COPY src/server/ /app/server/
COPY src/.babelrc /app/
```

```
RUN npm run compile
USER app
EXPOSE 3000
ENTRYPOINT npm start
```

In this revised Dockerfile, we use Alpine Linux instead of Ubuntu for smaller images, and we pin the version of Alpine for consistent builds. The container image based on Alpine Linux is 71% smaller:

```
$ docker images | awk '/chapter._ship/{ print $1 " " $7}'
chapter6_shipit-clicker-web-v2 154MB
chapter5_shipit-clicker-web 524MB
```

In the revised Dockerfile, we also create an `app` user so that Docker runs the application as a normal UNIX user, not the `root` user, as that can exacerbate security problems.

After installing the operating system packages and npm packages as silently as possible, we can copy the application files and the `.babelrc` configuration file into `/app`, and then run RUN `npm run compile` in order to prepare the production version of the node application, which we run as the `app` user with ENTRYPOINT `npm start`.

Re-examining the initial docker-compose.yml file

The initial `docker-compose.yml` file from the previous chapter gets the job done of starting both a web and a Redis container, but it has some deficiencies. The initial `docker-compose.yml` file was adapted from the barebones example in the Docker documentation at `https://docs.docker.com/compose/`, so it has some gaps in how ready it is for production use. Many developers adapt these examples without considering certain nuances that matter when you have to deploy an application to production. You can think of it as a starting point, rather than the final destination. The initial `docker-compose.yml` file is as follows:

```
---
version: '3'
services:
  shipit-clicker-web:
    build: .
    environment:
      REDIS_HOST: redis
    ports:
      - "3005:3000"
```

```
    links:
    - redis
  redis:
    image: redis
    ports:
    - "6379:6379"
```

The revised `docker-compose.yml` file for this chapter is much more robust. This file is inspired in part by the samples at `https://github.com/docker-library/redis/issues/111` and especially by an example by GitHub user `@lagden`, which has a nice example of a `docker-compose.yml` file that supports Redis:

```
---
version: '3'
services:
  shipit-clicker-web-v2:
    build: .
    environment:
        - APP_ID=shipit-clicker-v2
        - OPENAPI_SPEC=/api/v1/spec
        - OPENAPI_ENABLE_RESPONSE_VALIDATION=false
        - PORT=3000
        - LOG_LEVEL=${LOG_LEVEL:-debug}
        - REQUEST_LIMIT=100kb
        - REDIS_HOST=${REDIS_HOST:-redis}
        - REDIS_PORT=${REDIS_PORT:-6379}
        - SESSION_SECRET=${SESSION_SECRET:-mySecret-v2}
```

Note that we define all the environment variables explicitly for the application, and that several of them are defined with a `${VARIABLE_NAME:-default_value}` syntax that uses the value of an environment variable. These can be specified on the command line, in the usual configuration file: `$HOME/.profile`, `$HOME/.bashrc`, or the `.env` file in the same directory as the `docker-compose.yml` file:

```
  ports:
      - "${PORT:-3006}:3000"
    networks:
      - private-redis-shipit-clicker-v2
    links:
```

```
      - redis
  depends_on:
      - redis
```

The preceding `ports` section defines the networking configuration for the main container; it defines a private network called `private-redis-shipit-clicker-v2`, which links the two containers. Note the use of `depends_on` in this section. This means that the ShipIt Clicker container will wait until the Redis container is started before starting. Next, let's examine the Redis container definition:

```
  redis:
    command: ["redis-server", "--appendonly", "yes"]
    image: redis:5-alpine3.10
    volumes:
      - redis-data-shipit-clicker:/data
    networks:
      - private-redis-shipit-clicker-v2

  volumes:
    redis-data-shipit-clicker: {}

  networks:
    private-redis-shipit-clicker-v2:
```

This has many environment variable entries—for example, `LOG_LEVEL`, `REDIS_HOST`, and `REDIS_PORT`—that allow easy overrides. It allows the override of Redis host settings, both for easier debugging and to pave the way for easy connection to cloud Redis services. It starts Redis with command-line parameters that enable persistence and allocates a Docker persistent volume to store Redis append-only log files. Otherwise, the data would vanish every time the Redis container is restarted. It makes the network where Redis and the web server communicates private. This is especially important with Redis because, with the default configuration, the Redis server operates without any authentication or authorization—it is wide open to whoever can connect!

In this minimalistic, production-ready `docker-compose.yml` file, we expose the web server directly on port `80` to the world. This works, but modern browsers will show a security warning for plain HTTP content. It will work to get you to production, but many production applications require more security safeguards than running over plain HTTP. You can get around this by using either a proxy or external load balancer that terminates HTTPS on port `443`, or by configuring SSL certificates. We will cover this in more detail in later chapters.

One of the features of the `docker-compose` v3 configuration is that it sets the default behavior for when a container fails to *always restart*. This should happen even if the host is rebooted, and will definitely happen if a process exits due to an unhandled exception. If you need to configure the restart behavior of your application more directly, you can do so with the settings listed in the documentation at `https://docs.docker.com/compose/compose-file/#restart_policy`.

Preparing the production .env file

Clone the repository and prepare to configure `docker-compose`:

```
$ git clone https://github.com/PacktPublishing/Docker-for-
Developers.git
```
```
$ cd Docker-for-Developers/chapter6
```

In order to configure your application for production, you should create a file called `.env` in the directory where your `docker-compose.yml` file lives. If you want to change any of the defaults—for example, to change the level of debugging shown in production from `info` to `debug`—you should do so through creating and editing the `.env` file associated with the production deployment. Copy the file, `env.sample`, to `.env` and edit it to suit your preferences for production.

Handling secrets

This demo application uses environment variables and an `.env` file to store secrets. This is in accordance with the 12-factor application principles (see `https://12factor.net/config`), but it is certainly not the only way, or the most secure way, to deal with secrets. You could use a secret management system, such as HashiCorp Vault or Amazon Secrets Manager, to store and retrieve secrets. We will cover this in detail in both *Chapter 8, Deploying Docker Apps to Kubernetes*, and *Chapter 14, Advanced Docker Security – Secrets, Secret Commands, Tagging, and Labels*; but for now, let's just use environment variables for the secrets.

You should replace the secret in the environment variable, `SESSION_SECRET`, with a random secret and confirm whether you want to expose port `80` to the world. Use whatever editor you are comfortable with, whether that is `vi`, `emacs`, or `nano`:

```
cp env.sample .env
vi .env
```

Once you have set the environment variable overrides, you can deploy the application.

Deploying for the first time

Once you have copied your `.env` file in place, start the services in the background to deploy the application:

```
$ docker-compose up -d
```

Verify that the services are running, as follows:

```
$ docker-compose ps
       Name                 Command          State          Ports
    -------------------------------------------------------------------
    chapter6_redi      docker-              Up          6379/tcp
    s_1                entrypoint.sh
                       redis ...
    chapter6_ship      /bin/sh -c           Up          0.0.0.0:80-
    it-clicker-        npm start                        >3000/tcp
    web-v2_1
```

Check whether the system logs show any errors:

```
$ docker-compose logs
```

As long as you don't see a stream of error messages in the logs, you should then be able to reach the website at the IP address of the server—for example, at `http://192.0.2.10`—substituting your IP address. If you assigned a hostname using DNS, you should be able to reach it using that hostname—for example, at `http://shiptclicker.example.com`—substituting the full canonical domain name for this one.

Troubleshooting common errors

If you get an error like this, you need to ensure that the host is not running another web server, such as Apache HTTPD or NGINX:

```
docker.errors.APIError: 500 Server Error: Internal Server
Error ("b'Ports are not available: listen tcp 0.0.0.0:80: bind:
address already in use'")
```

If you get this issue, you should either uninstall the web server that is running on the host or change what port it uses to listen for requests. You could also change the port that ShipIt Clicker runs on by changing the PORT variable in the .env file. For Red Hat family systems, a server listening on port 80 is likely to be Apache HTTPd, and you can remove it with the following:

```
$ yum remove -y httpd
```

For Debian family systems, it is also likely to be Apache, and you will need to use the following command to remove it:

```
$ apt-get remove -y apache2
```

It is possible that you might have some other web server running. You can find out what the process name of your web server is with netstat:

```
$ sudo netstat -nap | grep :80
tcp6       0      0 :::80                    :::*
LISTEN        12037/httpd
```

You may not need to do any troubleshooting to get your application running in Docker, but in a single-host deployment scenario, you can use your system administration troubleshooting skills to figure out what might be going wrong.

Once you have the application running, you may find that you run some of the same operations repeatedly, such as rebuilding the application when you have made changes. This is where support scripts come in handy.

Supporting scripts

When running a site in production, you might have to do some operations frequently. It becomes tiresome to remember the exact sequence of the Docker commands required to restart and update the running system or to connect to the database.

You should continue to develop your application on your local workstation and use the production system to deploy changes to your users, once you have tested things locally.

With the improved networking setup in this chapter, it is no longer possible to connect directly to the Redis container via a direct TCP port, so we will use `docker exec` within a script to do that.

If you are in the `Docker-for-Developers/chapter6` directory, you can permanently add this directory to `PATH` with the following commands to make running these scripts more convenient:

```
$ echo "PATH=$PWD:$PATH" | tee -a "$HOME/.bash_profile"
$ . "$HOME/.bash_profile"
```

The most common operations for this application are probably restarting the application, deploying changes, and connecting to Redis to troubleshoot. For these operations, we will use the `restart.sh` script, the `deploy.sh` script, and the `redis-cli.sh` script.

Restarting

The `restart.sh` script will restart all the containers. You should run this after you make a change to the configuration file, `.env`. You could just run `docker-compose up -d`, but that alone will not tell you whether the changes took hold. This will also run `docker-compose ps` for you, which will show you whether your containers are running correctly after the change, including what the port mappings are. In the following example session, we remove the `.env` file entirely and then recreate it with just a single setting for `PORT=80`:

```
[centos@ip-172-26-0-237 chapter6]$ rm .env
[centos@ip-172-26-0-237 chapter6]$ deploy.sh
chapter6_redis_1 is up-to-date
Recreating chapter6_shipit-clicker-web-v2_1 ... done
               Name                              Command
State          Ports
---------------------------------------------------------------------
----------------------------------------------
chapter6_redis_1                      docker-entrypoint.sh redis
...    Up       6379/tcp
chapter6_shipit-clicker-web-v2_1    npm start
Up        0.0.0.0:3006->3000/tcp
[centos@ip-172-26-0-237 chapter6]$ echo 'PORT=80' > .env
[centos@ip-172-26-0-237 chapter6]$ restart.sh
```

```
chapter6_redis_1 is up-to-date
Recreating chapter6_shipit-clicker-web-v2_1 ... done
            Name                            Command
State       Ports
------------------------------------------------------------
-------------------------------
chapter6_redis_1                  docker-entrypoint.sh redis
...    Up        6379/tcp
chapter6_shipit-clicker-web-v2_1    npm start
Up        0.0.0.0:80->3000/tcp
[centos@ip-172-26-0-237 chapter6]$
```

You can see that the `chapter6_shipit-clicker-web-v2_1` application was recreated the second time that `restart.sh` was run, and that the server is now connected to the wildcard IPv4 `0.0.0.0` address on port `80`. This will allow the server to respond to an HTTP request without a special port number in the URL.

Deploying

The `deploy.sh` script pulls changes from the `git` upstream repository, builds the container, and restarts any containers requiring an update. You should use this after you have made changes to the code and tested them locally.

Redis

The `redis-cli.sh` script will allow you to connect to the running Redis server in the command line. It uses a `docker exec` command, which attaches to the running container and starts a new `redis-cli` command within it This is needed in part because now, Redis is running in an isolated network, and you should not be able to reach it via TCP sockets, even from the production host. This will let you troubleshoot any issues with the backend server.

Here is a sample session showing `redis-cli.sh` in action:

```
[centos@ip-172-26-0-237 chapter6]$ ./redis-cli.sh
127.0.0.1:6379> help
redis-cli 5.0.7
To get help about Redis commands type:
      "help @<group>" to get a list of commands in <group>
      "help <command>" for help on <command>
      "help <tab>" to get a list of possible help topics
```

```
        "quit" to exit

To set redis-cli preferences:
        ":set hints" enable online hints
        ":set nohints" disable online hints
Set your preferences in ~/.redisclirc
127.0.0.1:6379> keys *
1) "example/deploys"
2) "example/nextPurchase"
3) "example/score"
127.0.0.1:6379> get example/score
"209"
127.0.0.1:6379> quit
```

Note that you can use this `redis-cli.sh` script to connect to the Redis server, even though it is on a private virtual network that would be inaccessible if you had installed the standard `redis-cli` program on the host. Being able to rely on tools in a container can allow you to reach deep into the configuration of an application, even though it is protected from being directly exposed to the internet.

Exercise – keeping builds off the production server

The deployment script for this chapter does the simplest thing possible for updates: it rebuilds the container on the production server. This might, however, lead to resource exhaustion and bringing the production server down.

Given what you learned about Docker Hub in *Chapter 4, Composing Systems Using Containers*, how might you change the workflow of application development to revise the `docker-compose.yml` file and the `deploy.sh` script to avoid building the Docker container on the production server?

Write down one or two sentences describing the workflow that you would use and what alterations to the `docker-compose.yml` configuration file would be needed.

> **Note:**
> There are multiple ways to achieve these goals, and there is no single answer to how to achieve them. You can compare your answer with the `docker-compose.yml` file in the next chapter to see how your ideas compare to the solution for building the containers highlighted in that chapter.

Exercise – planning to secure the production site

Imagine that you hear from your boss that the ShipIt Squirrel code and production systems are going to get some attention from your company's chief information security officer, who is going to go through everything looking for weaknesses. He is concerned that in the rush to get this live, too many shortcuts have been taken, and he wants you to provide some more information to him. Please write down the answers to these three questions:

1. What could be done to secure communication between the clients and the server with SSL? Which of the following should you do?

   a. Terminate SSL within the program itself.

   b. Use an external load balancer to terminate SSL.

   c. Use a web server on the host, but outside Docker, to terminate SSL.

   d. Use Docker and a web server container to terminate SSL.

2. How do you plan on renewing the SSL certificate periodically?

3. Are there other weaknesses in the security of the current system that you can find, either at the Docker layer or the API layer?

Once you have deployed the application and considered some enhancements to its security, you should learn how to monitor the deployment so that you can find out when something goes wrong before the users of your application notice.

Answers for how to secure the production site:

Any of the four options for *Question 1* could work, but options *b* and *d* are the most robust and stable in practice. Option *a* is tricky to get right, and option *c* requires separate updates to the application environment.

Regarding *Question 2*, you can either purchase an SSL certificate from a vendor, which you must renew and reinstall every year, you can rely on the vendor of your load balancer to automatically renew your certificate (if they offer that as an option), or you can use Let's Encrypt to automatically renew the certificate. See the *Further reading* section of the next chapter for more about using Let's Encrypt to renew the certificate, as well as using a set of Docker containers to terminate SSL.

Question 3 is open-ended, but the first thing that you should notice is that there is no authentication or authorization built into the web services in the `chapter6` code base.

Monitoring small deployments – logging and alerting

One of the nice things about starting small is that you may be able to rely on very simple mechanisms for both logging and alerting. For any deployment using Docker and `Docker Compose` on a single host—for example, a deployment of ShipIt Clicker—you can use some basic tools and commands to deal with logging, and a variety of simple alerting services provided by third parties to deal with alerting.

Logging

For logging, in many cases, all that is required is to use the logs built into Docker. Docker captures the standard output and standard error file handles of every process it starts and makes them available as logs for each container. You can review the consolidated logs for all the services started since the last container restart with the following command, assuming you are in the directory where your `docker-compose.yml` file is present (`less -R` will interpret the ANSI color escapes that the `logs` command produces):

```
$ docker-compose logs 2>&1 | less -R
```

You can also do `docker ps` in order to find the name of the running containers so that you can retrieve their log streams:

```
[centos@ip-172-26-0-237 ~]$ docker ps
```

CONTAINER ID	IMAGE	COMMAND
CREATED		
STATUS	PORTS	NAMES
e947e7de33ef	chapter6_shipit-clicker-web-v2	"npm
start"	4 hours ago	
Up 4 hours	0.0.0.0:80->3000/tcp	chapter6_
shipit-clicker-web-v2_1		
3f91820e097b	redis:5-alpine3.10	„docker-
entrypoint.s…"	4 hours ago	
Up 4 hours	6379/tcp	chapter6_
redis_1		

Once you have the names of the containers, you can retrieve the individual log files for each running container separately. You can pipe them to `less`, or redirect the output of the logs to a file, for example:

```
[centos@ip-172-26-0-237 ~]$ docker logs chapter6_shipit-
clicker-web-v2_1 > shipit.log
[centos@ip-172-26-0-237 ~]$ tail shipit.log


> shipit-clicker@1.0.0 start /app
> node dist/index.js

{"level":30,"time":1580087119723,"pid":16,"hostname":"e947e7de3
3ef","name":"shipit-clicker-
v2","msg":"Redis connection established","redis_url":"redis://
redis:6379","v":1}
{"level":30,"time":1580087119934,"pid":16,"hostname":"e947e7de3
3ef","name":"shipit-clicker-
v2","msg":"up and running in development @: e947e7de33ef on
port: 3000}","v":1}
[centos@ip-172-26-0-237 ~]$
```

This procedure does require you to log into the production server and run some commands there, but in practice, this is a good way to examine the logs of an application running on a single host.

Alerting

To begin, it would be enough to monitor the HTTP server on port `80` of the production server to ensure it stays alive. If you have access to a network monitoring system for your company—for example, a Nagios or Icinga server—you could use that. If the system is accessible via the internet, you can use a free monitoring service, such as `https://uptimerobot.com`, to monitor the server.

In order to extend monitoring deeper, you might want to also monitor the internal services, such as Redis. This is more challenging in a simple setup like this one, though. We will go into more depth about advanced monitoring systems in *Chapter 10, Monitoring Docker Using Prometheus, Grafana, and Jaeger*.

The basic idea here is that you want to get either an email, an SMS message, or both if the system goes down.

Limitations of single-host deployment

What could go wrong with deploying a Docker application to a single host? Plenty! While single-host deployment offers operational simplicity, it has some major limitations. Let's look at some of the limitations in the following sections.

No automatic failover

If either the database server container or the web service container fails and cannot be restarted automatically, the site will be down and will require manual intervention. This might be as simple as noticing that your monitoring system says that the site is down, and so you need to SSH in and reboot the server. But sometimes, a single server will be so low on memory that it must be manually rebooted from a higher-level console or even power-cycled manually. This tends to lead to significant periods of time where an application is down and not available to serve requests.

Inability to scale horizontally to accept more load

What happens if the traffic for the system exceeds the current capacity? In single-host deployment, you may be able to switch the host to a larger computer with more memory and processors, which is called *vertical scaling*. That is much easier in a cloud environment than it is in an environment, where you have to deal with physical hardware, such as an on-premises or data center environment. It would be much harder to adapt these simple deployment techniques to a whole fleet of server instances—which is called *horizontal scaling*.

Tracking down unstable behavior based on incorrect host tuning

Depending on your hosting provider, the base operating system you start with, and how the Docker containers are configured, you might experience instability that is hard to track down. Maybe your host gets rebooted frequently due to the provider's network detecting unstable hardware or network conditions. Maybe you have configured your operating system to install automatic updates and applying them causes periods of outages. Maybe the application grows in memory until it triggers a failure of some kind.

For simplicity's sake, the examples in this chapter do not specify memory limits at an application or container level. This means that the Redis container could consume all available memory on the host since it lacks a `max_memory` setting in its application-level main configuration file. It also means that the node container running the Express web application could leak memory until the operating system **Out-Of-Memory (OOM)** killer terminates it or the Docker daemon.

One way of mitigating this problem is by configuring virtual memory on the host using a swap file or swap partition, which makes the system look as if it has more physical memory than it actually does. If you do not configure a swap file on the host, you may find that running the `deploy.sh` script will fail. You might not see any messages in the console when this happens, but if you check `/var/log/messages`, you will find traces of the Linux kernel's OOM killer terminating the `npm` install program or another part of the Docker container build process.

See the Docker documentation for more on the dangers of not configuring the memory for your containers and operating system appropriately:

`https://docs.docker.com/config/containers/resource_constraints/`

Loss of single host could be disastrous – backups are essential

If you have hosted your application on a single physical or virtual server, you should ensure that the system is backed up regularly. Many providers have an image backup service that you can configure to take daily backups and preserve them for some period of time for an extra cost. You could also script backups of the critical volumes using old-school methods, such as using TAR and SSH or using a modern backup system, such as `restic` (see `https://restic.readthedocs.io/en/latest/`), to back up the files and volumes to a cloud storage system.

Case study – migrating from CoreOS and Digital Ocean to CentOS 7 and AWS

One of the authors, Richard Bullington-McGuire, maintained a winter cycling competition website, `https://freezingsaddles.org/`, on a Digital Ocean droplet using CoreOS for more than a year. This system would frequently be knocked offline after a reboot, and it was difficult to track down exactly what the problems were that caused the periodic outages. Lack of console access to the Digital Ocean control panel and a lack of familiarity with CoreOS made troubleshooting the system even more difficult. To ensure that the system was backed up, `restic` was installed and configured to send backups to Amazon S3. After many frustrating system administration experiences, the system was moved over to AWS using Lightsail, running CentOS 7 as a host operating system. To guard against OOM conditions, the new system ran with a swap file equal in size to RAM. After this, the system stopped randomly failing every few days and operations became much more smooth. Additionally, the new system had daily automatic snapshot backups enabled, lessening the need to back up the system with an application-level tool such as `restic`. Even so, if the system reboots, the web server does not always come up smoothly, with manual intervention required to restore the service.

Summary

The simplest way to get your Docker-based application to production is to deploy it onto a single host with Docker Compose. If you have properly prepared the host with the right software, including Docker Compose, you can deploy your application there in a production-ready configuration. This can be completed in a matter of hours and can serve applications with low to moderate performance and availability demands efficiently. If you make the right adjustments to your configuration files, your application will be ready to deploy to production. By using shell scripts that encapsulate long, verbose commands, you can more easily handle regular maintenance and updates for your applications. In the simplest case, you can use external monitoring and alerting for this class of application and handle this concern with low effort.

You can apply what you have learned in this chapter to increase the sophistication of the Dockerfile and the `docker-compose.yml` file that support your application. You can craft simple shell scripts to automate the most common applications. You will have learned that you can rely on external monitoring through services such as `https://uptimerobot.com` to provide simple availability monitoring, and that you can use the built-in Docker logging facilities to provide insights into the operations of your application.

Once you have an application deployed, it would be a good idea to increase the level of automation surrounding it, particularly related to how you can build and deploy the application. In the next chapter, we will see how you can use Jenkins, a common continuous integration system, to automate deployment and testing.

Further reading

- *Docker Cookbook*: `https://www.packtpub.com/free-ebooks/ virtualization-and-cloud/docker-cookbook-second- edition/9781788626866`

- *Use Compose in production*: `https://docs.docker.com/compose/ production/`

- Open source monitoring tools: `https://geekflare.com/best-open- source-monitoring-software/`

- Free monitoring tools: `https://www.dnsstuff.com/free-network- monitoring-software`

- Is `docker-compose` suited for production? `https://vsupalov.com/ docker-compose-production/`

- Docker tip 2: the difference between `COPY` and `ADD` in a Dockerfile: `https://nickjanetakis.com/blog/docker-tip-2-the- difference-between-copy-and-add-in-a-dockerile`

If you are running a real production application on a single host with docker-compose, you should strongly consider securing your site with SSL. You can use Let's Encrypt and a host of Docker sidecar containers to achieve this:

- How to use Let's Encrypt, NGINX, and Docker to secure your site with SSL: `https://github.com/nginx-proxy/docker-letsencrypt- nginxproxy-companion`

- Using `docker-compose.yml` to configure Let's Encrypt with NGINX and Docker: `https://github.com/nginx-proxy/docker- letsencryptnginx-proxy-companion/blob/master/docs/Docker- Compose.md`

7
Continuous Deployment with Jenkins

In order to reliably use Docker containers in production, you need a process that will consistently build, test, and deploy your software. A team building very small applications might be satisfied with running tests and deployment scripts manually. However, discipline often breaks down, and people step on each other's toes. This often results in broken builds and tests that are not run before or after a production deployment. The aftermath is often downtime and unhappy customers. In order to make sure that we can build, test, and deploy software reliably, we can use continuous integration software. This type of software can reliably build, test, and deploy revisions in a disciplined and traceable way. A well-run modern project can even use this software to achieve continuous deployment, where even the smallest changes to the software can be quickly promoted to either a test or production environment.

In this chapter, we show how to configure Jenkins, one of the most popular continuous integration software systems, to facilitate deployment to the minimal environment shown in the previous chapter. We will use Jenkins to manage both the production installation and a new staging environment installation of the application used to test changes before they reach production.

By the end of this chapter, you will know when it might be a good idea to deploy Jenkins for CI and CD with Docker. You will learn how to set up a basic `Jenkinsfile` that can help Jenkins **secure shell** (**SSH**) to production hosts and run `docker-compose` commands to update the application. You will discover how to set up Jenkins parameterized builds that allow both changing and auditing configuration parameters. You will extend the simple production setup by adding an isolated staging environment to allow developers to make changes more confidently. Finally, you will know when this type of solution has exhausted its limits and when it is time to reach for more sophisticated tools.

In this chapter, we're going to cover the following main topics:

- Using Jenkins to facilitate continuous deployment

- The Jenkinsfile and host connectivity

- Driving configuration changes through Jenkins

- Deploying to multiple environments through multiple branches

- Complexity and limits to scaling deployments through Jenkins

Technical requirements

To complete the exercises in this chapter, you'll need Git and Docker on your local workstation, and you will need to have already set up a production application as described in the previous chapter. To complete the exercises about deploying to multiple environments, you will need another host to run a test environment, with similar specifications as the production host.

You will also need a Jenkins server. This chapter will go over some options for the simple setup and maintenance of a Jenkins server if you don't already have one available to you. If your company already runs a Jenkins server, you can use that—ask the system administrators for permission. This server will need to be able to reach your production server via SSH.

You will need to be able to create DNS entries in a zone you control, for both the staging server and the Jenkins server. You can use the same DNS zone as you used in the previous chapter.

The GitHub repository for this chapter is `https://github.com/Packt-Publishing/Docker-for-Developers`—please see the `chapter7` folder inside.

Check out the following video to see the Code in Action:

`https://bit.ly/3kL1EUU`

Example application – ShipIt Clicker v3

The version of *ShipIt Clicker* in this chapter is very similar to the one in the previous chapter. We will use it to test deployment through Jenkins to both a production and a staging environment.

Using Jenkins to facilitate continuous deployment

The world of continuous integration servers has come a long way in the last 20 years. One of the most popular systems is Jenkins (see `https://jenkins.io/`)—because it is free, flexible, and offers a huge variety of integrations and plugins. CloudBees (`https://www.cloudbees.com/`), the company behind it, also offers commercial support via a paid version. Your company might already be running Jenkins, in which case you may not need to do much setup to get your project to build and run.

We are going to use the Jenkins 2.x Pipeline project type, where a `Jenkinsfile` is committed to source control in GitHub and controls the steps Jenkins uses to build and deploy the project.

Avoid these traps

Before we set up Jenkins, we should make sure we avoid certain common traps people fall into when setting it up for the first time.

Avoid running Jenkins in Docker

Although you can use Docker to run a Jenkins server, doing so introduces some complications that are best avoided, especially when just trying to get a continuous integration server running for the first time. You would either need to use a feature called **Docker-in-Docker** (**dind**) or a customized Docker installation of Jenkins that has the correct ports and files mapped from the host in a very specific way. If you don't get it just right, you might run into trouble with not being able to build Docker containers since you can't double-mount a union filesystem, for example.

Setting up Jenkins itself running as a Docker container and working through the quirks would probably consume a ton of effort and time, and is beyond the scope of the advice we can give in this book.

Avoid running Jenkins on the production server

In a previous chapter, we set up a production server in the cloud to host an application. You might be tempted to have that same server you already have running do double-duty by having it run the Jenkins CI server as well. This would be economical, but it is risky as any problem with either the production configuration or the Jenkins server could both bring down production and knock your CI server offline. This would also complicate the network and web hosting virtual host configuration—it would be too easy to have these distinct services conflict, without a more sophisticated orchestration system.

Part of running robust systems is to have adequate isolation between processes and systems that have distinct purposes, so avoid doubling-up Jenkins and your production server; run it on a system separate from your production server.

Avoid running Jenkins on your local workstation

You might also be tempted to just install Jenkins on your local workstation to give it a test drive. However, you will find several major drawbacks to this approach:

- Your workstation probably does not have a stable IP address, necessitating dynamic DNS solutions, and possibly punching holes in firewalls and setting up NAT port redirections.

- You would have to run Jenkins on your system constantly to have it process and build changes to the software as commits get pushed.

- Jenkins can be pretty heavyweight to run alongside a full development environment—and it may slow your workstation down significantly.

If we should not run Jenkins as a Docker container, and we should not run it on our local workstation, where should we run Jenkins? Let's explore the options.

Using an existing Jenkins server

You don't have to set up Jenkins from scratch if you have access to a Jenkins server running a recent version of Jenkins in the 2.x series. Recent versions of Jenkins have excellent support for Docker, assuming that the hosts running the Jenkins builds have Docker running on them.

You will need to make sure that the following Jenkins plugins are present:

- SSH credentials
- Pipeline
- GitHub
- GitHub Organization

Ideally, the Jenkins server would already be set up with the GitHub Organization plugin and it should be configured so that it can automatically manage GitHub webhooks. If this is the case, you can either fork the sample repository or clone it and push it into your GitHub organization as a new repository and start deploying from there.

You will need enough permissions on the Jenkins server to create credentials, which we will use to hold secrets required for building and deploying the software.

Setting up a new Jenkins server

A convenient way to simplify the set of technologies you have to maintain is to use the same base operating system and Docker setup that the production host runs. The instructions and scripts here are tailored to a CentOS 7 installation, but you can follow the same basic steps for other operating system distributions with some modification of the specific commands used to set up and maintain the packages, for example using `apt-get` instead of `yum` to install operating system packages.

Begin by installing Docker and `docker-compose` just as you did in the previous chapter. Once that is done, test that Docker works with the `docker run --rm hello-world` command and then install Jenkins. If you are using CentOS 7, you can use the script at `https://github.com/PacktPublishing/Docker-for-Developers/blob/master/chapter7/bin/provision-jenkins.sh` to install both Docker and Jenkins together (replace `centos@jenkins.example.com` with the user name and IP address or hostname of your new Jenkins server):

```
$ ssh centos@jenkins.example.com < bin/provision-jenkins.sh
$ ssh centos@jenkins.example.com
```

If you are using another operating system, consult the Jenkins documentation online for installation instructions: `https://wiki.jenkins.io/display/JENKINS/Installing+Jenkins`

In order to configure CentOS 7 to allow network traffic to flow to Jenkins, you may have to configure its host firewall to allow inbound traffic.

Also, it is desirable to have Jenkins listen on a standard port such as port `80` or `443`. This can be accomplished in several ways, including having a web server act as a proxy for Jenkins, or using a load balancer to terminate SSL. A shortcut for allowing network traffic to flow to Jenkins on port `80` for CentOS 7 is as follows (if you used the `provision-docker.sh` script to provision Jenkins this is already done):

```
$ sudo firewall-cmd --zone=public --permanent --add-masquerade
$ sudo firewall-cmd --permanent --add-service=http
$ sudo firewall-cmd --permanent --add-forward-port=port=80:proto=tcp:toport=8080
$ sudo firewall-cmd --permanent --direct \
    --add-rule ipv4 nat OUTPUT 0 \
    -p tcp -o lo --dport 80 -j REDIRECT --to-ports 8080
$ sudo firewall-cmd --reload
```

The `firewall-cmd` invocation will allow you to reach Jenkins on port `80` instead of specifying port `8080`.

Once Jenkins is installed, you must retrieve a password from its logs to connect to the server:

```
$ sudo grep -A 3 password /var/log/jenkins/jenkins.log
```

Note the password given in the output of this command. If this does not work immediately, wait a few minutes and try again, as Jenkins may still be starting up.

Then, open a web browser and put in the IP address with the appropriate port, either `8080` or `80` depending on whether you have redirected connections. For example, enter `http://192.2.0.10:8080` and navigate to the site.

You should see a screen that says **Unlock Jenkins**:

Figure 7.1 – Unlock Jenkins

Use the administrator password from the /var/log/jenkins/jenkins.log file to sign in for the first time.

The next screen will prompt you to install plugins. Please install the suggested plugins:

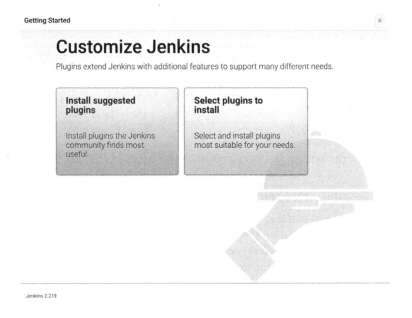

Figure 7.2 – Customize Jenkins

If your system has less than 4 GB of memory, you will want to run with a swap file. Run the `free` command to see if the server has any swap memory available. If not, issue these commands to create a 1 GB swap file and activate it:

```
$ free
                total         used         free      shared  buff/
cache    available
Mem:         1882296        89008      1533220        8676
260068     1612156
Swap:        2097148            0      2097148
$ sudo dd if=/dev/zero of=/swap bs=1M count=1024
1024+0 records in
1024+0 records out
1073741824 bytes (1.1 GB) copied, 2.94343 s, 365 MB/s
[vagrant@localhost ~]$ sudo chmod 0600 /swap
[vagrant@localhost ~]$ sudo mkswap /swap
Setting up swapspace version 1, size = 1048572 KiB
no label, UUID=2bd70cac-3730-45bb-8b77-982425fb7af5
[vagrant@localhost ~]$ echo /swap swap swap defaults 0 0 | sudo
tee -a /etc/fstab
/swap swap swap defaults 0 0
[vagrant@localhost ~]$ sudo mount -a
[vagrant@localhost ~]$ free
                total         used         free      shared  buff/
cache    available
Mem:         1882296        83120       481244        8668
1317932    1604256
Swap:        2097148            0      2097148
```

You should see that the system has non-zero swap memory in the output of `free`.

> **Jenkins security and HTTPS**
>
> For production use, you should configure Jenkins to run behind either an SSL-terminating load balancer or a web server configured with an SSL certificate that will listen on HTTPS. Please consult the Jenkins documentation or the many tutorials available on the internet regarding securing Jenkins with HTTPS on how to accomplish this. You should also consider restricting the set of IP addresses that can directly reach the Jenkins server as these servers are frequent targets for malicious actors. See the *Further reading* section at the end of this chapter for more about securing Jenkins.

In order to use Jenkins with Docker, you will need to install the Docker Pipeline plugin. From the Jenkins main screen, go to the **Manage Jenkins | Manage Plugins** menu, click on the **Available** tab, select the **Docker Pipeline** plugin, and then press the **Download now and install after restart** button. When Jenkins restarts, log in again.

Now that you have a Jenkins server available to you, you can proceed to configure it to talk to the production server.

How Jenkins can support continuous deployment

Jenkins can check out the sources for a project from version control, build the software, run tests, and run deployment scripts. Because it has Docker support, it can build a Docker container, push the container to Docker Hub or another container repository, and then run deployment scripts that connect to a server to tell it to update its running Docker containers. In order to support all these objectives, we must configure Jenkins to integrate with the production server, with a version control repository, and with Docker Hub. First, we will ensure that we can use Jenkins to connect to the production server.

The Jenkinsfile and host connectivity

To ensure repeatable builds, we are going to use Jenkins scripts to run build and deployment automation. Jenkins supports a type of script called a **declarative pipeline** script that allows a concise definition of steps needed to build, test, and deploy software. This script is conventionally known as a `Jenkinsfile`. Because these scripts are written using the Groovy language (see `https://groovy-lang.org/`), you can declare variables, write functions, and use many features of this very powerful language to help you build and deploy your software. Jenkins supports both a free-form scripting style and a more structured declarative style of script that uses a special Groovy DSL to provide more scaffolding for concise scripts.

See here for more information on how to write a `Jenkinsfile`: `https://www.jenkins.io/doc/book/pipeline/jenkinsfile/`

You can either directly enter these scripts into a Jenkins job definition or store them in version control. If you put a file called `Jenkinsfile` in the root of a version control repository, Jenkins can discover those files if it gets configured to talk to a version control system such as GitHub.

Testing Jenkins and Docker with a pipeline script

To test that Jenkins and Docker are working together, we will first enter a script through the console. At the top-level Jenkins screen, click on the **New Item** menu and then create a new job of type **Pipeline**. Call it Hello Docker:

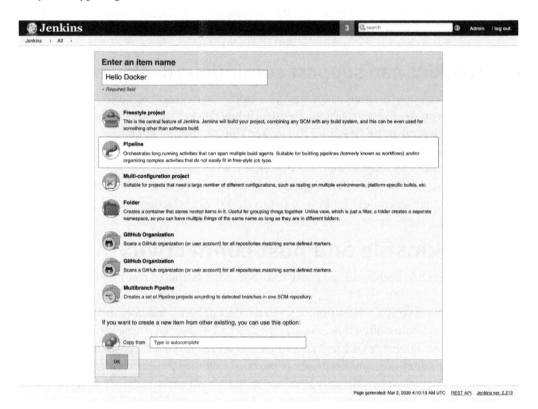

Figure 7.3 – New Item – Hello Docker pipeline

Then, in the **Pipeline** section, enter this script (see chapter7/Jenkinsfile-hello-world in the companion GitHub project):

```
pipeline {
    agent { docker { image 'alpine:20191114' } }
    stages {
        stage('build') {
            steps {
                sh 'echo "Hello, World (Docker for Developers
Chapter 7)"'
            }
```

```
            }
        }
    }
```

Save the job and click on the **Build Now** link, and Jenkins will create build **#1**. Follow the link for **#1** that appears on the left and then click on the **Console Output** button. You should see something like this:

Figure 7.4 – New Item – Hello Docker Console Output

You should see `Hello, World (Docker for Developers Chapter 7)` in the **Console Output** on the Jenkins web page. If you see out of memory errors here, ensure that you have a swap file on your Jenkins server. If you see an error about Docker not being a known agent type, go to the **Manage Jenkins | Manage Plugins** menu, and install the **Docker Pipeline** plugin.

Connecting to the production server via SSH

Next, we will configure Jenkins to connect to the production server via SSH. We need to do this in order to control the Docker subsystem on the remote server. We will generate an SSH key for Jenkins to use and add it to the production server's list of authorized keys.

Generating an SSH key and adding it to Jenkins credentials

On your local workstation, issue the following command to generate a 2,048-bit RSA SSH key pair and view it:

```
ssh-keygen -t rsa -b 2048 -f jenkins.shipit
cat jenkins.shipit
```

Copy the contents of the `jenkins.shipit` file to your clipboard, then go to your Jenkins home page, and in the left-hand menu, navigate to the **Manage Jenkins** link, then to the **Manage Credentials** link, then navigate to **System | Global credentials (unrestricted)** of the kind **SSH Username with private key**. Give it the ID of `jenkins.shipit` and enter the username of the non-root user from the production server (typically, `centos` for CentOS 7 cloud servers). Click on **Enter directly** and add the key and click on the **OK** button to save the credentials:

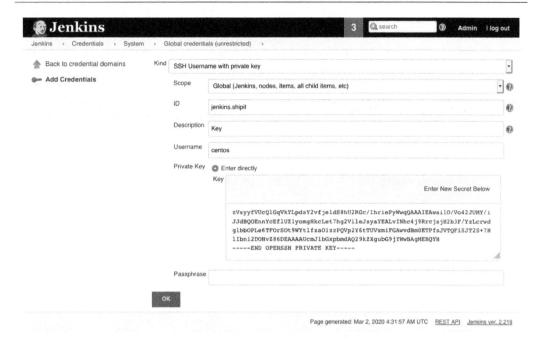

Figure 7.5 – Add Credentials – SSH key

Copy the SSH public key, `jenkins.shipit.pub`, from your local system to the production server and append it to the `~/.ssh/authorized_keys` file. By entering the following commands on your local workstation, replace `centos@192.2.0.10` with the username and IP address of your production server:

```
prod=centos@192.2.0.10
ssh $prod mkdir -p .ssh
ssh $prod tee -a .ssh/authorized_keys < jenkins.shipit.pub
ssh $prod chmod 700 .ssh
ssh $prod chmod 600 .ssh/authorized_keys
```

Test that the SSH key authentication is working by using the key to log in from your local workstation:

```
$ ssh -i jenkins.shipit $prod
Last login: Mon Mar  2 04:57:35 2020 from gateway.example.net
[centos@ip-172-26-13-202 ~]$
```

Once you have done this, you can create a test job that uses these credentials to SSH to the server.

Use a Jenkins Pipeline job to SSH to the production server

In the Jenkins web console, create a new Jenkins job with the **New Item** menu, give it the item name SSH to Production, and pick the **Pipeline** job type:

Figure 7.6 – Create Item – SSH to Production

In the job definition form, in the **Pipeline** section, for the **Definition** field, choose
Pipeline script and enter the following pipeline script into the **Script** field, but change
`centos@192.2.0.10` to the user and host for your production server, and save the job
script (see `chapter7/Jenkinsfile-ssh-proof-of-concept`) in the companion
GitHub project):

```
pipeline {
    agent any
    stages {
        stage('SSH') {
            steps {
                withCredentials([sshUserPrivateKey(
                    credentialsId: 'jenkins.shipit',
                    keyFileVariable: 'keyfile')]) {
                        sh '''
prod=centos@192.2.0.10
cmd="docker ps"
ssh -i "$keyfile" -o StrictHostKeyChecking=no $prod $cmd
                        '''
                }
            }
        }
    }
}
```

When you run this by clicking on the **Build Now** link, and view the console output, you
should see output similar to the following:

```
...
+ ssh -i **** -o StrictHostKeyChecking=no centos@34.238.248.192
docker ps
CONTAINER ID        IMAGE                               COMMAND
CREATED             STATUS                PORTS
NAMES
6c9ef1ca65f6        chapter6_shipit-clicker-web-v2      "npm
start"              6 weeks ago           Up 6 weeks
0.0.0.0:80->3000/tcp    chapter6_shipit-clicker-web-v2_1
...
3f91820e097b        redis:5-alpine3.10                  "docker-
```

```
entrypoint.s..."    7 weeks ago          Up 7 weeks           6379/
tcp                 chapter6_redis_1
```

If you do not see the output of `docker ps`, double-check the username, IP address, and SSH key. Check for any error messages that Jenkins emits about the `Jenkinsfile` or related to the `ssh` shell command to troubleshoot. You will need to get this to work in order to get the next stage to work reliably.

You can use Jenkins to connect to other hosts to run scripts that use `docker` and `docker-compose`. But you can also run `docker` and `docker-compose` directly on the Jenkins server if you need to. We will explore that later in the chapter.

Now that we can use Jenkins to connect to the production server via SSH, using a pipeline script, we can use that connection to make changes to the production server, including deploying new changes to the server.

Driving configuration changes through Jenkins

Next, we will learn how to make changes to the production system by running scripts from the Git repository hosted in Jenkins. We can use Jenkins both to build the Docker containers for the application and to deploy those containers on the production server. That way, any changes to either the program or to its `Dockerfile` or the `docker-compose.yml` file can be propagated through automation to the production system.

Here are some tips for integrating Jenkins with other systems, including GitHub, that can make your life easier. The first tip relates to the best way to configure Jenkins with a `Jenkinsfile`—by storing it in a version control system.

Using Git and GitHub to store your Jenkinsfile

In the previous section, we used `Jenkinsfile` entered directly into a Jenkins job to do some quick testing. That works well for doing exploratory work, but to build and manage a more complex set of scripts, you should use Git version control to store the `Jenkinsfile` and use GitHub to store and share the Git repository, since GitHub integrates nicely with Jenkins. This will let you make changes not only to your program but also to the deployment scripts in a controlled fashion.

For more information about why you should use the Git version control system in conjunction with GitHub, see this introductory guide: `https://guides.github.com/introduction/git-handbook/`.

We can combine the power of a script stored in GitHub with the Jenkins **Environment variables** feature, which lets you centrally store values that will be substituted in the same `Jenkinsfile` as the one in the repository for this book to deploy the demonstration project. This support for environment variable substitution will allow you to use the `Jenkinsfile` unchanged, even though your production server may be set up with a distinct user and host, while also using your SSH, Docker Hub, and GitHub credentials, which are similarly distinct.

In order to make further progress, you must make sure that Jenkins has a GitHub username and security token as a credential so that you can use Jenkins to check out GitHub repositories.

Ensuring Jenkins has a GitHub username and security token credential

In order to use Jenkins with GitHub, you will need to save a Jenkins credential that has a GitHub personal access token. In a web browser, sign in to GitHub, and go to `https://github.com/settings/tokens` and generate a token that has both the `repo` and `admin:repo_hook` scopes. Copy the generated token to the clipboard. Then, in another browser window, go to your Jenkins server and navigate through credentials to the Jenkins global credentials and create a **Global credentials (unrestricted)** credential of the type **Username with password** and put in your GitHub username, paste the security token from the clipboard, and give it an ID of `github.repo.username` and a description of **GitHub repo credentials (username)**, but replace `username` with your actual GitHub username. Press the **OK** button to save the credential.

Option 1 – Configuring Jenkins with a GitHub organization item

Jenkins has support for defining *items* that might be individual Jenkins jobs or collections of related jobs. Several of the types of items allow you to connect a version control system to Jenkins so that it will automatically define multiple Jenkins jobs. One of the most powerful of these is a `GitHub Organization` item. Using a `GitHub Organization` item will allow Jenkins to scan GitHub for every project that has a `Jenkinsfile`, and Jenkins will automatically set up a forest of child items for all the repositories in the GitHub organization where it finds a `Jenkinsfile`.

This is the easiest way to have Jenkins manage a set of related projects If you are using a new Jenkins server to explore Docker development, in a GitHub organization you control, try setting this up. If you are using a corporate Jenkins server, this may already be set up.

From your Jenkins installation's home page, click the **New Item** link and create an item with a name that matches your GitHub organization of type `GitHub Organization`. Use the credentials labeled as **GitHub repo credentials (username)** and make sure the name in the organization field matches your GitHub organization name.

You can set up a filter so that this scans only the projects you want for a `Jenkinsfile`. This might be a good idea if you have a huge number of repositories and branches in your organization, or if you only want your installation of Jenkins to build specific repositories—the repositories that might work with Jenkins—or there is some other Jenkins server that also builds a subset of the projects in your GitHub organization. If you want to do this, add a `Behavior` of type `Filter by name (with regular expression)` and construct a regular expression to match the names of only the repositories you want to include.

Using GitHub, fork the Docker-for-Developers repository (`https://github.com/PacktPublishing/Docker-for-Developers/`) to your organization. Alternatively, if you don't want to fork the repository, create an empty repository in your organization. Then, push your local copy of the repository to the freshly created repository, go into the GitHub organization item you created, and you should see a **Docker-for-Developers** item show up.

If you are using an individual GitHub account, and lack access to a GitHub organization, this may not be a good option, however. You could instead configure Jenkins with a multibranch pipeline item that retrieves the `Jenkinsfile` from a single GitHub repository.

Option 2 – Configuring Jenkins with a multibranch pipeline item

Using a multibranch pipeline item will allow Jenkins to scan GitHub for a single repository for every project that has a `Jenkinsfile`, and Jenkins will automatically set up a forest of child items for branches and pull requests for a single configured GitHub repository, for branches where it finds a `Jenkinsfile`.

Fork the Docker-for-Developers repository to your organization or create an empty repository in your account and push your local copy of the repository to GitHub. You need to do this before configuring the multibranch pipeline.

From your Jenkins installation's home page, click the **New Item** link and create an item with a name that matches your GitHub repository name of type `Multibranch Pipeline`. In **Branch Sources**, choose **GitHub**, and then fill out the GitHub form with the credentials labeled as **GitHub repo credentials (username)**, and put the URL of your GitHub repository in the **Repository HTTPS URL** field. Then, save the item. It will scan the repository and set up the individual Jenkins jobs for each Git branch.

At this point, whether you have used the multibranch pipeline or the GitHub organization item type, you should have a set of branches in your Jenkins.

Changing the origin of all checked out repositories

At this point, you should also change the URL for your Git repositories, both on your local workstation, and on the production server you set up in the previous chapter, to the new repository URL. Replace `example` with the name of your GitHub organization or user where you forked the repository:

```
git remote set-url origin https://github.com/example/Docker-
for-Developers.git
```

Checking that your GitHub repository is talking to Jenkins via a webhook

GitHub can communicate with other systems via webhooks, which are HTTP requests that the system triggers, targeting another system, when people do certain actions.

See here for more information about GitHub's support for webhooks and system integration: `https://developer.github.com/webhooks/`

When we set up the `GitHub Organization` item or the `MultiBranch Pipeline` item, Jenkins should have set up one of these webhooks in GitHub so that it can talk to Jenkins. If it did not, you can go to the **Settings** tab on GitHub for your GitHub repository, go to **Webhooks**, and add a webhook of the form `https://jenkins.example.com/github-webhook/` (replacing `jenkins.example.com` with your Jenkins server).

Now that we have configured Jenkins to be able to communicate with GitHub, we want to make sure that pushing a branch to GitHub triggers builds in Jenkins. Depending on your account's GitHub permissions and the Jenkins configuration, it might not have created the webhook automatically.

In a web browser, navigate to your GitHub repository and go to **Settings**, then to **Webhooks**, and verify that there is a webhook with your Jenkins server URL there.

What to expect now that Jenkins is connected to GitHub

Now that we have configured Jenkins to be able to check for the presence of a `Jenkinsfile` in the repository we are using, we can proceed. Jenkins will try to build the project you have just defined. The build will fail unless you provide Jenkins with additional variables and credentials, however.

In order to tie the specific configurations for the build to your environment, we will need to use Jenkins to set up some environment variables to store the less sensitive items, in addition to storing cryptographic keys and passwords using the **Credentials** feature.

Creating Jenkins environment variables for production support

Jenkins has support for setting environment variables that items (build and deployment jobs, for example) can reference. For secret variables, such as SSH private keys, or Docker Hub API credentials, you can use the **Credentials** system that we used in the previous section to store these securely. For values that are less sensitive, we can use the **Environment variables** settings available on the Jenkins **configuration** screen:

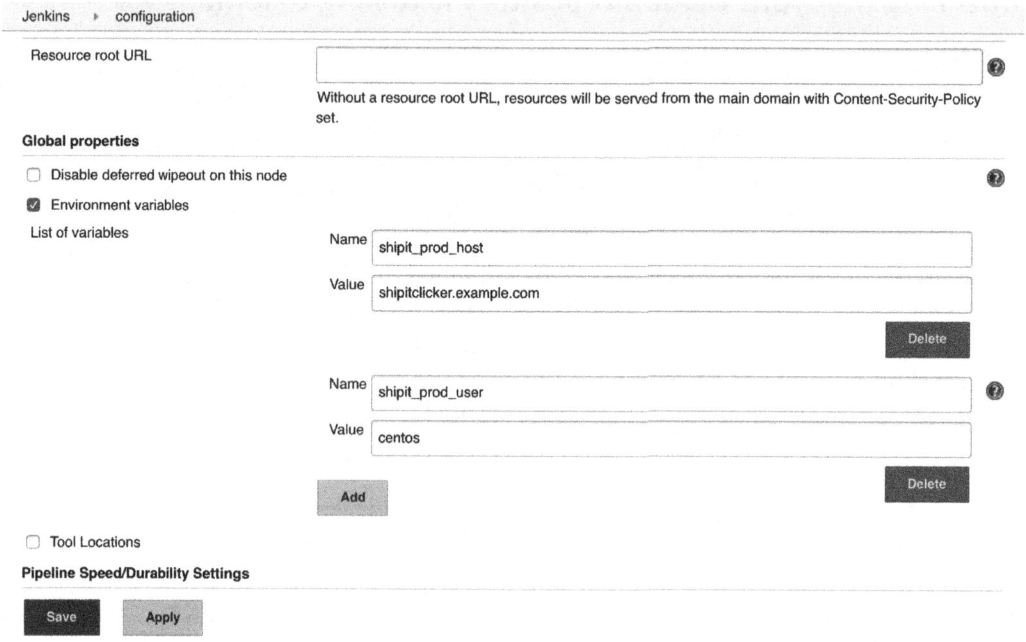

Figure 7.7 – Jenkins configuration – Environment variables for production host

In order to proceed, please double-check with the DNS provider that you use that your production host has a DNS name associated with its IP address. In *Chapter 6, Deploying Applications with Docker Compose*, we set up DNS names for the production server. Having a DNS name will make the configurations more readable and will make it easier for people to reach the server in a web browser. Set up variables for these keys and values:

- `shipit_prod_host`: Production server DNS domain name, for example, `shipitclicker.example.com`)

- `shipit_prod_user`: Production server username, for example, `centos`

Once you have set up these variables, hit the **Save** button. We will use these variables when we run the Jenkins job that updates the running containers. Before we do that though, we need a place to put the containers. In a previous chapter, you learned how to push a container image to Docker Hub. Next, we will automate that process.

Building Docker containers and pushing them to Docker Hub

In order to avoid building the containers on the production server, we will need to build them on Jenkins and then push the containers into a Docker container registry, such as Docker Hub. This allows a clean separation of building the Docker containers from deploying them. If you try to both build and deploy the container on a single small server, it is highly likely that at some point you will run into out of memory issues or other system stability problems. And on a production server, you want to maximize the stability of that environment.

While you could push the container to Docker Hub from your local workstation, part of the benefit of using Jenkins is that you can use it to automatically build and push containers to a central repository. To do that, you will need to give Jenkins credentials to Docker Hub.

Adding Docker Hub credentials to Jenkins credential manager

Log in to `https://hub.docker.com/` with your Docker account and create an API token for Jenkins to use from the `https://hub.docker.com/settings/security` security settings page. Copy that API token to the clipboard and in another web browser tab, visit the Jenkins credential manager and create another global unrestricted credential of type `Username with Password`. Give it an ID called `shipit.dockerhub.id` and put your Docker account username in the `username` field, and the access token in the `password` field and save it.

This will allow you to use your Docker Hub credentials to push a build to Docker Hub, and since we already have SSH credentials set up in Jenkins, we can use those to push a Docker image to Docker Hub after we build it, and then to connect to the production server in order to deploy the new software.

Ensuring the previous production environment is stopped

If the production environment from the previous chapter is running, you will need to stop it in order to deploy the new environment. This will ensure that the new production environment can bind to the correct TCP ports.

> **Note**
>
> In a situation where you have a real production application with valuable customer data, you would want to back up and restore any databases and other persistent storage to the new environment. The ShipIt Clicker application only uses Redis in order to save details about the production environment. For Redis, this can be done via the CLI using the SAVE command. You can then copy the resulting dump.rdb file into the Docker volume that this chapter's Redis container uses.

From your local workstation, SSH to the server and stop it (replace 192.0.2.10 with the IP address of your server):

```
cmd='cd Docker-for-Developers/chapter6; docker-compose stop'
ssh centos@192.2.0.10 "$cmd"
```

Now that the previous Docker containers are stopped, you may proceed with using Jenkins to build the software, push to Docker Hub, and deploy the containers on the production server. You only have to do this once, when you are first transitioning from the setup from the previous chapter to the environment managed by Jenkins in this chapter.

Next, let's trigger a production environment deployment through Jenkins.

Pushing to Docker Hub and triggering a production deployment

Now that we have all the environment variables and credentials in place, we can trigger a Jenkins build. Jenkins normally triggers a build when it detects a commit, but we can also force Jenkins to start a build. Go to the Jenkins job that is hooked up to the GitHub repository where the application code resides for the master branch and click on **Build Now**. Jenkins will start building the job and show the build number in the user interface:

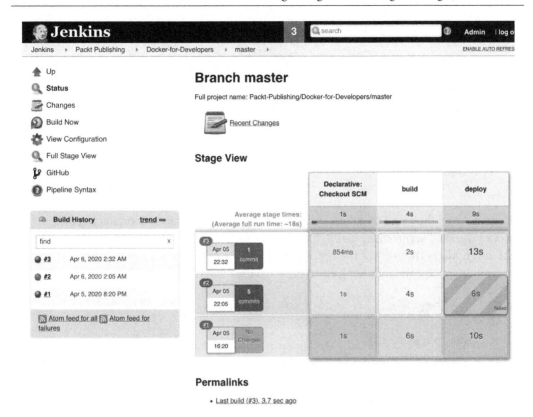

Figure 7.8 – Jenkins jobs in GitHub Organization – master branch

Before we check on the progress of the job, let's examine how it works.

Jenkins runs a combination of the `Jenkinsfile` and the script `chapter7/bin/dep-ssh.sh` in order to build and deploy the software. The `Jenkinsfile` checks out the repository, builds the Docker container, and pushes it to Docker Hub. The following excerpt from the `Jenkinsfile` shows the code that manages the checkout, build, and push process:

```
pipeline {
  agent any
  stages {
    stage('build') {
      steps {
        checkout scm
        script {
          docker.withRegistry(registry, 'shipit.dockerhub.id')
{
```

```
        def image = docker.build(
            getImageName(appName),
            "-f ${dockerfile} --network host ./chapter7"
        )
        image.push()
      }
    }
  }
}
```

The next stage, the `deploy` stage, runs when the branch is `master` or staging and invokes the shell script `chapter7/bin/dep-ssh.sh`, which connects to the server via SSH and updates the copy of the repository, pulls the built Docker containers, and restarts the containers. See the following excerpt from `dep-ssh.sh` for the most important part:

```
ssh -i "$keyfile" -o StrictHostKeyChecking=no "$targetEnv"
<<EOF
set -euo pipefail
cd Docker-for-Developers/chapter7
git fetch
git reset --hard HEAD
git checkout -f origin/"$GIT_BRANCH"
docker pull "$image"
set -a
DOCKER_IMAGE="$image"
PORT="$port"
bin/restart.sh
EOF
```

Now that you understand how the build and deploys are chained together, you should see whether the deployment to the production environment worked.

Verifying that the deployment worked

Click on the most recent build and then click on **Console Output** to follow the progress of the job. A successful run will show `Finished: Success` at the end of the console output.

The console output will show these basic steps:

1. The Git repository being cloned from GitHub.

2. The Docker container being built.

3. The Docker container being pushed to Docker Hub.

4. Jenkins connecting to the production server via SSH.

5. The script `chapter7/bin/ssh-dep.sh` runs on the production server, which then pulls the image from Docker Hub and restarts the Docker services.

If any of the preceding steps fail, the Jenkins job will fail. If that happens, double-check that the credentials and environment variables are correct. You can compare the output of your test run to the sample output, `chapter7/consoleOutput.txt`, in the companion GitHub repository to see whether your Jenkins run worked as expected.

If this has built successfully, you should be able to go to the same URL you used in the previous chapter (for example, `http://shipitclicker.example.com/` or `http://192.2.0.10/`) in order to see the application. Congratulations! Now every push to the master branch, including when pull requests get merged to the master branch, will deploy the production environment. This is one of the simplest ways to achieve continuous deployment.

You might want to be able to see your changes in a separate environment that is stable and always available so that if you make changes that might break the production environment, you can test them out in isolation. In the next section, we will learn how to set up a staging environment similar to the production environment and orchestrate deployments to it using Jenkins.

Deploying to multiple environments through multiple branches

Being able to deploy to a single production environment is valuable, but in order to support development and testing, it is useful to have at least one other environment other than the production environment to test with. That way, people testing the software who do not have a development environment can see the effect of changes you make, without you having to deploy them to the production environment.

In the next part of the chapter, we are going to create a second environment, a staging environment, to allow us to test changes before they are in production.

Creating a staging environment

You will need another host, similar in specifications to the one running the production environment, for the staging environment. Once you can SSH to that host, you could follow the instructions in the previous chapter about installing Docker and Git. Assuming you are running on CentOS 7, you can use the following script snippet to quickly provision Docker on that system and test that it is working (replace `centos@192.2.0.11` with the user and host you are using for your staging environment, and the GitHub URL with the URL of your organization's fork of the project repository):

```
$ staging=centos@192.2.0.11
$ ssh $staging < bin/provision-docker.sh
$ ssh $staging git clone https://github.com/PacktPublishing/
Docker-for-Developers.git
$ ssh $staging docker run --rm hello-world
```

Once you have Docker working on the staging system, you can enter the `exit` command to go back to your local workstation. Then, make sure that the staging system has the same SSH public key that the production system has. Do this from the directory that contains the `jenkins.shipit.pub` key file:

```
$ ssh $staging mkdir -p .ssh
$ ssh $staging tee -a .ssh/authorized_keys < jenkins.shipit.pub
$ ssh $staging chmod 700 .ssh
$ ssh $staging chmod 600 .ssh/authorized_keys
```

Now that the staging server has been prepared with the right SSH credentials and the essential software needed to run Docker applications, we will configure Jenkins to support this staging environment.

Creating Jenkins environment variables for staging support

In order to prepare Jenkins for deployments to the staging server, we will return to the **Environment variables** settings available on the Jenkins **configuration** screen. In order to proceed, please make sure that your staging host has a DNS name associated with it. Set up variables for these keys and values:

- `shipit_staging_host`: Staging server DNS domain name, for example, `shipit-staging.example.com`)
- `shipit_staging_user`: Staging server username, for example, `centos`

Deploying by force-pushing to the staging branch

The deployment scripts detect what branch is being processed and deploy to the right environment. This is done with a combination of directives in the `Jenkinsfile` and having the deploy script use environment variables set up through the `Jenkinsfile` and the Jenkins global configuration. Before we get to the example that shows how to use Git to force-push, we need to examine the `Jenkinsfile` and support scripts to see how they handle branch names.

How do the scripts know what server to use?

The `Jenkinsfile` will only run the deploy stage if the branch name is either `master` or `staging`:

```
stage('deploy') {
    when {
        anyOf {
            branch 'master'
            branch 'staging'
        }
    }
```

Next up, we are going to see some of the power of using a `Jenkinsfile`, showing off some of the Groovy language features such as variable interpolation and calling functions. The steps that follow in the `Jenkinsfile` define environment variables that the `chapter7/bin/ssh-dep.sh` script uses to help pick the right environment:

```
steps {
    echo "BRANCH_NAME is ${env.BRANCH_NAME}"
    echo "Deploying to ${getTarget()}"
    withCredentials([sshUserPrivateKey(
      credentialsId: 'jenkins.shipit',
      keyFileVariable: 'keyfile')]) {
        sh """
            set -a
            target=${getTarget()}
            image=${getImageName(appName)}
            keyfile=${keyfile}
            ./chapter7/bin/ssh-dep.sh
        """
```

These use Jenkins variable interpolation expressions to call Jenkins functions written in Groovy (`getTarget()` and `getImageName(appName)`) that set some of the environment variables that the `chapter7/bin/ssh-dep.sh` script uses.

The `getTarget()` function uses this ternary expression to pick whether to target the `prod` or `staging` environment:

```
def getTarget() {
   env.BRANCH_NAME == 'staging' ? 'staging' : 'prod'
}
```

Once the flow of control has passed to the `chapter7/bin/ssh-dep.sh` script, it uses the target environment variables to pick what environment to target and sets variables up so that the SSH command will pick the correct server:

```
port=${port:-80}
prod="${shipit_prod_user}@${shipit_prod_host}"
staging="${shipit_staging_user}@${shipit_staging_host}"
image=${image:-dockerfordevelopers/shipitclicker:latest}
if [[ "$target" = "staging" ]]; then
    targetEnv="$staging"
    targetHost="$shipit_staging_host"
else
    targetEnv="$prod"
    targetHost="$shipit_prod_host"
fi
```

In this way, the shell script sets up `targetEnv` so that the following SSH command can reach the correct server:

```
ssh -i "$keyfile" -o StrictHostKeyChecking=no "$targetEnv"
<<EOF
```

Now that you see how the variables in the `Jenkinsfile` and `chapter7/bin/ssh-dep.sh` interact, you are ready to use Git to initiate a deployment to staging.

Preparing to use Git to force-push a branch to staging

Although force-pushing branches in Git can be problematic, this is one of the times when it makes sense. If you consider the `staging` branch to be special, not something that you would ordinarily merge into the master, you can then repeatedly force-push work in progress from any branch to it.

On your local workstation, create a new branch in the Git repository called `experiment` by issuing the command `git checkout -b experiment`. Edit the `chapter7/src/public/index.html` file and change the text enclosed in the `<h1>` tags to `ShipIt Clicker Experiment`. Save the file and do a `git commit` command. Then, force-push the `HEAD` of your branch to GitHub as follows:

```
$ git push origin HEAD:staging --force
```

This will push the code you just committed to GitHub. Then, open a web browser to your Jenkins server and examine the item for your repository. You should shortly see that Jenkins has created a `staging` branch job and will build the software and push it to Docker Hub, and deploy it to the staging environment. Observe the Jenkins console log for the job for the `staging` branch and make sure that it is similar to the one for the production deployments from the `master` branch.

If your deployment worked, check with a web browser to see that the title of the application on the staging server is `ShipIt Clicker Experiment`—the text you changed.

At this point, we have used Jenkins to deploy a Docker application to both a production and a staging server. You might wonder what it would take to add a third or fourth environment, or what the drawbacks of this approach might be. Very complex scripts and environments might make it harder to deploy with Jenkins—let's examine that more closely.

Complexity and limits to scaling deployments through Jenkins

Since Jenkins is a general-purpose tool for building and scripting processes related to software development, it offers immense flexibility, but at the cost of complexity. While it can do almost any function related to continuous integration and deployment, it may take more scripting and setup than other systems, such as Spinnaker, CodeFresh, or WeaveWorks, that are more purpose-built. Some other continuous integration and deployment systems deal exclusively with Docker-focused workflows.

Using Jenkins to manage builds, tests, and deployments to one or two hosts is quite manageable. But when you start to scale out, it may become more complex and difficult to continue to use Jenkins to handle builds and deployments. The build and deployment scripts may also become too complex to manage due to the many different programming languages and approaches required. Let's examine these limits, starting with limits about managing multiple hosts.

Managing multiple hosts

The scripts shown in this chapter handled deployments to two environments: a production environment and a staging environment. However, if we wanted to have four more similar environments, say, development, QA, demo, and beta, we might have to spin up four additional hosts and extend our scripts accordingly. It could get to be a big, expensive mess pretty fast. Also consider what would happen if one host became too small to run the production site. You might need to run a fleet of instances and make sure that they all use the same database. Then, you would get into issues about how you might update and deploy that fleet of instances without downtime. The questions and problems start to get bigger if you use a brute-force scripting approach.

If you were going to use Jenkins to manage multiple hosts at scale, you would want to look into integrating it with services that offer additional abstractions to handle scaling and deployment, such as AWS EC2 Auto Scaling Groups, and AWS CodeDeploy. However, neither of those are focused on Docker-specific functionality. You could also use Jenkins to run scripts that used Kubernetes tools, such as kubectl or helm, in order to deploy the software to a Kubernetes cluster, if you have an organizational commitment to using Jenkins as your continuous integration environment.

The complexity of build scripts

One of the best things about Jenkins is that it allows you to script builds using the Groovy domain-specific language; however, this can be one of the worst things simultaneously. Groovy is a powerful and concise Java virtual machine-based language, but it is much less well known than many other scripting languages, such as Python, Ruby, and Bash. Furthermore, Jenkins uses a sandbox model to limit what type of Groovy statements are allowed.

This often means that implementers must split their build scripts between a high-level orchestration layer written in the Jenkins pipeline DSL dialect of Groovy and some other language. This project uses a combination of Groovy Jenkinsfile and Bash shell scripts to do this, which drive the Docker builds and deploys.

How do you know when you have hit the limit?

People who have had many years of experience using Jenkins and hand-rolled scripts to build and deploy software have learned to recognize a few signs that using Jenkins for your purposes has hit its limits:

- The installation of Jenkins itself becomes fragile and too complex for new people on the project to learn quickly.

- It becomes difficult to upgrade Jenkins because of plugin incompatibilities.

- The build scripts fail routinely, and people ignore the failures.

- It starts taking too long to build and deploy the software to meet the business needs.

- If you maintain many applications, the scripts used to build and maintain them become a maze of cut and paste spaghetti code.

If you see these signs, it might be time to consider using a more purpose-built approach, such as Spinnaker, GitLab CI, or CodeFresh as your CI and container pipeline management tool.

Summary

In this chapter, you have learned how to construct a continuous deployment pipeline using Docker, Jenkins, and GitHub. You learned how to establish connectivity between a Jenkins server and multiple host servers through SSH, scripted using a `Jenkinsfile`. You learned how to combine those techniques to drive configuration changes and Docker deployments to the production host using Jenkins. You also learned how to set up a second staging environment and use the Jenkins environment variables and credentials support in order to make a single set of scripts deploy to multiple environments. Finally, you learned about the limitations of using Jenkins to manage larger-scale deployments, and when it might be time to reach for other tools to manage continuous deployment.

Now that you have mastered the basics of using Jenkins to build and deploy software to both a production and a staging environment, you can apply this to your own projects. This will help you build and deploy your software more reliably.

In the next chapter, we will see how we can use Kubernetes and the **Amazon Web Services Elastic Kubernetes Service** (**AWS EKS**) to manage larger-scale, more robust clusters of servers that can host applications running in Docker.

Further reading

If you choose to use Jenkins to manage your Docker-based environments, you should look at these resources more closely:

- Using a `Jenkinsfile`: `https://jenkins.io/doc/book/pipeline/jenkinsfile/`

- Jenkins Docker integration docs: `https://jenkins.io/doc/book/pipeline/docker/`

- Securing Jenkins: `https://jenkins.io/doc/book/system-administration/security/`

- Using Let's Encrypt and Apache to secure Jenkins with SSL: `https://www.agileana.com/blog/serve-jenkins-over-https-with-apache-as-proxy-and-certbot-letsencrypt-ssl/`

- Using an NGINX reverse proxy or AWS ELB to secure Jenkins with SSL: `https://wiki.jenkins.io/display/JENKINS/Jenkins+behind+an+NGinX+reverse+proxy`

If you are running a real production application on a single host with `docker-compose`, you should strongly consider securing your site with SSL. You can use Let's Encrypt and a host of Docker sidecar containers to achieve this:

- How to use Let's Encrypt, NGINX, and Docker to secure your site with SSL: `https://github.com/nginx-proxy/docker-letsencrypt-nginx-proxy-companion`

- Using `docker-compose.yml` to configure Let's Encrypt with NGINX and Docker: `https://github.com/nginx-proxy/docker-letsencrypt-nginx-proxy-companion/blob/master/docs/Docker-Compose.md`

8
Deploying Docker Apps to Kubernetes

Recently, lots of container orchestrators have sprung up like mushrooms after a rainstorm, but one orchestrator is poised to dominate the market: Kubernetes, from the Cloud Native Computing Foundation. Google originally released Kubernetes with the intention of bringing the same level of sophistication to the world of open source container runtimes as it has been doing for years internally with the Borg clustering system.

We will begin by learning more about different Kubernetes distributions and why you might want to use each one. We will start with using Kubernetes on a local development workstation, and then install a sample application locally.

As we progress through the chapter, you will learn how to create a Kubernetes cluster on **Amazon Web Services (AWS)** through **Elastic Kubernetes Service (EKS)**, and deploy your application to a cluster running on multiple **Elastic Compute Cloud (EC2)** nodes. We will use AWS CloudFormation, an infrastructure-as-code system, to deploy the EKS cluster. Once we have deployed the cluster to AWS, we will learn about using labels and namespaces to organize our applications.

Running a Kubernetes cluster is more complex than the alternatives presented so far, but it opens up a huge universe of tools and techniques for running clustered applications with a vendor-neutral, cloud-native approach. Kubernetes is useful not only for cloud deployments, but also for on-premises deployments and local development.

In this chapter, we're going to cover the following main topics:

- Options for Kubernetes local installation
- Deploying a sample application – ShipIt Clicker v4
- Choosing a Kubernetes distribution
- Getting familiar with Kubernetes concepts
- Spinning up AWS EKS with CloudFormation
- Deploying an application with resource limits to Kubernetes on AWS EKS
- Using AWS Elastic Container Registry with AWS EKS
- Using labels and namespaces to segregate environments

Let's get started by getting Kubernetes running on our local workstation. Then, we will look at the various Kubernetes distributions available.

Technical requirements

For this chapter, you will need to set up Kubernetes on your local workstation, either through Docker Desktop or by installing a Kubernetes distribution, such as Minikube. In addition, to deploy your containers to AWS, you will need an account set up in advance.

You can sign up for an AWS account at the following URL if you haven't already done so:

`https://aws.amazon.com/`

The code files for this chapter can be downloaded from the `chapter8` directory at `https://github.com/PacktPublishing/Docker-for-Developers/`.

Check out the following video to see the Code in Action:

`https://bit.ly/3fXO5xy`

Options for Kubernetes local installation

You need to set up a local Kubernetes installation in order to build, package, and test your Docker application in preparation for deploying it to a production installation in the cloud. Please review the Kubernetes *Getting Started* documentation (`https://kubernetes.io/docs/setup/`). This documentation calls this local environment a **learning environment**. Think of the local environment as a way to learn about and test your application before you take the application to production with Kubernetes in the cloud. Let's continue by weighing up the options, starting with Docker Desktop's Kubernetes support.

Docker Desktop with Kubernetes

For most people, this is the easiest way to start experimenting with Kubernetes. You don't have to set up cloud accounts or do a complicated installation to get started if you choose to do this. To install Docker Desktop, follow the download links at `https://www.docker.com/products/docker-desktop`.

With recent versions of Docker Desktop, you can enable Kubernetes support and run and develop Kubernetes applications on your workstation. Open the Docker Desktop application on your workstation and go to the **Preferences** menu to open the **Settings** dialog. Tick the **Enable Kubernetes** box and hit the **Apply & Restart** button:

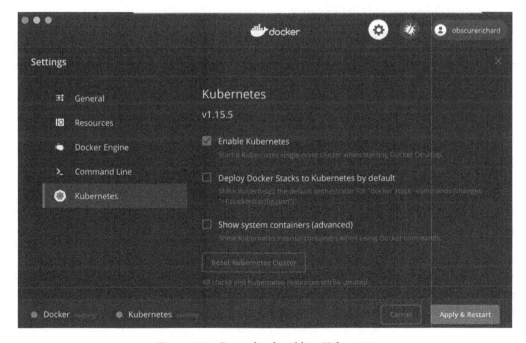

Figure 8.1 – Example of enabling Kubernete

This will activate a single-node Kubernetes cluster on your local workstation. Once you have enabled Kubernetes, you are ready to verify that your local installation works. See the following section to find out how to do this.

Minikube

If you don't want to run Kubernetes through Docker Desktop, you should probably use Minikube to set up a local Kubernetes single-node cluster environment. This is available on Windows, Macintosh, and a wide variety of Linux operating system distributions.

To install Minikube, follow the directions for your operating system found at `https://kubernetes.io/docs/tasks/tools/install-minikube/`, and then follow the instructions in the following section to verify that your Minikube installation works.

Verifying that your Kubernetes installation works

Interacting with Kubernetes is done mostly through the **command-line interface** (**CLI**). You can issue the following command to see whether your environment is functional; it will show all the running pods, including the system pods:

```
kubectl get pods -A
```

The output will look something like this:

```
$ kubectl get pods -A
NAMESPACE     NAME                                          READY   STATUS    RESTARTS   AGE
docker        compose-78f95d4f8c-6q47g                      1/1     Running   0          13d
docker        compose-api-6ffb89dc58-xmc7g                  1/1     Running   0          13d
kube-system   coredns-5644d7b6d9-trt7s                      1/1     Running   0          13d
kube-system   coredns-5644d7b6d9-x7z5f                      1/1     Running   0          13d
kube-system   etcd-docker-desktop                           1/1     Running   0          13d
kube-system   kube-apiserver-docker-desktop                 1/1     Running   0          13d
kube-system   kube-controller-manager-docker-desktop        1/1     Running   0          13d
kube-system   kube-proxy-9mq8k                              1/1     Running   0          13d
kube-system   kube-scheduler-docker-desktop                 1/1     Running   0          13d
kube-system   storage-provisioner                           1/1     Running   1          13d
kube-system   vpnkit-controller                             1/1     Running   0          13d
```

Figure 8.2 – Output of kubectl get pods

Now that you have Kubernetes running on your local workstation, you can develop and deploy applications using Kubernetes. Applications you develop and package with Kubernetes can be deployed with the same tools that you use locally – but at a much larger scale in the cloud. Before we deploy an application to the cloud, though, we should show that we can deploy a packaged application locally.

Deploying a sample application – ShipIt Clicker v4

Let's imagine that the ShipIt Clicker application introduced in previous chapters has been shipped to production and the team responsible for operations is nervous about the limits of scaling this application since it is only deployed on one server. In order to scale out this Docker application to multiple servers, the team has decided to migrate to Kubernetes and package the software for Kubernetes using the Helm package manager. To proceed, let's install Helm and test it out.

Installing Helm

Helm is to Kubernetes what a package manager is to a modern operating system. It allows developers to specify how their application is packaged and deployed in a Kubernetes cluster. Helm is not only a package manager, but also a templating system for generating Kubernetes configurations and applying those configurations in a controlled way. Helm allows developers to define the entire set of containers and their interrelated Kubernetes configurations. Once you have defined an application in Helm, it becomes simple to install and update that application.

You can install this on macOS easily with Homebrew using the following command:

```
brew install helm
```

For other operating systems, follow the Helm installation instructions at `https://helm.sh/docs/intro/install/`.

Once you have installed Helm, use it to install the stable Helm repository (so that we can install other software packages that Helm supports, such as the NGINX Ingress Controller) with the following command:

```
helm repo add stable https://kubernetes-charts.storage.
googleapis.com/
```

Once you have installed this, you can use Helm to install applications from the catalog to your local Kubernetes instance. You can also use Helm to install applications defined in local Helm charts. We will use Helm to deploy ShipIt Clicker to Kubernetes, in conjunction with another Helm package, the NGINX Ingress Controller. In this chapter, we will first deploy the ShipIt Clicker application to the local learning environment Kubernetes cluster, and later, we will deploy ShipIt Clicker to the cloud on Amazon EKS.

Deploying the NGINX Ingress Controller and ShipIt Clicker locally

Let's use Helm to install a packaged application, the NGINX Ingress Controller, and then use it to install ShipIt Clicker. An Ingress Controller is a Kubernetes networking proxy that allows requests from the outside to reach applications deployed to Kubernetes, with well-defined interfaces to help wire together the applications. The stable Helm repository contains the NGINX Ingress Controller. Install it as follows:

```
helm install nginx-ingress stable/nginx-ingress
```

Later in the chapter, we will explore Ingress Controller in more detail. Know for now that this simple installation is sufficient to expose services inside the Kubernetes cluster with the right configurations to localhost so that you can test them.

Next, we will build the ShipIt Clicker Docker container, tag it, and push it to Docker Hub. Kubernetes relies on pulling Docker images from a Docker image registry, so it is insufficient to only have the container on your local system. Issue these commands, replacing dockerfordevelopers with your Docker Hub username:

```
$ cd chapter8
$ docker build . -t dockerfordevelopers/shipitclicker:0.4.0
$ docker push dockerfordevelopers/shipitclicker:0.4.0
```

Edit the shipitclicker/values.yaml file and replace dockerfordevelopers with your Docker Hub username in this stanza:

```
# Default values for shipitclicker.
# This is a YAML-formatted file.
# Declare variables to be passed into your templates.

replicaCount: 1

image:
  repository: dockerfordevelopers/shipitclicker
  pullPolicy: IfNotPresent
```

Then, deploy ShipIt Clicker to the Kubernetes local environment. In this case, we will use a local Helm Chart instead of one from a network Helm Chart repository. The Helm Chart for ShipIt Clicker is in the GitHub repository, in the `chapter8/shipitclicker` directory. Install it with Helm, as follows:

```
$ helm install shipitclicker shipitclicker
NAME: shipitclicker
LAST DEPLOYED: Fri Apr 24 23:21:22 2020
NAMESPACE: default
STATUS: deployed
REVISION: 1
NOTES:
1. Get the application URL by running these commands:
   http://localhost
```

Visit `http://localhost/` to view the ShipIt Clicker application. You should see the running application splash screen.

Troubleshooting local installation

If you can't reach the application at `http://localhost/`, you might have another web server running on port `80`, such as Apache 2.

Now that we are running this on Kubernetes, you need to use Kubernetes commands to connect to services that are on the inside of the cluster and not exposed through the Ingress Controller.

To expose the Redis port from the Kubernetes cluster for testing, use the following commands:

```
$ brew install redis
$ kubectl port-forward deployment/shipitclicker 6379 &
$ redis-cli
> keys *
> quit
```

Now that you have deployed the ShipIt Clicker application to a local Kubernetes installation, you can proceed with deploying it to a larger cloud environment and configuring it for production readiness.

Choosing a Kubernetes distribution

So, how do we host Kubernetes beyond installing it on our workstations? When it comes to choosing a Kubernetes distribution, you are presented with a plethora of options, as we saw in *Chapter 5, Alternatives for Deploying and Running Containers in Production*. We are now going to revisit some of the most popular options to help you gain an understanding of the choices available based on your cloud provider or bare-metal data center setup, as well as see why we are choosing to use EKS to demonstrate the migration of the ShipIt Clicker sample application to Kubernetes.

Google Kubernetes Engine

Google Kubernetes Engine (**GKE**) is Google's key service for hosting containers in a Kubernetes-based environment. GKE (formerly known as Google Container Engine) was released in an Alpha state in November 2014 and went live in August 2015 for general usage.

It currently offers one of the most mature Kubernetes services offered by cloud providers, including the following features:

- A single cluster quick start option for trialing the service
- Container vulnerability scanning
- Built-in data encryption
- Multiple channels for upgrading, repairing, and releasing
- Integration with Google monitoring services
- Automatic scaling and load balancing
- Google-managed underlying hardware

Further documentation for interested readers can be found at the GKE website at `https://cloud.google.com/kubernetes-engine/docs`.

Let's now compare this with Amazon's offerings.

AWS EKS

Amazon's answer to serving and managing containers in the cloud is its EKS service. As with GKE, Amazon's Kubernetes services, EKS, offers a managed service. Unlike Google's offering, it came to the market later, not being available until early 2018. However, what EKS loses in maturity, it makes up for in features.

These features include the following:

- Serverless hosting via AWS Fargate (`https://aws.amazon.com/fargate/`)
- Server deployment options on EC2
- Zero-downtime upgrades and patching
- Auto-detection of unhealthy nodes
- Hybrid hosting solutions with AWS Outposts (`https://aws.amazon.com/outposts/`)
- Kubernetes Jobs for batch processing

You can read more about EKS on the official website at `https://aws.amazon.com/eks/features/`.

We'll be exploring EKS in more detail throughout this chapter and in subsequent chapters, mostly since it is the managed Kubernetes offering from the dominant cloud vendor. Other distributions have their merits, however, so we will also examine some of the other options out there. Next is Red Hat OpenShift.

Red Hat OpenShift

OpenShift is a collection of software developed by Red Hat geared toward containerized application architectures. Like GKE and EKS, OpenShift is Kubernetes-focused; however, where it diverges is with its focus on build-related artifacts and a native image repository.

Having used Jenkins in the projects presented in this book, you will now be familiar with **continuous integration and continuous deployment (CI/CD)** pipelines in relation to containers. One of the key features of OpenShift is its extension of the standard `kubectl` commands to include mechanisms that replicate the sort of CI/CD functionality that you might otherwise have to use software such as Jenkins or Spinnaker to get. This includes the ability to create builds, test runs, and deployments.

There are some other key features that also make OpenShift a desirable option:

- Automated upgrades and life cycle management
- Open source code base available on GitHub (`https://github.com/openshift`)
- Deploy in any cloud, in a data center, or on-premises
- An image registry
- Monitoring and log aggregation

For further information on Red Hat OpenShift, make sure to check out the documentation on GitHub (`https://github.com/openshift/openshift-docs`) or on the official website (`https://www.openshift.com/`).

Microsoft Azure Kubernetes Service

We've looked at the major players so far, but of course, couldn't go any further without mentioning Microsoft's contribution to the Kubernetes ecosystem. For users of Microsoft cloud products, **Azure Kubernetes Service (AKS)** provides a mechanism to serve Docker containers in a Kubernetes-based environment.

Let's take a brief tour of what AKS offers:

- The elastic provisioning of services
- Integration with the Azure DevOps and Monitor services
- Identity and access management with Active Directory
- Failure detection and container health monitoring
- Canary deployments
- Log aggregation

As you can see, for Azure users, it has a comparable set of features to those available in EKS and GKE. If you would like to learn more, please refer to the AKS documentation (`https://docs.microsoft.com/en-us/azure/aks/`). Here, you will also find a quick start guide for getting a taste of what the service has to offer.

Before running through the components that form the basis of Kubernetes, let's briefly review the other options available.

Reviewing other relevant options

EKS, OpenShift, GKE, and AKS represent the most popular Kubernetes services on the market. However, they are not alone. Digital Ocean offers an option for those wishing to get a taste of a managed service outside of deploying your own RedShift infrastructure or signing up to the big cloud providers. You can read more about it at `https://www.digitalocean.com/products/kubernetes/`.

Many readers will be familiar with IBM, and they too offer cloud-hosting services. If you want to try out Kubernetes in their cloud environment, you can find details on their website, including how to set up a free cluster (`https://www.ibm.com/cloud/container-service/`).

Anyone familiar with VMware might wish to explore their Kubernetes offering as well –VMware Tanzu Kubernetes Grid – which has strengths in building hybrid clouds (`https://tanzu.vmware.com/kubernetes-grid`).

Finally, those looking for a fully managed Kubernetes service or those who are already customers of Rackspace have the option of checking out their **Kubernetes as a Service (KaaS)** offerings (`https://www.rackspace.com/managed-kubernetes`).

That wraps up our whistle-stop tour of the hosting platforms available for deploying your containers.

For the remainder of this chapter, we will be using Amazon's EKS service. If you haven't created an account, we recommend you sign up for one here now:

`https://aws.amazon.com/`

> **Note**
> Users of other cloud providers may find that they can adapt the following sections to their own services if they wish.

Let's now dig into the core concepts of Kubernetes, including pods, nodes, and namespaces.

Getting familiar with Kubernetes concepts

Now that you know where you can deploy Kubernetes, let's dive into some of the key concepts (including objects, ConfigMaps, pods, nodes, services, Ingress Controllers, secrets, and namespaces) and how they work. Let's start by examining an architecture diagram that shows the relationship between the various components of the system:

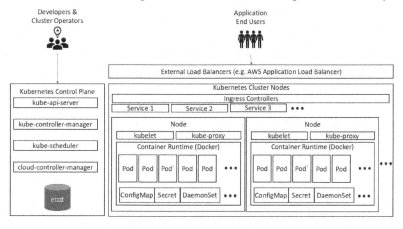

Figure 8.3 – Kubernetes architecture diagram

With Kubernetes, the cluster consists of a control plane that manages all aspects of the Kubernetes cluster (including the interface with the cloud provider) and a set of workers for the cluster, known as nodes, where the applications hosted by the cluster live. Developers and cluster operators interact with Kubernetes via the control plane through an API. The processes in the control plane communicate with the processes running on the individual worker nodes via the `kubelet` process, and the processes on the worker nodes are organized as pods that communicate with one another via the `kube-proxy` process that runs on each node.

Objects

The most fundamental concept in Kubernetes is an **object**. You use Kubernetes to create and maintain a collection of objects that might represent different elements of a cluster. All of the items explored in this section are Kubernetes objects. Kubernetes exposes APIs that let administrators create these objects and that some of the objects can use to discover and communicate with one another. You can use the `kubectl` utility to create, query, and modify all the different types of Kubernetes objects, as well as to configure the cluster.

The `kubectl` command-line utility can take YAML format files that describe the objects and use them to create and update the state of the system. This is the most basic way of defining, installing, and upgrading Kubernetes applications. The Helm tool we used to install applications takes this a step further by providing templating and life cycle capabilities.

We recommend configuring your application through Helm Charts. You briefly saw how to use Helm at the beginning of this chapter. A Helm Chart is simply a set of YAML configuration files that contain information about your containerized application.

You can create a new Helm Chart using the following command:

```
helm create my-chart
```

This sets up a Helm Chart structure with template files that are ready for customization.

ConfigMaps

Kubernetes handles application configuration with a concept known as a ConfigMap. Then, we need to define the configuration for the container itself. This is handled through a ConfigMap.

The key idea behind ConfigMaps is that you can separate the important configuration from the content of the images themselves. This is done in order to provide better portability of your microservices and applications.

ConfigMaps can be created directly through `kubectl` using the following command:

```
kubectl create configmap sample-configmap-name
```

A ConfigMap will contain information used by your application, and other key-value pairs, such as the namespace. The following example illustrates how an application's ConfigMap might look:

```
apiVersion: v1
kind: ConfigMap
metadata:
    name: shipitclicker-configmap
data:
    language: "JavaScript"
    node.version: "13.x"
```

A ConfigMap such as the one we just demonstrated would then be stored inside your Helm Chart directory in the templates folder – for example, `shipitclicker/templates/configmap.yaml`.

With this basic setup in place, you can then install your configuration through the `helm install` command. We will be exploring configuration in both its ConfigMap and Helm Chart formats in further detail throughout this chapter.

Pods

Pods in Kubernetes serve the purpose of grouping together *1* to *n* containerized components, which are then run in a shared context. They also include shared resources, such as IP addresses, storage, and definitions on how containers should be run. Multiple containers running together in a pod can communicate with each other on fixed ports on `localhost`, simplifying application configuration significantly.

When defining what should be run in a pod, the best approach is to think of it as holding all the necessary containers for a system or application. Multiple pods can then be added to Kubernetes to scale your application out horizontally. This allows you to create redundancy and helps cope with increases in traffic and load.

The shared context that the pods use is implemented through Linux concepts such as cgroups and namespaces. In *Chapter 12, Introduction to Container Security*, we will explore some of these concepts in depth in relation to container security.

Nodes

Machines that host Docker containers in Kubernetes' ecosystem are known as **nodes**, though you may also encounter the terms *minions* or *workers* – they all mean the same thing, but node is the official term. Kubernetes supports nodes that are either physical or virtual machines. Services such as Amazon's EKS provide the mechanisms for deploying node infrastructure. You deploy Kubernetes pods on nodes; the pods include both containers and shared resources.

In the learning environment that we are using, our local development workstation is the sole node in the cluster. Later in this chapter, we will be creating a Kubernetes cluster with nodes managed by EKS on AWS EC2. Kubernetes nodes run containers through pods and other Kubernetes objects, such as DaemonSets.

> **Alternative container runtimes**
>
> Kubernetes nodes could potentially run different container runtimes. Kubernetes not only supports Docker containers, but also other container technologies, including containerd, CRI-O, and Frakti. Since this book is about Docker, we will exclusively use the Docker runtime in our examples.

Services

A Kubernetes service is a way of declaring how your application exposes its interfaces to the world. It typically defines a network port that other Kubernetes pods can use to communicate with your application.

The Helm Chart for ShipIt Clicker emits a service template that defines a `ClusterIP` service definition:

```
$ helm template shipitclicker ./shipitclicker | less
...
# Source: shipitclicker/templates/service.yaml
apiVersion: v1
kind: Service
metadata:
  name: shipitclicker
  labels:
    helm.sh/chart: shipitclicker-0.1.10
    app.kubernetes.io/name: shipitclicker
    app.kubernetes.io/instance: shipitclicker
    app.kubernetes.io/version: "0.4.0"
```

```
      app.kubernetes.io/managed-by: Helm
spec:
  type: ClusterIP
  ports:
    - port: 8008
      targetPort: http
      protocol: TCP
      name: http
  selector:
    app.kubernetes.io/name: shipitclicker
    app.kubernetes.io/instance: shipitclicker
```

This declaration describes the fact that ShipIt Clicker exposes HTTP on port 8008 as a service on each pod. This lets other Kubernetes services discover and make connections to it.

Ingress Controllers

Kubernetes manages an internal network where the applications in a cluster can communicate with one another via a private network. By default, there is no way to reach applications running on the inside of a Kubernetes cluster from the outside. The Ingress Controller plays the role of a proxy and connection broker. Depending on whether you are deploying on-premises or in the cloud, different types of Ingress Controller have different uses. For example, earlier in this chapter, we installed the nginx-ingress Ingress Controller to allow us to reach applications running on our local Kubernetes installation. That controller is also useful when you want a vendor-neutral way of granting access to Kubernetes applications.

Other Ingress Controllers allow Kubernetes to work smoothly with different types of external load balancers, such as aws-alb-ingress-controller, which enables the use of an **Application Load Balancer** (**ALB**) in the AWS cloud, or k8s-bigip-ctlr, which enables the use of F5 BIG-IP load balancers, which are found in many data centers.

You can use Ingress Controllers to map domain names and HTTP paths to Kubernetes services. This makes it really easy to expose different services at different URLs. If you had a fleet of microservices, you could expose them at different API endpoints using this pattern. You can take advantage of Ingress Controllers by declaring an ingress object for your application that advertises how to connect your service to the outside world. For the ShipIt Clicker example, we use the following to map the service to `localhost` in the default namespace:

```
$ helm template shipitclicker ./shipitclicker | less
...
# Source: shipitclicker/templates/ingress.yaml
apiVersion: networking.k8s.io/v1beta1
kind: Ingress
metadata:
  name: shipitclicker
  labels:
    helm.sh/chart: shipitclicker-0.1.10
    app.kubernetes.io/name: shipitclicker
    app.kubernetes.io/instance: shipitclicker
    app.kubernetes.io/version: "0.4.0"
    app.kubernetes.io/managed-by: Helm
  annotations:
    kubernetes.io/ingress.class: nginx
    kubernetes.io/tls-acme: "true"
spec:
  rules:
    - host: "localhost"
      http:
        paths:
          - path: /
            backend:
              serviceName: shipitclicker
              servicePort: 8008
...
```

The Kubernetes system handles connections to applications hosted inside the cluster from the outside using this Ingress Controllers definition. This means that when you are first developing your application, you do not need to worry about how it is connected to the outside world. The Kubernetes configurations that enable Ingress Controllers can all be managed with Helm Charts, too.

Next, we will examine how Kubernetes deals with sensitive information – using secrets.

Secrets

Every application has values that need to be protected, from database passwords to API keys, so having a mechanism to store and retrieve them securely is an important function. In Kubernetes, this is handled with a mechanism called secrets. You can use a combination of configuration files and kubectl commands for sharing and modifying information that needs to be protected with your pods and their running containers. Once you have created a secret, you can use it in your application through a variety of mechanisms, including exposing a secret as an environment variable or creating a file that containers running in a pod can retrieve.

The key operations in Kubernetes related to secrets are as follows:

- Creating a secret
- Describing a secret
- Retrieving a secret
- Editing a secret

Let's explore these four concepts, starting with creating a secret.

Creating a secret

We can use several procedures to create a secret. This could be done by adding it manually on the command line or storing it in a YAML template file and using it from there.

To add a secret stored in a text document via the command line, we can use the following commands:

```
$ echo "new-secret" > secret.txt
$ kubectl create secret generic secex --from-file=./secret.txt
```

If we do this, kubectl will take care of encoding the secret for us using Base64 encoding.

Let's prepare a secret another way, with a configuration file. In order to prepare a text secret for this file, it must be Base64-encoded. You can do that from the command line in macOS or Linux with the following command:

```
$ echo -n "changed-api-key" | base64
Y2hhbmdlZC1hcGkta2V5
```

If we wanted to instead store the secret in a configuration file, and use `kubectl` to add it to Kubernetes, we could create the following `secret-api-token.yaml` file:

```
---
apiVersion: v1
kind: Secret
metadata:
  name: api-token
  namespace: default
type: Opaque
data:
  token: "Y2hhbmdlZC1hcGkta2V5"
```

Then, using the `kubectl apply` command-line option, we can create the secret:

```
kubectl apply -f ./secret-api-token.yaml
```

You will notice that the configuration file format for the secret is very similar to the example ConfigMap we examined.

Because `shipitclicker` uses Helm to manage its Kubernetes objects, it has support for secrets built into its templates. The one secret it references in the code in this chapter is related to a Node.js server-side framework setting for the Express framework used by the sample application that deals with server sessions. This secret is called `SESSION_SECRET`, and it is stored in the `chapter8/shipitclicker/templates/secrets.yaml` file:

```
---
apiVersion: v1
kind: Secret
metadata:
  name: {{ .Release.Name}}-secrets
  namespace: {{ .Release.Namespace }}
type: Opaque
data:
  SESSION_SECRET: "bXlTZWNyZXQtddjQK"
```

Notice that this uses template expressions for `name` and `namespace` in order to align with the other templates that Helm transforms.

We created this secret when we installed the `shipitclicker` Helm template earlier in the chapter when we used the `helm install` command. That is how you create secrets when you use a Helm template.

Now that we have seen several ways of creating secrets, we will show how we ask Kubernetes what secrets it knows about.

Describing a secret

Once a secret has been created, you can list it using the `kubectl get secrets` command. This will list the secrets in a similar way to this:

```
$  kubectl get secrets
NAME                                       TYPE                                     DATA   AGE
default-token-sm7kn                        kubernetes.io/service-account-token      3      15d
nginx-ingress-backend-token-slkjf          kubernetes.io/service-account-token      3      3h43m
nginx-ingress-token-v5jjp                  kubernetes.io/service-account-token      3      3h43m
sample-secret                              Opaque                                   1      15m
secex                                      Opaque                                   1      12m
sh.helm.release.v1.nginx-ingress.v1        helm.sh/release.v1                       1      3h43m
sh.helm.release.v1.shipitclicker.v1        helm.sh/release.v1                       1      3h30m
sh.helm.release.v1.shipitclicker.v2        helm.sh/release.v1                       1      3h1m
sh.helm.release.v1.shipitclicker.v3        helm.sh/release.v1                       1      112m
sh.helm.release.v1.shipitclicker.v4        helm.sh/release.v1                       1      104m
sh.helm.release.v1.shipitclicker.v5        helm.sh/release.v1                       1      102m
shipitclicker-secrets                      Opaque                                   1      102m
shipitclicker-token-lc9qv                  kubernetes.io/service-account-token      3      3h30m
```

Figure 8.4 – List of secrets

To learn more about the secret, use the `kubectl describe` command:

```
kubectl describe secrets/shipitclicker-secrets
```

The output of the preceding command is shown in the following screenshot:

```
$  kubectl describe secrets/shipitclicker-secrets
Name:          shipitclicker-secrets
Namespace:     default
Labels:        <none>
Annotations:   <none>


Type:  Opaque

Data
====
SESSION_SECRET:  12 bytes
```

Figure 8.5 – Output of the kubectl describe command showing the secret's metadata

You will see metadata about your secret displayed, including the key of the secret – in this case, SESSION_SECRET. It will not show the value of the secret, though.

Retrieving a secret

A typical way for a Kubernetes application to retrieve a simple secret is to define it as an environment variable passed to the container referencing the secret. See this excerpt from the rendered Helm chart templates:

```
# Source: shipitclicker/templates/deployment.yaml
apiVersion: apps/v1
kind: Deployment
metadata:
  name: shipitclicker
...
      containers:
        - name: shipitclicker
...
        env:
...
          - name: REDIS_PORT
            valueFrom:
              configMapKeyRef:
                name: shipitclicker-configmap
                key: REDIS_PORT
          - name: SESSION_SECRET
            valueFrom:
              secretKeyRef:
                name: shipitclicker-secrets
                key: SESSION_SECRET
```

You can see that the environment variables mapped to the deployment for the shipitclicker container reference both the configMapKeyRef and secretKeyRef entries.

To deal with more complex secrets that are complete files, such as SSH private keys, the mechanism is similar. See the Kubernetes secrets documentation for more scenarios at https://kubernetes.io/docs/concepts/configuration/secret/.

For troubleshooting purposes, we can retrieve a secret from Kubernetes from the command line:

```
$ template='go-template={{index .data "SESSION_SECRET"}}'
$ kubectl get secrets shipitclicker-secrets -o "$template" |
base64 -D
mySecret-v4
```

Now that we have seen how to retrieve a secret, we will examine how to edit secrets.

Editing secrets

If you wish to edit the secret after creating it, use the kubectl edit command:

```
kubectl edit secrets secex
```

This will open your default editor (by default, vi) and you can edit the secret. You will have to have the Base64-encoded replacement value ready. It will look something like this:

```
apiVersion: v1
data:
  secret.txt: Y2hhbmdlZC1hcGkta2V5LTI=
kind: Secret
metadata:
  creationTimestamp: "2020-04-25T20:54:31Z"
  name: secex
  namespace: default
  resourceVersion: "826562"
  selfLink: /api/v1/namespaces/default/secrets/sample-secret
  uid: ce8fbf27-33ba-461e-9bb8-1ca31fa3e888
type: Opaque
```

You can edit secrets directly this way. You might need to redeploy your application after updating a secret, depending on how it uses that secret. Having to manage this by hand can get complicated, which is one of the reasons why we use Helm to package applications.

Updating the ShipIt Clicker session secret

For applications deployed with Helm, it is usual practice to make changes through the Helm templates instead of using raw `kubectl` commands. Now, we will change the ShipIt Clicker `SESSION_SECRET` key using Helm by following this procedure:

1. Generate a Base64-encoded secret with the following command:

    ```
    echo -n "new-session-secret" | base64
    ```

2. Edit the template `chapter8/shipitclicker/templates/secrets.yaml` file.

3. Use the value outputted by the `openssl` command for the new `SESSION_SECRET` value.

4. Edit the `chapter8/shipitclicker/Chart.yaml` file and increment the chart's `version` number.

5. You have to do this every time you update a Helm Chart. Then, update the template with the following command:

    ```
    helm upgrade shipitclicker ./shipitclicker
    ```

As you can see, the basic commands to add and edit secrets are very simple. Using them in our application is slightly more complex. This should give you a taste of how to create a secret value and retrieve information on it to explore the feature.

> **Note**
>
> For further information on secrets, you can check out the latest Kubernetes documentation at `https://kubernetes.io/docs/concepts/configuration/secret/`.

In *Chapter 14, Advanced Docker Security – Secrets, Secret Commands, Tagging, and Labels*, we look into secret storage and usage in relation to Docker Swarm. While Docker Swarm is falling out of favor, with many teams switching to Kubernetes, it is important to understand these concepts when maintaining legacy systems. Additionally, you may find yourself in a position where you have to migrate systems from Docker Swarm to Kubernetes. The information provided in this chapter and *Chapter 14, Advanced Docker Security – Secrets, Secret Commands, Tagging, and Labels*, should help you map concepts from one technology to the other.

Namespaces

In order to partition resources within Kubernetes, we can use a concept called namespaces. Namespaces provide a mechanism to group container resources into non-overlapping sets, which then allows you to subdivide your Kubernetes resources, based on your business needs, within the same cluster. This could include everything from environments (development, staging, and production) to groups of microservices. One important factor you should consider is that applications in the same namespace can read any secret in that namespace, so it represents a security boundary as well.

It is tempting, once you learn of this feature, to want to use it everywhere, but the Kubernetes documentation cautions against this. The main namespaces content page (`https://kubernetes.io/docs/concepts/overview/working-with-objects/namespaces/`) states the following:

"For clusters with a few to tens of users, you should not need to create or think about namespaces at all."

Keep in mind, though, that different teams might want to segregate applications from one another, and namespaces are a good way to do that as they provide a security boundary. Later in this chapter, in the *Using labels and namespaces to segregate environments* section, we will explore using this concept to deploy our application to both a staging and production environment in AWS.

Next, let's set up AWS EKS with CloudFormation in order to deploy our application to the public cloud using Kubernetes.

Spinning up AWS EKS with CloudFormation

Now that we have walked through a local installation of Kubernetes and explored some of the cloud vendor options, we are going to try deploying containers to an AWS-hosted Kubernetes environment. This will be the EKS service we briefly introduced in the previous section of this chapter.

In order to achieve this, we will describe how to create and manage an EKS cluster using AWS CloudFormation, their infrastructure-as-code service. For more information on CloudFormation, be sure to check out the AWS guides and documentation at `https://docs.aws.amazon.com/cloudformation/`.

Assuming you have previously created an AWS account or followed the instructions under the *Technical requirements* section of this chapter, load up the AWS cloud console.

To proceed, we need to set up EKS. There are many ways to get a working EKS cluster that require varying amounts of work:

- Set up everything by hand, step by step through the AWS console. We *do not recommend* this approach as it requires deep AWS knowledge to carry out correctly, and will lead to a hard-to-replicate environment with poor controls.

- Write infrastructure-as-code templates from scratch in either AWS CloudFormation or Terraform to control all the resources needed. This is an approach that might work for you if you are an expert in either CloudFormation or Terraform and have an existing investment in CloudFormation or Terraform tooling, but we *do not recommend this for beginners*.

- Use the `eksctl` tool (see `https://eksctl.io`) to create a cluster with a simple CLI tool. This could work well if you are already familiar with AWS and want to put your cluster in a specific region and tweak more of the parameters of your cluster. We *only recommend this if you are familiar with AWS and EKS already*.

- Research and adopt infrastructure-as-code templates that someone else has already written. Both AWS and many other people have created CloudFormation and Terraform templates.

We are going to follow this last approach and use the AWS Quick Start CloudFormation templates for EKS to create our first cloud Kubernetes cluster.

Introducing the AWS EKS Quick Start CloudFormation templates

Amazon provides a handy set of CloudFormation templates called Quick Starts, built by their expert cloud architects to quickly get you up and running for a wide selection of AWS services and scenarios (`https://aws.amazon.com/quickstart/`).

We will be using an AWS EKS Quick Start template for the next section of this chapter.

However, before you deploy the EKS Quick Start CloudFormation templates, please take a moment to prepare your AWS account for deployment.

Preparing an AWS account

If you are just starting to use AWS, there are a few critical things to take care of before you proceed in order to protect your account. These precautions and preparations also apply if you choose a method other than using the AWS Quick Start CloudFormation templates to create your EKS cluster.

If you are already an experienced AWS user and have an AWS **Identity and Account Management** (**IAM**) user account with administrative privileges, you have an EC2 key pair in the us-east-2 region, and you know your public IPv4 address, you can skip ahead to the *Launching the AWS EKS Quick Start CloudFormation templates* section. Avoid using an assumed IAM role with administrative privileges to create the CloudFormation template, though – that can cause some of the child templates to enter an UPDATE_ROLLBACK_FAILED state, which is difficult to recover from.

Using an IAM administrator user and not the root account user

First of all, ensure that you are not using the AWS console as the root account user. This is a major security risk. You will need an AWS IAM user account with administrative privileges. If you have just created your AWS root account, you can set one up by following the AWS instructions at https://docs.aws.amazon.com/IAM/latest/UserGuide/getting-started_create-admin-group.html.

Once you have set up this user and enabled billing access for the IAM user as per instructions, go to the https://console.aws.amazon.com/iam/home#/home page and copy the IAM user's sign-in link to the clipboard. Edit your web browser bookmarks and use this URL to create an **AWS IAM Login** item. You will want to use this to sign in to your AWS account with your administrator account instead of using the root account.

On your local system, create an eks-notes.txt file and record the sign-in link there. Also, record the **User ARN** value of the administrator user from the https://console.aws.amazon.com/iam/home?region=us-east-2#/users/Administrator URL:

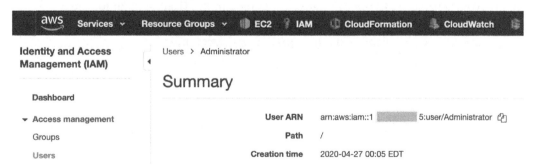

Figure 8.6 – AWS IAM user summary for the administrative user

This **Amazon Resource Name (ARN)** user is a string, much like a web **Uniform Resource Identifier (URI)**, but it is Amazon-specific. Now that we have set up an administrative user, let's set up **multi-factor authentication (MFA)** to protect both the root account and the administrator user.

Setting up MFA

We recommend that you protect both the root account and every IAM user account with administrative privileges using MFA. If someone compromises your root account, they could create huge bills by launching expensive cloud resources, steal your information, or even delete all your data. When you are getting started, we recommend that you use MFA with a virtual MFA device and supporting software such as Google Authenticator, Authy, or 1Password.

For added security, you have the option of using one of the supported hardware token solutions, but virtual MFA works fine. Please see the AWS MFA documentation for more details on setting up MFA:

```
https://aws.amazon.com/iam/features/mfa/
```

Signing in to the AWS console with the IAM user account

Ensure you have signed out of the root account. Then, use the sign-in URL from your `eks-notes.txt` document to sign in to the AWS console with your administrator IAM user account before proceeding.

Creating access keys for the IAM administrator user

In order to use the AWS command-line tools, you will need to generate AWS access keys. You can read more about access keys and other types of AWS credentials at `https://docs.aws.amazon.com/general/latest/gr/aws-sec-cred-types.html`.

In the AWS console, go to the IAM service and look in the **Users** section for the administrator user you just created. Then, navigate to the **Security credentials** tab and create new access keys by pressing the **Create access key** button:

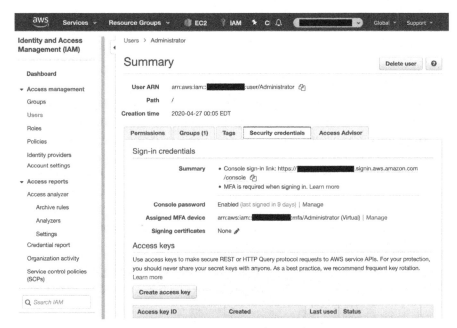

Figure 8.7– AWS IAM user summary for an administrative user

Download these access keys as a CSV file to your local system. You will need to open that file and examine the keys in order to configure the AWS CLI, which we will do next.

Configuring the AWS CLI on your local workstation

You are going to need a working AWS CLI installation on your local workstation to complete the configuration of the EKS cluster. If you don't already have this installed, follow the instructions to install it at `https://aws.amazon.com/cli/`.

Once it is installed, issue the `aws configure` command and use the access ID and secret key from the access key's CSV file you saved in the previous section to configure the CLI to use the administrator user. Verify that it works with the `aws sts get-caller-identity` command. Inspect the output to make sure that it does not show an error message, and then verify that the ARN that this command emits for the active user is the same one as for the administrator user shown in the IAM web console. The output should look something like this:

```
$ aws sts get-caller-identity
{
    "UserId": "AIDASDBK0BZBUC3RCCP42",
    "Account": "143970405955",
    "Arn": "arn:aws:iam::143970405955:user/Administrator"
}
```

Figure 8.8 – Output of aws sts get-caller-identity

You will need this set up when you configure the cluster for the ALB Ingress Controller later in the chapter.

Creating an EC2 key pair for the EKS cluster

In order to perform the initial configuration of the EKS cluster, you will need to SSH to an EC2 virtual server that the CloudFormation template sets up, known as the bastion host. A **bastion host** is a server set up for the purposes of being a single point of access to a protected network. In order to gain access to the bastion host, you will need an SSH key pair registered with AWS EC2. Having this configured can also help you gain access to the nodes in order to troubleshoot and inspect them. In order to do this, you need an SSH key pair registered with AWS EC2 in the us-east-2 region. Signed in as your IAM administrator user, go to https://console.aws.amazon.com/ec2, and then make sure you switch your region to **us-east-2** from the region picker:

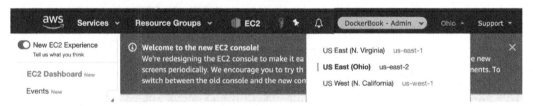

Figure 8.9 – Switching your AWS region

Then, find and click on the key pairs link in the menu on the left, create a new key pair called ec2-eks, and download it. You will need this key pair when you configure the EKS cluster. To prepare for that, copy this key pair to the .ssh directory under your local user home directory and set its permissions so that SSH will allow its use:

```
$ mkdir -p ~/.ssh
$ chmod 0700 ~/.ssh
$ cp ~/Downloads/ec2-eks.pem ~/.ssh/
$ chmod 0600 ~/.ssh/ec2-eks.pem
```

You will need this key to connect to the bastion host for your EKS cluster later. Next, make sure you know your public IP address.

Recording your public IP address in CIDR notation

We are going to restrict access from the internet to the Kubernetes cluster by restricting it to just the pubic IPv4 address you are currently using. This will keep malicious hackers and people who attack internet hosts from scanning your system. To do this, go to `https://whatismyip.com/` and copy your public IPv4 address in CIDR format, which is the raw numerical address with `/32` appended. For example, if it was `192.2.0.15`, the CIDR form of your IPv4 address would be `192.2.0.15/32`. On your local system, open your `eks-notes.txt` file and record the CIDR address there.

Launching the AWS EKS Quick Start CloudFormation templates

You can find the documentation on the AWS EKS Quick Start CloudFormation templates at `https://aws.amazon.com/quickstart/architecture/amazon-eks/`.

To get a complete picture of what this offers, read the deployment guide that AWS offers related to this quick start:

`https://docs.aws.amazon.com/quickstart/latest/amazon-eks-architecture/welcome.html`

At a minimum, review the outline on that page. When you want to proceed with deployment, click on the **How to Deploy** section. You will see that you have two options when deploying the CloudFormation templates, as follows:

- **Deploy to a new VPC** (`https://fwd.aws/6dEQ7`)
- **Deploy to an existing VPC** (`https://fwd.aws/e37MA`)

Before you begin, sign out of the AWS console if you are still signed in with the root account user, and sign in as a administrator user using the IAM sign-in URL you recorded in the `eks-notes.txt` file.

We recommend that you start by deploying this infrastructure to a new **Virtual Private Cloud** (**VPC**). Click on that link or use the preceding URL to go to the CloudFormation stack creation forms. Most of the items in these forms can be left at their defaults, but some must be filled out both to complete initial cluster configuration and to ensure that you do not accidentally create an unsecure configuration.

Guidance for EKS Quick Start CloudFormation creation

Creating the CloudFormation stack will require you to fill out a four-page CloudFormation parameters form by following the **Deploy into a new VPC** link in the previous section. This is the first page of that form:

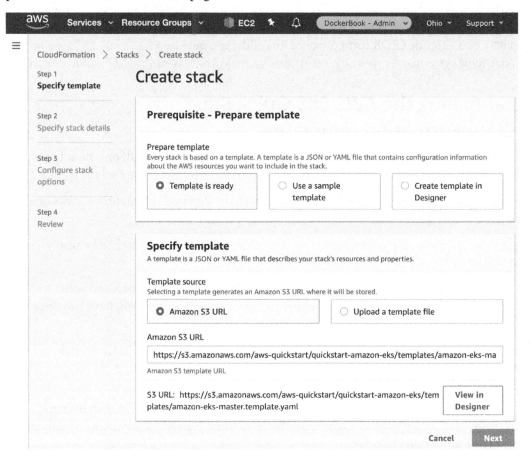

Figure 8.10 – CloudFormation form, page 1 of 4: Prepare template

This guidance will allow you to complete the items to get a working EKS cluster in about 30 minutes.

Create Stack – Prerequisite – Prepare Template

Leave all the items on this form at their defaults and hit the **Next** button. This will take you to the **Specify Stack Details** screen.

Specify Stack Details

You can leave almost all of these items at their defaults, but specify items for the following parameters:

- **Availability Zones**: `us-east-2a`, `us-east-2b`, and `us-east-2c`.

- **Allowed external access CIDR**: Enter your IPv4 CIDR address, such as `192.2.0.15/32`.

- **EKS cluster name**: Choose a short cluster name.

- **Maximum number of nodes**: 8.

- **SSH Key Name**: `eks-ec2`.

- **Additional EKS admin ARN (IAM Role)**: Leave this blank, unless you have another AWS IAM role in your account that you want to give access to.

- **Additional EKS admin ARN (IAM User)**: Leave this blank, unless you have another AWS IAM user in your account that you want to give access to.

- **Kubernetes Version**: 1.15.

> **Note**
>
> Do not use 1.16 or higher if you want to experiment with Spinnaker as described in *Chapter 9, Cloud-Native Continous Deployment Using Spinnaker*, as Spinnaker is not compatible with higher versions

- **EKS Public Access Endpoint**: Enabled.

- **EKS Public Access CIDRs**: Enter your IPv4 CIDR address, such as `192.2.0.15/32`.

- **ALB Ingress Controller**: Enabled.

- **Cluster Autoscaler**: Enabled.

- **EFS Storage Class**: Enabled.

- **Monitoring Stack**: Prometheus and Grafana.

Selecting these options will ultimately allow you to manage the EKS cluster from your local workstation using the `kubectl`, `helm`, and `eksctl` tools. Once these are specified, press the **Next** button at the bottom of the form. This will take you to the **Configure Stack Options** screen.

Configure Stack Options

Leave all of these at their defaults. Press the **Next** button at the bottom of the form. This will take you to the **Review** screen.

Review

Scroll to the bottom of the form and check both of the checkboxes acknowledging that this might create IAM resources with custom names and that it might require the CAPABILITY_AUTO_EXPAND capability. Press the **Next** button at the bottom of the form to create the CloudFormation template. Wait about 30 minutes and review the creation status of the template in the CloudFormation console—it should complete without issue. Check that all the CloudFormation templates reach the completed state before proceeding. It should look something like this:

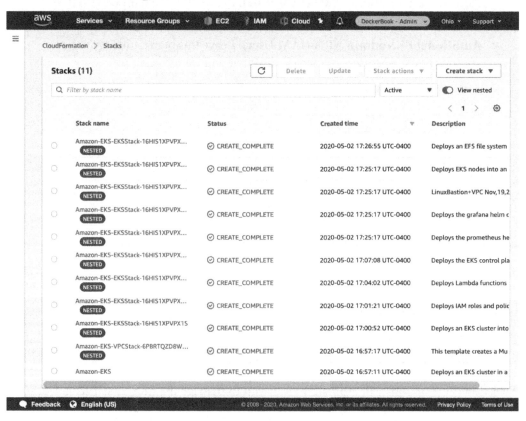

Figure 8.11 – The CloudFormation console with the CREATE_COMPLETE status

Now, your EKS cluster is ready for its initial configuration.

Configuring the EKS cluster

Having deployed the CloudFormation template, you will have an environment that contains the following AWS services:

- A VPC that serves as networking infrastructure for the cluster

- An EKS Kubernetes control plane managed by AWS

- An EC2 bastion host used to configure the cluster

- Kubernetes infrastructure, including three EC2 instances serving as nodes deployed across three AWS availability zones

- An ALB Ingress Controller that will allow outside access to cluster services

To gain initial access to the cluster, view the CloudFormation outputs for the stack and note the IPv4 address marked `BastionIP`. Then, SSH to the host with that address, replacing `192.2.10` with that IP address:

```
ssh -i ~/.ssh/eks-ec2.pem ec2-user@192.2.0.10
```

Once the deployment is complete, follow the AWS deployment guide to validate the cluster state:

`https://docs.aws.amazon.com/quickstart/latest/amazon-eks-architecture/step-3.html`.

Use some of the commands you have learned about, such as `kubectl get all -A`, `kubectl get nodes`, and `kubectl describe service/kubernetes`, to explore the cluster configuration from the bastion host.

The bastion node already has `kubectl`, `helm`, and `git` installed, so you have the option of using it to perform some cluster maintenance chores. The Helm installation even has the stable charts repository already installed, which you can verify with the `helm repo list` command.

> **Keep an eye on AWS costs**
>
> Once you have deployed the EKS infrastructure, AWS will start charging you by the hour while it is running. You will be responsible for all charges incurred while the EKS cluster and EC2 servers are running. Keeping this EKS cluster running might cost up to **$10-20 per day**. Please visit the **Billing & Cost Management** dashboard at `https://console.aws.amazon.com/billing/home?#/` in order to see your month-to-date and projected costs. We recommend that you have AWS generate cost and usage reports on a regular basis to help you track your spending. Information on enabling this can be found at `https://docs.aws.amazon.com/cur/latest/userguide/cur-create.html`.

Verifying that the ALB Ingress Controller is working

Because we enabled the ALB Ingress Controller optional add-in when we created the EKS cluster, we can skip the detailed directions in the ALB user guide (`https://docs.aws.amazon.com/eks/latest/userguide/alb-ingress.html`) to set up an ALB Ingress Controller for EKS. Since the ALB Ingress Controller is already set up, the cluster will automatically be able to create new Ingress Controllers and application load balancers when it finds a correctly annotated ingress object.

As an exercise, you can deploy the 2048 game described in the last section of the user guide to validate that the ALB works as expected.

Deploying an application with resource limits to Kubernetes on AWS EKS

In Kubernetes, we can set resource limits on an application in order to prevent it from consuming all the available CPU and memory resources in the cluster. This is desirable to protect the system from resource exhaustion, and to ensure that an application that has a memory leak or a bug that causes it to consume more CPU than expected does not bring down the entire cluster.

To demonstrate setting resource limits, we are going to deploy the ShipIt Clicker Docker container and Helm charts we deployed to our local Kubernetes installation in the *Deploying a sample application* section earlier in this chapter to the EKS cluster.

To demonstrate setting resource limits, we will now look at deploying the ShipIt Clicker application to Kubernetes, managed by the AWS EKS service, with CPU and memory limits enabled. We will also expose this application to the world using an Ingress Controller.

Configuring resource limits to guard against memory leaks and runaway CPU usage

Now that we are deploying to EKS, we want to be sure that our pod's containers are good citizens in the cluster. To do this, we will specify both resource requests and limits. Requests give Kubernetes guidance about how much of each resource it will initially allocate to the application, and will guide the orchestrator when it places the containers and pods on the nodes. Kubernetes will only schedule a pod on a node if it has adequate headroom to support a request. Limits give the orchestrator hard-maximum limits on how much CPU or memory to allocate. If a container exceeds its memory limit, its process will be killed with an **out-of-memory** (**OOM**) error.

We are going to use the Helm templates at `chapter8/shipitclicker-eks/` in order to make the first set of changes versus the basic Helm template we installed on our local system.

In `chapter8/shipitclicker-eks/values.yaml`, we are now specifying the CPU and memory requests and limits for the containers:

```
resources:
  limits:
    cpu: 500m
    memory: 512Mi
  requests:
    cpu: 500m
    memory: 512Mi
```

These apply both to the Redis and the ShipIt Clicker containers.

Annotating ShipIt Clicker to use the ALB Ingress Controller

Some changes are required for the `chapter8/shipitclicker-eks/values.yaml` file to make sure that the Ingress Controller annotations are compatible with the EKS setup. We need to switch up the annotations so that they are targeted toward EKS. Also, we will remove the host restriction and make sure that the configuration for paths has a wildcard in it. Since we use a `ClusterIP` service point, we also need to use the `ip` target type for the ALB Ingress Controller:

```
ingress:
  enabled: true
  annotations:
    kubernetes.io/ingress.class: alb
    alb.ingress.kubernetes.io/scheme: internet-facing
    alb.ingress.kubernetes.io/target-type: ip
  hosts:
#   - host: "*"
    - paths: ['/*']
```

Without these annotations, the ALB Ingress Controller would have trouble connecting to the services.

Deploying an EKS-ready ShipIt Clicker to EKS

SSH to the bastion host, clone the repository, and deploy the software with Helm:

```
$ git clone https://github.com/PacktPublishing/Docker-for-
Developers.git
$ cd Docker-for-Developers
helm install shipitclicker chapter8/shipitclicker-eks/
```

Check in the AWS EC2 console for evidence that an elastic load balancer is getting created. It may take a few minutes to become available. When it does, enter its DNS name in a browser and you should see the ShipIt Clicker game.

If you don't see it, troubleshoot by looking at the Ingress Controller logs:

```
kubectl logs -n kube-system    deployment.apps/alb-ingress-
controller
```

Now that we have the ShipIt Clicker application deployed to EKS and exposed to the world with an ALB Ingress Controller, let's examine how we can segregate environments so that different Docker containers can run without interfering with each other.

Using AWS Elastic Container Registry with AWS EKS

Using public images stored in Docker Hub is fine for some applications, but for more sensitive applications, you might want to store your Docker containers in a private Docker registry. AWS provides just such a registry: **Elastic Container Registry** (**ECR**). You can read more about the basics of ECR on the main product website at `https://aws.amazon.com/ecr/`.

In order to get a Kubernetes cluster to use images from a private repository, you must configure the cluster with the right credentials so that it can pull images from the repository. The process for most repositories is in the Kubernetes documentation at `https://kubernetes.io/docs/tasks/configure-pod-container/pull-image-private-registry/`.

However, AWS ECR uses an enhanced security system that relies on AWS IAM to grant temporary access tokens that are used to authenticate with ECR. Kubernetes has built-in support for this authentication process, as described in the documentation on images regarding using a private registry (`https://kubernetes.io/docs/concepts/containers/images/#using-aws-ec2-container-registry`).

When using ECR with Kubernetes, you use an ECR identifier in the specification for the images used in pod configurations or their Helm templates. Instead of using the default Docker Hub image specifications, you can specify images using the following syntax:

`ACCOUNT.dkr.ecr.REGION.amazonaws.com/imagename:tag`

The AWS documentation on EKS explains that the worker nodes that run the pods must have the correct IAM policies applied via IAM roles in order to get authentication tokens and retrieve the images:

`https://docs.aws.amazon.com/AmazonECR/latest/userguide/ECR_on_EKS.html`

Fortunately, the AWS CloudFormation templates we used to set up the EKS cluster produce worker nodes that already have the correct permissions applied, as do all clusters set up using the `eksctl` tool, if you set up your cluster with that alternative path. The access control rules described in ECR on the preceding EKS web page will grant EKS nodes permission to read any images stored in any ECR repository on the account.

So, to use ECR with EKS, all we should have to do is make sure our containers are pushed to an ECR repository in the same account with the EKS cluster, and that we use the ECR-style repository URIs as the identifiers for the containers that run in our Kubernetes pods.

Next up, let's create an ECR repository so that we can prepare for integrating ECR and EKS.

Creating an ECR repository

In a web browser, log in to the AWS console. Make sure you switch to the `us-east-2` region (the same region where your EKS cluster lives), and then click on the **Services** link and choose **Elastic Container Registry**. If you don't have any registries created yet, click on the **Get Started** button. The AWS console will prompt you for a namespace and repository.

Alternatively, visit the following URL to start the creation process:

`https://console.aws.amazon.com/ecr/create-repository?region=us-east-2`

Either way, you will see something like this:

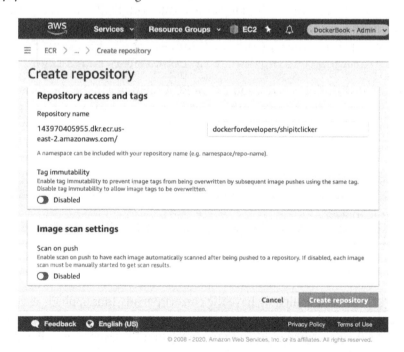

Figure 8.12 – The ECR Create repository form

Leave the other settings at their defaults. After you create the repository, note the URI for your repository; you will need it in order to push containers to the registry. You will see the URI on a screen that looks like this:

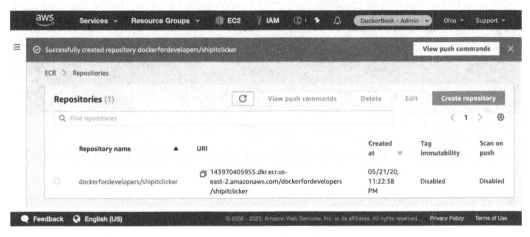

Figure 8.13 – The ECR Repositories page

Then, click on the **View push commands** button. This will give you detailed instructions on how to use the AWS CLI to get temporary credentials that you can use to accomplish a Docker push to the ECR repository.

Exercise – pushing ShipIt Clicker to the ECR repository

Follow the instructions shown after clicking on the **View push commands** button to build and deploy the ShipIt Clicker Docker container to ECR. The following commands are a less repetitive way of executing those steps (replace the REPO value with the hostname of your ECR registry from the URI generated in the **Create** form):

```
$ cd Docker-for-Developers/chapter8
$ REPO=143970405955.dkr.ecr.us-east-2.amazonaws.com
$ IMAGE=dockerfordevelopers/shipitclicker
$ aws ecr get-login-password --region us-east-2 | \
    docker login --username AWS --password-stdin $REPO
$ docker build -t $IMAGE:latest .
$ docker tag $IMAGE:latest $REPO/$IMAGE:latest
$ docker push $REPO/$IMAGE:latest
```

If this succeeds, you will see an output similar to the following:

```
$  docker push $REPO/$IMAGE:latest
The push refers to repository [143970405955.dkr.ecr.us-east-2.amazonaws.com/dockerfordevelopers/shipitclicker]
91886c2bec58: Pushed
803db8939aa3: Pushed
0e0a18348ee5: Pushed
62e05e3bb22a: Pushed
1348a1f0cfff: Pushed
f3acd9559398: Pushed
784ec316539a: Pushed
405463c769df: Pushed
ffac27138e4b: Pushed
da64c1c32e07: Pushed
latest: digest: sha256:c66f057ae0794e67705474fa480eaf653d0f8abe1eb6bd13354a23a4a1eefd89 size: 2409
```

Figure 8.14 – A Docker push to ECR

In the next chapter, we are going to use ECR to store Docker images that we build through Jenkins and deploy using Spinnaker and Helm.

Now that we have seen how we might store Docker container images in an ECR repository, we will examine how we can segregate environments using labels and namespaces.

Using labels and namespaces to segregate environments

We learned earlier in this chapter what a namespace is. Now, we will explore how we can use both namespaces and labels to create separate environments in both a local environment and in an EKS cluster.

Local example – labeled environments in the default namespace

Let's imagine you are developing the ShipIt Clicker application and want to keep a working stable environment deployed so that you can demonstrate it to others and compare new behaviors in code that you are changing to stable behavior. While you could use namespaces to segregate the application, it would be simpler to just deploy the Helm Chart again with deployments that have different labels. You can use multiple deployments with distinct labels, along with some template overrides, to accomplish this with Helm, without having to deal with the complexity of multiple namespaces.

To do this, we need to do the following:

1. Define a hostname to use to reach the service.

2. Configure the Ingress Controller for ShipIt Clicker to use that hostname.

3. Configure and bump the chart version in `chapter8/shipitclicker/Chart.yaml`.

4. Deploy the Helm Chart with a different name from the one already deployed, for example `shipit-stable`.

5. Test that we can reach the alternative environment.

Let's go through each of these steps in order to set up this stable environment using namespaces.

Adding multiple hostnames to the local environment

The time-tested way to add alternative names for your local environment is to edit your operating system hosts file – this is `/etc/hosts` on UNIX-inspired systems, such as Linux and macOS, or `C:\Windows\System32\Drivers\etc\hosts` on Windows systems. You must do so as a user with administrative privileges, though. You might add an entry such as `127.0.0.1 shipit-stable.internal.` to your hosts file, following some of the guidance at `https://tools.ietf.org/html/rfc6762#appendix-G` to pick a TLD that is unlikely to cause operational problems.

However, there is an easier way to do this now. You can use a hostname of the `name.A.B.C.D.nip.io` form and it will map to whatever IP address you give, thanks to the free `https://nip.io/` service. This enables the easy creation of `localhost` aliases as we can use `shipit-stable.127.0.0.1.nip.io` and similar names for local development.

Temporarily configuring the Helm Chart for the shipit-stable environment

Edit the `chapter8/shipitclicker/values.yaml` file to switch up the host so that it matches `shipit-stable.127.0.0.1.nip.io`, and bump the chart version. Then, use Helm to deploy the app using the command `helm install shipit-stable shipitclicker/`. You should then be able to see the application in your web browser by going to `http://shipit-stable.127.0.0.1.nip.io/`.

Staged environments – Dev, QA, staging, and production

In the EKS environment, you could also get a pretty good separation of environments just by deploying labeled stacks. You could label the stacks with a prefix or suffix name that indicates what environment they are. With ALB support, each separate service that is exposed to the world will get its own distinct load balancer, whether they are in different namespaces or not.

But there are some cases where you would want to use namespaces. For example, if you host both production and non-production resources in the cluster, you could make it so that the namespaces for the non-production resources use quotes. Refer to `https://kubernetes.io/docs/concepts/policy/resource-quotas/` for more information on quotas.

> **Exercise**
>
> Create a `qa` namespace with `kubectl` and use Helm to deploy ShipIt Clicker to that namespace. Then, set a memory quota on that namespace so that it never uses more than 1 GB of RAM.

For even more advanced practices regarding namespaces, you should consult the best practices documentation at `https://cloud.google.com/blog/products/gcp/kubernetes-best-practices-organizing-with-namespaces`.

Now that we have set up a separate environment that is segregated using namespaces, we have more flexibility in how we might deploy and manage our applications. Next, let's review what we have learned in this chapter.

Summary

In this chapter, we learned all about Kubernetes and options for hosting it in the cloud. We walked through some of the cloud-hosting platforms on the market and then completed a quick overview of the key components of Kubernetes.

Following this, we developed a process for deploying our Docker containers to AWS EKS, using AWS ECR as a Docker container registry. Here, you also got the chance to experiment with Amazon's CloudFormation technology, a platform for developing infrastructure as code.

Next, we studied Helm and Helm Charts and built on the ShipIt Clicker application. This was stood up in AWS with resource limits.

You should now feel comfortable with repeating this process for another project if you wish!

Now that our basic Kubernetes setup is ready to go, what other concerns do we need to address before we can use it for a scalable production project? We have seen how we can use Jenkins for continuous deployment, but it would be tedious to write all the scripts required to get the basic Jenkins system to manage a complex Kubernetes cluster and deploy applications to it reliably.

This chapter has presented a simplified set of Helm Charts that generate Kubernetes configurations that result in a running application, but there are some refinements we must make in order to make the application production-ready, just as we did in previous chapters with Docker Compose.

In the next chapter, we are going to introduce Spinnaker as a cloud-native CI/CD platform that will help us facilitate CI/CD for a Kubernetes for this exact task.

Further reading

These articles may help you get a better handle on some of the essential Kubernetes concepts:

- A gentle illustrated introduction to Kubernetes concepts through this tongue-in-cheek guide: `https://www.cncf.io/the-childrens-illustrated-guide-to-kubernetes/`

- Another Cloud Native Computing Foundation illustrated guide to Kubernetes concepts featuring Phippy: `https://www.cncf.io/phippy-goes-to-the-zoo-book/`

- Why is Kubernetes getting so popular? See this blog article: `https://stackoverflow.blog/2020/05/29/why-kubernetes-getting-so-popular/`

- Many applications require you to use private Docker image registries, whether that is Docker Hub, AWS ECR, or something else. Read this to find out how to integrate registry secrets into your Kubernetes configuration files: `https://kubernetes.io/docs/tasks/configure-pod-container/pull-image-private-registry/`

- While this is targeted at customers of Digital Ocean using their Kubernetes service, it does an excellent job of explaining NGINX Ingress Controllers: `https://www.digitalocean.com/community/tutorials/how-to-set-up-an-nginx-ingress-on-digitalocean-kubernetes-using-helm`

- The user guide for EKS. This is chock full of super-detailed information about running EKS: `https://docs.aws.amazon.com/eks/latest/userguide/what-is-eks.html`

- Deploy the Kubernetes dashboard. This is optional but will give you a nice web user interface to see more information about the cluster: `https://docs.aws.amazon.com/eks/latest/userguide/dashboard-tutorial.html`

- An example of an advanced configuration using Kubernetes namespaces might involve using the Kubernetes **role-based access control** (**RBAC**) system to further restrict how applications in different namespaces interact: `https://kubernetes.io/docs/reference/access-authn-authz/rbac/`

- Learn more about the options for EKS installations, including Terraform, using a hybrid strategy that mixes NGINX and ALB Ingress Controller, and more: `https://medium.com/@dmaas/setting-up-amazon-eks-what-you-must-know-9b9c39627fbc`

9

Cloud-Native Continuous Deployment Using Spinnaker

Deploying Docker containers as cloud-native applications to Kubernetes poses challenges that a specialized container-centric continuous deployment system can solve. Instead of writing custom deployment logic in those scripts that Jenkins runs, as we did when we deployed to a single host, we can use Spinnaker to deploy to Kubernetes. Because Spinnaker works with Jenkins, we can continue to use the Jenkins server that we already set up to build the Docker containers and prepare the Helm Charts for deployment. Using Spinnaker, we will deploy an application using its built-in support for Helm Charts and Kubernetes deployments. We will also explore some of Spinnaker's specialized deployment strategies and see how they apply to Kubernetes-centric environments.

In this chapter, we are going to learn when and why you would use Spinnaker in addition to Jenkins. We will learn how to improve your setup for supporting the deployment and maintenance of Kubernetes applications by learning to configure Spinnaker and integrating it with GitHub, Docker Hub, and Jenkins. We will learn how to deploy an app to Kubernetes using a Spinnaker pipeline and AWS **Elastic Container Registry** (**ECR**), as well as learn a bit about how Spinnaker's support for different deployment and testing strategies may or may not apply when you use it in conjunction with Kubernetes.

We will cover the following topics in this chapter:

- Improving your setup for Kubernetes application maintenance
- Spinnaker – when and why you might need more sophisticated deployments
- Setting up Spinnaker in your AWS EKS cluster with Helm
- Deploying ShipIt Clicker with a simple deployment strategy in Spinnaker
- Learning about Spinnaker's support for different deployment and testing strategies with respect to Kubernetes applications

Let's get started by reviewing the technical requirements for this chapter, and then we will move on to learning about the Spinnaker platform.

Technical requirements

You will need to have a working Kubernetes cluster in the cloud, as set up in the previous chapter. You could reuse that cluster or set up a new one for this chapter using the same method or by using `eksctl`. Please note that the Spinnaker version described in this chapter is not compatible with Kubernetes 1.16 and later; be sure to install this on a Kubernetes 1.15 cluster. You will also need to have a current version of the AWS **Command-Line Interface** (**CLI**), `kubectl`, and `helm` 3.x installed on your local workstation, as described in the previous chapter. The Helm commands in this chapter use the `helm` 3.x syntax. The AWS **Elastic Kubernetes Service** (**EKS**) cluster must have a working **Application Load Balancer** (**ALB**) Ingress Controller setup. We will also use the AWS ECR Docker repository set up in the previous chapter. You will also need to have the Jenkins server that was set up in *Chapter 7, Continuous Deployment with Jenkins*, available as Spinnaker relies on Jenkins for building software artifacts.

Spinnaker requires more resources than might be available on your local workstation, and we will want to connect it to outside services, such as Jenkins and GitHub, in a way that might not work with a local Kubernetes learning environment.

Check out the following video to see the Code in Action:

`https://bit.ly/2DUGumq`

Using the updated ShipIt Clicker v5

We will use the version of ShipIt Clicker in the `chapter9` directory in the following GitHub repository:

`https://github.com/PacktPublishing/Docker-for-Developers/`

This version has some changes from the previous version. It only has one copy of the Helm Charts in `chapter9/shipitclicker`, with several override YAML files for cluster deployment: `values-eks.yaml` and `values-spin.yaml`.

In the previous chapter, we kept multiple directories of redundant template and configuration files, but the only differences in the Helm Charts were the overrides in the `values` file. The copy in this chapter uses a more concise strategy. It turns out that you can use multiple YAML config files that override just the settings that have to change for each deployment or environment. In this chapter, we will transition the container repository for the sample application from Docker Hub to ECR, deploy it once manually, and then switch to deploying ShipIt Clicker using Spinnaker.

Improving your setup for Kubernetes application maintenance

In order to deploy and maintain Spinnaker, we need to be able to talk to the Kubernetes cluster from our local workstation. We also want to be able to use **Secure Sockets Layer** (**SSL**)-protected communications to Kubernetes-hosted resources. Let's take this step by step in order to prepare your local workstation and AWS account for more advanced deployments.

Managing the EKS cluster from your local workstation

In order to make it easier to administer the EKS cluster and work with it, you will want to set up your local workstation to talk to the cluster. In the previous chapter, we set up the AWS CLI with an AWS IAM administrator account and then used it to set up an EKS cluster. We will build on that in this chapter to make sure that we can efficiently manage the cluster and the applications in it from our local workstation.

Follow the instructions here on your local workstation to get `kubectl` and the rest of the Kubernetes utilities talking with your EKS cluster:

`https://aws.amazon.com/premiumsupport/knowledge-center/` `eks-cluster-connection`

The essential parts of the instructions in the preceding link involve executing an `aws cli` command from your local workstation. Issue this command to update `.kube/config` with an entry that will let you connect to the EKS cluster, but replace `EKS-VIVLKQ5X` with the name of your EKS cluster:

```
aws eks --region us-east-2 update-kubeconfig --name EKS-
VIVLKQ5X
```

Then, test whether you can communicate with the cluster:

```
kubectl get nodes
```

If this works, you will see a list of EC2 hosts that comprise your EKS cluster nodes.

Troubleshooting kubectl connection failures

If the preceding `aws eks` command yielded an error message or an access denied message, or it failed to complete, you will need to troubleshoot before proceeding. Follow the steps in the following sections, and also look at the AWS guide for troubleshooting this communication failure:

`https://aws.amazon.com/premiumsupport/knowledge-center/` `eks-cluster-connection/`

Making sure you have the right AWS CLI profile active

If you have multiple AWS CLI profiles, your default user might not match the one expected. You can either explicitly tell the AWS CLI to use a profile with the `--profile` parameter or you can set the `AWS_DEFAULT_PROFILE` variable to force it to use a particular profile, as follows, before issuing the `aws eks` command:

```
export AWS_DEFAULT_PROFILE=my-eks-profile
```

Now that we have set up the AWS CLI with the profile, we must double-check that we can still reach our EKS cluster by checking the CloudFormation template access control list.

Ensuring that your CloudFormation template is configured to allow access

In the previous chapter, when we set up the EKS cluster, we entered our IPv4 address in **Classless Inter-Domain Routing (CIDR)** form and set the CloudFormation parameters so that the EKS public access endpoint was enabled. Ensure that the setting to enable the public access endpoint is still enabled. Also, double-check the EKS public access CIDR setting and make sure it matches your current IPv4 address in CIDR form – for example, `192.2.0.15/32`. Double-check your address with `https://whatismyip.com/` to be sure. If these are not set correctly, update the CloudFormation stack with these values.

The CLI profile must match the IAM user that you used to create the EKS cluster with the AWS Quick Start.

This will configure IAM and EKS appropriately.

Switching between local and cluster contexts

When you have multiple Kubernetes contexts configured, you can switch between them via the `kubectl config get-contexts` and `kubectl config use-context` commands, as follows:

```
$ kubectl config get-contexts
CURRENT
NAME                                                                 CLUS
TER                                                             AUTHINFO
NAMESPACE
*          arn:aws:eks:us-east-2:143970405955:cluster/
EKS-8PWG7608    arn:aws:eks:us-east-2:143970405955:cluster/
EKS-8PWG7608    arn:aws:eks:us-east-2:143970405955:cluster/
EKS-8PWG7608
           docker-
desktop                                                      docker-
desktop                                                      docker-
desktop
$ kubectl config use-context docker-desktop
Switched to context "docker-desktop".
$ kubectl get nodes
NAME            STATUS    ROLES     AGE     VERSION
```

```
docker-desktop    Ready    master    21d    v1.15.5
$ kubectl config use-context arn:aws:eks:us-east-
2:143970405955:cluster/EKS-VIVLKQ5X

Switched to context "arn:aws:eks:us-east-
2:143970405955:cluster/EKS-VIVLKQ5X".

 $ kubectl get nodes
```

NAME	STATUS	ROLES
AGE VERSION		
ip-10-0-31-183.us-east-2.compute.internal	Ready	<none>
2d9h v1.15.10-eks-bac369		
ip-10-0-57-2.us-east-2.compute.internal	Ready	<none>
2d9h v1.15.10-eks-bac369		
ip-10-0-90-115.us-east-2.compute.internal	Ready	<none>
2d9h v1.15.10-eks-bac369		

In the preceding listing, we can see all the contexts we have defined. We can also see that when we use the docker-desktop context, we only see one node, but when we use the EKS context, we see multiple EC2 server nodes. For the rest of the chapter, we are going to target the EKS context for the Kubernetes-related commands.

Verifying that you have a working ALB Ingress Controller

In the previous chapter, we set up an EKS cluster with an ALB Ingress Controller in order to grant the world access to the ShipIt Clicker application. If you are reusing that EKS cluster and the ALB Ingress Controller is working OK, you can skip to the next section.

If you have set up a new cluster, you can either follow the instructions in the last chapter in order to get the ALB Ingress Controller working, or you can run one of the shell scripts included in this chapter as a shortcut if the new cluster lacks an ALB Ingress Controller.

To use the ALB Ingress Controller setup script, make a note of your EKS cluster name, and make sure you have installed both Helm and eksctl.

Then, run the deploy-alb-ingress-controller.sh script from your local workstation to set up the ALB Ingress Controller (replace EKS-8PWG76O8 with the name of your EKS cluster):

```
chapter9/bin/deploy-alb-ingress-controller.sh EKS-8PWG76O8
```

Now that you have the ALB Ingress Controller installed, you can proceed to get a domain managed in AWS and generate an SSL certificate.

Preparing a Route 53 domain and certificate

In order to secure the communications between your EKS cluster and the outside world, we are going to use the following services to manage **Domain Name Server** (**DNS**) entries and server certificates:

- **AWS Route 53**: `https://aws.amazon.com/route53/`
- **AWS Certificate Manager** (**ACM**): `https://aws.amazon.com/certificate-manager/`

In *Chapter 7, Continuous Deployment with Jenkins*, we configured Jenkins to use domain names to map entries for staging and production for ShipIt Clicker. In this chapter, we are going to use Route 53 to manage DNS entries and ACM to manage certificates to help secure communication.

You can either transfer the top-level domain you are using to Route 53, or you can delegate a subdomain of an existing domain you control, such as `eks.example.com`, to Route 53. See this AWS guide on delegating a subdomain to Route 53:

`https://docs.aws.amazon.com/Route53/latest/DeveloperGuide/CreatingNewSubdomain.html`

Once you have delegated the domain to Route 53, verify that you can view the SOA record for that domain (substituting your domain for `eks.example.com`):

```
$ host -t soa eks.example.com
eks.example.com has SOA record ns-1372.awsdns-43.org. awsdns-
hostmaster.amazon.com. 1 7200 900 1209600 86400
```

If this returns an SOA record similar to the preceding log, you are set. If it yields a not found error, you need to troubleshoot more.

Once your domain is resolving OK, go to the ACM console at `https://us-east-2.console.aws.amazon.com/acm/home?region=us-east-2#/` and generate a new public certificate containing both of the domain names – `*.eks.example.com` and `eks.example.com` (replacing `example.com` with your domain). The domain name starting with `*` is known as a wildcard certificate because it matches any domain name that has the same domain suffixes. Using that will allow us to have one certificate covering many domain names.

Use the DNS method of validation. Since you have that domain managed in Route 53, you can expand the domain and hit the shortcut **Create record in Route 53** button, which should look similar to the following:

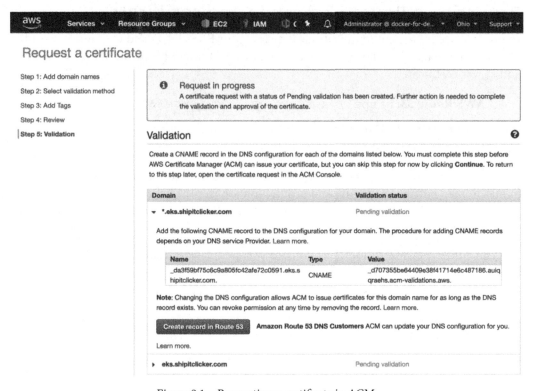

Figure 9.1 – Requesting a certificate in ACM

This will add validation records to your Route 53 zone, which will speed up the issuance of the certificates. The certificate might take from 5 minutes to 1 hour to get issued, unless there is a problem with the DNS validation records, such as the domain not being properly delegated from the name servers that are one level above it. Wait for the certificate to be issued and note the ARN of the certificate – you will need it later.

Building and deploying ShipIt Clicker v5

In order to verify that we have support for SSL-protected sites, we are going to deploy ShipIt Clicker to EKS and enable ALB load balancer support for HTTPS. In order to demonstrate that we can use the AWS ECR container registry, we will also push the container to ECR and use that registry to deploy the application.

Copy `chapter9/values-eks.yaml` to `chapter9/values.yaml`, and then edit the `values.yaml` file, as follows. Start by changing the name of the image at the start of the file and prefix it with the name of your ECR container registry (replace `143970405955` with your AWS account ID and make sure the region – here, `us-east-2` – matches the region you are using):

```
---
image:
  repository: 143970405955.dkr.ecr.us-east-2.amazonaws.com/
dockerfordevelopers/shipitclicker:0.5.0
```

Note that the `values.yaml` file has annotations indicating that the ALB should listen on both port `80` and `443`, and that it has a fully qualified domain name in the `host` setting. Edit the values in the following host entry so that the `shipit-v5.eks.example.com` domain name matches a domain name that would match the wildcard SSL certificate you have in ACM:

```
ingress:
  enabled: true
  annotations:
    kubernetes.io/ingress.class: alb
    alb.ingress.kubernetes.io/scheme: internet-facing
    alb.ingress.kubernetes.io/listen-ports:
'[{"HTTPS":443},{"HTTP":80}]'
    alb.ingress.kubernetes.io/target-type: ip
  hosts:
    - host: "shipit-v5.eks.example.com"
      paths: ['/*']
```

Now that we have prepared the `values.yml` file, we will build the container and push it to EKS.

Change the directory to `Docker-for-Developers/chapter9` and issue these commands to build and deploy the ShipIt Clicker to the cluster to test the ALB integration (replace `143970405955.dkr.ecr.us-east-2.amazonaws.com` with your ECR registry):

```
docker build . -t dockerfordevelopers/shipitclicker:0.5.0
```

```
docker tag dockerfordevelopers/shipitclicker:0.5.0
143970405955.dkr.ecr.us-east-2.amazonaws.com/
dockerfordevelopers/shipitclicker:0.5.0
```

```
aws ecr get-login-password --region us-east-2 | docker login
--username AWS --password-stdin 143970405955.dkr.ecr.us-east-2.
amazonaws.com
```

```
docker push 143970405955.dkr.ecr.us-east-2.amazonaws.com/
dockerfordevelopers/shipitclicker:0.5.0
```

```
helm install shipit-v5 -f values.yaml ./shipitclicker
```

After a few minutes, you should be able to verify that the Ingress Controller is working:

```
$ kubectl get ingress
NAME                        HOST
S                                   ADDRESS
PORTS    AGE
shipit-v5-shipitclicker    shipit-v5.eks.shipitclicker.
com    9bbd6f9c-default-shipitv5s-051a-795288134.us-east-2.elb.
amazonaws.com    80         90m
```

If this does not appear, check the Ingress Controller logs, as follows, for troubleshooting clues:

```
kubectl logs -n kube-system deployment.apps/alb-ingress-
controller
```

Next, we need to create a DNS address-mapping record, also known as an **A record**, to map the address for `shipit-v5.eks.example.com` to the address of the ALB shown in the HOSTS column in the preceding output of `kubectl get ingress`. Go to the Route 53 AWS console for your domain and create a new record of type A for `shipit-v5.eks`. Make this record an alias record and enter the DNS name from the HOSTS column of the ALB listed in the `kubectl get ingress` output. The form to do that should look something like the one in the following screenshot:

Figure 9.2 – Creating an A record as an alias in AWS Route 53

Press the **Create** button to save the record, and then wait 5 minutes for the DNS changes to propagate. Then, go to `https://shipit-v5.eks.example.com/` (replacing `example.com` with your domain name) to verify that you can view it over HTTPS.

Now that you've made sure that you can administer the EKS cluster from your local environment, pushed the demo application's container to ECR, deployed the demo application to Kubernetes using Helm, and configured the HTTPS support to secure an ALB Ingress Controller to reach a service hosted in EKS, you are ready to proceed with a Spinnaker installation.

Spinnaker – when and why you might need more sophisticated deployments

In order to reliably deploy your application, you could write many scripts by hand and use a continuous integration system. However, many people have thought about the problems inherent in deploying applications in Kubernetes. Kubernetes does have significant deployment capabilities, especially when you use the deployment controller. But this approach does not meet everyone's needs. Some people have developed specialized systems that reduce the complexity of handling these tasks. Systems such as Jenkins-X, Weaveworks, CodeFresh, and Spinnaker fit this niche. We are going to examine Spinnaker, a continuous deployment toolset, in more detail (`https://www.spinnaker.io/`).

We will begin by walking through Spinnaker's core concepts and highlighting where it shares terminology with other platforms, such as Kubernetes, including where the meanings are different.

Introduction to Spinnaker

Spinnaker is a **continuous delivery** (**CD**) platform that works across cloud vendors and is open source. Netflix originally wrote Spinnaker to help manage their multi-cloud deployments, using the immutable server pattern (see `https://martinfowler.com/bliki/ImmutableServer.html`). Spinnaker features an image bakery that involves combining application code with an operating system image and supporting libraries, and then saving (baking) an immutable machine image, such as an AWS **Amazon Machine Image** (**AMI**) or VMware **Virtual Machine Disk** (**VMDK**) image, to speed up deployments and minimize runtime configuration. Read more about the image bakery and its use in Spinnaker in the following articles:

- `https://netflixtechblog.com/how-we-build-code-at-netflix-c5d9bd727f15`

- `https://docs.armory.io/spinnaker-install-admin-guides/packer/`

This pattern works well at a scale, but the advent of Docker and container-centric runtimes, such as Kubernetes, provides a different approach to reach the same goals.

Spinnaker has been adapted to work with Kubernetes and Docker, as well as supporting its original deployment strategy of using an image bakery and the immutable server pattern. You can find the source code for the platform among other projects at the official GitHub repository:

`https://github.com/spinnaker`

Before we install the application, we should familiarize ourselves with some of the core concepts of this technology. The first one we will look at is application management.

Application management

We can use the management feature to administer and view our cloud resources. Using Spinnaker, we model our applications around concepts such as server groups and clusters. Refer to the Spinnaker documentation for a complete overview of these concepts:

`https://spinnaker.io/concepts/`

An application is the top-level container, which can be deployed on the infrastructure that Spinnaker maintains, including clusters and server groups. Each cluster then acts as a mechanism to organize server groups. Spinnaker considers Docker containers running in Kubernetes in pods as members of a server group. These Docker images may contain services such as ShipIt Clicker and any associated tools, such as the Datadog monitoring agents featured in *Chapter 15, Scanning, Monitoring, and Using Third-Party Tools.*

Now that we understand how a containerized project is represented in Spinnaker, we should consider how we can deploy it to our EKS cluster in AWS via this framework.

Application deployment

The application deployment piece of the puzzle is represented graphically in the Spinnaker user interface with a pipeline. A pipeline can either be started manually or kicked off automatically as part of a process triggered by other events, such as a source code control-system push. A pipeline tells us all the steps (called **stages**) along the way that need to be completed – for example, to take a Docker container, install it, and make subsequent updates to it in our cloud environment.

The following screenshot demonstrates what a deployment pipeline and its various stages look like:

Figure 9.3 – Spinnaker pipeline

Each of the stages in this pipeline can be thought of as a discrete task. Each task is executed in sequence or in parallel, depending on whether the pipeline forks. As we will see shortly, Spinnaker comes with a number of predefined stages that we can incorporate into our custom pipeline.

It is advantageous to tie the pipeline to your build server and your source code control repository so that when you push changes to your application and its Helm Charts, Spinnaker can package, test, and deploy them appropriately.

Now that we have briefly walked through the two major concepts of Spinnaker, let's get stuck into building out some infrastructure and a pipeline so that we can get a better handle of how the stages work and the types of deployment strategies that are possible.

Setting up Spinnaker in an AWS EKS cluster using Helm

Setting up a production-grade Spinnaker cluster requires some careful planning, but for learning purposes, we are going to use one of the simplified approaches. The complete Spinnaker setup guide can be found at https://www.spinnaker.io/setup/.

In order to demonstrate the proof of concept of using Spinnaker, we are going to use the Helm Chart found at the following link to deploy Spinnaker:

`https://github.com/helm/charts/tree/master/stable/spinnaker`

The Spinnaker Helm Chart warns against production use

Although this Helm Chart states that it is not suitable for production use, we can use it to demonstrate the proof of concept for building, testing, and deploying applications. The Spinnaker setup guide gives guidance for setting up production-grade Spinnaker systems. Most importantly, that includes making the Spinnaker installation separate from the cluster that also hosts the applications that end users consume. We are going to ignore that advice to save time and money in this chapter and make it easier to demonstrate. If you are going to adopt Spinnaker at scale, please take this advice to heart and set up Spinnaker according to their best practices documentation in a separate cluster.

Ensure you are connected to the correct Kubernetes context targeting your EKS cluster, and enter the following command to deploy Spinnaker to its own namespace:

```
$ kubectl create namespace spinnaker
```
```
$ helm install spinnaker stable/spinnaker --namespace spinnaker
--version 1.23.3 --timeout 600s
```

It may take several minutes for the Spinnaker deployment to complete. When it is done, you should see an output similar to the following:

```
NAME: spinnaker
LAST DEPLOYED: Sun May  3 14:33:10 2020
NAMESPACE: spinnaker
STATUS: deployed
REVISION: 1
TEST SUITE: None
NOTES:
1. You will need to create 2 port forwarding tunnels in order to access the Spinnaker UI:
   export DECK_POD=$(kubectl get pods --namespace spinnaker -l "cluster=spin-deck" -o jsonpath="{.items[0].metadata.name}")
   kubectl port-forward --namespace spinnaker $DECK_POD 9000

   export GATE_POD=$(kubectl get pods --namespace spinnaker -l "cluster=spin-gate" -o jsonpath="{.items[0].metadata.name}")
   kubectl port-forward --namespace spinnaker $GATE_POD 8084

2. Visit the Spinnaker UI by opening your browser to: http://127.0.0.1:9000

To customize your Spinnaker installation. Create a shell in your Halyard pod:

   kubectl exec --namespace spinnaker -it spinnaker-spinnaker-halyard-0 bash

For more info on using Halyard to customize your installation, visit:
   https://www.spinnaker.io/reference/halyard/

For more info on the Kubernetes integration for Spinnaker, visit:
   https://www.spinnaker.io/reference/providers/kubernetes-v2/
```

Figure 9.4 – Spinnaker Helm Chart installation

Next, we will connect to the freshly installed Spinnaker system.

Connecting to Spinnaker through the kubectl proxy

To carry out preliminary testing, pay attention to the advice in the output you receive from the `helm install` command you ran to create port forwarding tunnels in the previous section. It should be similar to the output shown in the preceding section. You should set up two separate console windows or tabs on your local workstation, and then run the pairs of commands listed in the output of the `helm install spinnaker` command in the NOTES section to set up the port forwarding tunnels, one per console window or tab. You can then go to `http://127.0.0.1:9000` in your browser to verify that Spinnaker is up and running.

Exposing Spinnaker via ALB Ingress Controllers

The directions for integrating Spinnaker with EKS (`https://www.spinnaker.io/setup/install/providers/kubernetes-v2/aws-eks/`) describe a solution using services with a LoadBalancer annotation to expose the services. However, since we have our ALB Ingress Controller, Route 53, and ACM already configured, it would be better to expose them using the ALB Ingress Controller. Edit the `chapter9/spinnaker-alb-ingress.yaml` file, and make the following changes in the ingress configuration for both `spin-deck` and `spin-gate` (there are two sets of configurations in the file):

- Replace `eks.example.com` with the domain name you have configured with the ACM wildcard certificate.

- Replace `192.2.0.10/32` with your public IP address in CIDR format (the same format you used to lock down the EKS API).

- Replace `192.2.0.200/32` with the public IP address of your Jenkins server.

> **Security notice**
>
> It is important to add the preceding IP address restriction because, out of the box, Spinnaker's user interface runs as the cluster administrator user. If you allowed `0.0.0.0/0` (the entire internet) access, someone could run processes as the cluster administrator and modify or take over your cluster. If you have a dynamic IP address, you might have to change this several times, starting with the CloudFormation template.

Then, apply the config template to create the ALB Ingress Controllers:

```
kubectl apply -n spinnaker -f spinnaker-alb-ingress.yaml
```

After a few seconds, issue the following command to verify that this worked (look for your domain name instead of eks.example.com):

```
$ kubectl get -n spinnaker ingress
NAME           HOSTS                               ADDRESS
PORTS    AGE
spin-deck    spinnaker.eks.example.com             9bbd6f9c-
spinnaker-spindec-5f03-917097792.us-east-2.elb.amazonaws.com
80       10m
spin-gate    spinnaker-gate.eks.example.com        9bbd6f9c-
spinnaker-spingat-712f-2021704484.us-east-2.elb.amazonaws.com
80       10m
```

The DNS names that this lists under the HOSTS column are the names we intend to use to call the services. The DNS addresses under the ADDRESS column are the actual DNS names that the ALB Ingress Controller has created using the AWS ALBs. To connect these two names, we need to create two DNS records in our domain in order to reach the Spinnaker services with the friendlier names. Note the DNS names of the ingress controllers from the ADDRESS column in this listing. Then, go to the AWS Route 53 console for your domain and create two new DNS entries of type A. Make them alias records.

Name the first one spinnaker and give it the value shown in the ADDRESS column for the entry named spin-deck.

Name the second entry spinnaker-gate and give it the value shown in the ADDRESS column for the entry named spin-gate.

The result of this will be two new DNS entries similar to the following (with your domain name instead of example.com):

- spinnaker.eks.example.com
- spinnaker-gate.eks.example.com

While you are waiting for 5 minutes or so for the DNS records to become available and the ALB to be fully activated, use Halyard to configure Spinnaker with the HTTPS version of these URLs.

Configuring Spinnaker using Halyard

Now that we have assigned friendly DNS names to our Spinnaker installation, we need to configure Spinnaker to make it understand that it must respect these names. From your local workstation, connect to the Halyard maintenance pod:

```
kubectl exec --namespace spinnaker -it spinnaker-spinnaker-
halyard-0 bash
```

Once you have connected to the pod, you will see a `spinnaker@spinnaker-spinnaker-halyard-0:/workdir$` prompt. Then, enter these commands, replacing `example.com` with your domain name:

```
$ hal config security api edit --override-base-url https://
spinnaker-gate.eks.example.com  --cors-access-pattern https://
spinnaker.eks.example.com
```
```
$ hal config security ui edit --override-base-url https://
spinnaker.eks.example.com
```
```
$ hal deploy apply
```

The last `hal` command will redeploy the Spinnaker application.

Wait 5 minutes for the DNS records to activate and the ALBs to be fully created. Once this is done, visit the Spinnaker site via its fully qualified domain name, replacing `example.com` with your domain name:

```
http://spinnaker.eks.example.com/
```

You should be redirected to the HTTPS version of the site.

Connecting Spinnaker to Jenkins

In order to get Spinnaker to receive artifacts from Jenkins, we must connect it using a Jenkins administrator API token. Spinnaker has instructions on this that can be found at `https://www.spinnaker.io/setup/ci/jenkins/`.

Go to the Jenkins server you used in a previous chapter. Sign in and go to the user configuration page at a URL similar to `https://jenkins.example.com/user/admin/configure` (substitute your Jenkins URL for `jenkins.example.com`). Then, generate an API token for Spinnaker:

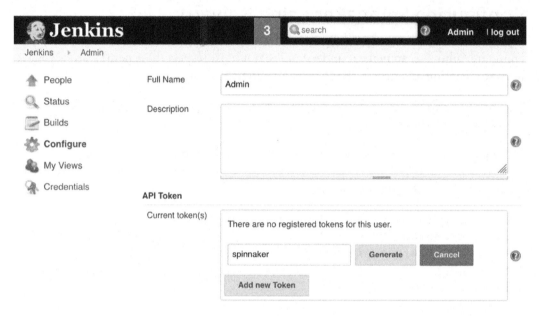

Figure 9.5 – Jenkins API token generation

As shown in the *Configuring Spinnaker using Halyard* section, connect to the `hal` maintenance pod from your local workstation:

```
kubectl exec --namespace spinnaker -it spinnaker-spinnaker-
halyard-0 bash
```

Then, issue these commands in the shell of that pod to configure Jenkins, replacing the values to the right of the equals sign for the BASEURL, APIKEY, and USERNAME values with those for your installation:

```
$ hal config ci jenkins enable
$ BASEURL=https://jenkins.example.com
$ APIKEY=12345678901234567890123456789 0
$ USERNAME=admin
$ echo $APIKEY | hal config ci jenkins \
  master add my-jenkins-master  \
  --address $BASEURL --username $USERNAME --password
$ hal deploy apply
```

Now that Spinnaker is set up to talk to Jenkins, we will move on to configuring Jenkins with an additional set of build jobs that Spinnaker will use.

Setting up Jenkins to integrate with both Spinnaker and ECR

In order to run the Spinnaker-specific jobs and integrate Jenkins with ECR, we are going to need to configure Jenkins with additional plugins and credentials so that it can push containers to AWS ECR, and also set up a new multi-branch pipeline item in order to use the Jenkinsfile for this chapter, stored in the GitHub repository as `chapter9/Jenkinsfile`.

In the following sections, we will make all the changes needed to make Jenkins work with both ECR and Spinnaker.

Installing the AWS ECR Jenkins plugin

Sign in to your Jenkins server as the admin user, and then navigate in the left menu to **Configure | Plugin Manager**. Click on the **Available** tab and type ECR into the **Filter** box. You will see something like this:

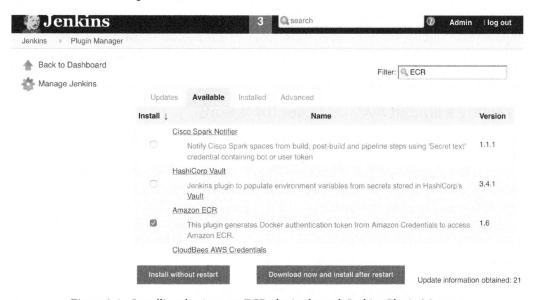

Figure 9.6 – Installing the Amazon ECR plugin through Jenkins Plugin Manager

Click on the **Install** checkbox next to the **Amazon ECR** plugin and select the **Download now and install after restart** button. You will see something as in the following screenshot:

Figure 9.7 – Installation in progress for the Amazon ECR Jenkins plugin

It might take Jenkins 5–15 minutes to restart before it is available again. Once it is available, sign in again as the Jenkins admin user. Next, we will create an AWS IAM user with limited privileges and configure Jenkins with those credentials.

Creating a limited AWS IAM user for Jenkins

In a previous chapter, we used the AWS console to create an administrator IAM user for the account. This time, we will use the AWS CLI in order to create a Jenkins user, with more limited permissions than the administrator user so that it can only manage ECR repositories and push Docker images to those repositories. This is in line with the security principle of granting the *least privilege* access required for a system only. To create the user, attach the appropriate policy, create the access keys, and issue the three `aws iam` commands in the following listing to set up the Jenkins user (the output that you should expect to see is in line with these commands):

```
$ aws iam create-user --user-name Jenkins
{
    "User": {
        "Path": "/",
```

```
            "UserName": "Jenkins",
            "UserId": "AIDASDBKOBZBU6ZX6SQ7U",
            "Arn": "arn:aws:iam::143970405955:user/Jenkins",
            "CreateDate": "2020-05-03T02:45:34Z"
        }
}
$ aws iam attach-user-policy --user-name Jenkins --policy-arn
arn:aws:iam::aws:policy/AmazonEC2ContainerRegistryPowerUser
$ aws iam create-access-key --user-name Jenkins
{
    "AccessKey": {
            "UserName": "Jenkins",
            "AccessKeyId": "AKIASDBKOBZBYFDCBLMR",
            "Status": "Active",
            "SecretAccessKey": "q+1z7wt/
FsbYOv5Yy7HRUSZI0OsLbANV7a8nIQDy",
            "CreateDate": "2020-05-03T02:46:00Z"
        }
}
```

Note the values associated with `AccessKeyId` and `SecretAccessKey` in the output of your commands. You will need those to configure a Jenkins credential for AWS access in the next section. Next, let's configure Jenkins with AWS credentials.

Configuring Jenkins with credentials for AWS and ECR

We need to tell Jenkins what our AWS credentials are so that it can push the Docker containers it builds to ECR. Furthermore, we also need to configure Jenkins to know what ECR registry to use. In *Chapter 6, Deploying Applications with Docker Compose*, we configured Jenkins with credentials for GitHub and Docker Hub. Now, we will configure additional credentials for the AWS IAM user and the ECR container registry.

While you are signed into the Jenkins server with the admin user, go to its home page and then navigate in the left menu to the **Credentials | System | Global credentials (unrestricted)** screen. Then, add a credential of the **AWS Credentials** type with the `shipit.aws.key` ID, the `ShipIt Clicker AWS API Keys` description, and the access key ID and secret access key from the previous section. You should see a credential form that looks like this:

Figure 9.8 – Configuring AWS credentials in Jenkins

Once you have done this, add an additional credential of the **Secret text** type with the following fields, but replace the values in the **Secret** field with the value of the ECR container host from the URL you used earlier this chapter when deploying ShipIt Clicker, omitting the `dockerfordevelopers/shipitclicker:0.5.0` reference at the end:

- **Scope**: **Global**
- **Secret**: `143970405955.dkr.ecr.us-east-2.amazonaws.com`
- **ID**: `shipit.ecr.container.id`
- **Description**: `ShipIt Clicker ECR container ID`

Save this credential by pressing the **OK** button.

Now that we have configured Jenkins with the credentials needed to connect to AWS and ECR, let's configure a new multi-branch pipeline for the code in this chapter.

Configuring Jenkins with a multi-branch pipeline for the Jenkinsfile

Next, we will configure Jenkins to use an additional multi-branch pipeline item that pulls from the same GitHub repository but is configured to use `chapter9/Jenkinsfile` instead of the Jenkinsfile at the root of the repository. Sign in to Jenkins, and from the home page, navigate to **New Item**. Create a new multi-branch pipeline item, name it `Spinnaker`, and then configure it with your GitHub repo credentials, similar to what is included in the following screenshot (replace `PacktPublishing/Docker-for-Developers`with the GitHub organization and name of the forked copy of the repository that you set up in *Chapter 7, Continuous Deployment with Jenkins*):

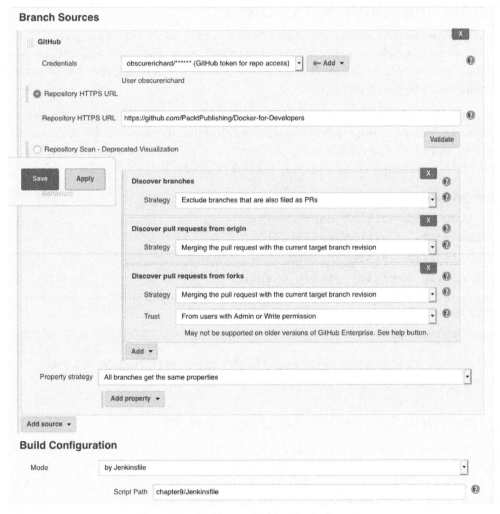

Figure 9.9 – Jenkins multi-branch pipeline setup

After you configure this, the new item should connect to the GitHub repository and build and push a container to AWS ECR. Inspect the console output from the master branch in this new item to make sure the build succeeds and that the Docker image gets pushed to the AWS ECR repository.

Now that you have configured Jenkins with the ECR plugin, created a Jenkins IAM user, configured Jenkins with the credentials for that user, configured Jenkins with new credentials to reflect the AWS integration, and added the new Jenkins multi-branch setup, you can proceed to connect other services to Spinnaker. Next, we will connect GitHub.

Connecting Spinnaker to GitHub

We will follow the guidance from `https://www.spinnaker.io/setup/artifacts/github/` to connect Spinnaker to Jenkins so that it can read artifacts from GitHub. Go to your GitHub user account and, in **Developer Settings**, generate an access token for Spinnaker with repo scope.

From your local workstation, connect to the Halyard maintenance pod, as shown in the *Configuring Spinnaker using Halyard* section, put the GitHub token in a file in the home directory, and then issue the following commands (replacing xxxx with your GitHub token and `my-github-user` with your GitHub username):

```
TOKEN=xxxx
GH_ACCOUNT=my-github-user
TOKEN_FILE=~/.github-token.txt
echo "$TOKEN" > $TOKEN_FILE
hal config artifact github enable
hal config artifact github account add $GH_ACCOUNT --token-file
$TOKEN_FILE
hal deploy apply
```

Once you have done this, Spinnaker should be able to talk to GitHub. Next, we will connect Spinnaker to Docker Hub.

Connecting Spinnaker to Docker Hub

You will also need to connect Spinnaker to Docker Hub so that it can read your repository and the `library/redis` repository. Integrating Spinnaker with Docker Hub requires you to whitelist all the repositories that your templates will use. The default Docker Hub integration has a short whitelist of the most common libraries.

We will follow the guidance from `https://www.spinnaker.io/setup/install/providers/docker-registry/` in order to add Docker Hub to Spinnaker.

Log in to your Docker Hub account and generate a new API token for the Spinnaker installation from `https://hub.docker.com/settings/security`.

From your local workstation, connect to the Halyard maintenance pod:

```
kubectl exec --namespace spinnaker -it spinnaker-spinnaker-
halyard-0 bash
```

Then, issue the following commands (replacing xxxx with your Docker Hub token and `my-dockerhub-user` with your Docker Hub username):

```
$ ADDRESS=index.docker.io
$ REPOSITORIES="library/redis dockerhub-user/shipitclicker"
$ USERNAME=dockerhub-user
$ PASSWORD=xxxx
$ REPOSITORIES="library/redis dockerhub-user/shipitclicker"
$ echo $PASSWORD | hal config provider docker-registry \
    account add my-docker-registry \
    --address $ADDRESS \
    --repositories $REPOSITORIES \
    --username $USERNAME \
    --password
$ hal deploy apply
```

Once Docker Hub is connected, you are ready to start setting up an application and pipeline in Spinnaker. But before we do that, let's talk about how to troubleshoot Spinnaker issues.

Troubleshooting Spinnaker issues

If you have any difficulties getting a Spinnaker pipeline execution to work, or have other issues setting up and configuring Spinnaker, the user interface has minimal error-reporting capabilities. It can seem opaque and daunting.

For example, let's imagine you have a typo in one of your artifact definitions – for example, `gitgub.com` instead of `github.com`. The pipeline might fail when it tries to retrieve that artifact due to a hostname failure lookup.

Rather than trying to figure out which of the Spinnaker pods might have recorded an error, you can just tail all the logs of all the Spinnaker pods at once:

```
kubectl logs -n spinnaker -f -l app=spin --all-containers
--max-log-requests 10
```

If you search your console output for the word exception, you may find a clue, such as this one found when troubleshooting Spinnaker:

```
com.netflix.spinnaker.clouddriver.artifacts.exceptions.
FailedDownloadException: Unable to determine the download
URL of artifact Artifact(type=github/file, customKind=false,
name=chapter9/helm.tar.gz, version=staging, location=null,
reference=https://api.gitgub.com/repos/PacktPublishing/
Docker-for-Developers/contents/chapter9/helm.tar.
gz, metadata={id=8ebb0ad7-2d14-4882-9b77-fde3a03e3c45},
artifactAccount=obscurerichard, provenance=null, uuid=null):
api.gitgub.com: Try again
```

Analyzing log files like this can really get you out of a jam. Next up, we will deploy ShipIt Clicker with Spinnaker.

Deploying ShipIt Clicker with a simple deployment strategy in Spinnaker

Let's get our hands dirty with Spinnaker by deploying our ShipIt Clicker application. For this, we will be using Helm Charts, and we will use the version of the application in the chapter9 directory.

> **Spinnaker requires Helm archive files to operate**
>
> In order to simplify the deployment of the Helm Charts, we have created an archive of the chapter9/shipitclicker Helm Chart directory in chapter9/helm.tar.gz, as Spinnaker expects an archive in this format as one of its inputs. We could instead output this archive to an AWS S3 object, or even as a GitHub release artifact, but that is beyond the scope of this chapter. If you change the Helm Charts in the chapter9/shipitclicker directory, be sure to update the helm.tar.gz archive and commit and push it before building with Spinnaker.

Adding a Spinnaker application

Go to your Spinnaker installation in the web browser at `https://spinnaker.eks.example.com` (replacing `example.com` with your domain). Add an application called `shipandspin`, then, in **Repo Project**, insert your GitHub username, and in **Repo Name**, insert the name of the repo where you have forked the `Docker-for-Developers` code:

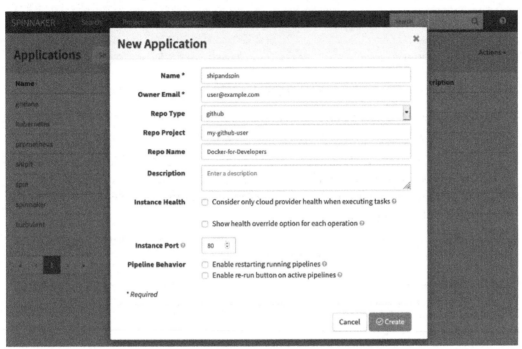

Figure 9.10 – The New Application dialog in Spinnaker

When you submit this form, it will take you to an infrastructure definition form. Stop here, and do not fill in or submit the infrastructure definition form. This form is intended for other types of Spinnaker deployments, not for Kubernetes-centric deployments. When you deploy your application, it will define infrastructure in Kubernetes that Spinnaker understands.

Adding a Spinnaker pipeline

Navigate to the **PIPELINES** screen:

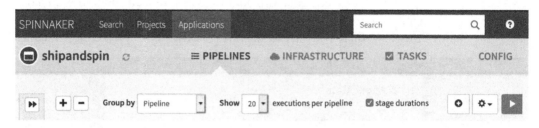

Figure 9.11 – A PIPELINES screen example in Spinnaker

Create a pipeline called `shipit-eks-staging`, and then add two artifacts – one for the Helm Chart and one for a `values-spin.yaml` override.

For the first one, pick the GitHub account, give it the `chapter9/helm.tar.gz` Helm artifact, and click **Use Default Artifact**. Then, give it the full URL of the artifact from the API, changing this to match your account and repository name (double-check that this is correct before submitting):

```
https://api.github.com/repos/PacktPublishing/Docker-for-
Developers/contents/chapter9/helm.tar.gz
```

Tell it to use the `staging` branch. It will look something like this when you have defined it:

Match against⊘	🗑Remove artifact
Account	○ obscurerichard ▼
File path ⊘	chapter9/helm.tar.gz
Display name	helm.tar.gz
If missing ⊘	
Use Prior Execution ☐	
Use Default Artifact ☑	
Default artifact⊘	
Account	○ obscurerichard ▼
Content URL ⊘	https://api.github.com/repos/PacktPublishing/Docker-for-Developer
Commit/Branch ⊘	staging

Figure 9.12 – Overriding the artifact: Helm Chart archive in Spinnaker

Give it another artifact for the `chapter9/values-spin.yaml` override file. Set the `chapter9/values-spin.yaml` file path and the `values-spin.yaml` display name, select **Use Default Artifact**, and then set `https://api.github.com/repos/PacktPublishing/Docker-for-Developers/contents/chapter9/values-spin.yaml` for **Content URL** and `staging` for the branch (replace`PacktPublishing/Docker-for-Developers`with the GitHub organization and name of the forked copy of the repository that you set up in *Chapter 7, Continuous Deployment with Jenkins*):

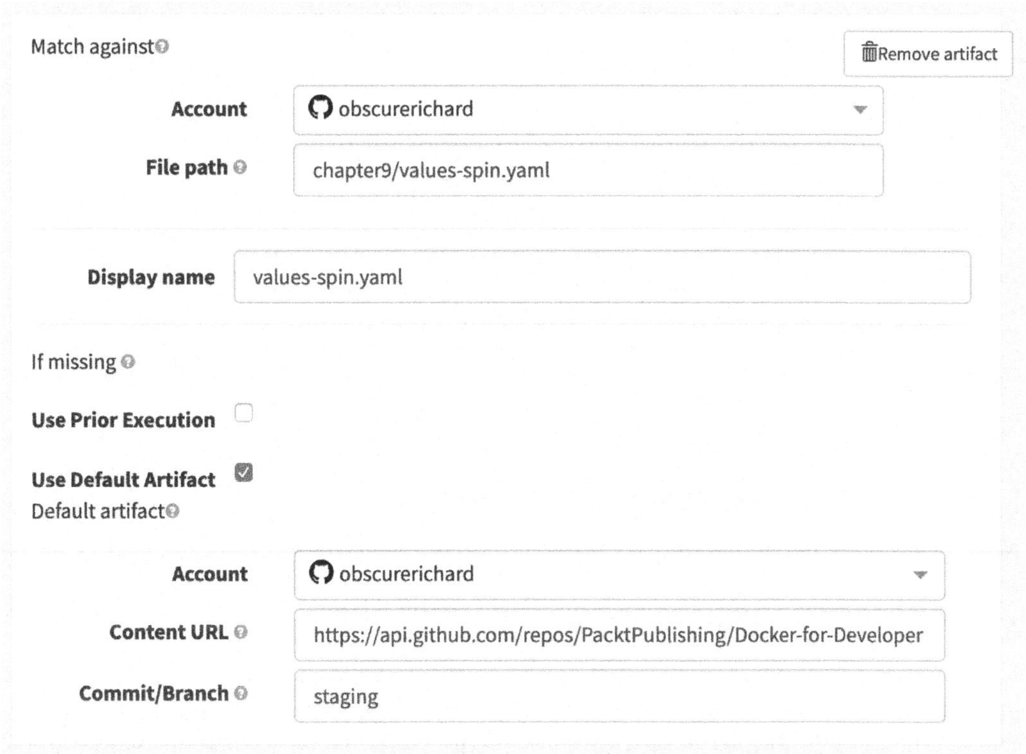

Match against	🗑Remove artifact
Account	◯ obscurerichard ▾
File path	chapter9/values-spin.yaml
Display name	values-spin.yaml
If missing	
Use Prior Execution	☐
Use Default Artifact	☑
Default artifact	
Account	◯ obscurerichard ▾
Content URL	https://api.github.com/repos/PacktPublishing/Docker-for-Developer
Commit/Branch	staging

Figure 9.13 – Overriding the artifact: Helm Chart archive in Spinnaker

Then, configure **Automated Triggers** to get triggers from your GitHub installation, as follows. Pick the job marked **job/staging**, which pulls from the branch that you learned to force push in a previous chapter. Be sure to also specify `build.properties` for **Property File**, which is a Jenkins archived file that this will use to get the version of the container that Jenkins built:

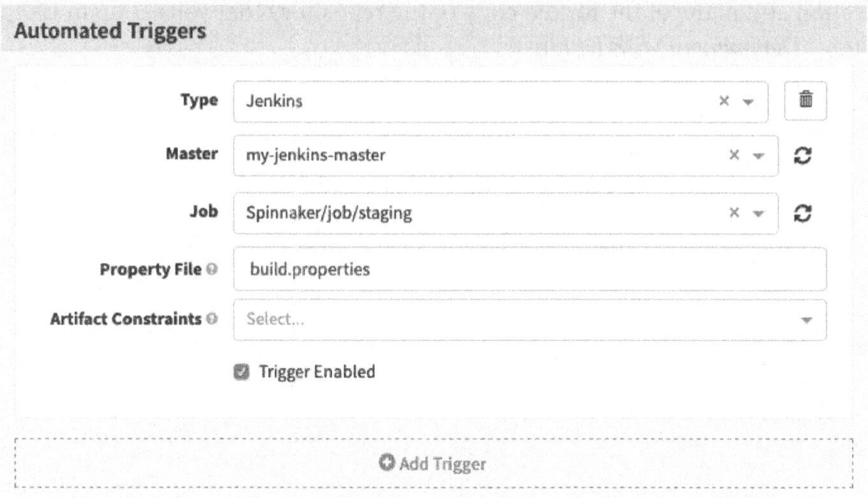

Figure 9.14 – The Jenkins Automated Triggers screen in Spinnaker

Go to the bottom of the form and save the **Configuration** stage.

Now, let's add the next stage, which creates the Kubernetes manifest from the Helm Charts.

Adding the Bake (Manifest) stage

After you have saved the configuration stage, you will still be at the bottom of the very long stage-definition web form. Go back to the top of the form and add an additional stage of the **Bake (Manifest)** type. Configure it with the `shipit-staging` name and tell it to deploy to the default namespace. Give it a **Template Artifact** setting of **helm.tar.gz**.

For **Overrides**, set **values-spin.yaml**. Add an override key-value pair with the `image.repository` name and the `${trigger["properties"]["imageName"]}` value. Add an override key-value pair with the `ingress.hosts[0].host` name and the `shipit-stage.eks.example.com` value, replacing `example.com` with your domain name.

We will set up a Route 53 DNS entry for the Ingress Controller that this creates as soon as it is deployed. The form should look something like the following:

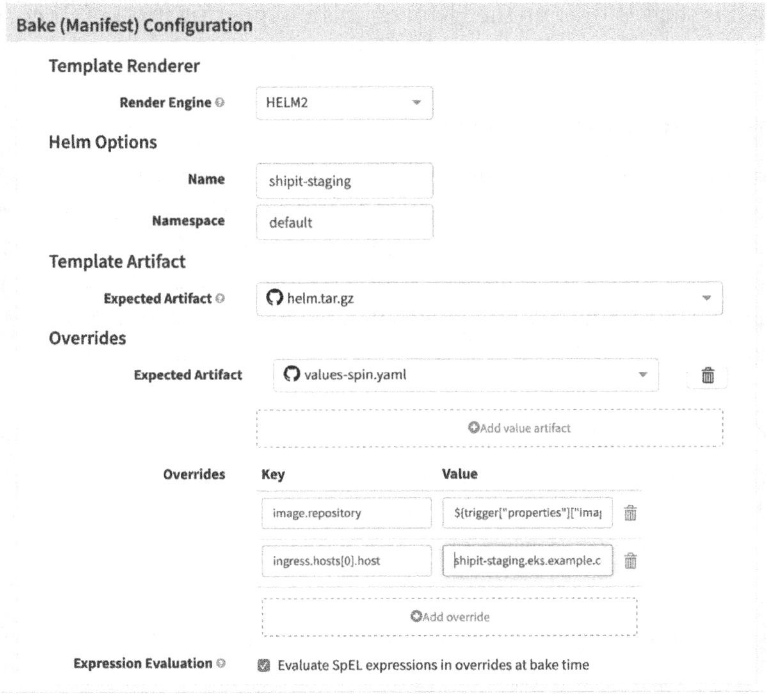

Figure 9.15 – The Bake (Manifest) template renderer configuration screen in Spinnaker

Then, at the bottom of the form, in the **Produces Artifacts** section, pick a **Base64** kind of artifact. Give it a name and display name of `kube-templates.yaml` and save the form. It should look something like this:

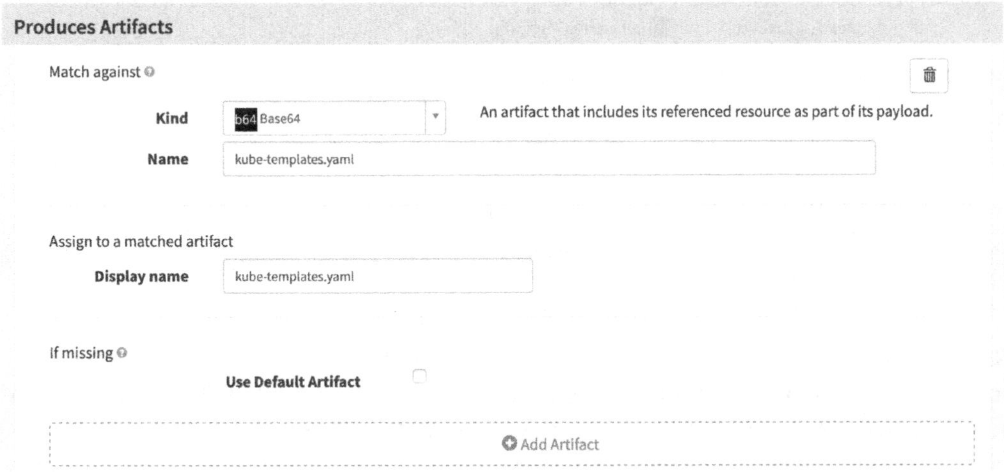

Figure 9.16 – The Bake (Manifest) Produces Artifacts section in Spinnaker

Configuring this stage will set up the Helm template-rendering process. Then, save the form. Next, we will set up the **Deploy (Manifest)** stage.

Adding the Deploy (Manifest) stage

After you have saved the previous configuration change, go to the top of the configuration form again and add another stage, **Deploy (Manifest)**. Pick the **default** account and tell it to override the namespace to deploy to the **default** namespace. Select `kube-templates.yaml` for **Manifest Artifact** to deploy. Do not select the **Rollout Strategy Options** setting, as this only works if you have one ReplicaSet and forego using **Deployments** as a Kubernetes controller. It will look something like this:

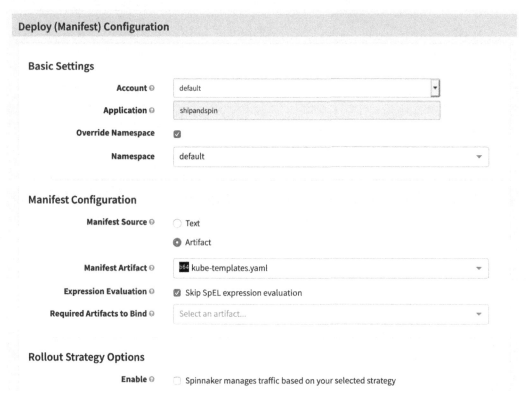

Figure 9.17 – Deploy (Manifest) Configuration in Spinnaker

Now, we are ready to trigger a deployment. Click on **PIPELINES** at the top of the screen and click on the **Start Manual Execution** link. It should reach out to GitHub for the latest build, and then bake the manifest using Helm Charts and deploy.

Because we used Jenkins to emit a `build.properties` file and used a **Spring Expression Language** (**SPEL**) expression to override the `image.repository` field in the template, we will be using the specific container that the Jenkins job connected to the trigger built. Refer to the following link for more information on SPEL expressions and Spinnaker pipelines:

`https://www.spinnaker.io/guides/user/pipeline/expressions/`

There might be some issues that you need to troubleshoot, particularly if you have made a typo in some of the required configurations. If all goes well, it should look something like this:

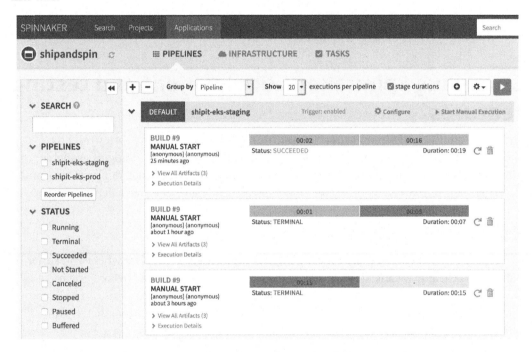

Figure 9.18 – Pipelines showing a completed job in Spinnaker

You can then explore the **Execution Details** and **INFRASTRUCTURE** panes, as Spinnaker will show you some information about the running application. It can even show you the logs from your running pods.

Setting up a DNS entry for the Ingress Controller

To see the running application from the outside, you will need to set up a DNS entry. Issue the `kubectl get ingress` command to determine the DNS alias of the Ingress Controller for `shipit-eks-staging`, and then set up the DNS alias in Route 53 for your domain to match the override you set up for `shipit-stage.eks.example.com` (replacing `example.com` with your domain).

You should be able to visit `https://shipit-stage.eks.example.com/` (replacing `example.com` with your domain) once this is complete and see the running ShipIt Clicker game.

Next up, we will learn about Spinnaker's support for different types of deployments and how they apply (or don't apply) to Kubernetes deployments.

Surveying Spinnaker's deployment and testing features

In the introduction to Spinnaker earlier in this chapter, we noted that you would have the opportunity to learn more about the various deployment methodologies available to you. Let's now dig into these concepts, including canary and red/black deployments, and describe their relevance to Spinnaker when used to manage Kubernetes deployments.

Canary deployments

Canary deployment is a method of exposing an application to its users where you run a subset of the traffic for the application through a new deployment while keeping most of the traffic for the application going to the currently deployed version. This can help you test whether the new version is suitable for production use without immediately funneling all the traffic through.

> **The Kubernetes v2 Spinnaker provider does not support canary deployments**
>
> Although this is one of Spinnaker's most desired features, the Kubernetes v2 cloud provider does not support canary deployments, so we won't use it for ShipIt Clicker. If we were using a non-Kubernetes cloud provider, such as the AWS, Google Compute Engine, or an Azure provider, this would be a more natural pattern to use. See `https://spinnaker.io/setup/install/providers/` for the full list of Spinnaker cloud providers.

Red/black deployments

Let's now look at how the red/black deployment methodologies work. This is another name for the better-known blue/green deployment strategy. With a red/black strategy, you keep two sets of servers or containers available during a deployment, with traffic flowing to only one at a time. Let's say red is taking traffic when the deployment begins. During the deployment, you would deploy to black. Once the health checks pass, you switch traffic to black, but keep red around so that if anything goes wrong, you can switch traffic back to red without having to redeploy.

Spinnaker announced support for red/black deployments through the Kubernetes v2 provider in 2019:

```
https://blog.spinnaker.io/introducing-rollout-strategies-in-
the-kubernetes-v2-provider-8bbffea109a
```

However, this has some significant limitations. It means you can't use the Kubernetes deployment objects and must instead use the lower-level ReplicaSet annotations. The Helm Chart generator produces a skeleton with a deployment in it that sits atop ReplicaSets, so if you want to use the Spinnaker red/black support with Kubernetes, you will have to alter your Helm Charts significantly. Refer to this advice on the Kubernetes v2 provider:

```
https://www.spinnaker.io/guides/user/kubernetes-v2/traffic-
management/#you-must-use-replica-sets
```

What Spinnaker *does* support for Kubernetes deployments that only use ReplicaSets are the following deployment strategies:

- **Dark**: Deploy to a new ReplicaSet that is not connected to the live load balancer.
- **Red/black**: Deploy a new ReplicaSet and switch back and forth between the new and old sets using Spinnaker.
- **Highlander**: Deploy a new ReplicaSet and destroy the old one as soon as the new one starts taking traffic (there can be only one ReplicaSet).

If you are using the Kubernetes deployment controller, the behavior you will get is very similar to the Spinnaker Highlander strategy. So, you may not need to use the Spinnaker support for advanced deployment strategies if you are using Kubernetes.

Rolling back

So, what happens if a deployment fails? Well, we will need to roll back to our previous release in a safe fashion. For the style of deployment where Spinnaker manages deploying machine images, it orchestrates this rollback. However, with the Kubernetes operator, it relies on the Kubernetes deployment mechanisms that use liveness and readiness probes in order to check that a deployment is valid.

Spinnaker does have some support for undoing a rollout of a set of templates directly through its interface. However, this may not work if all the resources in the templates do not have independent revisions, such as separately versioned and tagged Docker containers. See here for more information about rollbacks with Spinnaker and Kubernetes:

```
https://www.spinnaker.io/guides/user/kubernetes-v2/automated-
rollbacks/
```

Testing with Spinnaker

With Spinnaker, you can either use a manual judgement stage to provide time for people to do a manual test on an application or you can use a scripted pipeline stage to run an automated test suite in Jenkins versus your application. If you are deploying to multiple environments or using the red/black strategies, this can give you a better opportunity to execute tests versus your application before deploying it to production or exposing it to the world.

You can find more information on testing using either one of these strategies in their respective Spinnaker documentation at `https://www.spinnaker.io/guides/tutorials/codelabs/safe-deployments/` and `https://www.spinnaker.io/setup/features/script-stage/`.

Summary

In this chapter, we explored the topic of continuous deployment in AWS using the Spinnaker framework. We started by configuring Spinnaker to work with Jenkins, GitHub, AWS ECR, and Docker Hub. Then, we used it to deploy the ShipIt Clicker application to Kubernetes on EKS, securing both Spinnaker and the ShipIt Clicker application with SSL.

Following this, we learned about some advanced deployment strategies that Spinnaker offers, and what some of the trade-offs are that you would have to make when configuring your Kubernetes-driven Docker application to take advantage of them. We also learned how you can trigger the execution of tests (manual or automated) via Spinnaker. By using the lessons learned in this chapter in practice, you can construct continuous deployment systems that use a combination of simple Jenkins build jobs and Spinnaker pipelines to deploy Docker applications to Kubernetes. The skills you have acquired related to integrating Spinnaker with Kubernetes are also applicable to integrating other software packages with Kubernetes.

In the next chapter, we will explore monitoring our Docker containers with Prometheus, Grafana, and Jaeger.

Further reading

Use the following resources to expand your knowledge of Spinnaker and EKS:

- Spinnaker is not a build server, and other misconceptions: `https://www.armory.io/blog/spinnaker-is-not-a-build-server-and-other-misconceptions/`

- An AWS blog post describing a full installation of Kubernetes and Spinnaker with Jenkins and ECR: `https://aws.amazon.com/blogs/opensource/deployment-pipeline-spinnaker-kubernetes/`

- A good article on how Kubernetes services are exposed to the world: `https://medium.com/google-cloud/kubernetes-nodeport-vs-loadbalancer-vs-ingress-when-should-i-use-what-922f010849e0`

- The AWS official documentation on the ALB Ingress Controller: `https://docs.aws.amazon.com/eks/latest/userguide/alb-ingress.html`

- The Spinnaker CLI: `https://www.spinnaker.io/guides/spin/`

- A Kubernetes external DNS provider that you can use to annotate your templates to avoid having to manually set up DNS aliases: `https://github.com/kubernetes-sigs/external-dns`

Spinnaker is not the only advanced Kubernetes-aware CD system you should be aware of; you might consider these other alternatives as well, and carry out fresh research on this topic as this landscape is changing rapidly:

- Jenkins-X – an opinionated Kubernetes-focused CI/CD system: `https://jenkins-x.io/`

- Argo Project – workflows, CD, and more. A CNCF project at the incubating stage as of July 2020: `https://argoproj.github.io/`

- WeaveWorks – a GitOps system for CD using Kubernetes: `https://www.weave.works/technologies/ci-cd-for-kubernetes/`

10
Monitoring Docker Using Prometheus, Grafana, and Jaeger

In order to understand how an application behaves when it runs in production, developers and system operators rely on logging, monitoring, and alerting systems. These systems can both give insight into whether an application and its environment are operating normally and provide clues to follow if troubleshooting is needed. As systems become more complex, the need for deeper insights into both applications and their support software also grows. Systems that allow for deep inspection of all these concerns without having to alter the code that runs on the system can be said to have good **observability** characteristics.

In this chapter, you will learn how to instrument your application and its runtime environment to improve the observability of the entire system. You will learn about many aspects of logging, monitoring, and alerting. Specifically, you will learn how to view, query, and store logs from the Kubernetes cluster both within the cluster and in CloudWatch and Amazon **Simple Storage Service (S3)**. You will learn how to implement liveness and readiness probes specific to the needs of a cloud-native application, get alerts when something goes wrong, and capture application metrics with Prometheus. You will learn how to visualize performance and availability metrics using Grafana. Finally, we will dive deep into the application-specific metrics at the code and database layer using Jaeger.

We will cover the following topics in this chapter:

- Docker logging and container runtime logging
- Use liveness and readiness probes in Kubernetes
- Gathering metrics and sending alerts with Prometheus
- Visualizing operational data with Grafana
- Application performance monitoring with Jaeger

Next up, let's make sure that you are ready to test out these systems and learn how to use them in concert to achieve observability for your system.

Technical requirements

This chapter focuses on the integration of Kubernetes with some AWS services, including CloudWatch, Kinesis, and S3, so you must have a working AWS account with administrator privileges. You will need to have a working Kubernetes cluster in AWS, as set up in a previous chapter with AWS **Elastic Kubernetes Service (EKS)**. You could reuse that cluster or set up a new one for this chapter using either the AWS EKS Quick Start CloudFormation templates or `eksctl`.

You will also need to have a current version of the AWS CLI, `kubectl`, and `helm 3.x` installed on your local workstation, as described in the previous chapter. The `helm` commands in this chapter use the `helm 3.x` syntax. The EKS cluster must have a working ALB Ingress Controller setup.

You could use Spinnaker and Jenkins, as set up in previous chapters, to deploy the applications in this chapter, but it is not required.

Check out the following video to see the Code in Action:

`https://bit.ly/3iIqgvM`

Setting up a demo application – ShipIt Clicker v7

In order to have a sample application to instrument and monitor, we will use the version of ShipIt Clicker in the `chapter10` directory in the following GitHub repository:

`https://github.com/PacktPublishing/Docker-for-Developers/`

This version of the application has some important production-readiness updates in contrast to the version in the previous chapter. Instead of being tightly coupled with a specific Redis installation, this version uses a Redis server installed separately. We will need to deploy the Redis cluster onto Kubernetes before installing the latest version of ShipIt Clicker.

To prepare our Kubernetes environments, both in the local learning environment and the AWS cloud EKS cluster, we will first need to install Redis using Helm.

Installing Redis from the Bitnami Helm repository

In order to deploy this version, we are going to have to deploy the Redis server independently of the ShipIt Clicker pod. This represents a more realistic scenario than the one where the ShipIt Clicker Kubernetes pod had both the Redis server and the stateless application container running in it.

We are going to use the version of Redis maintained by Bitnami (`https://bitnami.com/`), which offers separate reader and writer endpoints. Deploy Redis first through Helm, both to your local Kubernetes installation and then to your cloud Kubernetes installation (replace `docker-desktop` and the AWS ARN with the context IDs for your installation when you run the following commands):

```
$ helm repo add bitnami https://charts.bitnami.com/bitnami
$ kubectl config use-context docker-desktop
$ helm install redis bitnami/redis
$ kubectl config use-context arn:aws:eks:us-east-2:143970405955:cluster/EKS-8PWG76O8
$ helm install redis bitnami/redis
```

This will deploy a Redis cluster with one node that accepts read and write, and multiple nodes that are replicas that are read-only. The version of ShipIt Clicker in this chapter has been adapted to use this external Redis service, which uses a Kubernetes secret to store a password needed for authentication.

> **Offensive terms – master and slave considered harmful**
>
> The Bitnami Redis template, and Redis itself, use *master* and *slave* terminology
> to describe the roles of nodes in a distributed system. Please know that
> while these terms are common in information technology, many people find
> this terminology backward and offensive. Other terms, such as primary/
> secondary or reader/writer, convey the same information without the negative
> connotations. See this article for more on this controversial issue:
>
> ```
> https://medium.com/@zookkini/masters-and-slaves-
> in-the-tech-world-132ef1c87504
> ```

Next, let's build and install ShipIt Clicker into our learning environment.

Installing the latest version of ShipIt Clicker locally

Next, we will build the ShipIt Clicker Docker container, tag it, and push it to Docker Hub,
as we did in previous chapters. Issue these commands, replacing `dockerfordevelopers`
with your Docker Hub username:

```
$ docker build . -t dockerfordevelopers/shipitclicker:0.10.0
$ docker push dockerfordevelopers/shipitclicker:0.10.0
$ kubectl config use-context docker-desktop
$ helm install --set image.repository=dockerfordevelopers/
shipitclicker:0.10.0 shipit-v7 shipitclicker
```

Inspect the running pods and services using `kubectl get all` to verify that the pod is
running, note its name, then inspect the logs with `kubectl logs` to see the startup logs.
There should be no errors in the log.

Next, let's install this version on EKS.

Installing the latest version of ShipIt Clicker on EKS through ECR

Now that you have built the Docker containers and installed this locally, install it to
AWS EKS via **Elastic Container Registry (ECR)**. Edit `values.yaml` to give this a
hostname in the Route 53 zone, such as `shipit-v7.eks.example.com` (replace the
ECR reference with the one corresponding to your AWS account and region, and replace
`example.com` with your domain name):

```
$ docker tag dockerfordevelopers/shipitclicker:0.10.0
143970405955.dkr.ecr.us-east-2.amazonaws.com/
dockerfordevelopers/shipitclicker:0.10.0
$ aws ecr get-login-password --region us-east-2 | docker login
--username AWS --password-stdin 143970405955.dkr.ecr.us-east-2.
```

```
amazonaws.com
$ docker push 143970405955.dkr.ecr.us-east-2.amazonaws.com/
dockerfordevelopers/shipitclicker:0.10.0
$ kubectl config use-context arn:aws:eks:us-east-
2:143970405955:cluster/EKS-8PWG76O8
$ kubectl config use-context arn:aws:eks:us-east-
2:143970405955:cluster/EKS-8PWG76O8
$ helm install shipit-v7 -f values.yaml --set image.
repository=143970405955.dkr.ecr.us-east-2.amazonaws.com/
dockerfordevelopers/shipitclicker:0.10.0 ./shipitclicker
```

Inspect the Kubernetes logs to make sure the application has deployed cleanly to
the cluster:

```
kubectl logs services/shipit-v7-shipitclicker
```

If all is well with the deployment, get the AWS ALB Ingress Controller ingress address,
as described in the previous chapter, and create DNS entries in the Route 53 console
for the deployed application with the ALB address. You should then be able to reach
your application at a URL similar to `https://shipit-v7.eks.example.com/`
(replace `example.com` with your domain name).

Configuring Jenkins and Spinnaker for this chapter

You might wonder whether you can use the same Jenkins and Spinnaker configuration
you set up previously for this chapter. You can, by making a few simple configuration
changes to the Jenkins job in the `Spinnaker` multi-branch pipeline item and the
Spinnaker pipeline definitions. Start by fixing up Jenkins. Edit the configuration of
the job and change the **Build Configuration | Script Path** item so that it references
`chapter10/Jenkinsfile`, and then hit the **Save** button:

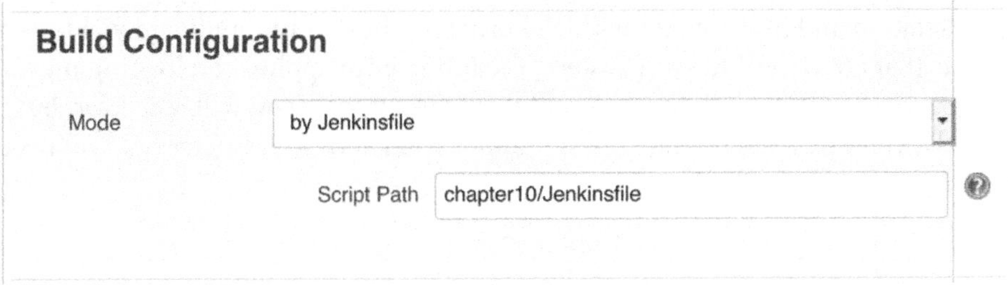

Figure 10.1 – The Jenkins Build Configuration setting for the Spinnaker multi-branch pipeline item

Jenkins will rescan the repository and use the files from `chapter10` instead of `chapter9`.

Then, go to Spinnaker and edit the pipeline for the staging environment in the configuration pipeline stage, and change all the `chapter9` references to `chapter10`.

You can then use `git push --force origin HEAD:staging` as described in the previous chapter to trigger a Kubernetes deployment from Spinnaker.

The Helm templates for ShipIt Clicker in this chapter have been packaged into an archive file, `chapter10/helm.tar.gz`, using the following commands:

```
$ cd chapter10
$ helm package shipitclicker
Successfully packaged chart and saved it to: /Users/richard/
Documents/Docker-for-Developers/chapter10/shipitclicker-
0.10.0.tgz
$ mv shipitclicker-*.tgz helm.tar.gz
```

If you alter the Helm Charts and you are using Spinnaker, be sure to use the preceding commands to repackage the `helm.tar.gz` file, as Spinnaker expects the charts in that specific file.

Next, let's take a detailed look at logging for both the Docker containers and the container runtime logs, such as those for the Kubernetes control plane.

Docker logging and container runtime logging

When you are trying to troubleshoot problems with your application, it helps to have detailed logs for both the application itself and from whatever system it runs. Every Docker container, whether it is run locally or with a cloud container runtime manager such as Kubernetes, produces its own logs that you can query.

In previous chapters, we've used both the `docker logs` command and the `kubectl logs` command in order to examine logs for the demo application when run both on a local workstation and in the cloud with Kubernetes. These commands can yield insight into events that are critical to your system, including both application logging messages and error and exception logs. They are still the bedrock tools you will reach for; but particularly when we need to scale out our application with Kubernetes, we will need a more sophisticated approach.

Understanding Kubernetes container logging

Every Docker container running in every Kubernetes pod produces logs. The Kubernetes runtime, by default, will temporarily store the last 10 MB of logs for every running container. This makes it possible to sample the logs for every running application using only the `kubectl logs` tool. When a pod is evicted from a node, or when a container restarts, *Kubernetes will delete these ephemeral log files*; it will *not* automatically save the logs to permanent storage. This is far from ideal if you need to troubleshoot a problem, especially if the problem happened long ago enough that those logs have rolled over and the older log entries are unavailable.

You can use `kubectl` to examine multiple logs at once, as shown in the previous chapter, with respect to showing multiple Spinnaker container logs, and you can use common command-line tools, such as `grep`, `awk`, `jq`, and `less`, to carry out further basic searching and filtering on logs. However, the issue with logs rolling over will thwart some search attempts.

Given the constraints on the basic features of the Kubernetes system with respect to both log retention and searching, it would be prudent to explore how we might want to mitigate these issues. Let's talk about the characteristics we would want from a log management system next.

Ideal characteristics for a log management system

Ideally, you would want to use a system for managing your logs that has some of the following characteristics:

- Having log messages be available to view in a central console
- Low latency from when a log event happens to when it is available for searches
- Collection of logs from multiple sources, including Kubernetes objects such as pods, nodes, deployments, and Docker containers
- An easy-to-use search interface, with the ability to save and reuse ad hoc queries
- A way to visualize a histogram of search results that includes the ability to zoom in on the graph by clicking and dragging over the graph (a feature known as *brushing*)
- A way to send alerts based on the contents of log messages
- A way to configure the retention period of the log messages

Various organizations have built many excellent log storage and analysis systems over the past 20 years, including the following third-party log management systems:

- Splunk (`https://www.splunk.com/`)
- Elasticsearch (`https://www.elastic.co/`)
- Loggly (`https://www.loggly.com/`)
- Papertrail (`https://www.papertrail.com/`)
- New Relic Logs (`https://newrelic.com/products/logs`)
- Datadog Log Management (`https://docs.datadoghq.com/logs/`)

Cloud providers also have built excellent integrated log storage and analysis systems, including the following:

- AWS CloudWatch (`https://aws.amazon.com/cloudwatch/`)
- Google Cloud Logging (`https://cloud.google.com/logging`)
- Microsoft Azure Monitor Logs (`https://docs.microsoft.com/en-us/azure/azure-monitor/platform/data-platform-logs`)

As a developer or system operator, you can use these systems to store and search log entries. However, in order to do so, you must use a **log shipper** to extract the logs from their origins and forward them to the log management system.

We will examine how to forward Kubernetes container logs to one of these systems shortly, but first, let's examine another critical system aspect: logging for the Kubernetes control plane that provides orchestration for nodes, pods, and the rest of the family of Kubernetes objects.

Troubleshooting Kubernetes control plane issues with logs

If you run your own Kubernetes cluster, where you manage the control plane servers, you may have a difficult time troubleshooting system-level issues. The Kubernetes troubleshooting guide offers guidance about looking at various log files on individual machines in the control plane cluster, which could be a painful exercise:

`https://kubernetes.io/docs/tasks/debug-application-cluster/debug-cluster/`

However, if you are using managed Kubernetes services, such as AWS EKS, you will not have direct access to these systems. You might ask, *how do I get those logs?* The managed Kubernetes service providers all have ways to ship those logs to another system in order to aid in troubleshooting. Fortunately, AWS EKS has an optional configuration setting that tells it to ship logs from its control plane directly to CloudWatch:

```
https://docs.aws.amazon.com/eks/latest/userguide/control-
plane-logs.html
```

If you used the AWS EKS Quick Start described in *Chapter 8, Deploying Docker Apps to Kubernetes*, to create your EKS cluster, it sets this up for you. You can go to the CloudWatch Logs console in the `us-east-2` region to verify: `https://us-east-2.console.aws.amazon.com/cloudwatch/home?region=us-east-2#logs:`

You will see a listing of log groups similar to the following:

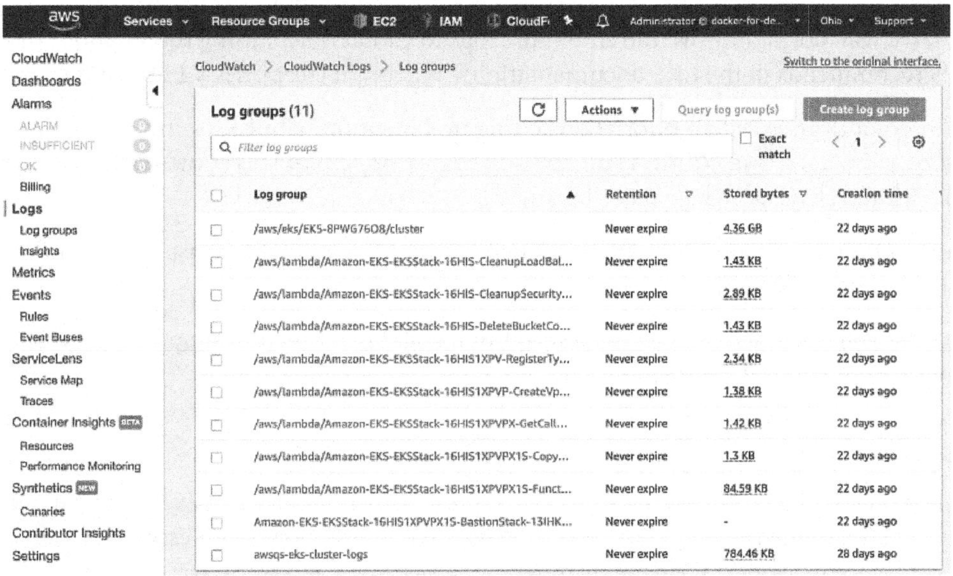

Figure 10.2 – CloudWatch log groups showing EKS control plane logs

The main Kubernetes control plan log group will be named similarly to `/aws/eks/EKS-8PWG7608/cluster`, but with your EKS cluster name. You can navigate to this and examine the logs there in detail through the console.

If you used `eksctl` to create your EKS cluster, you may not have enabled CloudWatch logging. You can use the instructions here to add CloudWatch logging to EKS through `eksctl`:

```
https://eksctl.io/usage/cloudwatch-cluster-logging/
```

Now that you have verified that your EKS cluster control plane is logging to CloudWatch and have learned how to get a basic viewing of the logs, let's proceed to capture the rest of the Kubernetes logs in CloudWatch Logs and analyze them with CloudWatch Logs Insights.

Storing logs with CloudWatch Logs

AWS operates a cloud-scale service to handle logging, time-series metrics, data ingestion, storage, and analysis called **CloudWatch**. Many AWS services, including EKS, offer logging integration through CloudWatch. As with so many AWS services, you only pay for what you use. You can learn more about the basics of CloudWatch at `https://aws.amazon.com/cloudwatch/`.

We saw in the previous section that AWS allows us to configure the EKS control plane to send logs directly to CloudWatch. This is good, but if we are going to manage our logs in a central place, we should try to store *all* of our logs there.

Next, we will look at how we can ship more logs to CloudWatch, using the solution that AWS recommends in the EKS documentation – Fluent Bit (`https://fluentbit.io/`).

AWS provides an excellent tutorial on setting up Fluent Bit with EKS at `https://aws.amazon.com/blogs/containers/kubernetes-logging-powered-by-aws-for-fluent-bit/`.

The scripts and configuration files described later in this chapter are inspired by and partially derived from that article.

Next, we will learn how we can use a script to install Fluent Bit and supporting AWS resources quickly and repeatably.

Installing Fluent Bit to ship logs to CloudWatch

While you could go through the steps in the previously referenced AWS blogs by hand, in order to streamline these operations and make them work more seamlessly with the AWS EKS Quick Start, you can use the `install-fluentbit-daemonset.sh` script in this chapter to install Fluent Bit as a DaemonSet in your EKS cluster, with a configuration that ships logs to CloudWatch Logs. Give it the name of the CloudFormation template for your EKS cluster CloudFormation template as a command-line parameter:

```
chapter10/bin/install-fluentbit-daemonset.sh Amazon-EKS
```

Setting up Fluent Bit to work with AWS requires a bit more work than it does with some other cloud platforms; for example, if you were using Google Cloud Platform's GKE, it would be installed automatically for you.

Once you have the logs for the containers streaming into CloudWatch, you can use the CloudWatch AWS console to view the container logs, as well as the control plane logs.

Changing the CloudWatch log retention periods

By default, CloudWatch will store logs indefinitely. To save on log storage fees, you should consider setting a relatively short retention period for your CloudWatch logs – such as 60 days. You can do that from the console or the command line, as follows, where this command sets the period for the `fluentbit-cloudwatch` log group created by the `install-fluentbit-daemonset.sh` script:

```
aws logs put-retention-policy --log-group-name fluentbit-
cloudwatch --retention-in-days 60 --region us-east-2
```

You might consider doing this for each of the CloudWatch log groups, even the ones created by the AWS EKS Quick Start CloudFormation template.

Next, let's see how we can store logs in S3.

Storing logs for the long term with AWS S3

In order to economically store log data for the long term, over a period of months or years, you can use an inexpensive cloud object storage system, such as Amazon S3 (`https://aws.amazon.com/s3/`).

If you have a serious need to retain logs for the long term – for example, if you have a sensitive financial application where regulations mandate 5 years of storage for all application logs – S3 could be a good fit. You can make long-term storage even less expensive by setting up S3 life cycle rules on the bucket to move objects to less expensive storage tiers, migrate them to Amazon Glacier (`https://aws.amazon.com/glacier/`), or expire and delete older records.

AWS published a blog article (`https://aws.amazon.com/blogs/opensource/centralized-container-logging-fluent-bit/`) that outlines a path that you could use to stream the logs into S3 using Kinesis Firehose as an additional Fluent Bit target. You could follow the instructions in the blog under the *Log analysis across clusters* section to get the logs streaming to S3 that way, but it will probably be challenging to do so as you would have to adapt the scripts to the EKS Quick Start in many ways, including changing the AWS region and dealing with the assumption that you used `eksctl` to set up your cluster.

A project called `CloudWatch2S3` that was inspired by that blog can help with this process by deploying one CloudFormation template. This has the advantage that it can send *all* of the CloudWatch log groups to S3, and you can install it by applying a single CloudFormation template. It can also collect CloudWatch logs from multiple AWS accounts should you choose to do that. Clone the GitHub repository at `https://github.com/CloudSnorkel/CloudWatch2S3` to your workstation and follow the directions there to set up the streaming of CloudWatch logs to S3. Before you proceed, you might consider creating an Amazon **Key Management Service** (**KMS**) key to encrypt the Kinesis Firehose and S3 bucket contents. Install the CloudFormation template using the AWS console or CLI, as you prefer.

Now that we have seen how to store logs in both CloudWatch and S3, it would be nice to learn how we might query those logs.

Analyzing logs with CloudWatch Insights and Amazon Athena

Now that you have logs stored in both CloudWatch and S3, you can query them with either CloudWatch Insights or Amazon Athena.

Analyzing logs stored in CloudWatch with CloudWatch Insights

The easiest way to perform queries on the logs stored in AWS is with CloudWatch Insights. This web-based query interface provides an interactive query builder and a way to visualize the results in both histogram and tabular data formats. It features a saved query manager, which is a key feature because it lets you build and refine a set of queries that can span one or more log groups. The documentation for CloudWatch Insights is available at `https://docs.aws.amazon.com/AmazonCloudWatch/latest/logs/AnalyzingLogData.html`.

You can explore the sample queries in the AWS console for that service to get a better feel for what CloudWatch Insights has to offer.

Analyzing logs stored in S3 with AWS Athena

When logs are stored in S3, you won't be able to query them in exactly the same way you would if you used CloudWatch Insights or another log management system. However, there are ways to efficiently query logs stored in S3. The most direct way is with a query tool called Amazon Athena:

`https://aws.amazon.com/athena/`

Athena will let you use a SQL-like query language on semi-structured data stored in S3 buckets. You pay by the query, according to how much data is scanned and how much processing time it requires. In order to get Athena to understand the structure of your S3 data, you would need to configure virtual tables using the AWS Glue catalog:

`https://docs.aws.amazon.com/athena/latest/ug/glue-athena.html`

Setting up the combination of AWS Glue and Athena is pretty complex and is beyond the scope of what we can show in this chapter. See the links in the *Further reading* section at the end of this chapter for more information on setting up Athena so that you can use it to query the data stored in S3.

Exercise – finding the number of ShipIt Clicker games played

The ShipIt Clicker demo application emits a log message every time a game is started of the form:

```
{"level":30,"time":1591067727743,"pid":17,"hostname":"ship
it-staging-shipitclicker-776c589c4f-z9tgg","name":"Shipit-
Clicker -shipit-staging","msg":"Game created in
Redis","key":"WWoor1SAYT_H98G4DDR-T","value":"OK","v":1}
```

Create a query in CloudWatch Insights that counts the total number of games that have been created. For CloudWatch Insights, you will have to select the `fluentbit-cloudwatch` log group.

Solution

Refer to the following file for the solution:

`https://github.com/PacktPublishing/Docker-for-Developers/tree/master/chapter10/cloudwatch-insights.txt`

Using the liveness, readiness, and startup probes in Kubernetes

Kubernetes has multiple types of health checks, called **probes**, to ensure that the Docker containers it runs are in shape to process traffic. You can read about them in detail at `https://kubernetes.io/docs/tasks/configure-pod-container/configure-liveness-readiness-startup-probes/`.

The types of probes deal with different concerns:

- **Liveness**: Determines whether an application can process requests at all.

- **Readiness**: Determines whether a container is ready to receive real traffic, especially if it depends on external resources that have to be reachable or connected.

- **Startup**: Determines whether a container is ready to start taking the other two types of traffic, intended for slow-starting legacy applications to give them time to start. As these are mostly needed for legacy applications, we won't cover them in detail.

You can configure probes to execute commands inside a running container, perform a TCP port check, or check an HTTP endpoint. Probes have sensible default values for timeouts and check intervals—by default, a probe will check every 10 seconds and will fail with a timeout with 1 second. By default, a probe must fail three times in a row before the probe enters the failure state, and it must succeed once before it enters a success state. You can override these values through template annotations, in `deployment.yaml` in your Helm Charts, for example.

If a liveness probe for a container fails enough times, Kubernetes will kill the container and restart it. If a readiness probe for a container in a pod is failing, Kubernetes will not direct any traffic for a service depending on that pod to the container. We are going to examine liveness and readiness probes in detail next.

Using a liveness probe to see whether a container can respond

For a service such as ShipIt Clicker, a good liveness check would be one where the application can rely solely on internally configured resources to respond – for example, relying on containers deployed in the same pod. In previous chapters, the liveness and readiness checks for this application were set to retrieve the / resource via HTTP. The liveness check stays the same for this chapter, as the ability to serve a simple HTML page is a good liveness check for an Express application. Observe the following excerpt from `chapter10/shipitclicker/templates/deployment.yaml`:

```
livenessProbe:
  httpGet:
    path: /
    port: http
```

This makes Express serve the file in `chapter10/src/public/index.html`. This makes a decent liveness probe, but it does not mean that a pod is ready to process requests that reach out to external resources. For that, we should use a readiness check.

Using a readiness probe to ensure that a service can receive traffic

Some applications have to complete a wave of initialization where they make database calls and call on external services before they are ready to take traffic. For ShipIt Clicker, the application must be able to contact Redis before it is ready to receive traffic. Next, we are going to examine a defect in the prior versions of ShipIt Clicker and the fix that had to be made to support both liveness and readiness probes, as these changes are illustrative of the type of changes that you might have in your application.

Changing ShipIt Clicker to support separate liveness and readiness probes

Previous versions of ShipIt Clicker would suffer a fatal exception if any connection to Redis failed. This would happen as soon as the initialization routines in `src/server/index.js` loaded, as the modules it loaded would instantiate the `RedisDatabase` class in `src/server/api/services/redis-service.js`, which would immediately connect to the Redis server. This class lacked a Redis error handler, so the error it threw was fatal and caused the process to terminate.

This failure would repeat immediately as Kubernetes tried to start another container and would trigger a series of crashes that engaged the Kubernetes crash loop detector.

The new error handler in the `RedisDatabase.init()` method in `chapter10/src/server/api/services/redis.service.js` looks like this, and will log all Redis errors to the console – and, therefore, to the Kubernetes logging system – to make it easier to troubleshoot:

```
    client.on("error", err => l.error({msg: "Redis error",
 err:err}));
```

This chapter's code also uses a lazy loading pattern to avoid having to immediately connect to Redis when the classes are instantiated. With lazy loading, you defer the creation of an object or resource until you actually need it. We achieve lazy loading by using by the `RedisDatabase.instance()` method, which uses the singleton design pattern for the Redis client connection:

```
instance() {
    return this._client ? this._client : this._client = this.
 init();
  }
```

```
async ping() {
  return this.instance().pingAsync();
}
```

Using lazy loading will allow us to defer connecting to the Redis server until a request arrives that really requires it. Recall that in this version of the application, we split the Redis server out from the ShipIt Clicker service and have it running separately. Given this, a readiness probe should reach out to the Redis server and make sure that ShipIt Clicker can indeed talk to it, before accepting traffic. This version has a new API endpoint, /api/v2/games/ready, which performs a Redis PING operation to ensure that the application is ready to take traffic:

```
readinessProbe:
  httpGet:
    path: /api/v2/games/ready
    port: http
```

If the Redis server is not available, this readiness probe will fail and Kubernetes will remove the container that fails the health check from the service.

Exercise – forcing ShipIt Clicker to fail the readiness check

Next, we will run an experiment to see what happens when the liveness probe passes but the readiness check fails. Use kubectl to switch to your local learning environment Kubernetes context. Temporarily alter the chapter10/shipitclicker/template/configmap.yaml file to break the Redis installation by changing the REDIS_PORT value to an invalid number, such as 1234. Then, use Helm to install the chart with the alternative shipit-ready-fail name. Use kubectl get pods to verify that the new pod is in the RUNNING state but has 0/1 pods that are marked READY. Your output should look something like this:

```
$ kubectl get pods | grep -E '^NAME|fail'
NAME                                              READY
STATUS      RESTARTS    AGE
shipit-ready-fail-shipitclicker-57c67d76cd-qklh6   0/1
Running     0           3m20s
```

The readiness checks for this installation of ShipIt Clicker will start failing immediately. If you describe the pod, you will see that it is no longer ready. When you are done, use Helm to uninstall the `shipit-ready-fail` chart and revert the value in the `configmap.yaml` file to its original value.

Gathering metrics and sending alerts with Prometheus

Prometheus is the dominant Kubernetes-based system for collecting metrics on cluster operations. Prometheus sports a wide range of features related to handling time-series data, visualizing data, querying it, and sending alerts based on metrics data.

This metrics data might include a variety of time-series data for CPU usage, both for nodes and for pods; storage utilization; application health, as defined by readiness probes; and other application-specific metrics. Prometheus uses a pull model where it polls endpoints for numeric data. Pods, DaemonSets, and other Kubernetes resources supporting Prometheus use annotations to advertise that Kubernetes should scrape them for metrics data via HTTP, usually via a `/metrics` endpoint. This can include data from Nodes, surfaced through a DaemonSet called `node_exporter` that runs on each Node.

It stores the metrics data it receives by associating this data with a metric name and a set of labels in key-value pair format, along with a millisecond-resolution timestamp. This labeling allows both efficient storage and the querying of the metrics in a time-series database. System operators and automated systems can then query this database to investigate the system's health and performance.

It not only provides a time-series database for metrics but also an alerting subsystem so that system operators can proactively take action when applications encounter trouble.

You can read more about the overall Prometheus architecture and its feature set at `https://prometheus.io/docs/introduction/overview/`.

Prometheus' history

While Prometheus was originally developed by SoundCloud in 2012, it became a **Cloud Native Computing Foundation** (**CNCF**) top-level project in 2016 and it is independent of any single company, just like Kubernetes itself. Its design is inspired by Google's Borgmon system.

Exploring Prometheus through its query and graph web interface

If you installed an EKS cluster using the AWS EKS Quick Start CloudFormation templates as described in *Chapter 8*, *Deploying Docker Apps to Kubernetes*, you should already have a working Prometheus application. If not, you can follow the instructions here to install it using Helm:

`https://docs.aws.amazon.com/eks/latest/userguide/prometheus.html`

You can connect to the Prometheus service and start exploring it by using `kubectl` to create a port forwarding proxy to the Prometheus console web application. You should connect the `prometheus-server` Kubernetes service to your local workstation as follows (replace the expression after `use-context` with your AWS EKS cluster ARN):

```
$ kubectl config use-context arn:aws:eks:us-east-
2:143970405955:cluster/EKS-8PWG76O8
$ kubectl port-forward -n prometheus service/prometheus-server
9090:80
```

Then, open a web browser and visit `http://localhost:9090/`, and you will see the Prometheus query console.

A good starter query to use to test Prometheus is the `node_load1` term, which shows the 1-minute load averages of the underlying Kubernetes nodes. Enter that into the query field and hit the **Execute** button, and then activate the **Graph** tab. You will see a graph showing those load averages.

The **Prometheus query language** is called **PromQL** and is quite different from other time-series database query languages. You will need to learn more about PromQL to formulate your own queries. Read more about that at `https://medium.com/@valyala/promql-tutorial-for-beginners-9ab455142085`.

While Prometheus can graph query results on its own, Kubernetes users typically use Grafana in conjunction with Prometheus to provide more sophisticated graphs and dashboards. We will explore Grafana further later in this chapter. Next, let's examine how you might add a Prometheus metric to an application.

Adding Prometheus metrics to an application

In order to integrate an application with Prometheus, you need to expose a specially structured HTTP API via a Prometheus client library. Prometheus offers official client libraries for several languages, and the community has created many other client libraries for different languages. You can read more about the general process in the Prometheus documentation at `https://prometheus.io/docs/instrumenting/clientlibs/`.

To demonstrate this integration, the version of ShipIt Clicker in this chapter exposes both a set of default metrics and a custom metric in the form of a counter, labeled `shipitclicker_deployments_total`. To do this, we integrate the Prometheus client for JavaScript applications using Node.js:

`https://github.com/siimon/prom-client`

To perform the integration, we installed and saved the prom-client Node module with an `npm install prom-client --save` command, and then integrated the client loosely following the provided example code at `https://github.com/siimon/prom-client/blob/master/example/server.js`.

The structure of a metrics-enabled ShipIt Clicker program

The Prometheus metrics publishing code in ShipIt Clicker is organized conventionally for a Node application written with the Express framework, with routes for metrics added to the main router in `chapter10/src/server/routes.js` in the same modular pattern as the routes for the game API. The main route imports `chapter10/src/server/api/controllers/metrics/router.js`, which defines the HTTP routes for `/metrics` and a special route for `/metrics/shipitclicker_deployment_total`, using the controller class defined in `chapter10/src/server/api/controllers/metrics/controller.js`. This controller has methods that integrate with a Prometheus service class defined in `chapter10/src/server/api/services/prometheus.service.js`, which integrates with the `prom-client` library and exposes both the default metrics and the custom `shipitclicker_deployments_total` metric. Refer to the following code excerpt from the service to see how we encapsulate the `prom-client` library:

```
import * as client from 'prom-client';
...
export class Prometheus {
...
    this.register = client.register;
```

```
    this.deploymentCounter = new client.Counter({
      name: 'shipitclicker_deployments_total',
      help: 'Total of in-game deployments in this ShipIt
Clicker process',
    });


    client.collectDefaultMetrics({
      timeout: 10000,
      gcDurationBuckets: [0.001, 0.01, 0.1, 1, 2, 5],
    });
  }
}
export default new Prometheus();
```

The controller classes that serve up the metrics have proper exception-handling and error-logging scaffolding that the baseline example from `prom-client` lacks. If you wanted to, you could easily adapt the router, controller, and service classes to a new application with minimal effort.

In order to simplify troubleshooting, the metrics are bound to the same HTTP port as the rest of the application: port `3000`. This means that you can retrieve the metrics from any installed version of ShipIt Clicker that has this code integrated – for example, from `https://shipit-v7.eks.example.com/metrics` (replace `example.com` with your domain name). You should see a long list of metrics, starting with the following:

```
# HELP shipitclicker_deployments_total Total of in-game
deployments in this ShipIt Clicker process
# TYPE shipitclicker_deployments_total counter
shipitclicker_deployments_total 0


# HELP process_cpu_user_seconds_total Total user CPU time spent
in seconds.
# TYPE process_cpu_user_seconds_total counter
process_cpu_user_seconds_total 2.5176489999999996
...
```

Now that we have seen the raw metrics, let's examine how the configuration that allows Prometheus to discover the demo application works.

Getting Prometheus to discover the ShipIt Clicker application

The installation of Prometheus configured through the AWS EKS Quick Start CloudFormation template is configured to perform service discovery of pods that support Prometheus metrics. In order for your Kubernetes pods to be discovered, they must be annotated with Prometheus-specific metadata, including the `prometheus.io/scrape: "true"` annotation. Refer to `chapter10/shipitclicker/template/deployment.yaml` for the annotations used to expose ShipIt Clicker to Prometheus:

```
template:
  metadata:
    labels:
      {{- include "shipitclicker.selectorLabels" . | nindent
8 }}
    annotations:
      prometheus.io/scrape: "true"
      prometheus.io/port: "3000"
```

As long as these annotations are on the pod, Prometheus will know that it must scrape the pod's `/metrics` endpoint for data.

Now that we have seen how the program and its configuration templates have been extended to support Prometheus metrics, let's query Prometheus for the custom metric.

Querying Prometheus for a custom metric

Play the game deployed at `https://shipit-v7.eks.example.com/` for a minute or two (replace `example.com` with your domain name). Then, connect to the Prometheus console using the port forwarding method explained earlier in this chapter, and issue a query for `shipitclicker_deployments_total`, then switch to the `Graph` tab. You should see a graph that shows an increasing number of deployments over time.

If you keep playing the game and keep re-issuing the query in the Prometheus console, you will see the number of deployments go up. The default scrape interval and targets that Prometheus uses are defined in a `prometheus.yml` file embedded in the `prometheus-server` ConfigMap in the `prometheus` namespace. By default, it is set to 30 seconds, so you will not see instantaneous changes in the query results from Prometheus.

Next, let's explore Prometheus' support for alerts.

Configuring Prometheus alerts

Prometheus has the capability to query itself periodically in order to detect important conditions – this is the basis of the alerts system. You can apply the powerful Prometheus query language to detect when parts of your system that have Prometheus metrics are overloaded, responding too slowly, or are not available.

For most applications, the foundational alert item must answer the question *is the application available*? If the application is up, it is ready and available to serve user requests. Prometheus has a metric called up that can help answer that question – it will have a value of 1 if the service is up, and 0 if it is down. If you query Prometheus for up, you will see the basic availability status of every service it monitors. You might want to raise an alert if any service has a value other than 1 for 5 minutes or more. That is the basic example given in the Prometheus documentation for alerts (refer to `https://prometheus.io/docs/prometheus/latest/configuration/alerting_rules/`). Next, we will show how to add the example `InstanceDown` rule from the documentation to our Prometheus service configuration.

The AWS EKS Quick Start templates have a Prometheus installation that has no alerts defined at the start, so we will have to define one or more ourselves. If you installed Prometheus on your local workstation, you would edit configuration files in the `/etc` directory to do this, and then trigger a configuration file reload. However, in a Kubernetes setup, there has to be another mechanism in place to allow the editing of these values.

The AWS EKS Quick Start Prometheus setup uses a Kubernetes ConfigMap in the `prometheus` namespace called `prometheus-service` that has multiple embedded YAML configuration files defined within it, and a container running in each Prometheus server pod (refer to `https://github.com/jimmidyson/configmap-reload`) that monitors the ConfigMap files for changes and then sends an HTTP `POST` to the Prometheus server running in the pod to get it to reload the changes. The ConfigMap files are updated once per minute inside the pods. The editing cycle for making config changes to alerts looks like this:

1. Edit the `prometheus-service` ConfigMap using `kubectl`.

2. Wait 1 minute for the ConfigMap changes to propagate to the pods.

3. View the alerts via the port-forwarded Prometheus console at `http://localhost:9090/alerts`.

In order to add the monitoring, we run the following command to edit the ConfigMap and add the rules under the `alerts:` stanza, as follows:

```
kubectl -n prometheus edit configmap/prometheus-server
```

Look at the top of the file and make the `alerts:` stanza match the following text:

```
apiVersion: v1
data:
  alerting_rules.yml: |
    {}
  alerts: |
    groups:
    - name: Kubernetes
      rules:
      - alert: InstanceDown
        expr: up == 0
        for: 5m
        labels:
          severity: page
        annotations:
          summary: "Instance {{ $labels.instance }} down"
          description: "{{ $labels.instance }} of job {{
$labels.job }} has been down for more than 5 minutes."
  prometheus.yml: |
```

After you have edited the file, save it and it will propagate to the pods within 1 minute.

Troubleshooting note – YAML format files are exacting

The capitalization and spacing in the **Alerts** section must be exact, or you may get parsing errors (visible in the logs from the `prometheus-server` pods) – or worse, a silent failure to add the alert you intended.

You should then be able to see the alert definition in the Prometheus console in the **Alerts** section; click on **InstanceDown** and it should show the alert definition:

Figure 10.3 – Prometheus alerts showing InstanceDown

Now that you have an alert defined, you can configure Prometheus to send notifications based on the alert.

Sending notifications with the Prometheus Alertmanager

One of the most powerful aspects of Prometheus is its support for sending notifications of alerts, powered by a component called **Alertmanager**. This component takes the raw alert information from Prometheus, performs additional processing on it, and then sends notifications. You can find an in-depth overview of Prometheus alerting at https://prometheus.io/docs/alerting/overview/.

This alerting system supports multiple channels, including email, PagerDuty, Pushover, Slack, and more through webhooks. We are going to configure a Slack integration to demonstrate sending an alert. In order to do this, we are going to alter the Alertmanager configuration, which is stored in a Kubernetes ConfigMap called prometheus-alertmanager.

To add the Slack integration, make sure you have a Slack account that is signed in via a web browser, then go to `https://api.slack.com/` and build a new app for Slack. In the **Features** configuration screen, configure a new incoming webhook and select a channel in Slack to receive the notifications. Then, copy the URL of the incoming hook to the clipboard and store it in a local text file. You will need that when you configure Alertmanager. Configure any other settings that you feel are relevant, including an icon for the Slack integration. Then, edit the ConfigMap for the Alertmanager using the following command:

```
kubectl -n prometheus edit configmap/prometheus-alertmanager
```

The ConfigMap will have an empty { } clause for the `global:` section, which we will remove, and then we add `slack_api_url` and the `slack_configs` section, as follows (replace the value in single quotes for the Slack API URL with your incoming webhook URL from the Slack application, and replace the channel with the hashtag name of your Slack channel where alerts should appear):

```
apiVersion: v1
data:
  alertmanager.yml: |
    global:
      slack_api_url: 'https://hooks.slack.com/services/A/B/C'
    receivers:
    - name: default-receiver
      slack_configs:
      - channel: '#docker-book-notices'
    route:
```

This will give you a very basic alerting setup that you can expand on in order to get notified of downtime. You can test that the Alertmanager is hooked up by sending a test alert via the Prometheus Alertmanager API. First, port-forward the Alertmanager service to your local machine:

```
kubectl -n prometheus port-forward service/prometheus-alertmanager 9093:80
```

In a different console window, issue the following command:

```
curl  -d '[{"status": "firing", "labels":{"alertname":"Hello
World"}}]' -H "Content-Type: application/json" http://
localhost:9093/api/v1/alerts
```

You should get a {"status":"success"} response from that curl command, and then you should see the Hello World alert in your Slack:

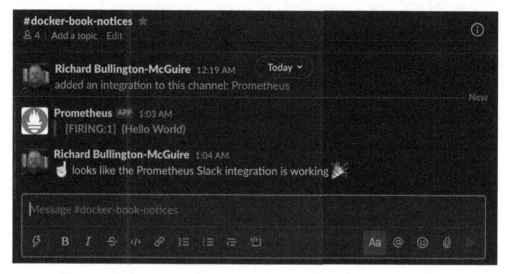

Figure 10.4 – Prometheus alert in Slack

Exercise – deploy a broken ShipIt Clicker, expect an AlertManager notification

Edit the chapter10/shipitclicker/templates/deployment.
yaml file to redirect Prometheus probes to port 3001 and deploy this broken ShipIt Clicker application using Helm to see the alerting in action. Call the application shipit-broken. Check the Prometheus console to verify that the alert enters the pending state. This should happen in less than 1 minute. Within 10 minutes, you should see an alert in Slack of the [FIRING:1] (InstanceDown shipit-broken shipitclicker 10.0.87.39:3000 kubernetes-pods default shipit-broken-shipitclicker-6658f47599-pkxwk 6658f47599 page) form. Once you get the alert, uninstall the shipit-broken Helm Chart, revert the change to deployment.yaml, and you should stop getting notifications about that specific issue.

Once you get the alert, uninstall the shipit-broken Helm Chart and you should stop getting notifications about that specific issue.

Exploring Prometheus queries and external monitoring in-depth

The topics about how to build Prometheus queries and how to extend Prometheus to monitor external systems are quite deep and beyond the scope of this chapter. Please consult the Prometheus documentation and the links in the *Further reading* section at the end of this chapter to learn more about creating Prometheus queries and configuring it to use additional metrics data sources.

Next, let's examine how we can use Grafana to visualize the data that Prometheus gathers.

Visualizing operational data with Grafana

Prometheus is often deployed with Grafana (`https://grafana.com/`) to provide sophisticated dashboards and a more sophisticated UI for monitoring. The installation of Kubernetes from the AWS EKS Quick Start includes Grafana, configured with a few dashboards. Let's explore the Grafana installation and see how it integrates with Prometheus.

Gaining access to Grafana

The Grafana installation is exposed by default over a Kubernetes LoadBalancer, which in EKS creates an AWS EC2-Classic **Elastic Load Balancer** (**ELB**). Find out what address it is listening on, as follows. Look in the `EXTERNAL-IP` field for the actual DNS name of the ELB:

```
$ kubectl -n grafana get service
NAME       TYPE            CLUSTER-IP     EXTERNAL-IP
PORT(S)          AGE
grafana    LoadBalancer    172.20.5.46    aaa-bbb.us-east-2.elb.
amazonaws.com    80:30669/TCP    39d
```

Put that DNS address into your web browser, prefixed with `http://`, and you will get the Grafana login screen. You will need to retrieve the administrative username and password from the Kubernetes secret to login:

```
$ kubectl -n grafana get secrets/grafana --template='{{index
.data "admin-user"}}' | base64 -D
[username redacted]
$ kubectl -n grafana get secrets/grafana --template='{{index
.data "admin-password"}}' | base64 -D
[password redacted]
```

Use these values to log in to the Grafana console. You can then explore the UI, including the dashboards and the Prometheus query explorer. Some of the dashboards might not have values fully populated, such as the **Kubernetes All Nodes** dashboard, but don't fret too much about it, as it is possible to add community-provided dashboards that are extremely detailed and fully populated with cluster-wide statistics. Look at the **Kubernetes Pods** dashboard and select different pods, including the Redis pods and the ShipIt Clicker pod, to get a feel for how to use the dashboards. Change the time window with the widget in the upper-right corner to show data for a day or a week, and then click and drag over an interesting area to zoom in.

Next, let's add a couple of community-provided dashboards to get a flavor for the full power that this system can deliver.

Adding a community-provided dashboard

Grafana provides a repository of both official and community-provided dashboards at `https://grafana.com/grafana/dashboards`.

These include a bewildering variety of dashboards. You should explore this in detail with your own needs in mind.

When you add a dashboard, one of the options presented is **Import**. Choose this and it will ask you for a dashboard ID or URL from the community site.

Here are four general-purpose dashboards that are worth adding to your installation:

- **Cluster Monitoring for Kubernetes**: This compact dashboard from Pivotal Observatory lets you see what pods are consuming the most CPU, memory, and network resources at a glance – `https://grafana.com/grafana/dashboards/10000`.

- **Kubernetes Cluster (Prometheus)**: A concise dashboard showing critical cluster-wide metrics – `https://grafana.com/grafana/dashboards/6417`.

- **1 Node Exporter for Prometheus Dashboard EN v20191102**: A cluster-wide complex dashboard that exposes many CPU, disk, and network metrics – `https://grafana.com/grafana/dashboards/11074`.

- **Node Exporter Full**: This exposes every possible metric from the **Prometheus Node Exporter**, a very popular dashboard on the site with over two million downloads – `https://grafana.com/grafana/dashboards/1860`.

Adding a new dashboard with a custom query

The steps to add a new dashboard with a custom query are as follows:

1. In the left menu, click on the + sign to add a new dashboard. Then, in the **New Panel** area, click **Add Query**. Add the following query to the field next to **Metrics**:

```
shipitclicker_deployments_total
```

It should look something like this:

Figure 10.5 – Grafana custom dashboard item definition

2. Then, in the **Panel** tab on the right, click on the **Panel Title** field. Name this panel `ShipIt Clicker Deployments`, and then click on the left-pointing arrow in the top-left corner of the screen to return to defining the widget.

3. In the top menu, click on the graph with the plus sign to add another widget:

Figure 10.6 – The Grafana add widget

4. Add another similar panel with the following query with the title `ShipIt Clicker Deployments Rate`:

```
rate(shipitclicker_deployments_total[2m])
```

5. Then, click on the gear icon in the top menu and change the name of the dashboard to `ShipIt Clicker Dashboard`, and then save the dashboard.

6. Next, take a break and play the ShipIt Clicker game for a few minutes. This will generate traffic that you will be able to see on the graph. A few minutes after you stop playing, your dashboard might look like this:

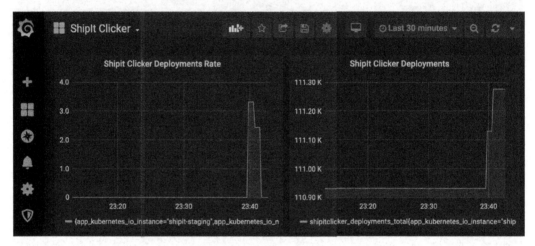

Figure 10.7 – The ShipIt Clicker custom dashboard in Grafana

Understanding rates and counters

Note that the rate dashboard drops back down to 0 after you stopped playing, but the one that counts only the total increases and stays as it is. Choosing a rate query for a variable ending in `total` in Prometheus is usually what you want to measure throughput.

Now that we have seen how to graph application metrics and build dashboards with Grafana, let's explore another topic: application performance monitoring and distributed tracing with Jaeger.

Application performance monitoring with Jaeger

We are now going to take a brief tour of Jaeger to see how it can be used for performance monitoring in a microservices architecture. One of the key problems faced when implementing performance and error tracking in a microservice architecture versus a monolithic application is that a microservices architecture is inherently a distributed environment.

Early attempts at solving this problem, such as OpenCensus (`https://opencensus.io/tracing/`), suffered from disparate terminology and approaches and incompatible systems. To solve this problem, the performance monitoring community created the OpenTracing API.

Understanding the OpenTracing API

The **OpenTracing** project (`https://opentracing.io/`) is designed to allow engineers to add performance-monitoring features to their projects using a common API specification that is non-vendor specific.

Some of the key features of OpenTracing that realize this goal are as follows:

- The API specification itself (`https://github.com/opentracing/specification`)
- Frameworks and libraries that implement the API specification
- Comprehensive documentation (`https://opentracing.io/docs/`)

Let's now look at the two most important core concepts of the specification: spans and tracing.

Spans

A span represents a unit of work and is the basic building block of this type of tracing system. Each span contains an operation name, the start and finish time, a **SpanContext**, and finally, **tags** and **logs** key-value pairs.

Your tag key-value pairs apply to the whole span and include information such as `db.type` and `http.url`. A list of conventional tags can be found on GitHub at `https://github.com/opentracing/specification/blob/master/semantic_conventions.md`.

The logs key-value pair is used to define logging messages that refer to a specific incident or event, rather than the span as a whole. For example, you could use this collection of key-value pairs to record debugging information.

The final concept in a span is the SpanContext, which is used to carry data across process boundaries. Its two key components are the state that denotes a specific span within a trace and a concept known as **baggage items**. These are essentially key-value pairs that cross a process boundary.

You can read more about spans at the OpenTracing website's documentation at `https://opentracing.io/docs/overview/spans/`.

Traces and tracers

The next concept we will look at is traces and tracers.

A trace is a way of grouping one or more spans under a single identifier known as the **trace identifier**. This can be used to understand a workflow through a distributed system, such as a microservices architecture.

The tracer is the actual implementation of the OpenTracing API specification that collects spans and publishes them. Examples of tracers that implement OpenTracing include Datadog (which we will explore in *Chapter 14, Advanced Docker Security – Secrets, Secret Commands, Tagging, and Labels*), Instana, Lightstep, and Jaeger.

If you want to read more around tracers and traces, you can find the official documentation at `https://opentracing.io/docs/overview/tracers/`.

Let's explore a tool that implements the OpenTracing API – Jaeger.

Introduction to Jaeger

Jaeger is an open source application-tracing framework that allows developers and system operators to gather information from a running application and determine both how the application spends its time and how it interacts with other distributed system components, using the OpenTracing API. The Jaeger website is `https://www.jaegertracing.io/`.

Jaeger's history

Jaeger, named after the German word for hunter, originally came from the transportation company Uber. Engineers there, led by Yuri Shkuro, built this distributed tracing framework. Inspired by the Google paper on their tracing framework, Dapper (`https://research.google/pubs/pub36356/`), and the Zipkin tracing framework (`https://zipkin.io/`), they created Jaeger as a cloud-native tracing framework. Uber has been using Jaeger since 2015 and contributed it to the CNCF in 2017; the CNCF promoted it to a top-level project in 2019. You can read more about the history of Jaeger on the Uber engineering blog at `https://eng.uber.com/distributed-tracing/`.

Jaeger's components

Some of the important components that make up the Jaeger ecosystem include the following:

- The client libraries available as packages or directly from GitHub
- Jaeger agents used to listen for spans
- The collector, responsible for aggregating data sent from agents
- Jaeger query, for analyzing data via a UI
- The Ingester, which allows us to gather data from Kafka topics and then write the data to services such as AWS Elasticsearch

Let's test Jaeger and see how it works in practice.

Exploring the Jaeger UI

To explore Jaeger, we can run the all-in-one latest image using Docker:

```
$ docker run --rm -i -p6831:6831/udp -p16686:16686
jaegertracing/all-in-one:latest
```

Then, we can open a web browser and visit `http://localhost:16686/` to see the UI. The Jaeger search interface itself is instrumented to send traces to the collector, so once you see the UI, reload the page once to make some more traces, and populate the **Service** drop-down box. Then, press the **Find Traces** button. It should look something like this:

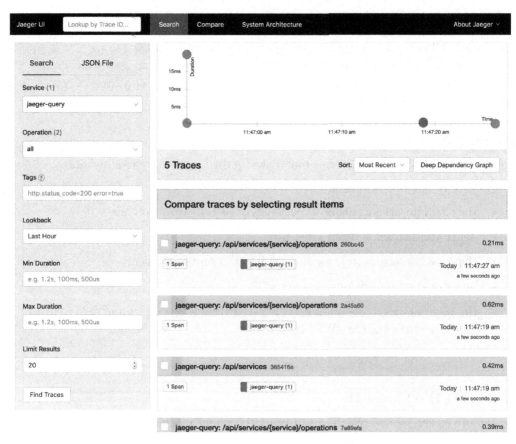

Figure 10.8 – The Jaeger UI search interface

When you are done exploring, stop the running Docker container by pressing *Ctrl + C*. Next, lets explore how you might instrument an application by seeing how ShipIt Clicker is integrated with OpenTracing and Jaeger.

Exploring the Jaeger client with ShipIt Clicker

The Jaeger client is available in a number of languages. Our example will use Node.js, but there is also support for Go, Java, and Python, among others. You can check the official client documentation at the following URL to learn more:

`https://www.jaegertracing.io/docs/1.18/client-libraries/`

ShipIt Clicker v7 already has a Jaeger client, a piece of OpenTracing JavaScript Express middleware, and the OpenTracing API client installed:

- The Jaeger client: `https://github.com/jaegertracing/jaeger-client-node`

- Express middleware: `https://github.com/opentracing-contrib/javascript-express`

- The OpenTracing client: `https://github.com/opentracing/opentracing-javascript`

If you have an Express application that you want to use with Jaeger, you would issue the following command to install the same combination of libraries:

```
$ npm install --save jaeger-client express-opentracing
opentracing
```

In the GitHub repository (`https://github.com/PacktPublishing/Docker-for-Developers`), the Jaeger client configuration in `chapter10/src/server/common/jaeger.js` has an example of how to configure the Jaeger client using a mixture of environment variables and default values. Both the `docker-compose` configuration files and the Helm templates for ShipIt Clicker have been updated to use some environment variables to configure Jaeger, to give `jaeger.js` the right context for those environments; this file imports the `jaeger-client` module, configures it, and exports a `tracer` object. We use the `tracer` object from the `express-opentracing` middleware in the `chaper10/src/server/common/server.js` file:

```
import tracer from './jaeger';
import middleware from 'express-opentracing';
...
export default class ExpressServer {
  constructor() {
...
    app.use(middleware({ tracer: tracer }));
  }
```

Using middleware or other software that can hook into common libraries processes provides us with lift and lets us avoid writing boilerplate code. The `express-opentracing` middleware object decorates the Express `res` response object with a `span` attribute, which lets us use an OpenTracing span from within our controllers and request handlers.

We can use a more explicit style also, where we create the spans and log entries programmatically:

1. To see this in action, inspect the ShipItClicker's API controller at `chapter10/ src/server/api/controllers/games/controller.js`:

    ```
    async incrementGameItem(req, res) {
      const key = `${req.body.id}/${req.body.element}`;
      const value = req.body.value;
      const span = tracer.startSpan('redis', {
        childOf: req.span,
    ```

2. The next stanza shows how to create a tag in the span that holds more detailed tracing information:

    ```
      tags: {
          [opentracing.Tags.SPAN_KIND]: opentracing.Tags.
    SPAN_KIND_RPC_CLIENT,
          'span.kind': 'client',
          'db.type': 'redis',
          'db.statement': `INCRBY ${key} ${value}`,
        },
      });
    ```

3. The preceding code initializes a child span for Redis, using the main span through `req.span`. Then, we immediately call Redis, log the results, and finish the span:

    ```
    try {
      var redis = await RedisService.incrby(key, value);
      span.log({ result: redis }).finish();
    ```

4. Next, we log a message in the span associated with the parent span:

    ```
      const msg = {
        msg: 'Game item Redis INCRBY complete',
        key: key,
        value: redis,
      };
      req.span.log(msg);
    ```

5. Now, we log the message using the regular logging mechanism and update the
    Prometheus custom metric if this request increments the `deploys` element:

```
l.info(msg);
if (req.body.element === 'deploys') {
    const incr = parseInt(req.body.value, 10);
    PrometheusService.deploymentCounter.inc(incr);
}
```

6. If we get this far, the Redis request has been successful, and we can return a JSON
    response to the client:

```
return res.json({
    id: req.params.id,
    element: req.params.element,
    value: redis,
});
```

7. If the request fails – for example, if Redis is unavailable – we must carry out error
    processing. First, we construct a message that has the detailed error in it:

```
} catch (err) {
    const msg = {
        key: req.body.id,
        element: req.body.element,
        message: err.message,
        stack: err.stack,
    };
```

8. Then, we log the error to both the OpenTracing span and our regular error log, and
    return a 404 Not Found HTTP response to the client:

```
span.log(msg).finish();
l.warn(msg);
return res.status(404).json({
    status: 404,
    msg: 'Not Found',
});
    }
}
```

The preceding code shows how you can use the tracer object to initiate a child span of the main span in `req.span`, and has logging elements that annotate both spans with the results of the Redis operation.

In order to make it easy to demonstrate the Jaeger integration, this chapter has a Docker Compose file, `chapter10/docker-compose.yml`, that integrates the ShipIt Clicker container, Redis, and Jaeger. You can run all of them by issuing the following commands from the `chapter10` directory:

```
docker-compose build && docker-compose up -d
```

You can then visit `http://localhost:3010/` to play the ShipIt Clicker game for a minute to generate some traces, then visit `http://localhost:16686/` to see the Jaeger query interface in action. Query the `shipitclicker-v7` service, click on one of the traces in the graph, and then expand the two spans and the logs revealed within and you should see something like this:

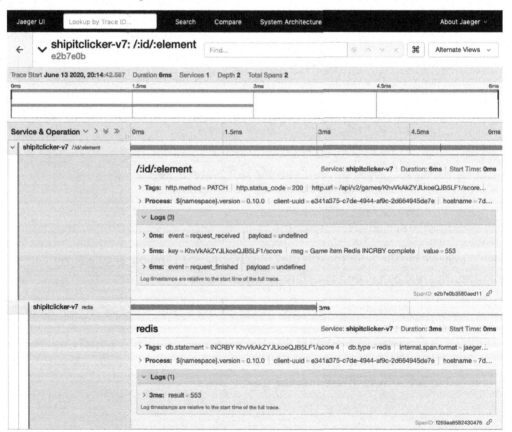

Figure 10.9 – Jaeger trace showing the ShipIt Clicker HTTP transaction and Redis spans

In contrast to the `docker-compose.yml` file presented in *Chapter 6, Deploying Applications with Docker Compose*, the one in this chapter is deliberately set up for development, not as a production-hardened configuration. It exposes both the Redis and Jaeger ports for convenience, so it is not suitable for production use without additional hardening. However, this makes it very convenient for debugging and developing the application. You can even run the ShipIt Clicker application code on your local workstation by running `npm run dev` and have it connect to the Docker-hosted Redis and Jaeger services – which is probably the fastest way to try out changes.

You could also install Jaeger in Kubernetes, both to your local learning environment and to the AWS EKS Kubernetes cluster. To do that, we will use the Jaeger Operator.

Installing the Jaeger Operator

We've seen how we can use Jaeger locally through both a raw `docker` command and through `docker-compose`. Next, we will learn how to deploy Jaeger to Kubernetes. The Helm Charts for Jaeger (`https://github.com/jaegertracing/helm-charts`) are not fully supported, and they may have issues with Helm 3. The Jaeger team is actively investing in Jaeger Operator as the primary method to install and maintain this system. A Kubernetes **Operator** is a special type of resource that orchestrates the installation and maintenance of a whole set of related objects and configurations, often comprising a complex distributed system.

To deploy to a Kubernetes environment, we can use the following GitHub repository as a guide:

`https://github.com/jaegertracing/jaeger-operator`

Use the set of `kubectl` commands listed there to install the operator namespace and the related Kubernetes objects for the Jaeger operator. Run not only the main `kubectl` commands but also the set of `kubectl` commands to give the operator cluster-wide permissions through a role binding. To get Jaeger to work smoothly with all the namespaces, edit the deployment and remove the value from the `WATCH_NAMESPACE` variable:

```
kubectl -n observability edit deployment/jaeger-operator
```

The part of the file with `WATCH_NAMESPACE` should then look as follows:

```
    spec:
      containers:
      - args:
        - start
```

```
        env:
        - name: WATCH_NAMESPACE
        - name: POD_NAME
```

Now that you have done this, you can install a Jaeger Operator instance that will itself spin up the services, pods, and DaemonSets for Jaeger. An example Operator definition suitable for development or lightweight production use that deploys Jaeger using a DaemonSet on all nodes using only memory for trace storage is in `chapter10/jaeger.yaml`. Install it with `kubectl`:

```
kubectl apply -n observability -f chapter10/jaeger.yaml
```

This will install all the required components, including a `jaeger-query` Ingress Controller that does not have any annotations, so the EKS cluster will not connect it to anything. See the `chapter10/jaeger-ingress.yaml` file for a version that has annotations to connect it to the internet with the ALB Ingress Controller. You can use the same basic procedures you used with other Kubernetes services and Route 53 to expose the Jaeger console from Kubernetes; or, you can leave it alone and connect to the Jaeger console only when you need to via port forwarding.

If you are installing this on your local Kubernetes learning environment, you could alternatively add NGINX Ingress Controller annotations to the Ingress Controller.

To further extend Jaeger, you might consider adding one of the storage backends, such as Cassandra or Elasticsearch, so that traces will persist beyond the lifetime of the Jaeger pod. We're going to leave it there with Jaeger, but feel free to explore it in more detail.

Next, we will review what we have learned in this chapter.

Summary

In this chapter, you have learned all about observability – how to perform logging and monitoring for Docker applications using both Kubernetes cloud-native approaches and using AWS services.

You learned about decoupling applications from common services (such as Redis) to increase production-readiness. In order to aid troubleshooting and the analysis of application and system problems, you learned how to extend logging beyond the running containers in a Kubernetes cluster into AWS CloudWatch and S3, as well as how to query those log storage systems using both CloudWatch Insights and AWS Athena. You saw how you might add more sophisticated Kubernetes liveness and readiness probes to an application, and how to make error handling more robust.

Then, you learned how to collect detailed metrics from both the application and the supporting systems using Prometheus, how to query those metrics, and how to set up alerts with the Prometheus Alertmanager. Prometheus and Grafana go hand in hand; you discovered how to configure Grafana dashboards provided by the community and how to add a custom dashboard that shows application-specific metrics. Finally, you learned how to use Jaeger and the OpenTracing API to instrument an application with traces that give deep insight into the performance of an application by using both open source middleware and explicitly annotating the application.

In the next chapter, we will explore how we can scale out the application using autoscaling, protect it from overloading using Envoy and the circuit breaker pattern, and perform load testing using k6.

Further reading

You can explore the following resources to expand your knowledge of observability, Kubernetes logging, Prometheus monitoring, Grafana, Jaeger, and managing Kubernetes clusters:

- Introduction to observability: `https://docs.honeycomb.io/learning-about-observability/intro-to-observability/`.
- Manage your Kubernetes clusters in style with k9s – a quick and easy terminal interface similar to Midnight Commander that is an alternative to using `kubectl` to query and control a Kubernetes cluster: `https://k9scli.io/`.
- Kail – Kubernetes' log tail utility: `https://github.com/boz/kail`.
- Getting started with Athena: `https://docs.aws.amazon.com/athena/latest/ug/getting-started.html`.
- Query data from S3 files using AWS Athena: `https://towardsdatascience.com/query-data-from-s3-files-using-aws-athena-686a5b28e943`.
- Getting started with Kubernetes – Observability: Are Your Applications Healthy? Liveness and Readiness Probes: `https://www.alibabacloud.com/blog/getting-started-with-kubernetes-%7C-observability-are-your-applications-healthy_596077`.
- *Kubernetes Liveness and Readiness Probes: How to Avoid Shooting Yourself in the Foot*: `https://blog.colinbreck.com/kubernetes-liveness-and-readiness-probes-how-to-avoid-shooting-yourself-in-the-foot/`
- Awesome Prometheus alerts – the mother lode of rules for not only Kubernetes but also other systems that Prometheus can monitor, available under a Creative Commons Attribution license: `https://awesome-prometheus-alerts.grep.to/rules`.

- Configuring Prometheus Operator Helm Chart with AWS EKS has good examples of more detailed Alertmanager configurations: `https://medium.com/zolo-engineering/configuring-prometheus-operator-helm-chart-with-aws-eks-c12fac3b671a`.

- Monitoring Distributed Systems – from the Google SRE book – pay special attention to the **four Golden Signals**: `https://landing.google.com/sre/sre-book/chapters/monitoring-distributed-systems/`.

- How to monitor Golden Signals in Kubernetes: `https://sysdig.com/blog/golden-signals-kubernetes/`.

- PromQL tutorial for beginners and humans: `https://medium.com/@valyala/promql-tutorial-for-beginners-9ab455142085`.

- Understanding delays on Prometheus alerting: `https://pracucci.com/prometheus-understanding-the-delays-on-alerting.html`.

- Kubernetes in Production – the Ultimate Guide to Monitoring Resource Metrics with Prometheus: `https://www.replex.io/blog/kubernetes-in-production-the-ultimate-guide-to-monitoring-resource-metrics`.

- Kubernetes Monitoring with Prometheus – the ultimate guide (part 1) – yes, it's funny that multiple articles claim to be the ultimate guide, but this one has really detailed information and a part 2 that also covers Grafana: `https://sysdig.com/blog/kubernetes-monitoring-prometheus/`.

- Kubernetes: Monitoring with Prometheus — exporters, Service Discovery, and its roles. Has a section on setting up a Redis exporter that you could use to explore ShipIt Clicker's operation better: `https://itnext.io/kubernetes-monitoring-with-prometheus-exporters-a-service-discovery-and-its-roles-ce63752e5a1`.

- Taking Advantage of Deadman's Switch in Prometheus: `https://jpweber.io/blog/taking-advantage-of-deadmans-switch-in-prometheus/` (combine with `https://deadmanssnitch.com/` for a complete Deadman's Switch alerting system).

- Using Prometheus Metrics in Amazon CloudWatch: `https://aws.amazon.com/blogs/containers/using-prometheus-metrics-in-amazon-cloudwatch/`.

- An alternative solution to the periodic export of CloudWatch logs to S3 via a scheduled Lambda function: `https://medium.com/searce/exporting-cloudwatch-logs-to-s3-through-lambda-before-retention-period-f425df06d25f`.

11
Scaling and Load Testing Docker Applications

Technology giants such as Google, Facebook, Lyft, and Amazon use container orchestration systems in part so that they can run their massive computing resources at very high levels of utilization. To do that, you must have a way to scale your applications across a fleet of servers, which might be dynamically allocated from a cloud provider. Even if you have a cluster that can scale out with high traffic and scale back in when demand subsides, you may still need additional tools to make sure it operates correctly. You also need to ensure that the service degrades gracefully if capacity limits are exceeded.

You can use a service mesh such as Envoy, Istio, or Linkerd to handle those concerns. Envoy is one of the simpler options in the service mesh arena; it provides both load balancing and advanced traffic routing and filtering capabilities. All these capabilities provide the glue needed to serve traffic to demanding users. Some of the more complex service meshes use Envoy as a building block since it is so flexible.

To prove that the scaling strategy works, you need to perform load testing. To do this, we will use k6.io, a cloud-native load testing and API testing tool.

In this chapter, you are going to learn how to use the Horizontal Pod Autoscaler, the Vertical Pod Autoscaler, and the Cluster Autoscaler to configure your Kubernetes cluster so that it scales out. You will learn about Envoy and why you might use it to provide a proxy layer and service mesh on top of Kubernetes. This includes how to create an Envoy service mesh on top of a Kubernetes cluster, as well as how to configure it with a circuit breaker. Then, you will learn how to verify that the service mesh and autoscaler mechanisms are working as expected. Finally, you will learn how to run a load test with k6.io and observe how the service fails when subjected to a stress test.

We will cover the following topics in this chapter:

- Scaling your Kubernetes cluster

- What is Envoy, and why might I need it?

- Testing scalability and performance with k6

Technical requirements

You will need to have both a local Kubernetes learning environment and a working Kubernetes cluster in the cloud, as set up in *Chapter 8, Deploying Docker Apps to Kubernetes*. You will also need to have a current version of the AWS CLI, as well as `kubectl` and `helm` 3.x installed on your local workstation, as described in the previous chapter. The Helm commands in this chapter use `helm` 3.x syntax.

For your local Kubernetes learning environment, you should have a working NGINX Ingress Controller configured, which you can install by running the `chapter11/bin/deploy-nginx-ingress.sh` script. You should also have a local Jaeger operator, which you can install by running the `chapter11/bin/deploy-jaeger.sh` script.

For the cloud-hosted cluster, you can reuse the AWS **Elastic Kubernetes Service** (**EKS**) cluster or set up a new one for this chapter using the same method or using `eksctl`. The EKS cluster must have a working ALB Ingress Controller set up. You should also have an **Elastic Container Registry** (**ECR**) set up to hold container images. We recommend that you also have working installations of Prometheus, Grafana, and Jaeger in your cloud-hosted Kubernetes cluster, as described in *Chapter 10, Monitoring Docker in Production with Prometheus, Grafana, and Jaeger*. You can run the `deploy-jaeger.sh` script against your cloud cluster as well.

Check out the following video to see the Code in Action:

`https://bit.ly/2CwdZeo`

Using the updated ShipIt Clicker v8

We will use the version of ShipIt Clicker provided in the `chapter11` directory of the following GitHub repository: `https://github.com/PacktPublishing/Docker-for-Developers/`.

This version of the application you use, similar to what we did in the previous chapter, depends on an externally installed version of Redis from the `bitnami/redis` Helm Charts when used in Kubernetes.

Understanding the differences from the previous version of ShipIt Clicker

In each chapter, we have made enhancements to ShipIt Clicker to illustrate changes related to the chapter content, as well as to polish the application the same way we would do as part of a production release process.

This version of ShipIt Clicker is similar to the one provided in the previous chapter, but it has one more API endpoint called `/faults/spin` that's used as a part of a *fault injection* testing strategy to induce CPU load on the nodes running the application, in order to test cluster autoscaling strategies. The `spin` endpoint will get slower the more frequently it is called but will recover and get faster if calls subside. This simulates the way that an application with poor performance behaves, without having to devise a complicated real set of poorly performing code and database servers. It provides an artificial CPU load that is convenient for testing CPU-based autoscaling. See the code in `chapter11/src/server/common/spin.js` and `chapter11/src/server/controllers/faults/controller.js` to see how this works.

This version of ShipIt Clicker also has an enhancement related to Prometheus metrics: it exposes these metrics on a separate port by configuring Express to listen on a separate port so that it serves up the `/metrics` endpoint. This helps us avoid exposing metrics that contain information about the application that an ordinary user does not need and makes it possible for multiple containers in the same pod as ShipIt Clicker to also expose Prometheus metrics. See the code in the `chapter11/src/server/index.js` file, which adds another HTTP listener and a router for metrics. The Helm templates in `chapter11/shipitclicker/templates/deployment.yaml` also have changes to support this new endpoint.

Next, we'll build and install ShipIt Clicker into our local Kubernetes learning environment.

Installing the latest version of ShipIt Clicker locally

In this section, we will build the ShipIt Clicker Docker container, tag it, and push it to Docker Hub, as we did in previous chapters. Issue the following commands, replacing dockerfordevelopers with your Docker Hub username:

```
$ docker build . -t dockerfordevelopers/shipitclicker:1.11.7
$ docker push dockerfordevelopers/shipitclicker:1.11.7
$ kubectl config use-context docker-desktop
$ helm install --set image.repository=dockerfordevelopers/
shipitclicker:1.11.7 shipit-v8 shipitclicker
```

Inspect the running pods and services using kubectl get all to verify the pod is running, note its name, and then inspect the logs with kubectl logs to see the startup logs. There should be no errors in the log.

Next, we'll install this version in EKS.

Installing the latest version of ShipIt Clicker in EKS through ECR

Now that you have built the Docker containers and installed this locally, we'll install it in AWS EKS via ECR. Edit chapter11/values.yaml to give this a hostname in the Route 53 DNS zone such as shipit-v8.eks.example.com (replace the ECR reference with the one corresponding to your AWS account and region and replace example.com with your domain name):

```
$ docker tag dockerfordevelopers/shipitclicker:1.11.7
143970405955.dkr.ecr.us-east-2.amazonaws.com/
dockerfordevelopers/shipitclicker:1.11.7
$ aws ecr get-login-password --region us-east-2 | docker login
--username AWS --password-stdin 143970405955.dkr.ecr.us-east-2.
amazonaws.com
$ docker push 143970405955.dkr.ecr.us-east-2.amazonaws.com/
dockerfordevelopers/shipitclicker:1.11.7
$ kubectl config use-context arn:aws:eks:us-east-
2:143970405955:cluster/EKS-8PWG76O8
$ helm install shipit-v8 -f values.yaml --set image.
repository=143970405955.dkr.ecr.us-east-2.amazonaws.com/
dockerfordevelopers/shipitclicker:1.11.7 ./shipitclicker
```

Inspect the Kubernetes logs to make sure that the application has deployed cleanly to the cluster:

```
kubectl logs services/shipit-v8-shipitclicker shipitclicker
```

If all is well with the deployment, get the AWS ALB Ingress Controller's address, as described in *Chapter 9, Cloud-Native Continuous Deployment Using Spinnaker*, and create DNS entries in the Route 53 console for the deployed application with the ALB address. You should then be able to reach your application at a URL similar to `https://shipit-v8.eks.example.com/` (replace `example.com` with your domain name).

Scaling your Kubernetes cluster

To support more traffic and more applications, your Kubernetes cluster may need to grow beyond its initial size. You can use both manual methods and dynamic programmed methods to do this, especially if you are working with a cloud-based Kubernetes cluster. To scale out an application, you need to control two dimensions: the number of pods running a particular application and the number of nodes in a cluster. You can't scale the number of pods infinitely on a cluster with the same number of nodes; practical limits related to CPU, memory, and network concerns will ultimately demand that the cluster scales out the number of nodes as well.

The method that's used to scale out a cluster will vary considerably, depending on the cloud vendor and Kubernetes distribution. The Kubernetes documentation explains both the general process and some specific instructions for clusters running in the Google and Microsoft Azure clouds:

`https://kubernetes.io/docs/tasks/administer-cluster/cluster-management/`

Generally speaking, you must start and configure a new server that is set up similarly to the existing cluster nodes, and then join it to the cluster by using the `kubeadm join` command:

`https://kubernetes.io/docs/reference/setup-tools/kubeadm/kubeadm-join/`

Kubernetes distributions and cloud vendors make this easier by relying on mechanisms such as machine images and autoscaling groups. We will show you how to scale your cluster by using Amazon EKS. In *Chapter 8, Deploying Docker Apps to Kubernetes*, we set up EKS with AWS Quick Start CloudFormation templates in the *Spinning up AWS EKS with CloudFormation* section. The following sections assume that you have used that method to set up a cluster that uses autoscaling groups.

Scaling the cluster manually

Given that we want to increase the number of nodes in our cluster, we will want to identify and follow the procedures that are specific to our Kubernetes installation. For Amazon EKS clusters, see the following documentation:

`https://docs.aws.amazon.com/eks/latest/userguide/launch-workers.html`

You could just launch an entirely new group of nodes, but you can often adjust a parameter or two in order to increase the size of your cluster. This is done when you increase the size of a cluster, which is called *scaling out*, and when you decrease the size of a cluster, which is called *scaling in*. Next, we will learn how to adjust a simple parameter so that we can scale out the number of nodes in the cluster.

Scaling nodes out manually

For the sake of simplicity, let's assume you used the AWS Quick Start for EKS CloudFormation templates to create your cluster initially. Since that uses CloudFormation to manage the cluster, you should prefer using CloudFormation to update the cluster's configuration. To manually scale your cluster out, go to the AWS console and update the CloudFormation deployment, changing the default values for **Number of nodes** and **Maximum number of nodes** from their current values to higher values, such as **4** and **8**:

Number of nodes
The number of Amazon EKS node instances. The default is one for each of the three Availability Zones.

```
4
```

Maximum number of nodes
The maximum number of Amazon EKS node instances. The default is three node.

```
8
```

Figure 11.1 – Updating the AWS EKS Quick Start CloudFormation template

Continue through the CloudFormation update forms and apply the changes. Look at the CloudFormation events for updates and wait a few minutes. You can then check that the update to the CloudFormation template worked fine. Then, you can check the size of the autoscaling group to make sure it has grown.

You could also update the autoscaling group sizes through the EC2 console, thereby setting the minimum, desired, and maximum number of nodes to **4**, **4**, and **8**, respectively. This will cause your deployed configuration to drift from its CloudFormation templates, however, which is undesirable as the actual state will no longer match the model that CloudFormation expects. See the following post for more on why that is problematic: `https://aws.amazon.com/blogs/aws/new-cloudformation-drift-detection/`.

If you used `eksctl` to create your cluster instead, you can follow the instructions at `https://eksctl.io/usage/managing-nodegroups/` to scale the node groups it creates.

Scaling nodes in manually

You can reverse the process to scale in the cluster (reducing its size), but beware that scaling a cluster in manually is trickier. Doing this safely involves a process called draining, which is described in the following Kubernetes documentation: `https://kubernetes.io/docs/tasks/administer-cluster/safely-drain-node/`. Just changing the autoscaling group's size on its own will terminate an instance without letting you choose which instance to terminate or giving you a chance to drain the instance. If you *really* wanted to do this, you would have to do all the following:

- Decrement the autoscaling group minimum size by one.
- Drain the node with `kubectl drain`.
- Terminate the node using an AWS CLI command that decrements the desired capacity.

After you've adjusted the autoscaling group's minimum size, you could issue the following commands (replace the node name and instance ID in each of these commands with the ones that match the node you want to terminate):

```
$ kubectl drain \
    ip-10-0-94-28.us-east-2.compute.internal \
  --ignore-daemonsets
$ aws autoscaling terminate-instance-in-auto-scaling-group \
    --instance-id i-09c88021d2324e821 \
  --should-decrement-desired-capacity
```

This process is involved and could easily lead to manual error. It will also lead to configuration drift from the CloudFormation template, so you should either seek to script it or rely on automatic scaling mechanisms instead.

Scaling pods manually through deployments

Manually scaling the number of pods in a deployment or ReplicaSet is quite easy, assuming that you have enough resources in your cluster. You can use the `kubectl scale` command to set the number of replicas. You might have to issue several `kubectl get` commands before you see all the replicas become ready, as shown in this transcript:

```
$ kubectl get deployment/shipit-v8-shipitclicker
NAME                       READY   UP-TO-DATE   AVAILABLE   AGE
shipit-v8-shipitclicker    2/2     2            2           57m
$ kubectl scale deployment/shipit-v8-shipitclicker --replicas=4
deployment.apps/shipit-v8-shipitclicker scaled
$ kubectl get deployment/shipit-v8-shipitclicker
NAME                       READY   UP-TO-DATE   AVAILABLE   AGE
shipit-v8-shipitclicker    2/4     4            1           58m
$ kubectl get deployment/shipit-v8-shipitclicker
NAME                       READY   UP-TO-DATE   AVAILABLE   AGE
shipit-v8-shipitclicker    4/4     4            4           59m
```

Next, we will examine how we can apply programmatic scaling to the cluster, for both nodes and pods.

Scaling the cluster dynamically (autoscaling)

Now that you've completed many of the exercises in the preceding three chapters, which explored the complex concepts that go along with the Kubernetes container orchestration system, you might be wondering: is all this effort worth it? In this section, we will explore the key feature that can make the pain of managing these systems worth it – autoscaling. By dynamically scaling the applications in a cluster, and the cluster itself, you can drive high utilization of cluster resources, meaning that you will need fewer computers (virtual or physical) to run your systems. When you combine dynamic scaling with the self-healing capabilities of the Kubernetes system, this becomes compelling, even though it has high complexity and a high learning curve in some areas.

Kubernetes supports several dynamic scaling mechanisms, including the Cluster Autoscaler, the Horizontal Pod Autoscaler, and the Vertical Pod Autoscaler. Let's explore each of these.

Configuring the Cluster Autoscaler

The **Cluster Autoscaler** is responsible for scaling the nodes in a cluster out to meet demand when the cluster has no more capacity to schedule pods, as well as for scaling in nodes that no longer have running pods on them. This system runs as a deployment in the `kube-system` namespace and uses cloud APIs to launch and terminate nodes.

If you used the AWS EKS Quick Start Cloudformation templates to create your cluster and told it to enable the Cluster Autoscaler, no further configuration is needed. If you used `eksctl` or another method to create the cluster, you may need to configure it further using the directions provided here: `https://docs.aws.amazon.com/eks/latest/userguide/cluster-autoscaler.html`.

You can verify that the Cluster Autoscaler is running by querying it:

```
$ kubectl -n kube-system get deployments | grep autoscaler
cluster-autoscaler-1592701624-aws-cluster-autoscaler    1/1
1              1
```

Now that we have learned a bit about the Cluster Autoscaler, let's discover how we might configure an application to take advantage of its features.

Configuring a stateless application to work with the Cluster Autoscaler

A stateless application, such as ShipIt Clicker, can tolerate starting and stopping any one of its pods and can run on any node in the cluster. It doesn't require special configuration to work with the Cluster Autoscaler. Stateful applications that mount local storage and some other classes of applications must avoid some scaling operations if possible and may require special handling. See the Autoscaling FAQ for more details: `https://github.com/kubernetes/autoscaler/blob/master/cluster-autoscaler/FAQ.md`.

You can give the Cluster Autoscaler a hint that it should not scale in pods beyond a certain point, and that it should strive to keep a certain number or percentage of healthy pods available by using a **PodDisruptionBudget** (**PDB**): `https://kubernetes.io/docs/tasks/run-application/configure-pdb/`.

We have configured ShipIt Clicker with a PDB in its Helm Chart. See `chapter11/src/shipitclicker/templates/pdb.yaml` for more information. You can find the default values for it in `chapter11/src/shipitclicker/values.yaml`. The defaults now have ShipIt Clicker configured to deploy two pods and have a PDB with a minimum of one pod available. This provides hints to the Cluster Autoscaler and other Kubernetes applications that it should always keep at least one pod alive, even as node maintenance is underway.

Next, we will demonstrate the Cluster Autoscaler in action.

Demonstrating the Cluster Autoscaler in action

In order to get the Cluster Autoscaler to make changes to the size of the cluster, we can start more pods than it has capacity to handle currently. To watch this process in action, it is helpful to tail the logs of the cluster-autoscaler service. Open a Terminal window and run the following commands to tail the logs of the service:

```
$ service=service/$(kubectl get services -n kube-system \
    | awk '/cluster-autoscaler/{ print $1 }')
$ kubectl logs -f -n kube-system "$service"
```

Every 10 seconds, you will see log entries indicating that the service is looking for *unschedulable* pods (which would cause the cluster to scale out the number of nodes) and for nodes that are eligible for scaling in.

Then, in a different Terminal window, manually scale the deployment of ShipIt Clicker to 50 pods:

```
kubectl scale deployment/shipit-v8-shipitclicker --replicas=50
```

Each of the t3.medium nodes in the default EKS cluster can handle approximately 4 to 16 ShipIt Clicker pods, depending on how many other pods are also running on each node. This will trip the Cluster Autoscaler and make it scale out by at least one additional node. You will see entries in the Cluster Autoscaler log noting that it has found unschedulable pods, and shortly afterward, that it has completed scaling.

To see the progress from the perspective of the nodes and pods in the deployment, issue the following commands every few seconds:

```
kubectl get nodes; kubectl get deployments
```

You will see nodes launching and more and more replicas becoming ready until the set of replicas stabilizes. Once that happens, scale it back down to a lower default state:

```
kubectl scale deployment/shipit-v8-shipitclicker --replicas=2
```

Once you've done that, you may notice that the nodes do not scale in immediately as they enter a cooldown condition for 10 minutes after a scale out operation completes. However, a minute after the cooldown period expires, the Cluster Autoscaler will notice that the CPU utilization of these nodes is close to zero and it will scale in the cluster, terminating the nodes that no longer have pods available. The Cluster Autoscaler will respect the PDB when it performs this scale in operation as well – allowing you to be as conservative as required when shrinking the number of pods and nodes in the cluster.

Now that you have learned how to scale the cluster nodes in and out using the Cluster Autoscaler, let's learn how to use the Horizontal Pod Autoscaler to set scaling policies.

Configuring the Horizontal Pod Autoscaler

The **Horizontal Pod Autoscaler** allows you to set up rules for scaling out sets of Kubernetes pods using rules that can take into account CPU utilization or other custom metrics. This service can also scale pods controlled by deployments, ReplicaSets, and replication controllers. You can read more about the theory of how it works here: `https://kubernetes.io/docs/tasks/run-application/horizontal-pod-autoscale/`.

This is the last big piece of the puzzle you need before you can achieve a cluster that automatically scales in and out in response to demand.

You need Metrics Server for the Horizontal Pod Autoscaler to work. We will install this next.

Installing Metrics Server

To have more detailed statistics available in your Kubernetes cluster for use by the software components that enable dynamic scaling (including the Horizontal Pod Autoscaler), you need to run the standard **Metrics Server**. It aggregates statistics across the cluster regarding the memory, CPU, and other resource utilization of the nodes and among the pods in a format that the various Kubernetes autoscaler mechanisms can understand and act upon. The AWS EKS guide talks about installing that here:

`https://docs.aws.amazon.com/eks/latest/userguide/metrics-server.html`

To install it, ensure your kubectl config context is set to your cloud cluster. Then, issue the following command from your local workstation:

```
kubectl apply -f https://github.com/kubernetes-sigs/metrics-
server/releases/download/v0.3.6/components.yaml
```

Once you have installed Metrics Server, verify that it is running:

```
$ kubectl -n kube-system get deployment metrics-server
NAME            READY   UP-TO-DATE   AVAILABLE   AGE
metrics-server  1/1     1            1           6m
```

Next, we will activate the Horizontal Pod Autoscaler for the ShipIt Clicker application to demonstrate how it works.

Activating the Horizontal Pod Autoscaler

The AWS EKS guide shows the steps needed to install the Horizontal Pod Autoscaler: https://docs.aws.amazon.com/eks/latest/userguide/horizontal-pod-autoscaler.html.

The main thing we need to install is the metrics service. It turns out that the Horizontal Pod Autoscaler is baked into Kubernetes itself. We can issue a command such as the following one to activate a Horizontal Pod Autoscaler for a deployment:

```
kubectl autoscale deployment shipit-v8-shipitclicker
--cpu-percent=50 --min=2 --max=50
```

If you need to edit these parameters, you can do so with the following command:

```
kubectl edit hpa/shipit-v8-shipitclicker
```

You can get a detailed view of what the Horizontal Pod Autoscaler has done recently by issuing this command:

```
kubectl describe hpa/shipit-v8-shipitclicker
```

To test whether the Horizontal Pod Autoscaler and Cluster Autoscaler are working as expected, we need to drive CPU load. That's where the `/faults/spin` endpoint comes in handy. Later in this chapter, in the *Testing scalability and performance with k6* section, we will see how to construct a realistic load test for the ShipIt Clicker application. However, to exercise autoscaling, we are going to use a brute-force method by using the Apache Bench utility that's run via Docker (replace `example.com` with your domain name):

```
$ url=https://shipit-v8.eks.example.com/faults/spin
$ docker run --rm jordi/ab -c 50 -t 900 "$url"
```

Use the `kubectl get deployments`, `kubectl get pods`, `kubectl get nodes`, and `kubectl describe hpa` commands repeatedly to watch the deployment replicas grow. Alternatively, use a Kubernetes monitoring tool such as k9s (`https://k9scli.io/`) to watch the pod and node counts grow over the first 10 minutes or so, and then subside in the 15 minutes afterward. You could also look at some Grafana dashboards and Jaeger traces, as described in the previous chapter, to see how the cluster is handling the load, or even look at the CloudWatch metrics that surfaced in the EC2 console for the active nodes.

Next, we will consider when we might use the Vertical Pod Autoscaler.

Configuring the Vertical Pod Autoscaler

The Vertical Pod Autoscaler is a newer scaling mechanism that observes the amount of memory and CPU usage that pods request, versus what they actually use, in order to optimize memory and CPU requests – it performs right-sizing to drive better cluster utilization. This is the most useful scaling mechanism for stateful pods.

However, the Vertical Pod Autoscaler documentation currently states that it is not compatible with the Horizontal Pod Autoscaler, so you should avoid configuring it so that it manages the same pods. You can explore using it for your application, but keep in mind the advice it specifies about not mixing it with the Horizontal Pod Autoscaler using CPU metrics. The installation procedure for the Vertical Pod Autoscaler is also more involved than configuring either of the other autoscalers, so we won't show all the steps in detail here – please refer to the Vertical Pod Autoscaler documentation for detailed configuration instructions: `https://github.com/kubernetes/autoscaler/tree/master/vertical-pod-autoscaler`.

In this section, we learned all about how we can scale our application using both manual and dynamic methods. In the next section, we will learn all about Envoy, a service mesh that provides some advanced controls and sanity regarding communications between pods in a Kubernetes cluster.

What is Envoy, and why might I need it?

Envoy (`https://www.envoyproxy.io/`) is a C++ open source **service mesh** and edge proxy geared toward microservice deployments. Developed by a team at Lyft, it is especially useful for teams developing Kubernetes-hosted applications, such as the ones you have seen throughout this book.

So, why exactly would we need to deploy Envoy? When developing cloud-based production systems that use multiple containers to host a distributed service, many of the problems you will encounter are related to observability and networking.

Envoy aims to solve these two problems by introducing a proxy service that offers runtime-configurable networking and metrics collection that can be used as a building block for creating higher-level systems that manage these concerns. Whether you're building out a small distributed application or a large microservice architecture designed around the service mesh model, Envoy's features allow us to abstract the thorny problem of networking in a cloud and platform-agnostic fashion.

The team at Lyft developed Envoy using the following concepts:

- **Out of process architecture**: Envoy is a self-contained process that can be deployed alongside existing applications.

- **A transparent communications mesh**: All applications communicate via `localhost` and are ignorant of the network topology. An L3/L4 filter architecture is used for networking proxying. You can add custom filters to the proxy to support tasks such as TLS client certificate authentication.

- **Language agnosticism**: Envoy works with multiple languages and allows you to mix and match application frameworks. For example, through the use of Envoy PHP and Python, containerized applications can communicate with each other.

- **HTTP L7 filters and routing**: As with L3/L4 filters, filtering is also supported at the L7 layer. This allows plugins to be developed for different tasks, ranging from buffering to interacting with AWS services such as DynamoDB. Envoy's routing feature allows you to deploy a routing subsystem that can redirect requests based on a variety of criteria, such as path and content type.

- **Load balancing and front/edge proxy support**: Envoy supports advanced load balancing techniques, including automatic retries, circuit breakers, health checking, and rate limiting. Additionally, you can deploy Envoy at the network edge to handle TLS termination and HTTP/2 requests.

- **Observability and transparency**: Envoy collects statistics to support observability at both the application and networking layer. You can combine Envoy with Prometheus, Jaeger, Datadog, and other monitoring platforms that support metrics and tracing.

Let's explore some of Envoy's features in more detail so that we can understand these concepts better.

Network traffic management with an Envoy service mesh

You should already be familiar with the concept of a load balancer, which is one type of network traffic manager. But what exactly is a service mesh? Why would you need to use one? How does Envoy help us in this regard?

A service mesh is an infrastructure layer dedicated to handling service-to-service communications, typically through a proxy service. The benefits of using a service mesh are as follows:

- Transparency and observability into network communications.

- You can support secure connections across the network.

- Metrics collection, including length of time for a retry to succeed when a service fails.

- You can deploy proxies as **sidecars**. This means they run alongside each service rather than within it. In turn, this allows us to decouple the proxying service from the application itself.

An example of a four-application service mesh can be visualized as follows:

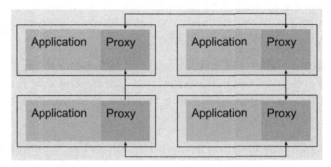

Figure 11.2 – Example of a service mesh with four microservices and sidecar proxies

Here, each of our containerized applications has a corresponding sidecar proxy. The application communicates with the proxy, which, in turn, communicates across the service mesh with the other containerized services we are hosting. The application does not know that the proxy exists and does not need any modifications to work with the proxy. All the configuration can be done by wiring ports together using the container orchestration system, in a way that is invisible to the application.

Now, let's gets our hands dirty and get Envoy up and running.

Setting up Envoy

Because of Envoy's architecture, you have flexibility in terms of how you can deploy the software:

- Configured explicitly as a sidecar container, with a static configuration file, alongside an application container
- Configured dynamically as part of a service mesh control plane, where the container might be injected into a Kubernetes pod as a component, using software such as Istio (https://istio.io/) or AWS App Mesh (https://aws.amazon. com/app-mesh/)

The second option offers additional power at the cost of adding major complexity.

The Envoy sample configurations (see `https://www.envoyproxy.io/docs/envoy/latest/start/start#sandboxes`) are all of the first variety, with explicit Envoy proxy configurations. To learn about Envoy, it is simpler to consider the explicit configuration examples. The version of ShipIt Clicker provided in this chapter has been modified so that you can add an Envoy sidecar container using a static configuration file when it is deployed in Kubernetes, with a minimalist approach that allows us to demonstrate Envoy's features.

Configuring ShipIt Clicker for Envoy

Now, let's examine the specific changes that need to be made for Envoy to be supported in ShipIt Clicker. The application JavaScript code does not require any changes; all the changes are in the Helm Charts. See the Helm Charts in `chapter11/shipitclicker` and compare them with the ones in `chapter10/shipitclicker`; you will see a new Envoy sidecar container defined in `chapter11/shipitclicker/templates/deployment.yaml`, configured with an image defined in `chapter11/shipitclicker/values.yml`:

```
- name: envoy-sidecar
  image: "{{ .Values.envoy.repository }}"
  imagePullPolicy: {{ .Values.envoy.pullPolicy }}
  command: ["/usr/local/bin/envoy"]
  args: ["-c", "/etc/envoy-config/config.yaml"]
```

The preceding lines in the template launch the Envoy container using a configuration file, `/etc/envoy-config/config.yaml`, defined in a ConfigMap. Envoy needs both a port definition for its administrative interface and a port definition for each service it manages or proxies:

```
ports:
  - name: envoy-admin
    containerPort: 9901
    protocol: TCP
  - name: envoy-http
    containerPort: 4000
    protocol: TCP
```

We can query the administrative API to ensure that Envoy is both live and ready to accept traffic, in accordance with Kubernetes best practices:

```
livenessProbe:
  httpGet:
    path: /server_info
    port: envoy-admin
readinessProbe:
  httpGet:
    path: /ready
    port: envoy-admin
```

To expose the configuration file to the container, we use a volume mount that exposes the `config.yaml` file:

```
volumeMounts:
  - name: envoy-config-vol
    mountPath: /etc/envoy-config/
volumes:
- name: envoy-config-vol
  configMap:
    name: {{ .Release.Name }}-envoy-sidecar-configmap
    items:
      - key: envoy-config
        path: config.yaml
```

The `config.yaml` file is defined in `chapter11/shipitclicker/templates/configmap-envoy.yaml` and has definitions for listeners and clusters for the following:

- An ingress proxy for the ShipIt Clicker container inside the pod

- An egress proxy for the Redis Kubernetes service that can be reached at `redis-master` in the cluster

- An ingress proxy that allows Prometheus to scrape metrics from the Envoy sidecar in the pod

The ConfigMap for ShipIt Clicker in `chapter11/shipitclicker/templates/configmap.yaml` has been modified so that it connects to `localhost:6379` for Redis, which Envoy listens for and proxies out via a TCP L4 proxy to the Redis service. This listens elsewhere in the cluster at `redis-master:6379`.

The Kubernetes service in `chapter11/shipitclicker/templates/service.yaml` now calls the `envoy-http` port instead of directly calling the application container's port.

Why not use the Envoy Redis protocol proxy?

The example files used here use a plain TCP proxy, instead of Envoy's Redis protocol proxy (see `https://www.envoyproxy.io/docs/envoy/latest/api-v3/extensions/filters/network/redis_proxy/v3/redis_proxy.proto` and `https://github.com/envoyproxy/envoy/tree/master/examples/redis`).

This is because the ShipIt Clicker application has a Redis password authentication set up that is not compatible with Envoy's Redis proxy. ShipIt Clicker is set up to use a password it retrieves from a Kubernetes Secret that the Bitnami Redis Helm Chart stores. However, Envoy does not pass through this password; when configured with the Redis protocol proxy, it emitted an error message stating `Warning: Redis server does not require a password, but a password was supplied` when ShipIt Clicker tried to authenticate. It turns out that if you use the Envoy Redis protocol support, you must configure the proxy itself with password authentication for the client, and optionally the server, through the configuration file stored in a ConfigMap. However, the password that the Bitnami Redis server uses is only available as a Kubernetes secret, so reworking the system to support this would add complexity.

As an exercise, you could install Redis without a password and remove the password from the configuration for ShipIt Clicker if you wanted to do this. If you did this, you could also switch Redis implementations to the Bitnami Redis Cluster Helm Chart (see `https://github.com/bitnami/charts/tree/master/bitnami/redis-cluster`), and then use the Envoy support for Redis clusters in order to implement the reader/writer split pattern.

So far, we've seen how to deploy Envoy to create a service mesh. Next, we are going to explore the circuit breaker pattern.

Configuring Envoy's support for the circuit breaker pattern

The circuit breaker pattern is a mechanism that's used to configure thresholds for failures. The goal here is to prevent cascading failures spreading across your microservice platform and to stop continuous requests to a non-responsive service.

Configuring the pattern on Envoy is relatively simple. We can configure circuit breaking values as part of an Envoy cluster definition via the `circuit_breakers` field.

To see how this works, examine the following ConfigMap file, which contains a definition of a circuit breaker (`chapter11/shipitclicker/templates/configmap-envoy.yaml`):

```
        circuit_breakers:
            thresholds:
            - priority: DEFAULT
                max_connections: {{ .Values.envoy.maxRequests }}
                max_pending_requests: {{ .Values.envoy.
maxRequests }}
                max_requests: {{ .Values.envoy.maxRequests }}
                max_retries: {{ .Values.envoy.maxRetries }}
```

This threshold definition specifies the maximum number of connections Envoy will make and the maximum number of parallel requests. In our example, we have a configuration for a default priority threshold and a second one for high priority (used for HTTP 1.1) and the maximum number of requests (used for HTTP/2). If the rate of traffic that Envoy detects exceeds these thresholds, it will throw an error and deny the requests, without passing the request to the target service. Notice that since we are using Helm Charts, we specify the actual values using the Helm template variable substitution with the values coming from `chapter11/shipitclicker/values.yaml` or one of the override mechanisms for Helm Chart values. The default values are from a section of the `values.yaml` file that specifies Envoy-specific values:

```
envoy:
  repository: envoyproxy/envoy:v1.14.2
  pullPolicy: IfNotPresent
  accessLog: "/dev/null"
  maxRequests: 1024
  maxRetries: 2
```

These default values are suitable for production for this application, but how can we test that the circuit breaker works, without inducing a massive load? We will show you how do that next.

Testing the Envoy circuit beaker

In order to test that the Envoy circuit breaker is working properly, we'll deploy ShipIt Clicker to the cloud Kubernetes cluster with an artificially lowered request limit and perform a quick load test to verify that it works. Issue a Helm `upgrade` command, followed by a `kubectl rollout restart` command, similar to the following, to set the maximum simultaneous requests to `10` (replace `image.repository` with your ECR repository reference):

```
$ helm upgrade shipit-v8 -f values.yaml --set image.
repository=143970405955.dkr.ecr.us-east-2.amazonaws.com/
dockerfordevelopers/shipitclicker:1.11.7 --set envoy.
maxRequests=2 ./shipitclicker
Release "shipit-v8" has been upgraded. Happy Helming!
NAME: shipit-v8
LAST DEPLOYED: Sun Jun 28 22:34:15 2020
NAMESPACE: default
STATUS: deployed
REVISION: 17
NOTES:
1. Get the application URL by running these commands:
   http://shipit-v8.eks.example.com/*
$ kubectl rollout restart deployment/shipit-v8-shipitclicker
deployment.apps/shipit-v8-shipitclicker restarted
```

Next, we'll use Apache Bench to test the deployed application, starting with a single concurrent request:

```
$ url=https://shipit-v8.eks.example.com/faults/spin
$ docker run --rm jordi/ab -c 1 -n 400 $url | grep requests:
Completed 100 requests
Completed 200 requests
Completed 300 requests
Completed 400 requests
Finished 400 requests
Complete requests:      400
Failed requests:        0
```

Here, you can see that when run with only one concurrent request, all the requests succeeded. Next, we'll increase the concurrency to 50 simultaneous connections:

```
$ docker run --rm jordi/ab -c 50 -n 400 $url | grep requests:
Completed 100 requests
Completed 200 requests
Completed 300 requests
Completed 400 requests
Finished 400 requests
Complete requests:        400
Failed requests:          72
```

If we set the concurrency to 50 simultaneous requests, many of them will fail as the circuit breaker kicks in. We've already seen how to set up a basic circuit breaker with two thresholds for our cluster. More advanced circuit breaker patterns exist, including breaking on latency and retries. We'll leave you to explore this further if you think your applications will need it.

Now that you have tested the circuit breaker with low connection thresholds, reset the thresholds to their original values and redeploy the application to help set up the application for more load testing.

If we had a good measurement of how much real user traffic each pod could handle without failing, we could use this to set a better value for the circuit breaker. However, Apache Bench is a blunt instrument that does not let us simulate a realistic user load. For that, we need to use a more sophisticated load test framework. Now, we'll take a look at how we can test scalability with k6, a Docker-based load testing framework.

Testing scalability and performance with k6

The k6 framework (`https://k6.io`) is a programmable open source load testing tool. We are going to show you how to use it to generate a more realistic load pattern than you could generate using a simple load generator such as **Apache Bench (ab)**.

This framework is quite simple to set up and use thanks to its Docker image, which is available on Docker Hub. You can find the Quick Start instructions at `https://k6.io/docs/getting-started/running-k6`.

To create a load test using k6, you need to use JavaScript using k6's library routines. To perform a smoke test, your script would need to look something like this:

```
import http from 'k6/http';
export default function() {
```

```
      http.get('https://shipit-v8.eks.example.com/');
}
```

This script is roughly equivalent to using the `ab` utility to stress test a web server. Create a file called `hello.js` using the preceding source code, replacing `shipit-v8.eks.example.com` with the fully qualified domain name of one of your websites.

Following Docker best practices, you should ensure that you add the `--rm` flag to the Docker command line so that you do not accumulate stale containers in your local installation:

```
$ docker run --rm -i loadimpact/k6 run - < hello.js
```

This will run k6 and retrieve the URL specified in `hello.js`.

There are just a few key concepts you must know about:

- You must provide a default function.
- K6 is *not* Node.js. It has no event loop.
- Your default function is known as a **Virtual User (VU)**.
- Code defined outside of the default function is evaluated once, on program startup.
- The default function is run repeatedly until the test is over.
- You can run your test with as many VUs as you want, and for as long as you want.

> **Note**
> There are many command-line options you can use with k6 to ramp up and down VUs over time, as well as to specify how long to run the test and how many VUs to simulate. The defaults have only one VU, and only one test iteration.

Let's use some of those options to run the test with more users and for a longer duration:

```
$ docker run --rm -i loadimpact/k6 run --vus 50 --duration 30s
- < hello.js
```

Running k6 like this will perform a load test almost identical to an Apache Bench load test, with a concurrency of 50 and a duration of 30 seconds.

However, since you have the full power of JavaScript available, you can write more nuanced load tests using a variety of strategies.

Recording and replaying network sessions

An alternative to writing a script such as `hello.js` by hand is to use a record-and-replay strategy. Many load testing frameworks support this paradigm, including k6. To do this, use the Chrome browser and its **Inspect** feature. You can use the debugger's **Network** tab to capture and save network traffic to and from the application's backend.

You start with an empty (cleared) network history in the debugger. Then, you load and play the game. Each click will cause API requests to occur between the application running in the browser and the backend.

When you are satisfied with your recording, right-click on the **Network** pane and choose **copy all as HAR**. This puts the HAR-formatted text in the system clipboard:

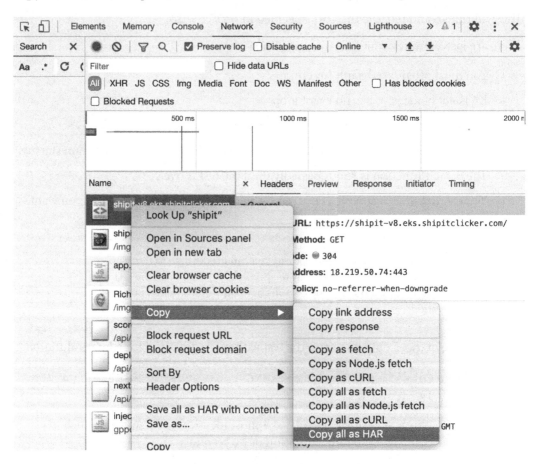

Figure 11.3 – Google Chrome inspector debugging console – Copy all as HAR

Paste from the clipboard into a file named `chapter11/src/test/k6/session.har`. Then, run a conversion script to transform the HAR file into a JavaScript file at `chapter11/src/test/k6/har-session.js`, and run another shell script that will run k6 via Docker with the right arguments to initiate a one-user, 60-second test:

```
$ chapter11/bin/k6-convert-har.sh
$ chapter11/bin/k6-run-har.sh
```

The `k6-run-har.sh` script is set up to use environment variables that override the VUs with the USERS variable, and to override the test duration with the DURATION variable. So, you can prefix the script with those variables like this and run a 10-user test for 300 seconds:

```
$ USERS=10 DURATION=300 chapter11/bin/k6-run-har.sh
```

There are some wrinkles to note about using this playback and record strategy, though: the process is quite literal, and results in a file that has no delays between requests. Running the test will induce a large, machine-speed load on the target service. There is no randomization of the delays that should happen between requests, which is something you want to do in order to closely model the load that a real user's session would put on a service.

To create a more realistic test, we are going to have to do some JavaScript programming.

Hand-crafting a more realistic load test

In the `chapter11/src/tests/k6/` directory, there is a `test.js` script designed to realistically test ShipIt Clicker, whether it's deployed locally or in the cloud.

This script mimics a human playing the game by using these strategies:

- Fetches the HTML, stylesheets, images, and JavaScript files that make up the application
- Performs HTTP post to start a new game
- Gets the initial score, deployments, and nextPurchase values
- Attempts to simulate the click stream a human player would make

The HTTP requests were identified by playing the game in a web browser such as Google Chrome, using its **Inspect** feature, and viewing the **Network** tab as the game loads and is played. Then, we wrote a test that simulated the series of requests in a way that is closely modeled after real user behavior, including having realistic random delays.

Let's examine the code in `chapter11/src/test/k6/test.js`. Here, we import the `http` class and the `sleep()` method from the k6 supplied libraries:

```
import http from "k6/http";
import { sleep } from "k6";
```

We pass parameters to the `test.js` script as environment variables:

- The `DEBUG` environment variable lets us trigger more verbose logging.

- The `MOVES` environment variable contains the number of moves per game.

- The `TARGET` environment variable would be something like `http://192.2.0.10:3011` for `localhost` development, where `192.2.0.10` is the IPv4 LAN address of your workstation.

These parameters get retrieved from the `__ENV` object, as follows:

```
const DEBUG = __ENV.DEBUG;
const MOVES = __ENV.MOVES;
const target = __ENV.TARGET;
```

The `ENDPOINTS` array gets used to iterate through the three main elements that the game tracks:

```
const ENDPOINTS = ['score', 'deploys', 'nextPurchase'];
```

The `deploy()` method simulates a human clicking on the **Deploy** button in the app; it calls `http.patch()` twice – once to update the deployment count and once to update the score:

```
const deploy = id => {
  validate(
    http.patch(
      `${target}/api/v2/games/${id}/deploys`,
      JSON.stringify({
        id: id,
        element: 'deploys',
        value: 1,
      }),
```

```
      params
    )
  );
```

This function also updates the score:

```
  validate(
    http.patch(
      `${target}/api/v2/games/${id}/score`,
      JSON.stringify({
        id: id,
        element: 'score',
        value: 1,
      }),
      params
    )
  );
};
```

The `validate()` method that the `deploy()` method calls simply verifies that the server returns a valid response:

```
  validate(
    http.patch(
      `${target}/api/v2/games/${id}/score`,
      JSON.stringify({
        id: id,
        element: 'score',
        value: 1,
      }),
      params
    )
  );
};
```

The `getStaticAssets()` method simulates the user's browser fetching the HTML, CSS, images, and JavaScript that make up the game:

```
const getStaticAssets = () =>
  [
    target,
    `${target}/stylesheet.css`,
    `${target}/img/shipit-640x640-lc.jpg`,
    `${target}/img/Richard-Cartoon-Headshot-Jaunty-180x180.
png`,
    `${target}/app.js`,
  ]
    .map(http.get)
    .map(validate);
```

The `getGameId()` method simulates the start of a new game:

```
const getGameId = () => {
  const uri = `${target}/api/v2/games/`;
  const response = validate(http.post(uri, {}, params));
  return JSON.parse(response.body).id;
};
```

The `getScores()` method retrieves the existing scores using the `map` functional programming technique to both iterate over the endpoints and to run a validation function on the HTTP response:

```
const getScores = id => {
  return ENDPOINTS.map(element =>
    http.get(`${target}/api/v2/games/${id}/${element}`)
  ).map(validate);
};
```

The `putScores()` method is used to reset all the game scores, such as when a new game begins:

```
const putScores = (id, score) => {
  return ENDPOINTS.map(element =>
    http.put(
      `${target}/api/v2/games/${id}/${element}`,
```

```
        JSON.stringify({
            id: id,
            element: element,
            value: score,
        }),
        params
    )
  ).map(validate);
};
```

The default function is the one that k6 loops through for each virtual user:

```
export default function() {
  const startDelay = random_gaussian(6000, 1000) / 1000;
  log.debug(`Loading static assets, then wait ${startDelay}s to
start game`);
  getStaticAssets();
  sleep(startDelay);
```

After this function loads the static assets, it sleeps for a random delay to simulate a user waiting at the splash screen:

```
  const gameDelay = random_gaussian(1500, 250) / 1000;
  const id = getGameId();
  log.debug(
    `Game ${id}: Reset game scores, then wait ${startDelay}s to
start game`
  );
  getScores();
  putScores(id, 0);
  sleep(gameDelay);
```

After another delay, when simulating the user seeing the game screen, the test program enters a loop where it starts rapidly simulating clicks:

```
  log.info(`Game ${id}: Simulating ${MOVES} moves, starting in
${gameDelay}s`);
  for (let i = 0; i < MOVES; i++) {
    const moveDelay = random_gaussian(125, 25) / 1000;
```

Notice that we use a randomly generated delay between moves with a Gaussian distribution that has a mean of 125 milliseconds and a standard deviation of 25 milliseconds. This simulates clicking at about 8 clicks/second, which is the rate we measured when playing ShipIt Clicker on an iPhone – in 1 minute, we recorded 480 clicks:

```
    log.debug(`Game ${id}: move #${i}, then sleep ${moveDelay}
s`);

    deploy(id);

    sleep(moveDelay);

  }

  log.info(`Game ${id}: Done with ${MOVES} moves`);

}
```

The `default` function that's used for each virtual user fetches the same URLs that a user's browser would fetch on first page load. Note all the random delays that realistically simulate the delays that a real user would make. In a tight loop, the test simulates the user clicking as fast as a human would. The delay between clicks is subtly randomized using a random number with a normal distribution to simulate the fact that a human cannot click with robotic precision.

The `chapter11/bin/k6-run.sh` script runs the test using the same environment variable pattern override that the `k6-har-run.sh` script did, but with more variables. It allows you to set these parameters:

- USERS: Number of users
- DURATION: Duration in seconds
- MOVES: Number of moves in a game
- STAGES: Specify a set of k6 stages, which can vary VUs over time

The script requires a command-line argument, which is the URL target for the test. As mentioned earlier, this might be something like `http://192.2.0.10:80/` to test against the application infrastructure deployed on your workstation. Or, it could be the application as it was deployed to your cluster in the cloud, such as `https://shipit-v8.eks.shipitclicker.com/`.

Running a stress test

In order to run a stress test, you want to ramp up the amount of load on an application until it starts showing signs of failing. We can try doing that using the `script.js` k6 program and the `k6-run.sh` test harness. The key element that we must specify is the `STAGES` parameter:

```
$ MOVES=400 STAGES=900s:100 chapter11/bin/k6-run.sh https://
shipit-v8.eks.example.com
```

You will likely find that with the default settings of two pods, this initial test will not show any signs of failure. You can use the `kubectl` command, plus Prometheus, Grafana, and Jaeger to monitor the test progress, plus the CPU and memory utilization in the cluster, as described in the previous chapter. For example, here is a screenshot of Grafana after the preceding load test:

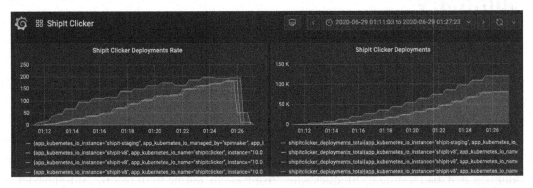

Figure 11.4 – The Grafana dashboard showing the rate of ShipIt Clicker deployments during the load test

In order to get this deployment to fail during the stress test, we don't want it to automatically scale out. So, we will delete the Horizontal Pod Autoscaler:

```
kubectl delete hpa/shipit-v8-shipitclicker
```

We also want to stress test a single pod in order to see how much it can take, so we will shrink the number of replicas in the deployment to only `1`:

```
kubectl scale deployment/shipit-v8-shipitclicker --replicas=1
```

At this point, we can rerun the stress test using the preceding `k9-run.sh` command. Watch the output. You will probably see some failed requests, which should be logged in the k9 output with a warning that looks something like this:

```
time="2020-06-29T05:52:31Z" level=info msg="WARNING:
PATCH https://shipit-v8.eks.example.com/api/v2/games/
t2iAHlWtnhJhbsXfJI3zB/deploys: status 503"
```

Once we are done stress testing, we can recreate the Horizontal Pod Autoscaler and reset the number of replicas for the deployment to a higher number.

At this point, we've learned how to use k6 to create a realistic load test and used it to perform a stress test of ShipIt Clicker.

Summary

In this chapter, we explored the topic of scaling out clusters in Kubernetes by using the Cluster Autoscaler and the Horizontal Pod Autoscaler. We then explored the topic of service meshes and set up a minimalistic Envoy service mesh in order to provide proxying and transparent network communications for complex microservice architectures.

Following this, we looked at how we could use the circuit breaker pattern to prevent a service from becoming overwhelmed by traffic. Then, we used connection thresholds to test that the circuit breaker worked, in conjunction with a simple load test technique, using Docker and Apache Bench. After this, we learned about progressively more sophisticated load testing techniques when using k6, including both record-and-playback and detailed hand-crafted load tests designed to mimic real user behavior.

This brings us to the end of our *Running Containers in Production* section of this book. We're going to move on and look at security next. Here, we will learn how to apply some techniques to the projects and skills we have developed so far in this book to improve our container security posture. So, let's move on to *Chapter 12, Introduction to Container Security*.

Further reading

Use the following resources to expand your knowledge of autoscaling, the Envoy service mesh, and load testing:

- Envoy presentation from Lyft: `https://www.slideshare.net/datawire/lyfts-envoy-from-monolith-to-service-mesh-matt-klein-lyft`.

- *Performance Remediation Using New Relic and JMeter*, a three-part article series by the *Docker for Developers* co-author Richard Bullington-McGuire. This covers load testing and performance improvement basics. You can adapt these techniques to Kubernetes using Prometheus, Grafana, Jaeger, and k6.io: `https://moduscreate.com/blog/performance-remediation-using-new-relic-jmeter-part-1-3/`.

- Using a Network Load Balancer with the NGINX Ingress Controller on Amazon EKS – an economical and flexible alternative to using the ALB Ingress Controller for many scenarios: `https://aws.amazon.com/blogs/opensource/network-load-balancer-nginx-ingress-controller-eks/`.

- *Kubernetes Autoscaling 101: Cluster Autoscaler, Horizontal Pod Autoscaler, and Vertical Pod Autoscaler*: `https://levelup.gitconnected.com/kubernetes-autoscaling-101-cluster-autoscaler-horizontal-pod-autoscaler-and-vertical-pod-2a441d9ad231`.

- Velero to backup and restore your Kubernetes cluster. Backup and restore your entire cluster, a namespace, or objects, filtered by tags: `https://velero.io/`.

- Expose Envoy Prometheus metrics as `/metrics`. See this issue for the workaround that's integrated into ShipIt Clicker's Envoy configuration that lets you expose Envoy's metrics to the Prometheus metrics scraper by adding an additional Envoy mapping: `https://github.com/prometheus/prometheus/issues/3756`.

- Microservicing with Envoy, Istio, and Kubernetes: `https://thenewstack.io/microservicing-with-envoy-istio-and-kubernetes/`.

- Jaeger Native Tracing with Envoy – an advanced tracing strategy: `https://www.envoyproxy.io/docs/envoy/latest/start/sandboxes/jaeger_native_tracing`.

- Redis with Envoy Cheatsheet – setting up Redis and Envoy using TLS and Redis Auth: `https://blog.salrashid.me/posts/redis_envoy/`.

- *Introduction to Modern Network Load Balancing and Proxying*, from Lyft's Matt Klein: `https://blog.envoyproxy.io/introduction-to-modern-network-load-balancing-and-proxying-a57f6ff80236`.

- *Matt Klein on the Success of Envoy and the Future of the Service Mesh*: `https://thenewstack.io/matt-klein-on-the-success-of-envoy-and-the-future-of-the-service-mesh/`.

- *Cost Optimization for Kubernetes on AWS*. Once you get a handle on scaling, the next step is to reduce costs. The EKS cluster might cost between $10-20 per day to run with the defaults given in the AWS EKS Quick Start CloudFormation templates: `https://aws.amazon.com/blogs/containers/cost-optimization-for-kubernetes-on-aws/`.

Section 3: Docker Security – Securing Your Containers

In this section, we introduce the topic of security. Here, you will build upon the skills you have learned throughout the book in order to understand how security techniques can be adopted to protect your container-based environments from malicious actors. From expanding our use of monitoring to introducing new tools to the DevOps pipeline, you'll be left in a position to start exploring more advanced topics and projects.

This section comprises the following chapters:

12
Introduction to Container Security

When developing technical projects, security should be a fundamental concern. We live in a world surrounded by security threats, from malware and viruses to data breaches. Being the victim of cybercrime or information leaks can have increasingly negative consequences, especially under regulations such as the EU's **General Data Protection Regulation (GDPR)**.

When breaches or compromises do happen, having the ability to limit their scope through good architectural practices is a must. This is achieved through the concept of limiting what is called lateral movement. By this, we mean using one breached system to access another, thereby providing the attacker with the ability to traverse through your system, compromising further systems and stealing data.

Thankfully, containerization, when deployed correctly, can help you improve your security posture through a variety of features that will be explored in the final section of this book. First, however, we should explore the technical fundamentals of Docker's security architecture so that we can start to build upon it. Some of the concepts in this chapter will be a recap of ideas we have explored elsewhere in this book, framed in a security setting. This should help to not only cement those concepts in your learning process but also help you to understand how to secure your application development projects.

In this chapter, we're going to cover a brief overview of the security architecture of containers and how this relates and compares to virtualization, as well as how Docker Engine and containerd work from a security perspective and the concepts they have inherited from Linux. We will also look at an overview of best practices that you can implement that leverage Docker's security architecture. This will provide a foundation for exploring the topic deeper in the following chapters.

We will cover the following topics in this chapter:

- Virtualization and hypervisor security models
- Container security models
- Docker Engine and containerd – Linux security features
- A note on cgroups
- An overview of best practices

So, let's start by reviewing how containers and virtualization differ and how security is a fundamental component of both.

Technical requirements

For this chapter, you will need to have access to a Linux machine running Docker. We recommend that you use the setup you have been using so far in this book.

If you have jumped to the security section as your starting point, we recommend you install the Docker Community Edition from `https://docs.docker.com/v17.09/ engine/installation/`.

Check out the following video to see the Code in Action:

`https://bit.ly/3gW33FD`

Virtualization and hypervisor security models

In previous chapters, we explored how Docker works and how it compares to other technologies, such as FreeBSD jails and virtualization. Building on what we learned here, we will now seek to understand the security model that underpins Docker better.

To start with, let's look at how security is implemented by virtualization tools so that we can then understand how Docker matches and differs from them.

Virtualization and protection rings

When using **virtual machines (VMs)**, you may have come across the term hypervisor. This is a program that orchestrates how the VMs run on your system and interact with the underlying hardware. Some hypervisor products, known as type 1 hypervisors, run directly on top of the hardware. Others, such as VirtualBox, are installed via your existing operating system and allow you to load additional operating systems as VMs.

How the hypervisor works with the underlying hardware is governed by what is known as protection rings. These rings dictate the layers of privilege, effectively deciding which aspects of a computer system's software, such as the operating system, drivers, and desktop applications, can access which parts of the underlying hardware.

Typically, you will see the protection ring modeled as a set of concentric circles, such as the following:

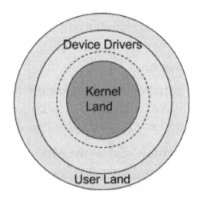

Figure 12.1 – Protection ring example

Sometimes the **device drivers** ring may show as two separate rings as well (denoted by the dotted circle in the diagram).

Each hardware architecture will differ slightly in its adaptation of the protection ring model and, in turn, the operating systems that run on it may also run code at different levels than expected. However, it is typical to find ring 0—that is, the ring at the center with the most privilege—denoted as the **kernel ring** (sometimes called **kernel land**).

Malicious software will often try to attack the kernel in order to gain full access over the system and run low-level system processes. This software is usually known as kernel-mode rootkits. Therefore, protecting the kernel is a must, as well as ensuring that if a system is breached with a malicious application, library, or package, it cannot escalate privileges to gain kernel access is paramount.

Outer rings may then handle device drivers and applications. Each is assigned a ring and the outer ring containing user applications is often known as **user land**. Gates handle how each ring can speak to the ring below it. As with the kernel, there is a risk of malicious software infecting applications that run at these levels including user-mode rootkits that run at level 3.

With these threats in mind, the protection ring model helps prevent the programs that you install on your desktop from maliciously accessing the underlying hardware and bypassing the kernel. Therefore, malware writers are forced to look for security holes and other means of obfuscating their attacks, such as injecting their code into other processes. You can think of these layers of security as providing a set of doors that need to be breached, rather than an attacker just being able to walk in and be given direct access to the underlying hardware.

These layers of segmentation, while not foolproof, help to provide what is known as a layered approach to security. The idea here is that by adding one layer of security to another, we make it increasingly difficult for an attack to be pulled off.

Virtualization and malware

Since we are interested in virtualization and subsequently, how this compares to Docker containers, we are, of course, interested in how virtualization fits into this model. How does virtualization protect against rootkits and other malware?

Many modern hardware architectures, such as the ARMv7-A, include a hypervisor as a privilege level in our ring model that is more privileged than the operating system level. This allows the hypervisor to switch between operating systems that are running at the next ring above.

Some architectures also implement what is known as **ring -1**. This allows the hypervisor to run at a further deeper security ring, with the guest operating system kernels running at ring 0. If, for example, you are running VirtualBox on top of an x86 platform, depending on whether hardware virtualization exists, VirtualBox will run either at ring -1 or ring 0.

VMs are useful for conducting malware analysis for a number of reasons, including the fact the machine can be locked down, so it is a self-contained environment. Once the investigator is done analyzing the code and its effects, the VM can be deleted without having to reinstall the whole operating system of the machine, or (if configured correctly) risk the malware gaining access to the underlying hardware.

So, in summary, protection rings provide a mechanism to provide a way to segment software so that it can only access certain resources. In a virtualization model, a hypervisor can run in the ring with the most privilege to switch between operating systems. A hypervisor can be installed via an existing operating system, such as Windows, or be deployed on bare metal, such as the VMware ESXi product. It can also be used to create a sandbox environment that prevents malicious code from infecting the underlying hardware or operating system.

So, how does this compare to Docker and how does the protection ring model apply?

Docker and protection rings

Like VMs, Docker containers provide an isolated environment for running your code on top of an existing operating system. This operating system can be either virtualized or installed directly onto bare metal.

So, how does this work? You may remember that Docker containers run on top of Docker Engine, which in turn sits on top of the operating system via an intermediate component called **containerd**. This is in comparison to the type 1 hypervisor, which runs on top of the infrastructure, as we discussed previously, with the guest operating systems running on top of the hypervisor.

Docker containers, therefore, all run on top of the same operating system, regardless of whether it is virtualized or not. In fact, in some instances, such as if you run Linux containers on Docker on Windows, you may notice that it uses an intermediary step. This consists of running a virtualized version of Linux, which in turn runs the Docker engine. In this scenario, all the containers are running on the same virtualized Linux operating system.

> **Note**
> Docker Engine Enterprise Edition also supports native Windows containers.
> You can read more about them at `https://www.docker.com/products/windows-containers`.

The key concept to all of this is that isolation happens at the container level, rather than—or in addition to—the VM level. So, at a basic level, Docker does not provide the same sandboxing that the VM itself does.

The following diagram demonstrates the difference:

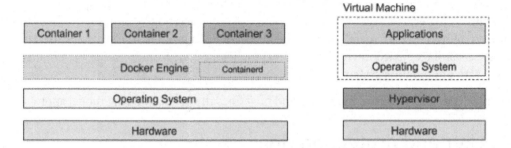

Figure 12.2 – Example of isolation in Docker and VMs

In the preceding diagram, if we run Docker on the VM stack, we would replace the **Applications** layer with the **Docker Engine/Containerd** and container layers.

As you can probably see, this provides a layer of security in addition to that provided by the underlying host operating system or, when applicable, the additional layer of the hypervisor. However, this layer of security when operating on top of the host operating system and not via a VM does mean that if the Docker Engine contains a security vulnerability, you have an additional layer of risk.

The Docker containers' access to the underlying system/kernel, therefore, is mediated by the engine, which in turn makes system calls via containerd (and, in most cases, is called via `runc`).

> **Note**
> If you want to read about containerd and runc in more detail, check out the official website at `https://containerd.io/`.

Here, we have provided a level of isolation between each container and the underlying operating system and hardware. Docker Engine does not run at ring 0 or ring -1, but rather at ring 3, meaning while it is susceptible to other forms of attack, it does not have direct access to the hardware as the hypervisor does.

> **Note**
> Even with this layered approach to security, flaws have been found in the past. You can read more at `https://www.twistlock.com/labs-blog/breaking-docker-via-runc-explaining-cve-2019-5736/`.

Additionally, each container is a separate self-contained set of libraries and applications that can only communicate with each other via Docker Engine. By default, as we noted, the containers do not have access to the underlying operating system that Docker Engine is hosted on. In fact, any calls to access system resources at the underlying OS level have to be explicitly configured when setting up the Dockerfile. The Docker containers, therefore, run at ring level 3, aka user land, with additional layers of security in place.

Now that we have an understanding of the ring model and how Docker and virtualization work in conjunction with it, let's look at container security models and what they have inherited from Linux's best practices and techniques.

Container security models

Moving up from the hardware layer and how the hypervisor and base operating system mediate access to it, we can begin to review what happens at the software layer running at ring level 3. To explore this, there are two key features of Docker's container security model that we need to understand:

- Applications are isolated from the underlying host system.

- Containerized applications are isolated from each other.

So, how does Docker achieve these objectives? The answer to this is, as you may have guessed, via Docker Engine and related components, such as containerd. These components have inherited a number of key Linux features and concepts with major benefits for security, including the following:

- **runc**: A lightweight container runtime

- **Namespaces**: A Linux method for partitioning kernel resources

- **Control groups (cgroups)**: A kernel feature for limiting resources such as CPU usage

Additionally, it also allows the implementation of other security features found in the Linux kernel, such as the following:

- **SELinux**: The Linux kernel security module for handling access control security policies

- **AppArmor**: A Linux feature for restricting application capabilities

- **TOMOYO**: A Linux security module for handling **mandatory access control** (**MAC**)

- **GRSEC**: A collection of security enhancements for the Linux kernel

These tried and true best practices allow containers to be isolated from one another and from the host operating system in a secure fashion. We will now delve deeper into Docker Engine and containerd to get a better understanding of how these security features are implemented.

Docker Engine and containerd – Linux security features

Docker Engine, which you installed previously, acts as the coordinator for all your application containers. In addition to the engine are other key components that make up the Docker ecosystem. Initially, many of the components were baked into Docker Engine, but over the years, in order to make the engine smaller and faster, some components, such as the runtime mechanism for managing containers, were broken down into separate projects.

One example of this is the containerd project. containerd, which implements `runc`, allows container management and is used in a number of related projects beyond Docker, including Kubernetes CRI.

> **Note**
>
> You can download and view the source code for containerd from GitHub at `https://github.com/docker/containerd` and `runc` at `https://github.com/opencontainers/runc`.

containerd solves the problem of aggregating a number of features in the Linux kernel and providing an abstraction layer to handle **system calls (syscalls)**. Docker Engine, therefore, sits on top of this and uses it to interact with the underlying operating system. An example of a task handed off to it from Docker Engine is attaching a process to an existing container.

This modular approach is not limited to the engine and how it interacts with the operating system. For example, containers and the engine do not need to reside on the same machine. Therefore, hosting options can be broken up.

This distributed model works as Docker implements a client-server model with the engine being the server and each of your containers acting as clients. Some of the key features of this architecture are as follows:

- The server running as a Linux daemon process (`https://man7.org/linux/man-pages/man7/daemon.7.html`).

- A Docker **command-line interface** (**CLI**) where you can run containers from. This is represented by the `docker` command in your terminal.

- Communication between the containers and the engine handled over a REST API.

It is important to note that the communication channel between the containers and the engine can be encrypted using SSL/TLS.

SSL/TLS is the de facto standard for encrypting traffic between web endpoints. You will have seen it used on websites when accessing content via the HTTPS protocol. Later on, we will explore how you can enable SSL/TLS to help protect the Docker daemon socket.

Docker provides an extensive set of features for configuring complex networks, and you can read more about it in detail at the Docker website at `https://docs.docker.com/v17.09/engine/userguide/networking/`.

The isolation that this client-server architecture provides between the host OS and your various containers (whether located on the same machine or distributed) works on the premise of least access. This means that each Docker container effectively only has access to the resources it needs, such as to the disk or network resources, and nothing more. Additionally, one Docker container cannot access the processes of another container.

This model of least access is aided by the implementation of Linux namespaces to isolate processes from one another. Running Docker on Windows via a virtualized Linux environment hosting the engine is one way that Windows users can reap the benefits of this technology.

> **Note**
> If you would like to learn more about how native Windows containers achieve process and Hyper-V isolation, you can refer to the Windows Containers website at `https://docs.microsoft.com/en-us/virtualization/windowscontainers/manage-containers/hyperv-container`.

342 Introduction to Container Security

Docker Engine, when deploying a container, will generate a number of these Linux namespaces. They are as follows:

- The **process ID (PID)** namespace
- The **mount (MNT)** namespace
- The **networking (NET)** namespace
- The **inter-process communication (IPC)** namespace
- The **Unix time-sharing (UTS)** namespace
- The USER namespace

We'll now look at each of these in a little more detail to understand the security implications.

PID namespaces

As you may know, each process in the Linux operating system resides in a tree structure and is assigned an ID called the PID. The PID namespace allows the separation of processes. By implementing the PID namespace, we can prevent our container from viewing the system processes. Aside from the security benefit of this, it has the additional benefit that system PIDs, such as PID 1, can be reused.

If you want to grant your containers access to system processes, you will, therefore, have to encode this into your Dockerfile explicitly. This follows the previously mentioned principle of granting the least access. So, think carefully before you implement any features this way.

MNT namespaces

The MNT namespace allows a container to have access to its own collection of root directories and file mounts. This method allows you to create a private filesystem and so segment which files are accessible to which container, reducing the risk of a compromised container getting access to files it shouldn't or accidental file corruption.

NET namespaces

Docker, as we discussed briefly, has a variety of networking tools at its disposal. By default, when you deploy a container, it will have its networking features enabled. This will allow them to make outgoing connections. By default, the container will use the same DNS servers as configured by the host and have a MAC address assigned to it. The IP address in IPv4 and IPv6 can be set using the relevant flags. If you chose to override the MAC address via the available flag, you should be aware that there is no mechanism to automatically check whether the MAC address is unique. Duplicate MAC addresses will likely result in a MAC address collision.

If you wish to disable networking as part of your security posture for a particular container, this can be achieved by overriding the settings using the `--network` flag when you execute the run command. Setting the flag to none will disable all external access, leaving only the loopback address accessible.

A number of other configuration options are available to customize your container network settings, and these can be accessed under the help menu.

IPC namespaces

The IPC namespace is used to provide separation of named shared memory segments, along with message queues.

IPC namespaces are locked down to prevent processes in one namespace accessing those within another. The benefit of this model is that a container can safely deploy a set of services that require memory segment utilization, such as the types of applications you might find in FinTech.

UTS namespaces

The UTS namespace allows us to set the domain and hostname for processes running in the namespace. This namespace is a default feature, so all containers have it enabled, and it allows you to assign a different hostname per container.

USER namespaces

The final category of namespace we will discuss is the USER namespace. This is a mechanism that allows you to map users and groups to a container. Once mapped, users can be assigned different user IDs.

One extremely useful benefit of this feature from a security perspective is that it helps to prevent your container from being leveraged for privilege escalation attacks. Examples of how to achieve this include not only running applications as an unprivileged user but also mapping the root user within the container to a less-privileged user at the Docker host level. Therefore, processes running at root within the container have this privilege level limited to the container they operate within.

A note on cgroups

Linux **cgroups** are a mechanism used to control the number of processes that can be spawned and so prevent a system from suffering severe performance loss or worse, crashing.

By using cgroups, we can set a limit to the number of processes that can be spawned through the `fork()` and `clone()` operations. Once a limit is hit, it's not possible to generate any further processes under the cgroup. Additionally, cgroups support the ability to set CPU and memory limits. You can read about their comprehensive list of options at `https://www.man7.org/linux/man-pages/man7/cgroups.7.html`

Using this feature enables you to have more granular control over the system resources that your container is using. In an unfortunate event where a container is compromised, preventing it from over-consuming system resources is a useful mechanism to limit the damage until you can remediate the problem.

Having looked at how Docker Engine and containerd use best practices from Linux, let's now move on to look at some best practices that we can use that also implement some of the features we have discussed so far.

An overview of best practices

In the following chapters, we will be delving into techniques to ensure your containers are secure. You'll be happy to know that there are a number of best practices that you can use off the bat to ensure that you are thinking about and implementing security at the most basic level.

The first thing to understand, and that you may have already picked up on, is that Docker containers, compared to VMs, do not provide the same level of security. We gave an example earlier of how a VM can be used for malware analysis due to its sandboxed environment. Therefore, from a security perspective, you should approach containers as a mechanism that is used to optimally package system resources and applications for development and delivery (with some very useful security built in) but not treat them as a micro-VM.

With this in mind, let's look at some best practices we can apply when using Docker.

Keeping Docker patched

As with any application you run, it is important to keep Docker patched. Unpatched security vulnerabilities in Docker Engine, for example, can be leveraged by nefarious actors who gain access to one of your containers in the case of a breach.

The Docker Desktop application in macOS, for example, provides an option to check for updates, and the preferences allow you to automatically check for updates:

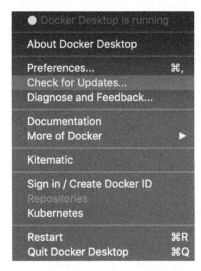

Figure 12.3 – Example of checking for updates on macOS

When implementing Docker, you may also wish to manually upgrade the software based on security patches or whether you are using the Docker Enterprise edition.

A list of each patch/release can be found on the Docker website with a list of the features added or issues addressed:

```
https://docs.docker.com/engine/release-notes/
```

You will notice here that some of the items are listed with the **CVE** prefix, which stands for **common vulnerabilities and exposures**. The CVE list is a collection of publicly disclosed security issues. When a security problem with Docker is identified, it may be listed in the CVE database, and then when it is fixed, the CVE ID for the issue will be listed in the release notes.

As a final note on this topic, also remember to keep the underlying operating system that Docker is running on patched and hardened, too.

Securing the Docker daemon socket

In addition to ensuring that Docker is regularly patched, we also need to safeguard the daemon socket. This means locking it down to prevent an attacker from using it to gain root access to the underlying host. Docker security documentation provides an extensive guide to doing this; however, we will summarize it here.

> **Note**
>
> To read more about the daemon socket, review the official documentation on Docker's website at `https://docs.docker.com/engine/reference/commandline/dockerd/#daemon-socket-option`.

You can find the domain socket file on Linux systems at `/var/run/docker.sock`.

This file should only be accessible via root permissions or accounts in the Docker group.

We are now going to set up encrypted access over TLS/SSL to the Docker daemon to add another layer of protection.

As you may be aware, unencrypted TCP sockets are enabled through using the `-H` flag and include the TCP protocol, host, and port number. The port for unencrypted connections by convention is `2375`. Going forward, if you have been using that method, we recommend you stop and use the built-in TLS/SSL support.

Before we can connect over the secure channel between our client and host, we need to generate the following files:

- **Certificate authority** (**CA**) private and public keys
- Server key
- Server **certificate signing request** (**CSR**)
- Signed certificates
- Client key
- Client CSR

Depending on your operating system, the steps to generate these OpenSSL files will be different. The Docker website provides a handy list of steps for this process. Windows users can use a Linux VM to perform these steps as well:

`https://docs.docker.com/engine/security/https/`

Implementing encryption can be achieved in the following fashion by enabling the Docker daemon to use the CA, server certificate, and server key. In this example, we will run the daemon on 0.0.0.0 and on port 2376:

```
dockerd --tlsverify --tlscacert=tlsca.pem
 --tlscert=tlsservercert.pem --tlskey=tlsserverkey.pem
 -H=0.0.0.0:2376
```

Now, we can test connecting to it. First, make sure that the client certificate, key, and CA are available. Then, run the following command:

```
docker --tlsverify --tlscacert=tlsca.pem --tlscert=tlscert.pem
 --tlskey=tlskey.pem -H=$HOST:2376 version
```

You should now be able to successfully connect to the Docker daemon over the encrypted channel.

Docker won't fix bad code

Docker can do a lot to help negate the effects of security problems, but it cannot fix bad code. The same best practices apply when writing applications that apply when deploying on an EC2 instance, VMware, or any other platform.

A great place to start with application security is the OWASP top 10. OWASP also offers a number of helpful cheat sheet guides for application security development, in addition to their standard documentation.

You can find them at https://cheatsheetseries.owasp.org/.

Always set an unprivileged user

We touched on the subject of the USER namespace and how it can aid you in securing your Docker setup. One practice you should implement is to make sure you configure containers to use an unprivileged user where possible. Doing this from the start will help you get into good habits.

The two easiest methods to do this are as follows:

- Add a user to the Dockerfile.
- When running Docker, add the --user flag to the run command.

In the first case, this can be achieved in the following fashion:

```
FROM alpine

RUN addgroup -S secureusers && adduser -S secureuser -G
secureusers

#Execute any root commands prior to needing to switch users
USER secureuser
```

With the second option, we can apply the flag to the command line as follows:

```
docker run --user 5000:500
```

Here, we have included the user ID and group ID.

Now that we have some basics in place, let's quickly review what we have learned before we further dig into some of the fundamentals and get our hands dirty.

Summary

Over the course of this chapter, we learned about how VMs and Docker work in conjunction with the underlying operating system, hardware, and each other.

Following this, we explored the various features that Docker has implemented from Linux to bake in security concerns.

Finally, we looked at some best practices that apply regardless of the applications we are developing. Now, let's jump into some security fundamentals and learn about Docker image security, commands, and the build process in the next chapter.

13
Docker Security Fundamentals and Best Practices

As we wish to ensure that our containers are hardened for both development and production environments, there are many techniques and best practices we can implement to achieve this task. In many cases, it is simply a case of modifying existing commands or behaviors you've learned throughout this book to add an extra layer of security to your practices.

Within this chapter, we will be building upon the foundational knowledge we have of Docker and container security. This will involve hands-on exercises in building and modifying containers. Covering subjects as varied as image security through the usage of Docker commands and signed images, upon completing the following exercises, you should feel comfortable in applying these skills in a real-world development and DevOps environment.

In this chapter, we're going to cover the following main topics:

- **Docker image security**: Here, we will learn about image security, including using minimal base images, signed and verified images, and avoiding data leakage.

- **Security around Docker commands**: Here, we will gain an understanding of how to use Docker commands securely, including using COPY instead of ADD when building out Docker images.

- **Security around the build process**: Here, we will learn about the best practices for build processes, including multi-stage builds.

Let's get started by looking at Docker image security and some best practices we can implement.

Technical requirements

For this chapter, you will need to have access to a Linux machine running Docker. We recommend that you use the setup you have been using so far in this book.

In addition to this, you will need an account on Docker Hub in order to access images located there. If you have not already set one up, you can do so at https://hub.docker.com.

If you have an existing container or service running SSH, this can be used later in this chapter. If not, do not worry. We provide a link to an example Dockerfile from the official Docker documentation you can use instead if you wish.

Check out the following video to see the Code in Action:

https://bit.ly/30WkOPE

Docker image security

As you have worked through the material in this book, you will have become increasingly familiar with images. These are a fundamental building block in the Docker ecosystem. An image is the combination of the filesystem and parameters that, when run by Docker, becomes your container.

Having made sure Docker itself is patched and secured, that our application code is robust, and that when we run the containers they will have limited privileges, we also want to ensure that the image itself is secure.

One of the benefits of Docker is that services such as Docker Hub allow us to share and reuse container images. However, we need to be careful that what we are downloading is secure and has not been uploaded by a malicious party:

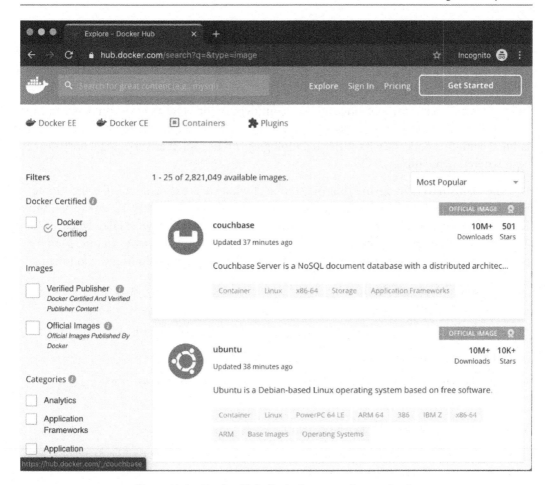

Figure 13.1 – Docker Hub displaying example repositories

You should always be cautious, however, even with legitimate/official websites.

There have been several cases in the past where malicious images have been uploaded to Docker Hub, with the hope that these will be downloaded by unsuspecting parties. Examples of malicious code have included images purporting to be related to **tomcat**, **mysql**, and **cron**. A compromised container containing a kernel exploit, for example, could lead to an attack on the underlying host.

Kromtech Security Center in one particular time frame in 2018 found 17 malicious Docker images on Docker Hub. You can read about this situation in their report, *Cryptojacking invades cloud. How modern containerization trend is exploited by attackers*, at `https://kromtech.com/blog/security-center/cryptojacking-invades-cloud-how-modern-containerization-trend-is-exploited-by-attackers`.

Your first step, therefore, in any project when using third-party tools and code should be to verify that the source of these artifacts is trustworthy. It is also important to stay on top of security alerts to make sure you do not inadvertently download images with damaging flaws.

In the case of Docker images, once you are confident of the validity of origin, you can then add additional verification processes to check the artifact itself is safe. In fact, you may be familiar with this concept with other technologies you use, such as verifying a file integrity hash when downloading an OS.

One mechanism to help ensure that the source of what we are downloading is legitimate is to use the signed Docker Certified images served from Docker Hub. As we saw with the Kromtech report, we can never be too careful, even with legitimate hosts like Docker Hub. These certified images have been reviewed by the host and certified as authentic. Many popular application environments are available on Docker Hub, including the following:

- Splunk Enterprise Edition: `https://hub.docker.com/_/splunk-enterprise`

- Datadog: `https://hub.docker.com/_/datadog-agent`

- Dynatrace: `https://hub.docker.com/_/dynatrace`

- Oracle Java 8 SE (Server JRE): `https://hub.docker.com/_/oracle-serverjre-8`

You can find more at the Docker Hub website here:

```
https://hub.docker.com/search?q=&type=image&certification_
status=certified
```

Let's now take a hands-on approach to checking the legitimacy of an image, including interacting with Docker Hub. Load up your command-line tool and then move on to the next section.

Image verification

The first concept we need to understand is that of content trust. This is the security model in Docker applied to images.

Docker's Content Trust (DCT) model at its heart is a mechanism to use digital signatures to prove the integrity of images hosted on platforms such as Docker Hub. With DCT enabled, users can then ensure they do not pull untrusted images (that is, unsigned images) unless they make explicit exceptions.

By default, Docker has DCT disabled, which will allow you to pull images without verifying the safety of them. This opens you up to the risk of downloading an artifact that is infected with malware or another security vulnerability.

Thankfully, we can use the DOCKER_CONTENT_TRUST flag to ensure that when we pull an image, it is verified. This works by checking whether the image has been signed by its creator or whether we are using an explicit hash associated with an image. To enable it system-wide, include it in your .bashrc file as follows:

```
$ vim /<path>/<to>/.bashrc
export DOCKER_CONTENT_TRUST=1
:x
$ source /<path>/<to>/.bashrc
```

If, for any reason, you wish to interact with an untagged image, you can temporarily disable the setting by using the --disable-content-trust flag in your command.

The DOCKER_CONTENT_TRUST flag can be limited to a single shell in addition to system-wide coverage. To quickly enable it in a new shell when you spawn, type the following:

```
$ export DOCKER_CONTENT_TRUST=1
```

Just remember that when you close the shell, you will need to enable the flag again, or set the system-wide property as explained earlier in the .bashrc file.

In practice, with this setting enabled system-wide (or in an individual shell), it means that command-line operations that interact with a tagged image will need to have one of two things. These can be either content hashes appended to the image or the image itself will need to be one that has already been signed in advance through the use of signing keys.

> **Signing keys**
>
> Signing keys are a set of components that are used to sign an image. They consist of an offline key, which forms the basis for DCT to trust an image tag, along with a tagging key for signing tags themselves and finally, a set of server-managed keys for enforcing security guarantees.

So, from a practical perspective, what exactly does this result in when running commands? Let's see a quick example using the image called shipitclicker.

If we wish to pull the `shipitclicker` image while the DOCKER_CONTENT_TRUST flag is enabled, we can append a hash to the image using the @ symbol. Consider the following, for example:

```
$ docker pull dockerfordevelopers/shipitclicker@
sha256:b20caa037ac2c36a9845f719ebb12952bbb3e749d4b05fcdcd8d
38201a7de795
```

As long as the content hash `sha256:b20caa037ac2c36a9845f719ebb12952bbb3e749d4b05fcdcd8d382 01a7de795` exists, the command will succeed. Otherwise, imagine that we wanted to pull the latest version of this image or version number, such as the following, for example:

```
$ docker shipitclicker:v0.1
```

In this scenario, we then would need to ensure that the image had been signed, or the command will fail. The `pull` command is not the only operation that interacts with trusted content. Others include the following:

- $docker push
- $docker build
- $docker create
- $docker run

We can test this out now. We've created the `shipitclicker` image in advance for you to pull from Docker Hub, located in the Packt Docker book repository at `https://hub.docker.com/r/dockerfordevelopers/shipitclicker`.

You can attempt to pull this image using the following command:

```
$ docker pull dockerfordevelopers/shipitclicker:v0.1
```

You should now see a *request denied* error similar to the following:

```
Error: remote trust data does not exist for docker.io/
dockerfordevelopers/shipitclicker: notary.docker.io does
not have trust data for docker.io/ dockerfordevelopers/
shipitclicker
```

Ensuring that this flag is enabled in an automated build process is also a must, as it prevents unverified images from making their way into your environments by accident.

This very simple approach of using DCT can go a long way to ensuring you avoid using untrusted content from Docker Hub. Now let's look at the base images a little closer.

Using minimal base images

So we know that we are pulling in signed images or specific hashes, but is there anything we need to consider around the type of image we are using in our containers? The answer to this is *yes*.

You should ask yourself when using an image whether the whole OS, complete with all its pre-installed packages, is required? In some cases, this can introduce vulnerabilities, as you may be including unpatched libraries and other code in your container. The best approach, therefore, is to start with something basic and then build up from there. This will help to reduce your overall attack surface.

Let's grab a minimal image from Docker Hub now so we can work with it throughout the rest of this chapter. The image we are going to use is `shipitclicker:v0.1`, which we just tested with `DOCKER_CONTENT_TRUST` and is based on Alpine.

> **Note**
> If you are interested in checking it out and haven't already done so, the Alpine image is only 5 MB in size and is part of the Official Images program on Docker Hub. These are a set of repositories that provide all the essential basics, while also ensuring all security patches are applied regularly. In addition to this, the official Docker images are also signed, so can therefore guarantee some of the security precautions that were just discussed around image verification in this chapter.

The first thing you will need to do is disable `DOCKER_CONTENT_TRUST` in your current shell, or grab the hash of the image so that you can now pull it. If you wish to disable `DOCKER_CONTENT_TRUST`, you can do this via the following command in your current shell:

```
$ export DOCKER_CONTENT_TRUST=0
```

Just remember, if you shut the shell down and create a new one, you will need to run this command again. We recommend you leave the flag set to 1 and instead pull the hash version.

You can find the hash under the **Tags** tab for the repository, as the following
link demonstrates:

```
https://hub.docker.com/r/dockerfordevelopers/shipitclicker/
tags
```

From here, select the digest value displayed under the version you are interested in.
This will then display the sha256 hash, such as the following, for example:

```
DIGEST:sha256:39eda93d15866957feaee28f8fc5adb545276a64147445c
64992ef69804dbf01
```

The following screenshot shows where you can find the hash for use in your docker
pull commands:

dockerfordevelopers/shipitclicker:0.1
DIGEST: sha256:39eda93d15866957feaee28f8fc5adb545276a64147445c64992ef69804dbf01

OS/ARCH	SIZE	LAST PUSHED
linux/amd64	2.68 MB	a few seconds ago by rpigui

Figure 13.2 – Information on a Docker image

The portion of the string containing sha256 onward can then be used in the pull request:

```
$ docker pull  dockerfordevelopers/shipitclicker@
sha256:39eda93d15866957feaee28f8fc5adb545276a64147445c64992ef
69804dbf01
```

You should now see something similar to the following in your terminal:

```
sha256:39eda93d15866957feaee28f8fc5adb545276a64147445c64992ef
69804dbf01: Pulling from dockerfordevelopers/shipitclicker
Digest: sha256:39eda93d15866957feaee28f8fc5adb545276a64147445c
4992ef69804dbf01
```

Running the docker images command should now show it present on your system.

When it comes to building your own images, another consideration is using the
.dockerignore file to help keep the overall container size down.

With the `.dockerignore` file included in the build context directory, any files listed in the file will not be added to the image. This, as you will see shortly, has another handy benefit. From an image size perspective, and in light of our general drive cleanliness as a best practice, we can use it to avoid binaries such as Python `.pyc` files and similar being accidentally added to the image. The following example `.dockerignore` file demonstrates how we can do this:

```
# ignore .pyc and .git files/directories
.git
**/*.pyc
```

This approach is very simple, and if you are used to using `.gitignore` files, it will already be familiar.

Now we have our minimal base image, we should take a look at some methods to restrict privileges when we create containers, so as to prevent accidental security breaches.

Restricting privileges

In the previous chapter, we looked at assigning a user and a group to restrict privilege escalation when starting the image. We can build on this by also using a useful parameter called `no-new-privileges`.

The flag leverages a feature of the underlying Linux kernel known as `no_new_privs`. The basic idea of this feature was to ensure that any processes, including child processes, cannot gain additional privileges when spawned. With this option enabled, applications will not be able to use features such as `setuid`.

> **Note**
>
> The `setuid` feature allows users to run and execute certain programs with escalated privileges. This poses a security threat, as an attacker can exploit it to execute code and programs they would not normally have access to.

Processes spawned via this feature also cannot unset the `no_new_privs` flag on themselves, thus preventing an attacker from disabling this feature and escalating privileges via `setgid` or `setuid`.

To enable the `no-new-privileges` feature when running a container, you will need to include the `--security-opt` flag and add it as a parameter.

Let's try this out with the image we just downloaded:

```
$ docker run -d -it --security-opt=no-new-privileges
dockerfordevelopers/shipitclicker@sha256:39eda93d15866957
feaee28f8fc5adb545276a64147445c64992ef69804dbf01
```

The image should now be running in this mode. Remember that we can get the container name by running the following command:

```
$ docker ps -a
```

Disabling the ability for a container to gain further privileges can also help us to prevent container breakout. The term **breakout** is used to refer to a case when a compromised container can access sensitive data on the underlying host. In a scenario where a container is exploited and the exploit allows the attacker to elevate privileges (if, for example, the previously discussed flag wasn't included), they may then attempt to pivot and compromise other containers through Docker, or exploit the host itself for some other gain.

As we will learn later in this chapter, there are ways to harden our system further, by restricting the privileges (known as capabilities) of a container when we run it.

We'll now look at some more flags we can add, along with some other techniques to ensure that the data we are using remains safe.

Avoiding data leakages from your image

In Linux, we can implement users and groups to ensure that only those who need access to read and write files can do so. This fine-tuned system of access permissions is important to help prevent data leakage. Another useful method we can use to protect the filesystem used by the image is to set the filesystems and any volumes to a read-only state.

Let's start by looking at a volume we may want to mount. We're going to run a new container based off the shipitclicker image and mount a local filesystem to it. In order to achieve this, in addition to the --mount flag, we will include a readonly statement within the run command.

Start by creating an empty folder on your local OS, which we can use to mount the filesystem:

```
$mkdir testfiles
```

Next, try running the following command. It will mount the local folder and run the container and attempt to write a file to the /mnt/testfiles directory called test.file:

```
$ docker run --mount source=testfiles,destination=/mnt/
testfiles,readonly dockerfordevelopers/shipitclicker@
sha256:39eda93d15866957feaee28f8fc5adb545276a64147445c64992ef
69804dbf01 sh -c 'touch /mnt/testfiles/test.file'
```

You should now see an error informing you that the filesystem is read-only:

```
touch: /mnt/testfiles/test.file: Read-only filesystem
```

Using this mechanism, we can read files mounted to the container, but avoid a situation where the container can write files back to it, thus accidentally writing keys or other data into a directory on the host where they should not be located.

> **Note**
> An important point to remember is that the root account can override any file permissions and thus can read any files in the container. If somebody gets root access, they can exfiltrate your data!

What about protecting the filesystem in the container itself, for example, the /tmp directory? Thankfully, Docker provides us with an easy method to do this, via the --read-only flag. We can try this out and see how it works in practice. First, stop the container we just created. Remember, you can get the container's name when you run the docker ps -a command.

Once you have the container name, stop the container. We've used nervous_sinoussi here to represent the name; replace this with your container's own unique name:

```
$ docker stop nervous_sinoussi
```

Now, we are going to recreate the container using the --read-only flag. Included in the run command will be an example of trying to write a file called test to the /tmp directory. With the --read-only flag enabled, we should get an error informing us this is not permitted.

Let's remove the container we created previously in order to keep our environment clean:

```
$docker container rm nervous_sinoussi
```

So, try running the following command, including your container name:

```
$ docker run --read-only dockerfordevelopers/shipitclicker@
sha256:39eda93d15866957feaee28f8fc5adb545276a64147445c64992e
f69804dbf01 sh -c 'echo "Testing" > /tmp/test'
```

You should now see an error such as the following:

```
sh: can't create /tmp/test: Read-only filesystem
```

Checking the list of Docker processes running, you will see the command executed and exited. Let's clear this container out and try rerunning the command without the flag and echo out the contents of the file we create:

```
$ docker run dockerfordevelopers/shipitclicker@sha256:
39eda93d15866957feaee28f8fc5adb545276a64147445c64992ef69804
dbf01 sh -c 'echo "Testing" > /tmp/test | echo "File content
is: $(cat /tmp/test)"'
```

Confirmation that the filesystem was written to will now be displayed via the `echo` command, which prints the contents of `/tmp/test`:

```
File content is: Testing
```

Therefore, to avoid this second scenario where the filesystem can be written to, always include the `--read-only` flag.

Additionally, remember not to include sensitive information such as private keys and API tokens inside the Dockerfile. There are a number of services you can use to avoid this situation including HashiCorp Vault, Docker Swarm, and services built into cloud providers like AWS, such as SSM. *Chapter 14, Advanced Docker Security – Secrets, Secret Commands, Tagging, and Labels*, will cover these in more detail.

With some of these best practices in mind, now let's look at the commands we would use to build our own images and what security concerns we need to take into consideration.

Security around Docker commands

We will shortly be exploring the build process and how we can harden this from a security perspective. In order to do this, however, we will first dig into some of the commands we will use in a little more detail so we know which ones are safe to use, and which pose a potential threat. Let's start by looking at the COPY and ADD commands.

COPY versus ADD – what's the story?

When you come to build an image, you will want to copy files from the host over to it. Typically, there are two methods for doing this. If you've done any research online, you may have seen comments along the lines of "don't use the ADD command." So why is this?

The ADD command allows us to recursively copy files over to the image, much like a cp -r command might do in Linux if we also piped it through zip when necessary. In short, it expands archive files and creates any directories that don't exist on the target.

The input to the command is provided as a URL that can reference either a local or remote (archive) file. As you can imagine, when pulling from a remote location, there are a number of risks to consider

- Has the file been modified on the remote host and compromised?

- Do you know the origin of the file on the remote host?

- What considerations are there regarding **Man-In-The-Middle (MITM)** attacks?

An example of how this command might be used in a Dockerfile can be seen here:

```
ADD https://github.com/PacktPublishing/Docker-for-Developers/
archive/master.zip /tmp/ch13/
```

In this case, the zipped version of the repository hosted on this book's GitHub account would be downloaded and expanded into the tmp directory.

Previously, we discussed using the .dockerignore file to help keep image sizes small. In addition to this benefit, they can help to prevent files accidentally being added if you include the ADD command. For example, you can ensure that configuration .ENV files or similar are not copied over.

The COPY command works slightly differently to ADD. Like ADD, it copies files recursively. However, you must provide an explicit source and destination folder. This means you have to declare the locations the files are coming from and going to. A ZIP file copied from A to B will still remain a ZIP file, and not be expanded while avoiding any unintended consequences.

We can see an example of the syntax for this command as follows:

```
COPY master.zip /tmp/ch13
```

It is safer to break down the process of adding files into multiple steps, such as downloading the files, scanning them, and then copying them over. When accessing remote content, you should always use an SSL/TLS connection as well. This can prevent MITM attacks being a problem by implementing a cryptographically secure and authenticated communication route.

> **Note**
>
> An MITM attack is one where a malicious party secretly eavesdrops, relays, or alters communications between two parties.

We've just looked at how the COPY command can avoid some of the issues of ADD, but what about recursive copying? Are there risks here?

Recursive COPY – use with caution

Recursive copying, as you may be aware, copies the contents of one location to another, and includes all the nested subfolders and files.

It's possible to accidentally copy files into the image you did not mean to when using the recursive copy command in Docker.

Let's look at an example. In this following screenshot, we can see an example directory, and included in it is a folder called oops and a my_secret file. This file contains a hypothetical secret such as an API token that has been accidentally left in the folder:

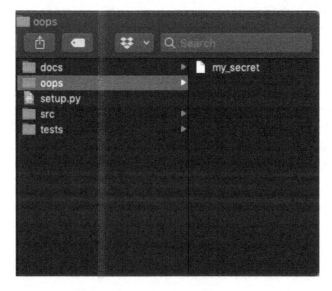

Figure 13.3 – Example of a secret accidentally left in the source code

Imagine that we were to run the following command:

```
COPY . .
```

Along with the parent directory in which all the folders reside, this secret file would also be copied over, as the command will recursively copy everything, including the `oops` directory and our nested file.

In order to avoid these negative effects, it is always a good practice to update your `.dockerignore` file to ensure that sensitive file types are excluded.

As we noted earlier, if you are familiar with `.gitignore`, adding file types to your `.dockerignore` file should be simple. Here are some quick rules to remember:

```
# comment - the line is ignored

* # matches anything up to the * e.g. *.txt matches all text
files

**# matches any number of folders e.g. **/*.txt matches all
text files in build context

! #can be used to exclude a specific file e.g. !id_rsa.pub

tmp? # Any files or folder that start with tmp and include a
subsequent character are
              #ignored

*/tmp* # Will exclude any directories or files starting with
tmp directly below root

*/*/tmp* # Similar to the above however works for two
directories below root
```

Using these mechanisms, you can ensure a variety of files are excluded from the container, such as `*.pem` and `*.ENV` files.

Therefore, if you do plan to use recursive copying in your Dockerfile, ensure the `.dockerignore` file is up to date and that you have audited your application to ensure that everything being copied over is as intended.

Let's now turn our attention to the build process and how we can improve security at this stage. Here, we will see how commands such as COPY come into play as part of a larger process.

Security around the build process

We've seen how we can pull images and run them in a secure fashion. But what about building our own container images? As you are now familiar with, some commands pose additional risks when added to the Dockerfile. In this section of the chapter, we will look at how we can secure the build process using the techniques we have learned so far. This will include using a minimal base image (`shipitclicker`) as a starting point and then using the security tweaks we have tested against this image when running it as a container.

Using multi-stage builds

As we previously covered, we need to be careful about secrets and ensure they are not accidentally leaked. One way to avoid this is to not include them in the Dockerfile. However, what about at the build stage? It's likely you will need to use private keys in conjunction with the build process from time to time, for example, to pull code from a remote service that is protected with public key encryption.

One method to use keys securely is through the use of multi-stage builds. This process uses a disposable intermediate layer, which ensures that data isn't accidentally leaked into the final build process. Let's look at a simple example. If you wish to run this code, you will need to have an SSH server running and add your public key to it.

If you don't have one running already, to build a container that runs SSH, you can reuse the Dockerfile located at `https://docs.docker.com/engine/examples/running_ssh_service/`.

Next, let's take a look at an example of the multi-stage build process and how we can use it in conjunction with accessing an SSH service.

Copy the following code to a new Dockerfile you can work with. On your container running the SSH server, add a file called `file.txt` and then update the Dockerfile code to include your user, IP/hostname, and the path to the file you just created.

Let's do a quick walkthrough of what is going on here before we build it:

```
FROM  dockerfordevelopers/shipitclicker@sha256:39eda93
d15866957feaee28f8fc5adb545276a64147445c64992ef69804dbf01 as
intermediate

WORKDIR /test
ARG ssh_prv_key
RUN echo "$ssh_prv_key" > /tmp/id_rsa_test
```

```
RUN chmod 600 /tmp/*
RUN apk add openssh
RUN scp -i /tmp/id_rsa_test user@server:/path/to/file.txt .

FROM dockerfordevelopers/shipitclicker@sha256:39eda93
d15866957feaee28f8fc5adb545276a64147445c64992ef69804dbf01

WORKDIR /test
COPY --from=intermediate /test .
```

This code does a number of things. First, it takes our shipitclicker image as an intermediate build step.

Following this, it sets the WORKDIR to test and creates an ARG value called ssh_prv_key. This ARG value will allow us to pass in the path to the RSA private key that will be needed to connect to the remote SSH server.

Based upon our input, we echo it out as a file and then set permissions on the file to 600. Then, we install openssh so we can use the scp command-line feature. The interesting bit comes next.

The RUN scp command takes the private key we injected and uses it to connect to the remote server to retrieve a file called file.txt, which is then copied back to the present directory. This step completes the first stage of the build.

In the second stage, we once again use the shipitclicker image and use the same WORKDIR, that is, test. The final line, however, is where the magic happens. It copies from the intermediate step we completed in step 1, the file that was retrieved from the remote server, and replicates it to the final build stage.

As you can see from the result, the final container does not contain the private key we used to retrieve the file from the remote SSH server, and thus will not accidentally end up in the final container.

To build out this Dockerfile once you have a remote location to copy the file from, you can use the following command:

```
$docker build --build-arg ssh_prv_key="$(cat ~/.ssh/id_rsa_
test)" .
```

As you can probably guess from looking at this, the ssh_prv_key build argument is simply the value of our private key concatenated out into the variable.

Once we have built our container, when we run it, we want to ensure that it does not consume more resources than required. This can help to mitigate damage in the case of an unfortunate security breach.

As a final note, multi-stage builds can also aid in keeping the images small, which is a desirable quality, as already discussed. Let's now take a look at how we limit capabilities and resource usage in Docker further.

Limiting resources and capabilities when deploying your builds

You can limit a variety of resources available to your container, including CPU usage and memory. This can help prevent denial-of-service attacks. In this scenario, the container is exploited to use up the underlying resources of the host, thus causing overall performance degradation, or worse, the underlying host to crash.

Additionally, access control mechanisms are an important piece of the puzzle to ensure that as well as limiting the resources used by a container, we also limit privileges and access.

Limiting resources

In order to avoid the types of DOS attacks mentioned earlier, we can use a combination of flags to restrict how much of the underlying host resources a container can consume.

The first area we will look at is memory. Docker gives us the ability to restrict how much memory a container can use through a combination of hard and soft limits.

We can set a hard limit on a container using the -m/--memory flag. This will set aside the amount you specify and will not allow the container to exceed this. In the case that a container does become compromised, the hard limit feature will prevent a runaway malicious process from consuming more and more of the underlying host's RAM.

When setting the memory limit, ensure that you adjust it in line with what your application is intended to do. Too little memory may prevent an issue if the container were compromised, but may, in turn, not be enough to run your application.

The –memory flag can also be combined with the –memory-reservation flag. This second feature allows you to specify a soft limit smaller than the –memory one. When Docker discovers that the underlying host has an issue, such as low memory, it will activate this feature. Once activated, Docker will attempt to restrict the amount of memory available to the container.

As with memory, we also need to be aware that an exploited container can also consume more CPU resources than expected, which can, in turn, have negative side effects for the host.

> **Note**
>
> If you are using Docker 1.12 or lower, you will need to use the `–cpu-period` and `–cpu-quota` flags instead of the `–cpus` flag.

Using the `–cpus` flag, you can define how many CPUs a container has access to. If you have multiple CPUs (for example, four) and set the value to `–cpus="2"`, the container is restricted to only being able to use up to two CPUs and no more.

We've seen how we can use some flags to restrict the resources a container has available to it at runtime. Let's look at some additional flags we can use to further restrict potential security risks when we run our container.

Dropping capabilities

Some techniques you can use to help avoid other risks include dropping capabilities when running containers. Capabilities are a feature of Linux that divide privileges associated with the root/super user account into individual components.

The list of capabilities that a container usually has are `chown`, `dac_override`, `fowner`, `fsetid`, `kill`, `setgid`, `setuid`, `setpcap`, `net_bind_service`, `net_raw`, `sys_chroot`, `mknod`, `audit_write`, and `setfcap`. To understand what each capability allows, please refer to the Linux man-pages documentation at `http://man7.org/linux/man-pages/man7/capabilities.7.html`.

To remove capabilities such as `chown`, you can use the `–cap-drop` flag when running a container. Refer to the following for an example:

```
$ docker run -d -it --cap-drop=chown   --security-opt=no-new-
  privileges dockerfordevelopers/shipitclicker@sha256:39eda
  93d15866957feaee28f8fc5adb545276a64147445c64992ef69804dbf01
```

Removing powerful capabilities that your production containers do not need can help harden you against attacks that seek to break out of the container.

That ends this chapter on techniques to improve your fundamental security posture. Before we move on to some more advanced techniques, let's quickly re-cap what we have learned so far.

Summary

In this chapter, we have reviewed some basic steps you can take to ensure that when you pull images and build and run containers, your attack surface will be reduced.

We learned about how to ensure that we only pull safe images from Docker Hub. Additionally, we saw how we can use read-only permissions to prevent write access to filesystems.

Multi-stage builds were discussed to show how we can break down our container build process into steps to ensure that SSH keys and similar are not accidentally included in the final product. The `.dockerignore` file was briefly reviewed from a security perspective, and finally, we discussed how to restrict system resources and implement access control through removing capabilities.

In the next chapter, we will look at how we can automate some of the security processes by using scanning tools and implement monitoring.

14

Advanced Docker Security – Secrets, Secret Commands, Tagging, and Labels

We've seen several examples so far of the need to use files that contain secrets. We can think of secrets as a generic term for the types of sensitive data that would typically be stored in config and ENV files, such as database access credentials or API tokens. Docker provides a handy method for securing this type of data and sharing it. For legacy systems using swarm mode instead of Kubernetes, having an understanding of how to apply security to these environments is important, as you may have to retroactively fix environments in your career.

Along with managing secret data, we can also use labels and tags to help ensure we are working with security in mind. You've seen tags already in the previous chapter and we will explore these further later in this chapter.

Additionally, we will explore how metadata labels can be used to provide extra information about a container and how to use the `security.txt` file.

In this chapter, we're going to cover the following main topics:

- An introduction to securely storing secrets in Docker
- What secrets are and why we need them
- A walk through the Raft log file
- Adding, editing, and removing secrets from a swarm
- Using tags more effectively to ensure we use secure images
- Implementing metadata labels and the secrets.txt file

Let's get started by looking at what Docker secrets are and why they are beneficial.

Technical requirements

For this chapter, you will need to have access to a Linux machine running Docker. We recommend that you use the setup you have been using so far in this book.

In addition to this, you will need an account on Docker Hub in order to access images located there. If you have not already set one up, you can do so via the following link:

```
https://hub.docker.com
```

Finally, in order to explore using Docker secrets, you will need to set up at least two containers and use Docker's swarm feature. You can read more about swarm mode here: `https://docs.docker.com/engine/swarm/`

Check out the following video to see the Code in Action:

```
https://bit.ly/3iDsjkA
```

Securely storing secrets in Docker

An inevitable part of working with complex, networked software projects is having to deal with secret data. This can be a range of things such as private keys for SSH access, SSL certificates, passwords, and API keys.

In order to share secrets securely with multiple containers, you will, of course, need to avoid attempts to store the secret in the container itself in a fashion that allows a potential attacker to access it. This layer of abstraction is not only useful for managing different sets of credentials based upon the environment, but also provides an extra layer of security should the container be compromised in some fashion.

Thankfully, Docker comes with a useful feature for achieving this goal. It is simply called Docker secrets. In order to use this feature or the Kubernetes equivalent, you will need to implement swarm services or Kubernetes itself. As we have recommended elsewhere in this book, you may wish to avoid swarm services if possible, in favor of Kubernetes. However, you may have to work with legacy systems where they are in use, so understanding secrets in this case is important. With this in mind, containers should, therefore, run as a service.

Mirantis, having purchased Docker, has pledged open-ended support for Docker Swarm as of February 2020 (`https://www.mirantis.com/blog/mirantis-will-continue-to-support-and-develop-docker-swarm/`). You may be familiar with this concept from *Chapter 5, Alternatives for Deploying and Running Containers in Production*; however, if you need a refresher you can follow the steps provided on the Docker website for getting started with swarm mode as an alternative to Kubernetes if you wish:

`https://docs.docker.com/engine/swarm/swarm-tutorial/`

The secrets feature in both swarms and Kubernetes allows you to manage data such as passwords and API keys centrally and then securely share it with the containers of your choice. This avoids having to hardcode values in an insecure fashion within the container, or having to allow all containers access to the sensitive data.

Additionally, secrets, when shared with other containers in a swarm by Docker secrets, for example, are transferred over a secure connection encrypted via SSL/TLS. Let's now take a deeper look at how Docker secrets work at a fundamental level, including an important feature called the Raft log.

The Raft log

In order to share content between swarm nodes, we need to ensure there is both consensus and fault tolerance. In short, this means that all nodes in the network agree on some set of values to maintain a consistent state.

The algorithm that Docker Swarm uses is called Raft. You can read more about the technical details in the paper *In Search of an Understandable Consensus Algorithm*, available at the Raft GitHub account:

`https://raft.github.io/raft.pdf`

Docker Swarm uses a file known as the Raft log file as part of its implementation of the algorithm. The benefit of this file is that it can be used for storing secrets, which subsequently have to be shared across 1 to *n* nodes. When a secret is added via the `docker secret` command, a value is added to the Raft log file and is then made available via a temporary filesystem, as seen in this example:

```
/run/secrets/apikey
```

And this in essence is how a secret can be shared between multiple Docker containers in a swarm. Reading the secret in an application will depend on what language you are using. For example, if you were modifying the ShipIt Clicker application you would be using JavaScript. If we had a secret such as an API key file, we could access it directly in the JavaScript source code using the `fs` module, as the following example demonstrates:

```
fs.readFile('/run/secrets/apikey', 'utf8')
```

As you can see, this is a fairly simple approach.

Although this file is encrypted, we can also add an extra layer of security through locking.

Swarms can be locked using the `--autolock` flag in order to prevent an attacker from decrypting the Raft log file.

Refer to the Docker documentation for more details:

`https://docs.docker.com/engine/swarm/swarm_manager_locking/`

Now you have a basic understanding of how the Docker secrets feature works, let's look at how we use it.

Adding, inspecting, and removing secrets

We will now begin exploring the various commands associated with secrets.

Feel free to also substitute the commands in this section with their Kubernetes equivalent if you wish to try those instead. You can find the list of `kubectl` commands at `https://kubernetes.io/docs/concepts/configuration/secret/`.

Or you can refer back to *Chapter 8, Deploying Docker Apps to Kubernetes*, where we created, described, retrieved, and edited secrets via `kubectl`.

In relation to Docker, we will start by creating secrets first.

Creating

The `create` command is how we add a new secret to the Raft log file. Its basic format is the following:

```
docker secret create [OPTIONS] SECRET [file|-]
```

You may notice this is similar to the command in `kubectl`, which is `kubectl create secret`.

When creating a secret, we can use the `-l` flag to add a label to the secret, such as the following:

```
docker secret create -l key=val api_key -
```

This allows us to label values, so we know which environment they are destined for. For example, we can add a key value for the environment such as **Quality Assurance (QA)**, **Development (DEV)**, and **Production (PROD)**.

A secret can also be a file. For example, if we want to add a private key, we might do the following:

```
docker secret create my_key ./id_rsa
```

If you wish to add/update a secret to a running service, you will need to use the `--secret-add` flag on the `update` command. See the following, for example:

```
docker service update --secret-add <secret> <service>
```

Having added a secret, let's explore how we can now review it.

Inspecting

There are a number of techniques we can use to examine Docker secrets. To list any secrets that have been added to the Raft log file, we can use the `ls` command:

```
$ docker secret ls.
```

On running this command, the current secrets will be displayed, as shown in the following example:

ID	NAME	CREATED	UPDATED
123345	my_key	2 weeks ago	2 weeks ago

We can gather more information about this secret using the `inspect` command.

The format for this is the following:

```
docker secret inspect [OPTIONS] SECRET [SECRET...]
```

So, using the preceding example, we could run the command as follows:

```
$ docker secret inspect my_key
```

This will then return a JSON object containing the ID, version created and updated dates, and the `spec` object containing the labels and name. An example of this output is now provided:

```
[
    {
        "ID": "ae4kfwe6s56sgop7vn1kxap59",
        "Version": {
            "Index": 10
        },
        "CreatedAt": "2020-01-26T07:15:29.674382561Z",
        "UpdatedAt": "2020-01-26T07:15:29.674382561Z",
        "Spec": {
            "Name": "my_key",
            "Labels": {
                "env": "dev",
                "rev": "20200126"
            }
        }
    }
]
```

We've added and inspected secrets, so now we shall explore how to delete them when we no longer need them.

Deleting

Removing a secret is as easy as adding one, and uses the same syntax as its Linux equivalent for removing files, that being `rm`.

The format of the command is as follows:

```
docker secret rm SECRET [SECRET...]
```

In Kubernetes, the equivalent would be `kubectl delete secret`.

To remove our example secret from earlier, we would run the command as follows:

```
docker secret rm my_key
```

If you wish to remove a secret being used by a current service, you will need to use the `--secret-rm` flag with the `update` command, such as in the following example:

```
docker service update --secret-rm <secret> <service>
```

As you can see, adding, removing, and inspecting secrets is simple. Let's now try the preceding commands out using the SSH file from *Chapter 13, Docker Security Fundamentals and Best Practices.*

Secrets in action – examples

It's now time to try out the commands we just reviewed (`create/inspect/ls/rm`). Make sure your setup is configured to use swarms. You can also re-use the image from the previous chapter for this section. This can be obtained using the following command:

```
$ docker pull docker pull dockerfordevelopers/shipitclicker@
sha256:39eda93d15866957feaee28f8fc5adb545276a64147445c64992ef
69804dbf01
```

> **Important note**
>
> Remember, you can use the `docker swarm init` command to initialize the swarm. Use the `--advertise-addr` flag with the IP address of your initial container as well.

Previously, we used the following command to add an SSH private key for use with SCP to a single container:

```
$ docker build --build-arg ssh_prv_key="$(cat ~/.ssh/id_rsa_
test)" .
```

To add this key to our swarm, we would use the following command:

```
$ docker secret create -l env=dev ssh_prv_key ~/.ssh/id_rsa_
test
```

Here, we have created a new secret with the same name as the build argument we used previously, and we output the content of our private key to it. We also included a label, which has a `key=val` pair denoting the environment we are working in. In this case, it is the development environment.

Let's now check that we have added it correctly. We can do this by running the `ls` command:

```
$ docker secret ls
ID          NAME          CREATED         UPDATED
To5jj...    ssh_prv_key   1 minutes ago   1minutes ago
```

Here, we see the ID of the secret and the name. This looks good! Now let's execute the `inspect` command on the key using the `NAME` value:

```
$ docker secret inspect ssh_prv_key
```

You should now see a JSON object displayed, similar to the following:

```
[
    {
        "ID": "to5jjgshjqaddhf56ty89rss42",
        "Version": {
            "Index": 17
        },
        "CreatedAt": "2019-11-25T07:11:03.335174723Z",
        "UpdatedAt": "2019-11-25T07:11:03.335174723Z",
        "Spec": {
            "Name": "ssh_prv_key",
            "Labels": {
                "env": "dev",
                "rev": "20181125"
            }
        }
    }
]
```

If you have multiple containers in your swarm, then you can grant them access to this secret. The following example demonstrates how we can send the secret we just created to a new container that uses our example image:

```
$ docker service create --name second_container
--secret source=ssh_prv_key,target=second_ssh_prv_
key,mode=0400 dockerfordevelopers/shipitclicker@
sha256:39eda93d15866957feaee28f8fc5adb545276a64147445c64992ef
69804dbf01
```

Here, the --secret source value is set to the name of the Docker secret we created. We are then going to store it in the variable defined in the target value. For clarity, we have called this second_ssh_prv_key. The mode has been set to 0400 to make the secret accessible and then chosen our tagged image as the source image for the create command.

To confirm the secret is available, we can check the temporary filesystem we discussed earlier. For this, you will need to grab the container ID of the new container. You can use the docker ps command for this.

Next, use the container ID as follows:

```
$ docker exec -it <id> cat /run/secrets/second_ssh_prv_key
```

You should see that the contents of the secret are the same as those you passed into the first container, namely the private SSH key we have been testing with so far.

> **Other options**
>
> In addition to using native Docker and Kubernetes tools, a variety of other options exist for storing secrets in cloud-based systems. AWS, GCP, and Azure offer native support, and HashiCorp provides a comprehensive cloud-agnostic secrets-managing mechanism in the form of HashiCorp Vault, at https://www.vaultproject.io/.

We are now going to build upon our knowledge of Docker secrets by understanding how tags can be used.

Docker tags for security

We've just seen how we can make sure we are sharing secrets securely between containers in a swarm. In *Chapter 12, Introduction to Container Security*, we gained an appreciation for how to use tags combined with other security features, to ensure we use the correct image.

Now, we'll see how these two worlds can intersect by using tags with secrets and labels so we can annotate which environment a given secret and tag are used in.

As a good security practice, we should always use different secrets for different environments. For example, the passwords for database access in your development, staging, and production instances should not be the same. Typically, as part of your development process, you will likely be using newer versions of containers in research, development, and QA environments compared to production.

We can use Docker tags to help ensure that once we have credentials/secrets set up for a development environment, we are also pulling in the right image as well; that is, the one we intended to use for development purposes with the development credentials we created. Using fixed tags provides a layer of security through immutability and prevents an experimental image that may contain security flaws from accidentally being used outside of the development environment.

Typically, a methodology such as semantic versioning (https://semver.org/) should be in place. This will result in tags using a format that communicates the level of change you should expect when using the release. Major version numbers indicate a backward-incompatible set of changes. A minor release is usually a new feature to an existing release. Finally, we have a patch release, which could be a small security fix or similar. A typical format might be the following:

```
1.1.2
```

When choosing the tag, in line with your versioning system, choose the one that most closely matches the environment you want to deploy in. For example, choose :1.1.2-dev over :1.

In this instance, you know you will be pulling the patch release. You can then deploy credentials via docker secret, specifically for this build and for the environment you are deploying it to. One useful method is to pair up the secret label with the tag version you are using, as in the following code, for example:

```
$docker secret create   --label ver=1.1.2-dev \
                         --label env=dev \
                         ssh_prv_key ~/.ssh/id_rsa_test
```

In this example, a secret has been created (an SSH key) and we know it should be used with tag version `1.1.2` and that this is a development environment. Here, the labels provide annotations to give us the context of the secret. Simple techniques like this can help to provide more information to an engineering team and avoid a production credential from accidentally being used with an experimental development container or in the wrong environment.

We've seen how we can combine tags, secrets, and labels. Let's now look at other labeling options.

Using labels for metadata application

Metadata labels are a way of annotating your containers with extra information to provide development teams with useful facts. This can be useful for other developers on your team when they need to understand key features of the image, such as its version and a description.

We saw with the `docker secrets` command how we could add labels via the command line. With metadata labels, we can also add labels to the Dockerfile so that when we build out a new container, this information is baked in.

A label takes the following format:

```
LABEL key=value
```

Building upon our preceding example, we can set the version inside of our container via the Dockerfile as follows:

```
LABEL "version"="1.1.2-test"
LABEL "description"=" Development environment container for
testing the newest security patch. Not for production release
yet"
```

Once you've built out a container, you can view any of the metadata you have added using the `docker inspect` command:

```
"Labels" :{
        "version"="1.1.2-test",
        "description"=" Development environment container for
testing the newest security patch. Not for production release
yet"
}
```

When releasing software for public consumption, you should consider also linking to a `security.txt` file. Like a code of conduct or contributors' guide, this provides a mechanism to alert security researchers on how to responsibly disclose any security issues they may find with your software.

You can automatically generate a `security.txt` file from the following website:

`https://securitytxt.org/`

Save this file to your code repository, and then link it via LABEL in your Dockerfile as in the following example:

```
LABEL "security.txt"="https://respository.example.com/my_
project/security.txt"
```

That wraps up our guide to secrets, tags, and labels. Let's recap what we have learned so far.

Summary

In this chapter, we learned all about Docker secrets, the counterpart to Kubernetes secrets. We saw how this feature can be used to securely share sensitive data between containers in a swarm if you need to work with this technology instead of Kubernetes. We also learned this can be useful for segmenting sets of credentials based upon the environment you are working in. Finally, we walked through how we can create, inspect, and delete them.

Following this, we looked at tags once again and discussed how these can be used to ensure the right image is being pulled from the right environment. A combination of environment-based secrets and tags were shown to help you secure your development processes further.

Finally, we discussed how containers can be annotated with metadata labels. This also included using the `security.txt` file.

In the next chapter, we will explore how third-party tools can be used to help secure our containers and enforce some of the practices we have learned so far.

15
Scanning, Monitoring, and Using Third-Party Tools

So far, we have explored how we can manually configure our Docker containers to ensure security is a priority. In this chapter, we will look at some of the tools available to automatically scan our images and monitor our production loads. This will provide a jumping off spot for you to expand your Docker-based projects further, based upon your cloud provider if you use one.

We will start off by looking at DevOps solutions such as Anchore Engine for scanning images for security vulnerabilities, review `docker stats` and learn how it is useful, set up cAdvisor for local monitoring, and understand how Datadog can be used as a cloud-based solution for gathering container stats.

This chapter will also briefly review AWS security options including GuardDuty for monitoring production environments and cover some of the features that Microsoft Azure offers. You'll gain an understanding of what tools are available to **Google Cloud Platform** (**GCP**) users and deploy the Datadog Agent to your container environment.

In this chapter, we're going to cover the following main topics:

- Scanning and monitoring – cloud and DevOps security for containers
- Securing your containers using AWS
- Securing your containers using Azure
- Securing your containers using GCP

Let's get started by looking at techniques for monitoring containers, scanning for security issues.

Technical requirements

For this chapter, you will need to have access to a Linux machine running Docker. We recommend that you use the setup you have been using so far in this book.

In addition to this, you will need an account on Docker Hub in order to access images located there. If you have not already set one up during previous chapters, you can do so via `https://hub.docker.com`:

In order to use many of the programs explored in this chapter, you will need to download them from the web. We'll provide links in each section where relevant so you know where to get them from. In some instances, you may need to set up an account in order to use a service or download a tool.

Check out the following video to see the Code in Action:

`https://bit.ly/30VfWu8`

Scanning and monitoring – cloud and DevOps security for containers

Before we begin to look at specific tools for monitoring and scanning your containers, we shall first define exactly what we mean by the term monitoring in a security context.

As you have seen throughout this book, containers provide a mechanism to serve up applications in small self-contained environments. However, we need to ensure that released software does not suffer from performance degradation while running. For example, we need to know if a container is consuming a lot of resources and thereby impacting the overall performance of our environment. You may already have some understanding of this concept from *Chapter 10, Monitoring Docker Using Prometheus, Grafana, and Jaeger.*

Additionally, monitoring allows us to look for anomalies that may indicate that the system is under attack or has been compromised in some fashion. While elsewhere in this book monitoring has been focused on ensuring system stability and performance, we will use those concepts from a security angle. Security scanning applications are an important part of any tool chain, but may not pick up every issue, especially newer exploits. Therefore, looking for negative side effects of a malicious software's presence is an important defense mechanism. As such, combining scanning prior to release, monitoring post release, and incident response are important parts of running a production container system.

A note on sandbox environments

One concept that may also be useful to understand is a sandbox environment. A sandbox provides an environment for isolating and testing untrusted code. These environments are useful for reviewing containers you believe may be infected with malware without risking impacting live systems or development environments your team uses.

In this chapter, we are going to start by looking at the scanning stage in the CI/CD (DevOps) pipeline, before investigating how monitoring tools can be used in conjunction with them to protect our systems. Let's get started with Anchore Engine for scanning our containers.

Scanning using Anchore Engine

When building out a DevOps pipeline, scanning our containers for security issues is an important consideration. One of the final steps in a typical CI process is to build the container itself, having tested the software we intend to deploy to it. As you have seen throughout this book, we have experimented with a number of technologies deployed within containers. While there are many security tools for each language, whether it be JavaScript or PHP (which are sadly out of scope for this book), we shouldn't fail to lessen our manual security burden at the container level by using automated tools.

While we have seen the importance of pulling down signed images, it certainly doesn't hurt to scan them. As the saying goes, *better safe than sorry!*

If we discover that an image we have included in our build is compromised or a tag violates an internal work security policy or compliance, we know that the whole build is thus vulnerable to attack and can in turn prevent it from reaching our production environment.

Therefore, we can think of the security scanning process as the following two interrelated steps:

1. Looking at the image we are including in the `Dockerfile`, and also the configuration in the `Dockerfile` itself.

2. Ensuring that the container matches any internal requirements that we may have such as not using blacklisted images. In this case, the image may have not been blacklisted purely for security reasons, but also for performance.

In order to accommodate these two factors, we need a container scanning tool that allows us the flexibility of defining our own policies on top of standard security considerations.

One of the most popular open source tools on the market that allows us to meet both these goals is Anchore Engine. You can find the official website at: `https://anchore.com/engine/`.

In addition to a large number of features we will shortly investigate, it is also an open source project. So, if you wish to contribute to it, make sure to check out the GitHub repository at `https://github.com/anchore/anchore-engine`.

At its heart, Anchore is an engine for scanning containers for security issues. It can easily be hooked into your CI pipeline to provide vulnerability and policy scanning prior to deployment. Let's take a look at getting it installed and running a basic scan against the latest Alpine image.

Installing Anchore Engine

Installing Anchore Engine is straightforward. First, we need to start with the engine portion of the product. Let's create and navigate into a new directory called `aevolume`:

```
$ mkdir ~/aevolume
$ cd ~/aevolume
```

Next, pull down the latest version of Anchore Engine:

```
$ docker pull docker.io/anchore/anchore-engine:latest
```

We can now run Docker's `create` command:

```
$ docker create --name ae docker.io/anchore/anchore-
engine:latest
```

> **Use curl to grab the docker-compose.yaml**
>
> You can also copy the `docker-compose.yaml` via curl using:
> ```
> curl https://docs.anchore.com/current/docs/engine/
> quickstart/docker-compose.yaml > docker-compose.
> yaml
> ```

Copy over the `docker-compose` file to your current directory and then remove the `ae` folder that was created:

```
$ docker cp ae:/docker-compose.yaml ~/aevolume/docker-compose.
yaml
```
```
$ docker rm ae
```

Finally, run the `pull` and `up` commands as follows:

```
$ docker-compose pull
```
```
$ docker-compose up -d
```

Next, we need to install the CLI that can interact with the engine. You have several options here, including the Docker container:

```
$ docker pull anchore/engine-cli:latest
```

You can also use one of the methods listed here, which will install the CLI locally onto your machine: `https://github.com/anchore/anchore-cli`.

The Python version of the CLI can be installed using the following commands:

```
apt-get update
```
```
apt-get install python-pip
```
```
pip install anchorecli
```

If you have pulled the container image and wish to use the default credentials, run the following command to be dropped into the CLI shell:

```
$ docker run  -it anchore/engine-cli
```

In the following section will be use the Python command line version of the CLI to interact with the engine.

You can now execute the CLI commands against the engine from within the container shell, or from the CLI if you've installed it manually. The following example demonstrates calling the endpoint via the CLI, passing in the credentials and endpoint, and requesting the system status information:

```
$ anchore-cli --u admin --p foobar --url http://localhost:8228/
v1/ system status
```

You should now see some status results in your console indicating the engines are up:

```
Service analyzer (anchore-quickstart, http://engine-
analyzer:8228): up
```
```
Service simplequeue (anchore-quickstart, http://engine-
simpleq:8228): up
```
```
Service policy_engine (anchore-quickstart, http://engine-
policy-engine:8228): up
```
```
Service apiext (anchore-quickstart, http://engine-api:8228): up
```
```
Service catalog (anchore-quickstart, http://engine-
catalog:8228): up
```
```
Engine DB Version: 0.0.12
```
```
Engine Code Version: 0.6.1
```

Now let's review the scanning step.

Adding and scanning images

Let's try out Anchore Engine by running a scan on the latest Alpine container. You'll remember that Alpine is the base operating system that our shipitclicker image version 0.1 has been using so far. Therefore, confirming this is free of issues is a good first step.

When we run a scan, it checks the image against what is known as a set of **policies**. Policies in Anchore are collections of whitelists and checks that the image must pass.

The process to kick off a scan is as follows:

1. Let's add the Alpine image using the CLI command by executing the following:

```
$ anchore-cli --u admin --p foobar --url http://
localhost:8228/v1/ image add alpine:latest
```

2. When this completes successfully, you should see something similar to the following. This tells us the image was added:

```
Image Digest: sha256:ddba4d27a7ffc3f86dd6c2f92041af252a1
f23a8e742c90e6e1297bfa1bc0c45

Parent Digest: sha256:ab00606a42621fb68f2ed6ad3c88be54397f
981a7b70a79db3d1172b11c4367d

Analysis Status: not_analyzed

Image Type: docker

Analyzed At: None

Image ID: e7d92cdc71feacf90708cb59182d0df1b911f8ae022d29
e8e95d75ca6a99776a

Dockerfile Mode: None

Distro: None

Distro Version: None

Size: None

Architecture: None

Layer Count: None


Full Tag: docker.io/alpine:latest

Tag Detected At: 2020-02-04T16:22:19Z
```

3. Our image hasn't been analyzed by Anchore yet. This is where we extract and classify metadata. So, let's move the image into this state as follows:

```
$ anchore-cli --u admin --p foobar --url http://
localhost:8228/v1/ image wait alpine:latest
```

4. Once complete, we can now run a vulnerability scan on the Alpine image using this command. Here, we are checking for operating-system-level package vulnerabilities using the os property. In addition to os, we have the option of checking for non-os (this includes language-specific packages such as Python PIP and Ruby GEM types) and all:

```
$ anchore-cli --u admin --p foobar --url http://
localhost:8228/v1/ image vuln alpine:latest os
```

If everything is successful and the image passes, you will not see any vulnerabilities displayed on the screen.

If a vulnerability is found, it will come back in the following format:

```
Vulnerability ID  Package      Severity   Fix
Vulnerability URL
CVE-1111-1111      package.zip  Negligible None https://
somewebsite
```

By default, the basic Anchore installation policy will scan for CVE issues and Dockerfile problems, such as those we have explored in the previous few chapters.

Now you have the scanning engine in place, you can begin to build out your own policies and scan against them. For more information, refer to the Anchor policy documentation:

```
https://docs.anchore.com/current/docs/using/cli_usage/
policies/
```

Also, to see examples of policies you can copy and modify, check out the Anchore Hub page on GitHub:

```
https://github.com/anchore/hub
```

Whether defining custom policies or reusing others, these JSON files can be added using the CLI:

```
$ anchore-cli policy add /path/to/image/policy/bundle.json
```

Once added, they can then be activated using the `activate` command:

```
$ anchore-cli policy activate <Policy ID>
```

If you need to know a policy ID, you can use the `policy list` command from the CLI:

```
anchore-cli --u admin --p foobar policy list
```

As an experiment, you might like to run the default or your own policies against the other images in the Docker for Developers Docker Hub repository:

```
https://hub.docker.com/r/dockerfordevelopers/shipitclicker/tags
```

This covers the basics of getting up and running. If you wish to add scanning to your DevOps pipeline, Anchore integrates with a number of CI/CD systems, including the following:

- CloudBees
- GitHub
- GitLab

- CircleCI

- Codefresh

Integration instructions for each platform can be found on the Anchore website:

`https://docs.anchore.com/current/docs/using/integration/ci_cd/`

Anchore also includes a plugin for Jenkins, so you can experiment with integrating it with the Jenkins setup we completed earlier in this book:

`https://plugins.jenkins.io/anchore-container-scanner/`

Let's quickly mention another tool before we move on to looking at monitoring tools.

A brief mention of Chef InSpec

Another tool you may be interested in reviewing when considering scanning container infrastructure is Chef InSpec.

Chef InSpec is an open source framework like Anchore but geared toward testing and auditing all of your applications and infrastructure. This includes running auditing tests against Docker. If you are looking for an all-in-one solution for infrastructure beyond just your container environment, this may meet your needs.

> **Note**
>
> A complete walk-through of InSpec is out of scope of this book, however, if you would like to read more about it, you can find further information in the document portal at the InSpec website: `https://www.inspec.io/docs/`.

In summary, we can scan our containers before deploying them to check if they are secure. Let's now move on and look at Docker stats for container monitoring.

Native monitoring locally using Docker stats

Now we have deployed our containers and believe that they are secure, we should consider using monitoring tools to review performance and help investigate problems when they arise.

Before exploring some of the complex and comprehensive tools available in the cloud, we can use Docker's native stats tool to get a quick overview of the container's health. This can be useful if you are quickly testing a container in an isolated sandbox environment due to a suspicion that some software on it may be using up resources in an anomalous fashion – for example, if you suspect a web application may be infected by a coin miner that wasn't picked up at the CI stage.

> **Note**
>
> Running a container in a VM sandbox, as well as allowing you to probe performance metrics, allows you to safely scan it for security issues without risking infecting the underlying machine.

To access data on your container's performance, you can execute the following command:

```
$ docker stats <container id>
```

For each container, you will see CPU usage, memory usage, the memory limit (MEM), % NET I/O, and finally, BLOCK I/O. The following example demonstrates a typical output:

```
CONTAINER CPU % MEM USAGE/LIMIT MEM % NET I/O  BLOCK I/O
ebb12326ae94 1% 73.63 MiB/490 MiB 15.02% 90.2 MB/275.5 MB 26.8
MB/873.7 MB
```

While the stats command is useful when doing local development or if you wish to get a quick snapshot of how a system is performing, it would be nice to gather a more comprehensive set of metrics. One method of achieving this is to use the Stats API. We'll now briefly look at this and also consider some of the security implications around it.

Using the Stats API

The Stats API is a more comprehensive set of results, returned in JSON format, and is available on the Docker socket:

```
$ /var/run/docker.sock
```

You'll remember from the *Securing the Daemon Socket* section in *Chapter 12, Introduction to Container Security*, that we need to ensure an attacker cannot compromise the socket and then use it to gain root access to the underlying host. We can do this by encrypting the traffic using TLS. Refer back to this chapter if you need help in getting this set up.

The Stats API operates using a REST architecture and thus takes HTTP requests as queries. You can see examples on the official documentation site at https://docs.docker.com/engine/api/latest/.

Requests to the API can be made from the command line using netcat or `curl`, with a third-party tool such as Postman, or you can write your own script using Python, Bash, or similar, to hit the endpoint.

Using `curl` as an example, you can replace the value in this command with your own and execute it:

```
$ curl -sk <options> https://<ip>:<port>/<rest endpoint>
--cert <path/to/cert.pem> --key <path/to/key.pem -cacert <path/
to/ca.pem>
```

You should see a JSON object returned with the results. These are more comprehensive than using the Docker command, and may be more useful if you wish to save them as JSON files for further analysis, for example, if gathering data on a container you may believe is compromised.

In addition to the native Docker tools, Google provides **Container Advisor** (**cAdvisor**) for gathering metrics on your container. We will now briefly take a look at this, as a third option for local monitoring.

cAdvisor for container monitoring

cAdvisor is a Google-managed software project for providing container insights into container performance and resource usage. The source code for cAdvisor is available on GitHub at the following URL:

`https://github.com/google/cadvisor`

To test it out, you can use the standard demo container provided by Google. Simply run the following command to pull it down from Google Container Registry and start it up:

```
$ sudo docker run \
    --volume=/:/rootfs:ro \
    --volume=/var/run:/var/run:ro \
    --volume=/sys:/sys:ro \
    --volume=/var/lib/docker/:/var/lib/docker:ro \
    --volume=/dev/disk/:/dev/disk:ro \
    --publish=8080:8080 \
    --detach=true \
    --name=cadvisor \
    gcr.io/google-containers/cadvisor:latest
```

You can now access cAdvisor's web portal on port `8080` of `localhost`. If you have other services running on this port, such as Jenkins, you can change the cAdvisor port in the preceding command.

Try accessing `http://localhost:8080/containers/` and you should see the dashboard shown in the following screenshot:

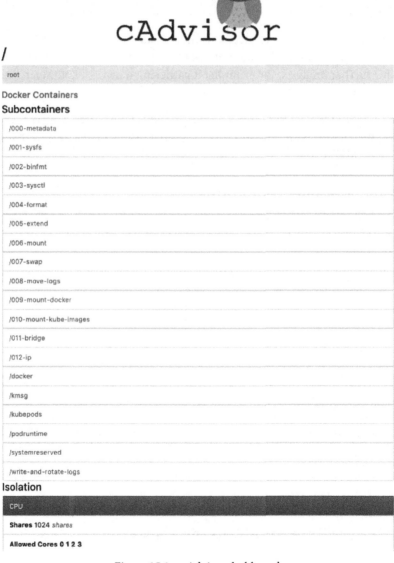

Figure 15.1 – cAdvisor dashboard

From this dashboard, you can explore a variety of metrics ranging from filesystem and memory to CPU and processes. Monitoring these for poor performance can be a useful tool to monitor security issues as we have noted elsewhere.

For example, if resource usage seems to be abnormally high, this can be an indication of software that it isn't functioning properly, or a potential security issue, such as malware running on the container.

All of this is very useful for small local systems and perhaps a quick investigation of a potentially compromised container, but what about monitoring our containers in a production environment and gathering actionable data if we believe a security issue may exist? Well, we can look at one of the many third-party tools that exist that allow us to gather metrics and build comprehensive dashboard and alerting systems.

To demonstrate this, we are going to look at one of the most popular tools on the market for gathering monitoring data for Kubernetes and Docker environments, Datadog.

Aggregating monitoring data in the cloud with Datadog

For commercial projects where environments are deployed to a cloud environment or on your own data center, we need a platform that is capable of aggregating data from a variety of inputs and then presenting it in a fashion you can work with.

Datadog is one such product capable of achieving this and provides plugins for both simple Docker and advanced Kubernetes-based environments. It is also supported on a number of platforms, including major cloud providers such as AWS. Datadog (`https://www.datadoghq.com/`) offers a free 14-day trial so you can experiment with their container features and decide if they meet your needs. You'll find this a worthy rival to some of the tools explored in earlier chapters.

So, now let's take a look at the agents you can run for Kubernetes and Docker on your nodes to start sending data back to Datadog.

Datadog agents for Docker and Kubernetes

Once you have an account set up at `https://www.datadoghq.com/`, you can install the Datadog Agent on a test node to monitor performance.

> **Tip**
>
> We'd recommend starting with a test environment before trying to deploy the production. We also recommend that, before deploying to your production environment, you familiarize yourself with the Docker and Kubernetes agent documentation at: `https://docs.datadoghq.com/agent/docker/?tab=standard`.

The following examples will cover installing Docker Agent and also the Kubernetes agent. Each example uses a cluster with only a single node for demonstration purposes. You are welcome to reuse the Docker container from *Chapter 12, Introduction to Container Security*, or one of the other containers used elsewhere in this book.

Installing and monitoring Docker Agent

Your first task is to install the Docker Agent on the host. The Datadog Docker Agent is responsible for collecting the metrics and passing them back to your account dashboard.

Installing the agent is now incredibly easy. From within your host, execute the following Docker command to include the Datadog Agent:

```
$ docker run -d --name dd-agent \
    -v /var/run/docker.sock:/var/run/docker.sock:ro \
    -v /proc/:/host/proc/:ro \
    -v /path/to/cgroup/:/host/sys/fs/cgroup:ro \
    -e DD_API_KEY={API_KEY} \
    datadog/docker-dd-agent:latest
```

Based upon your OS version, and the version of the agent you have installed, you can then confirm it is running by checking the list of commands here:

`https://docs.datadoghq.com/agent/guide/agent-commands/?tab=agentv6v7#agent-status-and-information`

From the Datadog dashboard you should now see data being returned. You can now begin to explore the metrics that come back from your containers, and set alerts when issues arise:

Figure 15.2 – Example of the Datadog dashboard showing metrics

The next area you may be interested in exploring is the **Security** option in the menu. Select this and follow the wizard to set up security monitoring. Once complete, you can enable and disable security **Detection Rules**, as the following screenshot demonstrates:

Figure 15.3 – Detection rules in Datadog

For more on setting monitors and alerts for containers in Datadog, please refer to the documentation here:

`https://docs.datadoghq.com/monitors/`

Let's now look at the Kubernetes agent equivalent.

Installing and monitoring the Kubernetes agent

As with our previous Docker example, we need to install the agent first. To do this, we can deploy a DaemonSet via Helm. The following instructions use Helm version 3.

> **Tip**
>
> Remember to run add `helm repo add stable, https://kubernetes-charts.storage.googleapis.com`, if you haven't already, to add stable to your repositories.

You can download the official Helm file (`values.yaml`) containing the configuration from GitHub at (`https://github.com/helm/charts/blob/master/stable/datadog/values.yaml`).

Next, you will need to grab your API key from your account. With the API key, we can now complete the installation process. In the following command, replace `{API_KEY}` with your own:

```
helm install datadog-agent -f values.yaml  --set datadog.
apiKey={API KEY} stable/datadog
```

You should see a confirmation in your terminal that the deployment was successful:

```
NAME: datadog-agent
LAST DEPLOYED: Wed Jun  3 10:23:37 2020
NAMESPACE: default
STATUS: deployed
REVISION: 1
TEST SUITE: None
NOTES:
Datadog agents are spinning up on each node in your cluster. After a few
minutes, you should see your agents starting in your event stream:
    https://app.datadoghq.com/event/stream
```

Figure 15.4 – Datadog Agent deployment

Now you have deployed the agent, it will start to collect metrics from Kubernetes:

Figure 15.5 – Example dashboard metrics

As part of this installation process, the `kube-state-metrics` Helm chart is also included. This Helm chart installs the `kube-state-metrics` service (`https://github.com/kubernetes/kube-state-metrics`).

A variety of data is collected by this service and you can view the exposed metrics at `https://github.com/kubernetes/kube-state-metrics/tree/master/docs`.

For example, you may be interested in the metrics around secrets, so you can see what data is being gathered by reviewing the Kubernetes log collection document. You can also enable log collection via Helm. To do this, update the `datadog-values.yaml` file to set the `enabled` and `containerCollectAll` key-value pairs both to `true`. Once you have done this, run `helm upgrade` to update your Datadog Helm chart.

With the metrics from your nodes being sent back to the Datadog default Kubernetes dashboard, you can start to configure alerting and monitoring and explore the many features Datadog offers.

For example, you can create a custom dashboard that displays the number of security signals discovered:

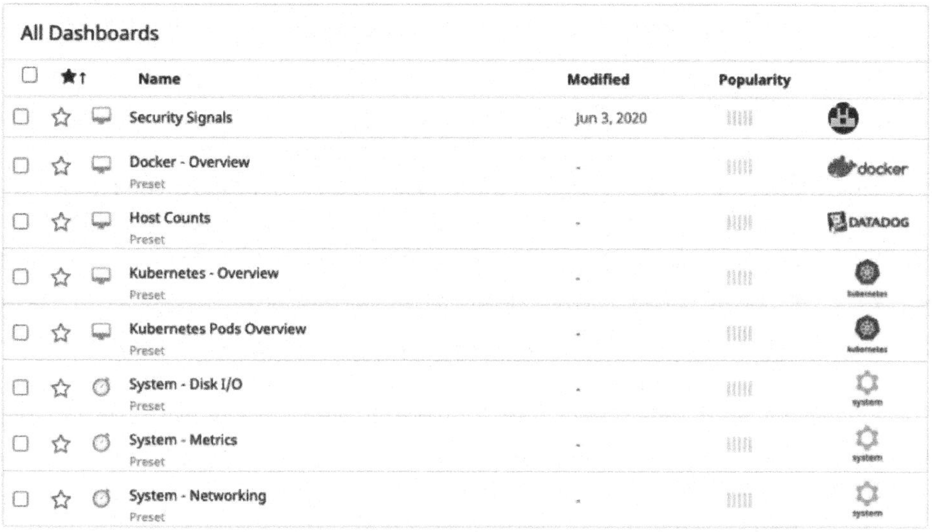

Figure 15.6 – Dashboard list

We've briefly seen how we can use third-party tools to monitor our containers in a security context. This can help to alert us about security issues that may manifest their symptoms as performance problems.

Let's now look at some of the tools provided by the major cloud platforms out there. Both Datadog and the CI/CD scanning pipeline we discussed can be integrated with the providers listed in the following sections, to provide an even more comprehensive security posture.

Securing your containers using AWS

There are a number of approaches we can take to securing containers in the cloud. We will start by looking at **Amazon Web Services**, commonly known as **AWS**. This section of the book assumes you are already familiar with working in AWS for hosting container-based projects. If you use a different service, such as Azure or GCP, then please feel free to skip ahead to the *Azure container security* and *Google container security options* sections respectively. The topic of AWS and container hosting is also discussed in *Chapter 5, Alternatives for Deploying and Running Containers in Production*, and *Chapter 8, Deploying Docker Apps to Kubernetes*. Let's take a look at the tools used for monitoring in AWS.

Security alerts for AWS with GuardDuty

A number of tools exist either in AWS or as third-party plugins that can be used to monitor your Amazon environment hosting your container infrastructure.

Amazon's major tool for monitoring security issues within a VPC is GuardDuty (`https://aws.amazon.com/guardduty/`).

We've seen how we can monitor container health with Datadog, but also saw how important it is to monitor the environment that supports our infrastructure. Complex production instances often use AWS services that sit outside of **Elastic Kubernetes Service (EKS)**, **Elastic Container Service (ECS)**, and **Elastic Compute Cloud (EC2)**. Examples include the IAM roles you might have used to set up CloudWatch metrics or S3 buckets earlier in this book.

AWS GuardDuty provides a mechanism to monitor our cloud-based environment to ensure that any attacks within the VPC that hosts our containers can be tracked down. This is achieved by being integrated with CloudWatch, which allows us to trigger certain security actions based upon the type of alert we see, such as triggering a lambda function, or sending the events on to a third-party application or an S3 bucket for storage.

If you wish to enable GuardDuty, you will need a VPC setup hosting your containers, such as the one configured in *Chapter 8, Deploying Docker Apps to Kubernetes*.

With this in place, you can now create a rule to allow CloudWatch to send events for anything that GuardDuty discovers. This is especially useful for spotting whether containers are generating suspicious network traffic in your VPC.

Using the AWS CLI, we can now enable CloudWatch to start sending the previously mentioned events. To do this, execute the following command:

```
$ aws events put-rule --name PacktContainerSecurity --event-
pattern "{\"source\":[\"aws.guardduty\"]}"
```

With these events enabled, you have a number of options for next steps. You could, for example, attach a lambda function that will handle events that are triggered and act on them, or integrate CloudWatch GuardDuty events with your Datadog setup, as outlined here:

```
https://github.com/DataDog/datadog-serverless-functions/tree/
master/aws/logs_monitoring
```

If you wish to write the results of CloudWatch GuardDuty events to the S3 bucket created in *Chapter 10, Monitoring Docker Using Prometheus, Grafana, and Jaeger*, in the *Storing logs for the long term with AWS S3* section, then you can attach the lambda function as an event rule:

```
$ aws events put-targets --rule PacktContainerSecurity
--targets Id=1,Arn=arn:aws:lambda:<zone>:<ARN
digits>:function:<function>
```

An example of a lambda function that can be used to write to the S3 bucket is provided by AWS at the following link:

```
https://aws.amazon.com/blogs/database/monitoring-your-security-
with-guardduty-in-real-time-with-amazon-elasticsearch-service/
```

Once you have modified this lambda to your needs and added it between the < and > brackets, you can include the required permissions by running the following command:

```
$ aws lambda add-permission --function-name <function>
--statement-id 1 --action 'lambda:InvokeFunction' --principal
events.amazonaws.com
```

This should act as a jumping-off point for you to explore GuardDuty in more detail and expand upon the setup you have created over the course of this book.

> **Another way to store findings to S3**
>
> You can also use the steps provided by AWS here for exporting GuardDuty findings to an S3 bucket: `https://docs.aws.amazon.com/guardduty/latest/ug/guardduty_exportfindings.html`

Other security features in AWS you may be interested in checking out include the following:

- Amazon Inspector for analyzing application security:
  `https://aws.amazon.com/inspector/`

- AWS Security Hub for creating a unified central security center:
  `https://aws.amazon.com/security-hub/`

- Amazon Detective for detecting potential security issues:
  `https://aws.amazon.com/detective/`

Each of these services can be enabled through your AWS web console. Let's now move on and take a look at some of the options available in Microsoft Azure.

Securing your containers using Azure

Azure is Microsoft's flagship cloud service and provides a number of tools you can use to deploy and monitor Docker containers. This section assumes some familiarity with both Azure and the Log Analytics service.

Container monitoring in Azure

Microsoft's Container Monitoring solution provides a mechanism to manage Docker and Windows hosts from a single place and supports Kubernetes and Docker Swarm, both of which have been discussed in this book.

If you are already using Microsoft's AKS service, you may be familiar with the monitoring services available on the AKS page, however, it is also possible to monitor containers across your whole Microsoft infrastructure in Azure.

To enable the monitoring of your containers, you will need to start by enabling the feature by adding it to Log Analytics. You can do this by clicking the **GET IT NOW** button on the Azure Marketplace website:

`https://azuremarketplace.microsoft.com/en-us/marketplace/apps/microsoft.containersoms?tab=overview`

Once this is complete, you can create a new Log Analytics workspace. From this new workspace, record the name you chose, and also obtain the workspace ID and key. These are available under the **Advanced settings** of your workspace and can be found under the **Connected Sources | Linux Servers** options.

For the purpose of this overview, we are going to assume an environment of a single host as we did for Datadog running on Linux. In this scenario, you will need to install the Log Analytics agent as follows:

```
$ wget https://raw.githubusercontent.com/Microsoft/OMS-Agent-
for-Linux/master/installer/scripts/onboard_agent.sh && sh
onboard_agent.sh -w <workspace_id> -s <workspace_key>
```

You can now restart the agent using the following command:

```
$ sudo /opt/microsoft/omsagent/bin/service_control restart
[<workspace_id>]
```

Now let's try running the monitor against the container as follows:

```
$ sudo docker run --privileged -d -v /var/run/docker.sock:/
var/run/docker.sock -v /var/lib/docker/containers:/var/lib/
docker/containers -e WSID="<workspace_id>" -e KEY="<workspace_
key>" -h=`hostname` -p 127.0.0.1:25225:25225 --name="omsagent"
--restart=always microsoft/oms
```

We can modify the event data we collect under the **Data** option of the Log Analytics workspace. From here, we can add syslog and also enable the Linux Performance Counters.

Once the solution is enabled, you will see the **Container** tile appear. You can then drill into the **Container** dashboard to gather metrics.

Now we have some monitoring in place, let's look at some security features that are available in Azure for container-based platforms.

Using Security Center to secure your containers in Azure

With monitoring in place, you can now move on to looking at Microsoft's container security tools. The recommended native tool for achieving this in Azure is the Security Center service.

You can sign up to add it to your Azure account by clicking the **Turn on Security Center** button at https://azure.microsoft.com/en-us/services/security-center/ and sign up for an Azure account at the same time if you wish.

Once you have the feature enabled, you will see that Security Center provides a number of features, including the following:

- Container runtime protection
- Vulnerability management
- Environment hardening

We'll take a look at each of these briefly.

Container runtime protection

Security Center's runtime protection for container environments allows you to generate real-time threat metrics that can be used to plan remediation efforts. The threat detection mechanism is broken down into two core areas:

- **At the host level**: At this level, we can monitor for containers acting in a malicious or suspicious fashion, including an exposed Docker daemon or a privileged command run within the container.

- **At the AKS cluster level**: AKS cluster-level threat detection analyzes the Kubernetes audit logs for suspicious activity such as highly privileged role creation or a coin miner being detected.

These two features combined can help to look at the layers of your container stack and detect suspicious activity.

Vulnerability management

Here, you can use the Container Registries bundle to scan new images when they are pushed. Security Center integration with third-party security provider Qualys scans the container for some of the vulnerabilities we've discussed in this book.

When an issue is detected, it will be logged on the dashboard with a recommended remediation step.

Environment hardening

Security Center provides a variety of tools for monitoring the security of your container environment. One of the most important features is running bench mark tests, such as the CIS Docker Benchmark, to alert you if your environment's configuration is weakened. An example of a CIS control is checking whether containers have unrestricted network traffic being exchanged between each other.

You can download a copy of the CIS Docker Benchmark for free from the CIS website:

`https://learn.cisecurity.org/benchmarks`

> **Note**
>
> InSpec users may be interested in downloading the InSpec profile for CIS Docker Benchmarking at `https://github.com/dev-sec/cis-docker-benchmark`.

When Security Center spots a problem with your environment, it will flag it on the **Recommendations** page of the dashboard for you, so you can start remediating the issue.

We've briefly looked at what is available in Azure. Let's wrap up with a quick tour of some of GCP's features.

Securing your containers using GCP

Google offers a number of tools for monitoring containers in both Anthos and **Google Kubernetes Engine** (**GKE**).

For those unfamiliar with Google's offerings, Anthos is a platform that is designed for hybrid and multi-cloud deployment and allows you, among other features, to deploy container-oriented platforms such as Kubernetes. GKE is Google's enterprise-grade Kubernetes platform offered via **Google Cloud Platform** (**GCP**) and can be thought of as a rival to Amazon's EKS. Googles Container Registry is a platform for storing images that can be reused across your projects.

For the following sections, it is assumed that you have some prior knowledge of GCP. If you would like to know more about getting started with GCP, please visit the following link:

`https://cloud.google.com/gcp/getting-started`

Let's start by looking at container security in GCP.

Container Analysis and Binary Authorization in GCP

A useful feature that Google offers is the **Container Analysis** scanner for Container Registry. This feature allows you to scan images for security issues and exposes an API for your use to pull down the metadata results. If you enable this feature on your account, it will scan all new images that are pushed to the registry, however, for existing images you will need to re-push them to trigger the scan.

The two core features of Container Analysis are the following:

- **Incremental scans**: This handles the scanning of new images and generates the metadata related to them.

- **Continuous monitoring**: The metadata generated by incremental scans is continuously analyzed to see if it matches new sets of security vulnerabilities.

When running scans, a severity level for effective severity (the level defined by the Linux distribution owner) and **Common Vulnerability Scoring System** (**CVSS**) score is assigned to a matching issue.

> **Note**
> If you would like to know more about CVSS, please visit the CVSS website:
> `https://www.first.org/cvss/specification-document`.

Severity levels are categorized as follows:

- Critical

- High

- Medium

- Low

- Minimal

These results are stored within your Container Registry account and can be viewed from there. Additionally, they can be retrieved by the RESTful API. For an overview of the REST commands available, please refer to the Container Analysis API documentation:

`https://cloud.google.com/container-registry/docs/reference/rest`

To explore Container Analysis further, you can enable it within your account and test it out by pushing an existing image to the registry. For example, you could use one of the `shipitclicker` projects we have used throughout this book. To do this, remember to tag the image first:

```
$ docker tag <source_image> <hostname>/<project_
id>/<image>:<tag>
```

The hostname will be one of the four following storage regions:

- `gcr.io` (US)

- `us.gcr.io` (US)

- `eu.gcr.io` (EU)

- `asia.gcr.io` (Asia)

Then, to push to the registry, use the `docker push` command in the following format:

```
$ docker push <hostname>/<project_id>/<image>:<tag>
```

It's as simple as that, you can then pull the container image as and when you need to and use the Container Analysis service. In addition to conducting analysis on containers, we can enforce rules around using signed images to complement this.

Google have built a deploy-time security feature geared toward preventing untrusted container images from making it into GKE. This is called **Binary Authorization** (`https://cloud.google.com/binary-authorization`).

Binary Authorization is built around **Kritis**, which defines a specification for the deployment authorization of Kubernetes applications. You can read more about it here on GitHub:

`https://github.com/grafeas/kritis/blob/master/docs/binary-authorization.md`

Using this service will allow you to enforce rules around requiring Docker images to be signed by trusted authorities. This involves a process known as attestations. Effectively, each container image has a unique hash (called a digest), which is signed by the signer. You might remember we saw how digests can be used earlier in this book, in *Chapter 13, Docker Security Fundamentals and Best Practices.*

When a digest is signed, this is known as an attestation. When we come to deploy a container image, we can use a Binary Authorization attestor to verify the attestation. This allows us to prevent unauthorized – that is, unsigned – container images being used.

If you are interested in learning more, to set up Binary Analysis you can follow the simple steps documented here:

`https://cloud.google.com/binary-authorization/docs/quickstart`

Let's now take a look at another feature of GCP, Security Command Center.

Understanding your attack surface with Security Command Center

The final tool we will quickly take a look at is Google's Security Command Center. For this, you will need to have set up an organization and project in GCP to work with. If not, please refer back to the preceding section for a link to Google's own quick-start guide.

To enable Security Command Center for this new organization and project, follow these steps:

1. Log into Cloud Console at `https://console.cloud.google.com`.

2. Add the following two roles via **IAM &Admin** in your web console, by selecting your **Project** and **Organization** and then adding the permissions next to your username: `organizationAdmin (roles/resourcemanager.organizationAdmin)` from **Resource Manager | Organization Administrator** and `securitycenter.admin (roles/securitycenter.admin)` from **Security Center | Security Center Admin**.

3. Save the changes and navigate to the Security Command Center page in the web console.

4. Select the organization you added in step 2 from the drop-down list called **Organization**.

5. You will now be presented with the **Enable asset discovery** page.

6. Enable the **All current and future projects** option.

7. Asset discovery will now begin.

Once Security Command Center has finished scanning your resources, you will be able to see the results on the dashboard. By default, anomaly detection is enabled, however, Google provides a number of security sources you can integrate, or you can plug in container-specific third-party services.

A full list of the potential sources you can integrate can be found here:

`https://cloud.google.com/security-command-center/docs/how-to-security-sources`

With these two basic services set up, you are now free to explore integrating other third-party providers such as Twistlock or experiment with these services to get comfortable rolling them out to a production environment.

That concludes our whistle-stop tour of a few of the major cloud providers' offerings. Let's summarize what we have looked at.

Summary

In this chapter, we've provided you with some pointers for where you can take your cloud skills to next. This has included looking at scanning tools such as Anchore, reviewing metric-gathering platforms such as Datadog, and looking briefly at some of the features offered by the major cloud providers.

These cloud platforms included AWS, Microsoft Azure, and GCP. Each of these companies also provide a number of other cloud-based container infrastructure products you may wish to explore further.

We hope this high-level overview has provided you with some thoughtful insights on how to apply these skills to your own projects. Each topic in this chapter should act as a jumping-off point to explore each tool further, or provide you with the basics to start experimenting with monitoring in a cloud-based container environment. For those of you working with local projects, tools such as Docker stats and cAdvisor will provide a handy mechanism for monitoring container performance.

Now we will move on to the final chapter, where we shall recap what we have studied throughout the book and leave you with some takeaway points for where to take your learning to next.

Further reading

Don't forget you can visit each provider's website for a list of these further features:

- Containers on AWS: `https://aws.amazon.com/containers/services/`

- Container services in Azure: `https://azure.microsoft.com/en-us/product-categories/containers/`

- Container options in GCP: `https://cloud.google.com/container-options`

16
Conclusion – End of the Road, but not the Journey

You have now reached the final chapter of this book. Over the previous 15 chapters, a variety of topics have been covered. As you may have noticed, the book was grouped into three areas—development, DevOps with monitoring, and finally security. So, let's take the time to recap what we studied in each area and where we can go next.

First, we will run through an overview of what we learned in the book. Next, a summary of the skills we acquired on the development front will be presented. After this, we will explore where we can go next to learn more about DevOps with containers and expand our newly learned skills. Our penultimate review will consider what we learned about security and how we can stay on top of it. Then, we will finish up with a general conclusion on everything we've studied.

In order to review these items, we've broken them down into the following topics in this chapter:

- Wrapping up – let's get started
- What we learned about development
- Next steps for taking your DevOps knowledge further
- A summary on security and where to go next

Grab your containerized environment and get ready for our last foray together into the world of Docker.

Technical requirements

For this chapter, you will need to have access to a Linux machine running Docker. We recommend that you use the setup you have been using so far in this book. This is so you can follow up with some of the tools and techniques recommended in this chapter if you wish.

Check out the following video to see the Code in Action:

```
https://bit.ly/2CpGTfZ
```

Wrapping up – let's get started

Over the course of this book, we have explored the world of containerization. As the technology becomes ever more ubiquitous in companies and projects across the world, having a solid handle on the basics and the toolsets supporting containers becomes ever more useful.

Before we close the book, we are going to wrap up by reviewing what we have learned on the development front. After this, we will discuss what steps can be taken next to build on your DevOps skills and finally do a quick tour of some security projects that may be of interest.

You may wish to have your project from *Chapter 9, Cloud-Native Continuous Deployment Using Spinnaker*, ready in order to augment it with some of the recommended projects in this chapter.

Remember you can revisit the source code for setting up this project here:

```
https://github.com/PacktPublishing/Docker-for-Developers/tree/
master/chapter9
```

With that said, let's look at what we have learned about developing in a Docker-based environment.

What we learned about development

In the first section of this book, *An Introduction to Docker – Containers and Local Development*, we got into the basics of Docker and containers, and how they are used for development purposes.

First, we introduced the topic of containerization and related technologies such as virtualization. Following this, we sized up the differences between Docker containers and virtual machines to see how they compared for development purposes. In *Chapter 3, Sharing Containers using Docker Hub*, we got our first taste of using Docker Hub to store and retrieve images from a third-party location. Finally, having looked at pre-built containers and container images, we explored the scenario where multiple containers must work together to form a more complex system.

These four chapters in this section, taken together, provide the basics for local development and understanding the tooling required to make you a successful engineer in this area. To build upon this knowledge, understanding design patterns for container-based systems would be a logical next step for you to explore.

Going deeper – design patterns

The first section of this book provided a guide to hands-on development. Just because you are using containers does not mean that architectural patterns for software development have to be abandoned!

So, you may be asking what a design pattern is if you are new to the subject. In short, patterns are reusable blueprints for solving common architectural problems. Much as engineers and architects in the construction industry reuse workable models for constructing buildings, we can use a similar approach for building software systems.

The following container-oriented patterns provide a great jumping-off point for you to explore the subject further once you have finished this book. In fact, you may recognize some of them from earlier chapters, which is why we have included them here. Let's now take a brief tour of five of them and look at which services and projects in this book have implemented them.

A single container – keeping it simple

When we first embarked on the projects in this book, we kept things simple and used a **single container** pattern. This is the simplest pattern you can adopt in a container-based environment and the ShipIt Clicker application uses it.

The sidecar design pattern – useful for logging

We've looked at logging throughout this book and log-monitoring systems are common implementors of something known as a **sidecar** pattern. In its simplest form, we have a container such as the ShipIt Clicker one, and then a second container with a log monitoring tool. This could be Grafana, Datadog, or one of the other tools we experimented with. As you start to build out your own projects, this simple pattern makes a great starting point. Deploy your application on a container, and then use a second container to handle log processing. You will also remember from our exploration of Envoy that the sidecar pattern is used here to allow us to create a service mesh without having to directly edit our applications to handle complex networking problems.

Leader and elections – adding redundancy

We've seen how highly available systems are desirable, and how tools such as Kubernetes can help us achieve this goal through orchestrating multiple containers across pods. A common design pattern used in conjunction with Kubernetes is the **leader and election** approach. Here, data can be split across multiple nodes to provide redundancy; for example, the data may be replicated across containers.

If, for some reason, our container crashes, the other containers will elect a new leader and Kubernetes will spin up a new node to plug the gap.

The ambassador design pattern – an approach to proxying

Proxying is an important part of many systems, especially in microservice architectures. As you have seen, in Docker-based environments, we can have multiple containers residing on the same virtual network. Each of these containers is assigned a name, which allows containers to communicate with one another.

An example of where we can use the **ambassador** pattern is in communicating between a backend caching service, such as Redis, and a set of applications. In this instance, the applications communicate with a single Redis proxy node, believing it to be Redis itself. However, the proxy node then distributes the traffic across multiple other Redis nodes on the network.

> **Redis**
>
> Redis (`redis.io`), as you may remember from earlier chapters, is an in-memory, open source caching and message brokering system. It allows you to store a variety of data structures in memory such as lists, sets, and hashes, and can additionally be used as a primary database if you wish (`https://redislabs.com/blog/goodbye-cache-redis-as-a-primary-database/`).

The tool Envoy, which we examined in *Chapter 11, Scaling and Load Testing Docker Applications*, is very useful for deploying an ambassador-style approach. If you are interested in trying it out with Redis, then check out Dmitry Polyakovsky's article, *Envoy Proxy with Redis* (`http://dmitrypol.github.io/redis/2019/03/18/envoy-proxy.html`).

Redis can be obtained from Docker Hub as a container (`https://hub.docker.com/_/redis/`). Let's now look at our final design pattern before moving on.

The adapter design pattern – solution reuse

Having a consistent way to communicate information between containers is important, and this is especially the case when aggregating metrics. For example, if different containers produce logs in different formats, we need to be able to ingest this data in a common format. This is where the **adapter** pattern comes in. We can use this pattern to develop a uniform interface and subsequently receive log files from multiple containers, standardize them, and then store the data in a centralized monitoring service.

We saw in *Chapter 10, Monitoring Docker Using Prometheus, Grafana, and Jaeger*, that Prometheus is a useful tool for container monitoring. However, Prometheus requires a uniform interface from which to pull metrics, that being the metrics API. Where an application does not expose endpoints that are compatible with Prometheus, we can deploy an interface using the adapter pattern that wraps the target service containers with a Prometheus-compatible set of endpoints. This then allows Prometheus to pull data from the containers we are interested in seamlessly via the intermediate interface container.

Reading more on design patterns

Using container-based design patterns helps to ensure that the right model is being used for your system, only introducing as much complexity is as needed, while ensuring the system is resilient and easier to manage.

If you would like to learn more about container patterns in Kubernetes and Docker, be sure to check out the book, *Kubernetes Design Patterns and Extensions*, by Packt.

Next steps for taking your DevOps knowledge further

The second section, *Running Containers in Production*, was geared toward DevOps practices such as **continuous integration** and **continuous deployment (CI/CD)**, container orchestration with Kubernetes, and monitoring with tools such as Jaeger.

To start with, we looked at options around hosting containers in cloud-based systems and hybrid environments. Next up, we explored the simple option of serving up our application on a single host with Docker Compose. After this, experimenting with Jenkins provided us with our first introduction to CI/CD tools and how these can be used with Docker. With the concept of CD under our belt, it was then on to *Chapter 8, Deploying Docker Apps to Kubernetes*, which gave us our first taste of Kubernetes for container orchestration. Subsequently, the topic of special container-native cloud deployment options in the form of Spinnaker was then trialed, including understanding what deployment methodologies are useful for production environments. The penultimate chapter of section two of this book explored monitoring tools for performance, such as Jaeger, Prometheus, and Grafana. Finally, we closed this section with a discussion looking at Envoy service meshes, proxying, and scaling and load testing projects in a production environment.

The seven chapters in this section provided a wealth of projects that gave you an understanding of some of the core concepts companies face when hosting and serving container-based applications in a production environment. However, there are still plenty of interesting techniques and topics to learn in order to take your DevOps skills to the next level.

Chaos engineering and building resilient production systems

With a complex production system in place, containers being orchestrated in the cloud, and CD happening, how do we ensure our systems are resilient against faults and unexpected crashes? This is where the concept of chaos engineering comes into play.

Chaos engineering is the practice of understanding that code and infrastructure are inherently complex and therefore we should approach the engineering and testing process with this in mind. There are five concepts to chaos engineering that can be summarized as follows:

- **Develop a hypothesis around steady state behavior**: Measure outputs from the system over a short period of time to gather a baseline. This baseline is known as the steady state and could include metrics such as the error rate, response and latency times, and traffic loads.

- **Test a variety of real-world events**: When testing for real-world events that could impact a production system, consider testing software failures, mangled inputs, containers crashing, and other events that could degrade performance.

- **Experiment in production**: Testing in production may seem like anathema. However, each environment is different and, for authentic results, testing in production is a must.

- **Minimize the impact, aka blast radius**: Running tests in production, however, does not absolve us of the responsibility to ensure that any degradation of performance is temporary and easily recovered from. Always make sure your experiments are well contained.

- **Run automated experiments in a continuous fashion**: Using an automated approach allows you to reduce the labor overhead and for tests and experiments to run at all hours of the day.

One such tool developed by Netflix implementing this concept is Chaos Monkey. Chaos Monkey is a platform to which you deploy your infrastructure that will randomly terminate containers that run in a production environment. The goal is to test how a production system will respond/recover and to allow engineers to tune the system to be more resilient.

You've already seen how to set up Spinnaker, so as a next step, you can integrate Chaos Monkey into your existing pipeline. Chaos Monkey also works with AWS and Kubernetes. The source code can be found at `https://github.com/Netflix/chaosmonkey`.

If you are interested in installing Chaos Monkey and adding it to the existing CI/CD Spinnaker pipeline that you built in *Chapter 9, Cloud-Native Continuous Deployment Using Spinnaker*, you can follow the official installation guide at `https://netflix.github.io/chaosmonkey/How-to-deploy/`.

Once it's up and running, you can now test Chaos Monkey in your Spinnaker-based container environment to see how it copes with terminating services and what corresponding metrics are displayed in your monitoring tools.

If you are interested in combining Chaos Monkey with security techniques, be sure to check out Packt's video guide on how you can use Chaos Monkey to **fuzz test** applications you host:

```
https://subscription.packtpub.com/video/virtualization_and_
cloud/9781788394901/94651/94677/chaos-monkey-and-fuzz-testing
```

> **What is fuzz testing?**
> Fuzz testing is the process of testing random, invalid, and incompatible randomized data inputs to an application to see how it responds.

In addition to Chaos Monkey, the following tools also offer mechanisms for building and testing resilient systems:

- **Gremlin**: A chaos engineering platform that can be used with Kubernetes, Mesos, ECS, and Docker Swam, available at `https://www.gremlin.com/`.

- **Mangle**: VMware's open source platform for orchestrating chaos engineering that supports Kubernetes and Docker, available at `https://vmware.github.io/mangle/`.

- **Chaos Mesh**: A cloud-native chaos engineering platform geared toward Kubernetes environments. It can be deployed via Helm, and is available at `https://github.com/pingcap/chaos-mesh`.

We've briefly covered chaos engineering as a concept you could explore further from a DevOps perspective. Let's now recap what we studied under the banner of security.

A summary on security and where to go next

The final section of this book, *Docker Security – Securing Your Containers*, was dedicated to the subject of security. First, we looked at how containers work with the underlying hardware from a security perspective. We studied container and hypervisor security models and quickly dipped our toes into security best practices.

Security fundamentals and best practices came next and provided us with guidance on the best approach to handling our Dockerfile and building minimal base images. After this, we looked at how secrets can be handled in Docker Swarm. This provided insight for readers who may need to maintain legacy systems or migrate from Swarm to Kubernetes. We also looked at how tags, metadata, and labels can be used from a security perspective.

The penultimate chapter of this book, *Chapter 15, Scanning, Monitoring, and using Third-Party Tools*, gave us a whistle-stop tour of Google, Amazon, and Microsoft's container security features in the cloud. We also installed Anchore for security scanning, looked at some extra monitoring tools that may be useful, and briefly tried out Datadog for container monitoring, which, in turn, can be used in a security context.

With these basics under your belt, the following are ideas for some next steps regarding container security projects that build upon this knowledge.

Metasploit – container-based penetration testing

Now that we've built secure containers, and hopefully a secure application too, you can explore penetration testing in a container-based environment, such as the one you deployed via Spinnaker. Penetration testing is the process of looking for security flaws in a system that can then be leveraged to gain access, exfiltrate data, disrupt performance, or turn the compromised system into a platform to launch other attacks.

A popular tool for performing penetration tests is the **Metasploit** framework (`https://www.metasploit.com/`). Metasploit is an open source framework for developing and deploying security exploit code against a remote target, such as a container running in your environment. Metasploit is available in a container format from Docker Hub, at `https://hub.docker.com/r/metasploitframework/metasploit-framework`.

With this tool in place, you can test vulnerabilities found in containers with tools such as Anchore. Vulnerabilities may include, for example, old versions of software installed on a container that may be open to attack. To grab the latest copy, run the following code:

```
docker pull metasploitframework/metasploit-framework
```

You can then run the container as follows:

```
sudo docker run --rm -it metasploitframework/metasploit-framework
```

Once loaded, you will be dropped into the Metasploit shell, called `msfconsole`:

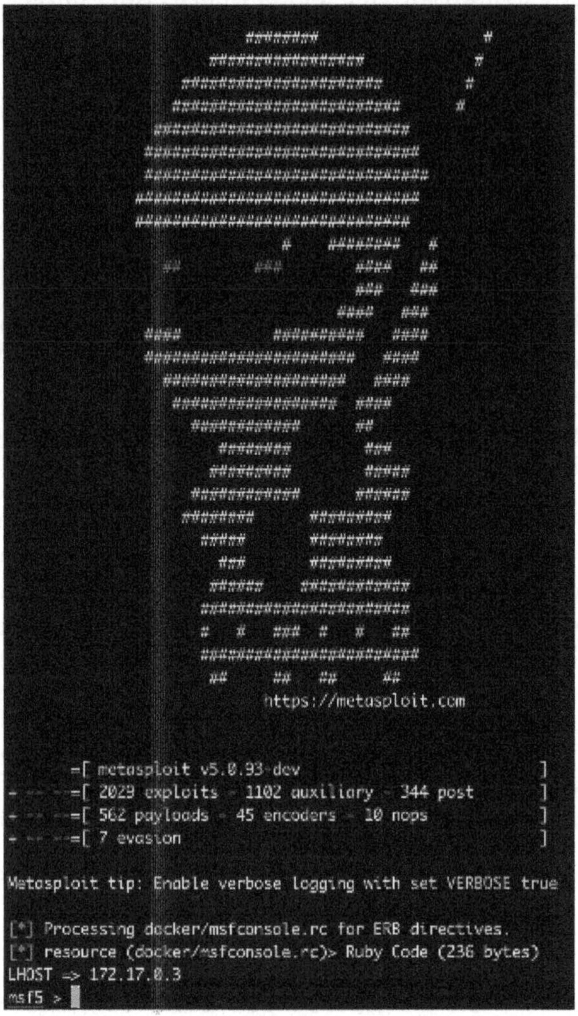

Figure 16.1 – Example of a Metasploit container running

From here, you can begin to explore the commands available and consider projects you can run from inside the container. A free course on using Metasploit can be found on the Offensive Security website at `https://www.offensive-security.com/metasploit-unleashed/`. Once you are familiar with the basic commands, consider exploring some of the following features in Metasploit.

Unprotected TCP socket exploit

You will remember that we discussed how leaving the TCP socket for Docker exposed could be exploited by attackers. Metasploit provides an example of how this can be achieved. Try running Docker via `2375/tcp` on a second machine and load up the `docker_daemon_tcp` module (`https://www.rapid7.com/db/modules/exploit/linux/http/docker_daemon_tcp`) in the Metasploit container we just set up. You can now target the compromised socket via this module and create a Docker container with the `/` path mounted with read and write permissions on the underlying target host that is running the container.

Testing third-party vulnerable containers – Apache Struts

The following is just one example of the many vulnerable containers available for downloading and experimenting with. This container, created by `piesecurity`, includes a vulnerable version of Apache Struts (`https://hub.docker.com/r/piesecurity/apache-struts2-cve-2017-5638/`).

Apache Struts is a popular framework built in Java for developing web applications. In 2017, a vulnerability was discovered in the framework that allowed an attacker to execute code remotely on the server running it. One of the most well-known victims of this vulnerability was Equifax, who suffered a catastrophic data breach.

You can deploy and run this container loaded with Struts via Spinnaker and test out the exploit yourself. Once installed, use the Metasploit module `struts2_content_type_ognl` (`https://www.rapid7.com/db/modules/exploit/multi/http/struts2_content_type_ognl`). This will allow you to launch an attack that creates a reverse shell on the compromised container and demonstrates how security flaws inside third-party frameworks can be exploited even when running in Kubernetes and Docker.

If you'd like to dig into this further, the book *Advanced Infrastructure Penetration Testing* from Packt provides guidance for using the Metasploit Framework and testing container-based environment security.

Summary

We hope you have enjoyed reading this book. It aimed to provide a comprehensive guide to Docker development, both locally and in the cloud. Throughout the 16 chapters, our goal was to demonstrate not only how to develop applications in containers, but how they can be built, deployed, scanned, and monitored.

Whether you plan to build a new project from scratch, are maintaining legacy systems on Docker Swarm, or migrating to a Kubernetes-based environment, *Docker For Developers* is the type of book you can dip back into again to refresh your knowledge or seek guidance as required.

We hope you have enjoyed your journey into the world of containers as much as we have enjoyed sharing this knowledge with you. Good luck with your future projects!

Other Books You May Enjoy

If you enjoyed this book, you may be interested in these other books by Packt:

Continuous Delivery with Docker and Jenkins - Second Edition

Rafał Leszko

ISBN: 978-1-83855-218-3

- Get to grips with docker fundamentals and how to dockerize an application for the CD process
- Learn how to use Jenkins on the Cloud environments
- Scale a pool of Docker servers using Kubernetes
- Create multi-container applications using Docker Compose
- Write acceptance tests using Cucumber and run them in the Docker ecosystem using Jenkins
- Publish a built Docker image to a Docker Registry and deploy cycles of Jenkins pipelines using community best practices

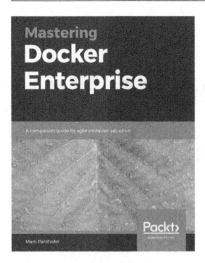

Mastering Docker Enterprise

Mark Panthofer

ISBN: 978-1-78961-207-3

- Understand why containers are important to an enterprise
- Understand the features and components of Docker Enterprise 2
- Find out about the PoC, pilot, and production adoption phases
- Get to know the best practices for installing and operating Docker Enterprise
- Understand what is important for a Docker Enterprise in production
- Run Kubernetes on Docker Enterprise

Leave a review - let other readers know what you think

Please share your thoughts on this book with others by leaving a review on the site that you bought it from. If you purchased the book from Amazon, please leave us an honest review on this book's Amazon page. This is vital so that other potential readers can see and use your unbiased opinion to make purchasing decisions, we can understand what our customers think about our products, and our authors can see your feedback on the title that they have worked with Packt to create. It will only take a few minutes of your time, but is valuable to other potential customers, our authors, and Packt. Thank you!

Index

C

Made in the USA
Coppell, TX
26 April 2021

54555191R00260